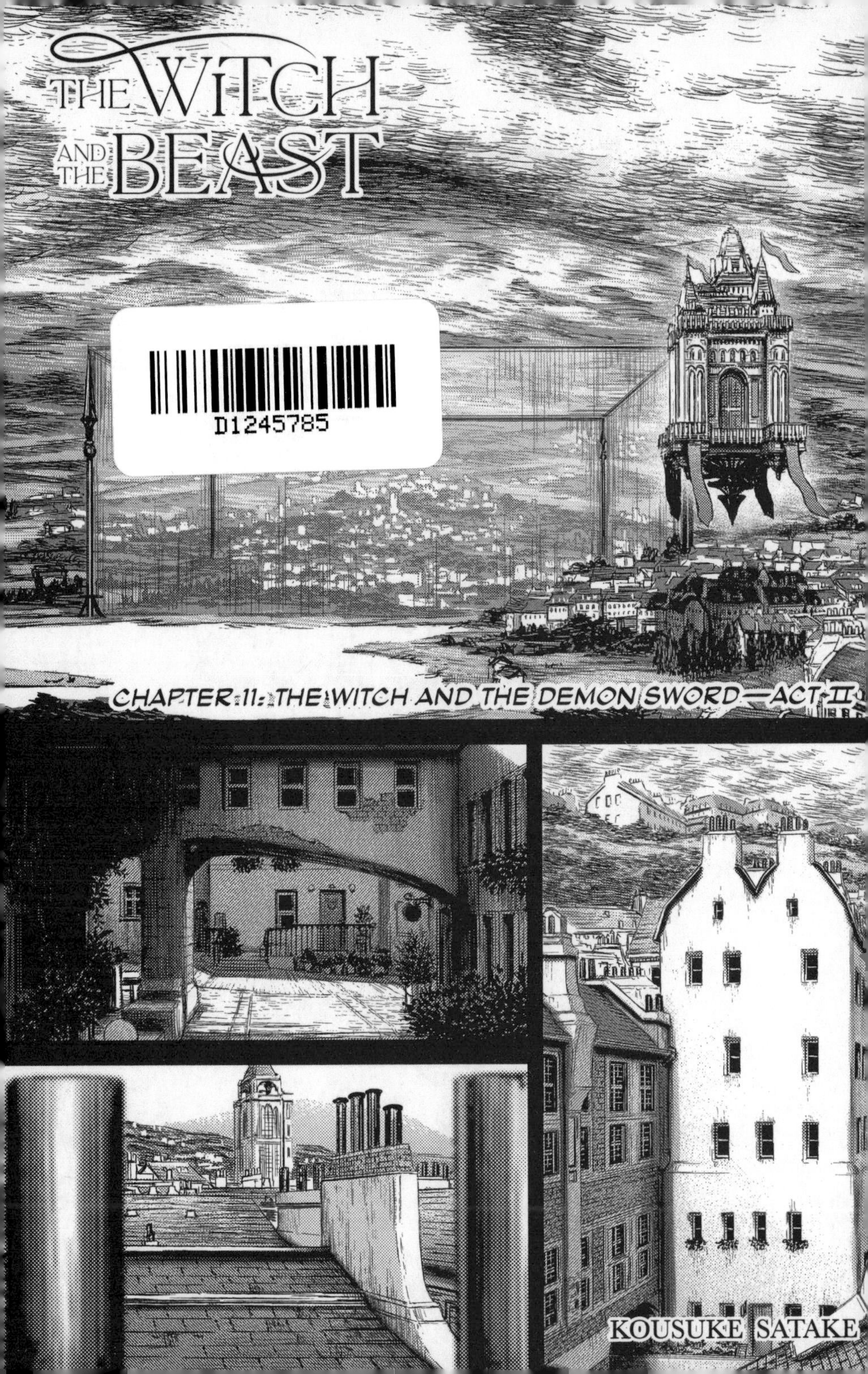
THE WITCH AND THE BEAST
CHAPTER 11: THE WITCH AND THE DEMON SWORD—ACT II
KOUSUKE SATAKE

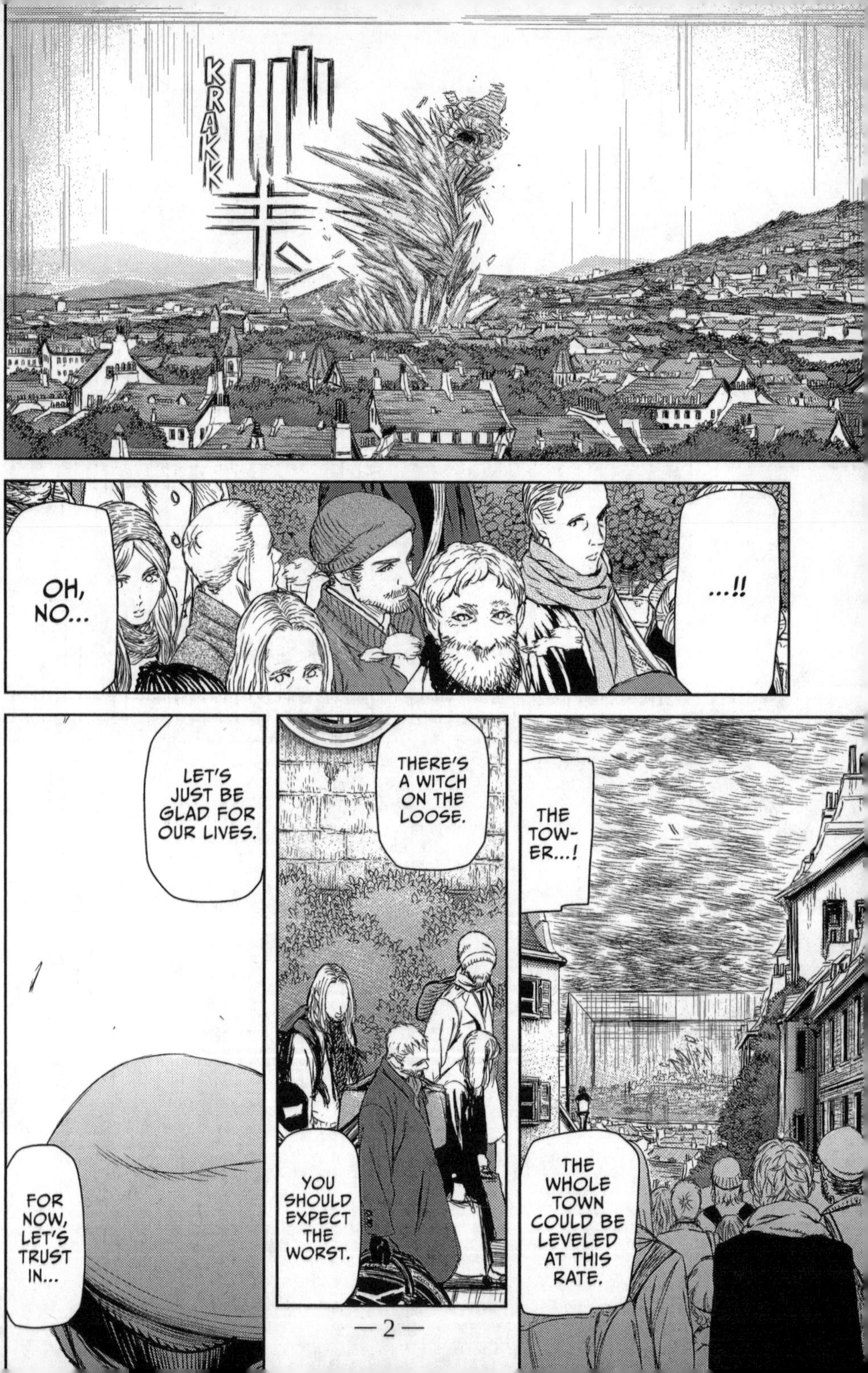
KRAKKK
...!!
OH, NO...
THE TOWER...!
THE WHOLE TOWN COULD BE LEVELED AT THIS RATE.
THERE'S A WITCH ON THE LOOSE.
YOU SHOULD EXPECT THE WORST.
LET'S JUST BE GLAD FOR OUR LIVES.
FOR NOW, LET'S TRUST IN...

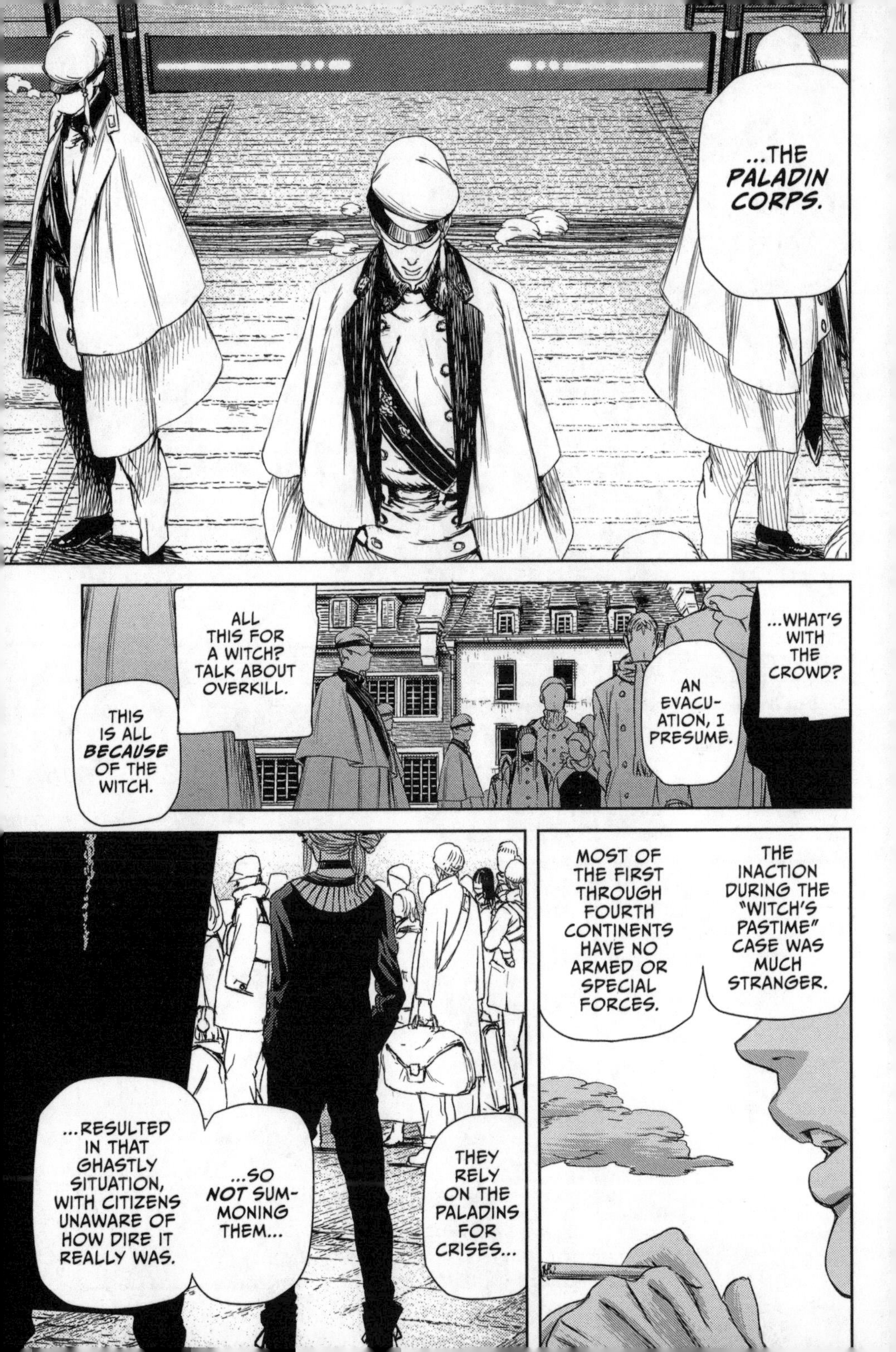
...THE *PALADIN CORPS.*
...WHAT'S WITH THE CROWD?
AN EVACUATION, I PRESUME.
ALL THIS FOR A WITCH? TALK ABOUT OVERKILL.
THIS IS ALL *BECAUSE* OF THE WITCH.
THE INACTION DURING THE "WITCH'S PASTIME" CASE WAS MUCH STRANGER.
MOST OF THE FIRST THROUGH FOURTH CONTINENTS HAVE NO ARMED OR SPECIAL FORCES.
THEY RELY ON THE PALADINS FOR CRISES...
...SO *NOT* SUMMONING THEM...
...RESULTED IN THAT GHASTLY SITUATION, WITH CITIZENS UNAWARE OF HOW DIRE IT REALLY WAS.

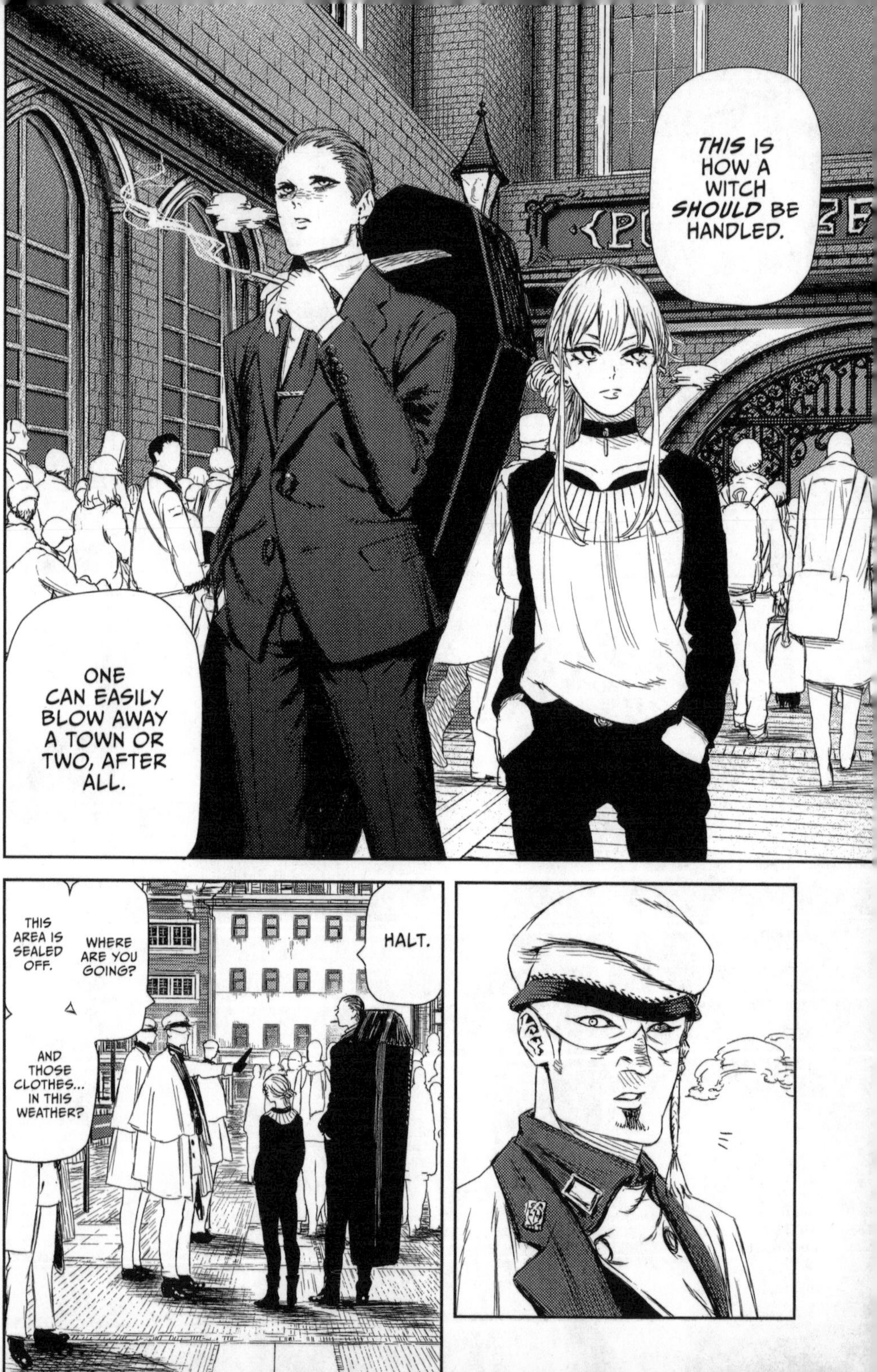

THIS IS HOW A WITCH *SHOULD* BE HANDLED.
ONE CAN EASILY BLOW AWAY A TOWN OR TWO, AFTER ALL.
HALT.
WHERE ARE YOU GOING?
THIS AREA IS SEALED OFF.
AND THOSE CLOTHES... IN THIS WEATHER?

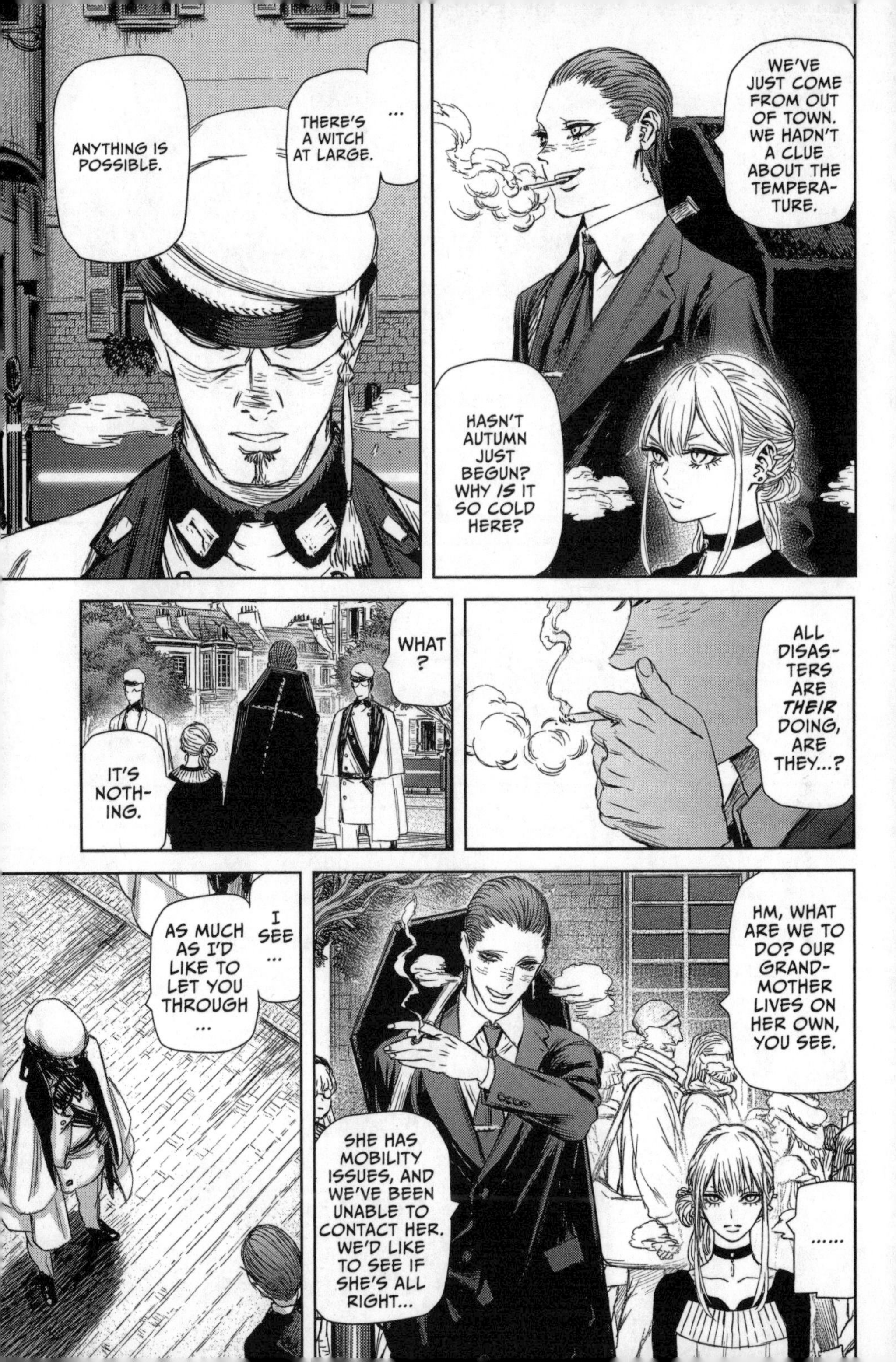
WE'VE JUST COME FROM OUT OF TOWN. WE HADN'T A CLUE ABOUT THE TEMPERATURE.
HASN'T AUTUMN JUST BEGUN? WHY *IS* IT SO COLD HERE?
...
THERE'S A WITCH AT LARGE.
ANYTHING IS POSSIBLE.
ALL DISASTERS ARE *THEIR* DOING, ARE THEY...?
WHAT?
IT'S NOTHING.
HM, WHAT ARE WE TO DO? OUR GRANDMOTHER LIVES ON HER OWN, YOU SEE.
SHE HAS MOBILITY ISSUES, AND WE'VE BEEN UNABLE TO CONTACT HER. WE'D LIKE TO SEE IF SHE'S ALL RIGHT...
......
I SEE...
AS MUCH AS I'D LIKE TO LET YOU THROUGH...

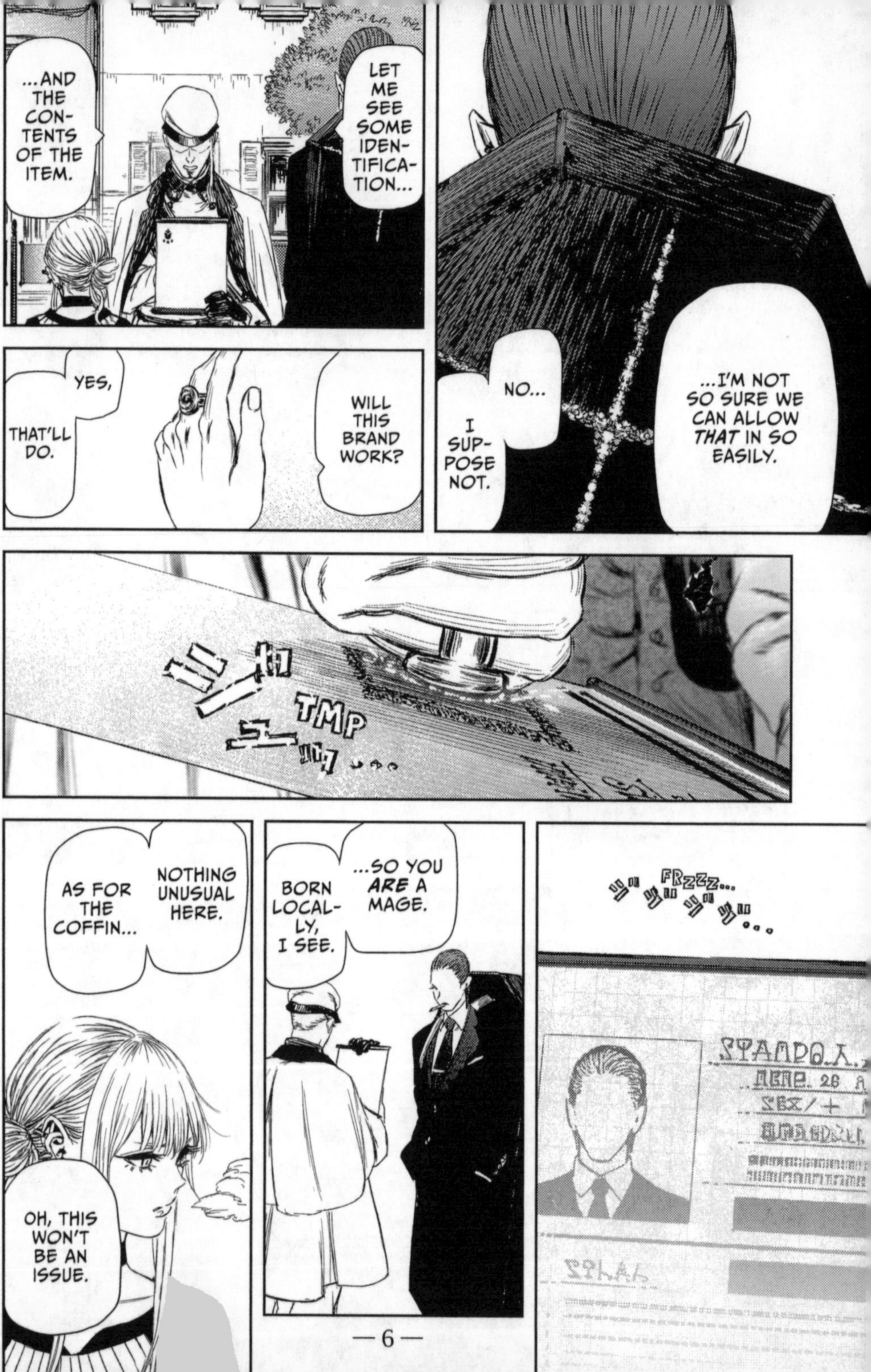
...I'M NOT SO SURE WE CAN ALLOW *THAT* IN SO EASILY.
NO...
I SUPPOSE NOT.
LET ME SEE SOME IDENTIFICATION...
...AND THE CONTENTS OF THE ITEM.
WILL THIS BRAND WORK?
YES,
THAT'LL DO.
TMP
FRZZZ...
...SO YOU *ARE* A MAGE.
BORN LOCALLY, I SEE.
NOTHING UNUSUAL HERE.
AS FOR THE COFFIN...
OH, THIS WON'T BE AN ISSUE.

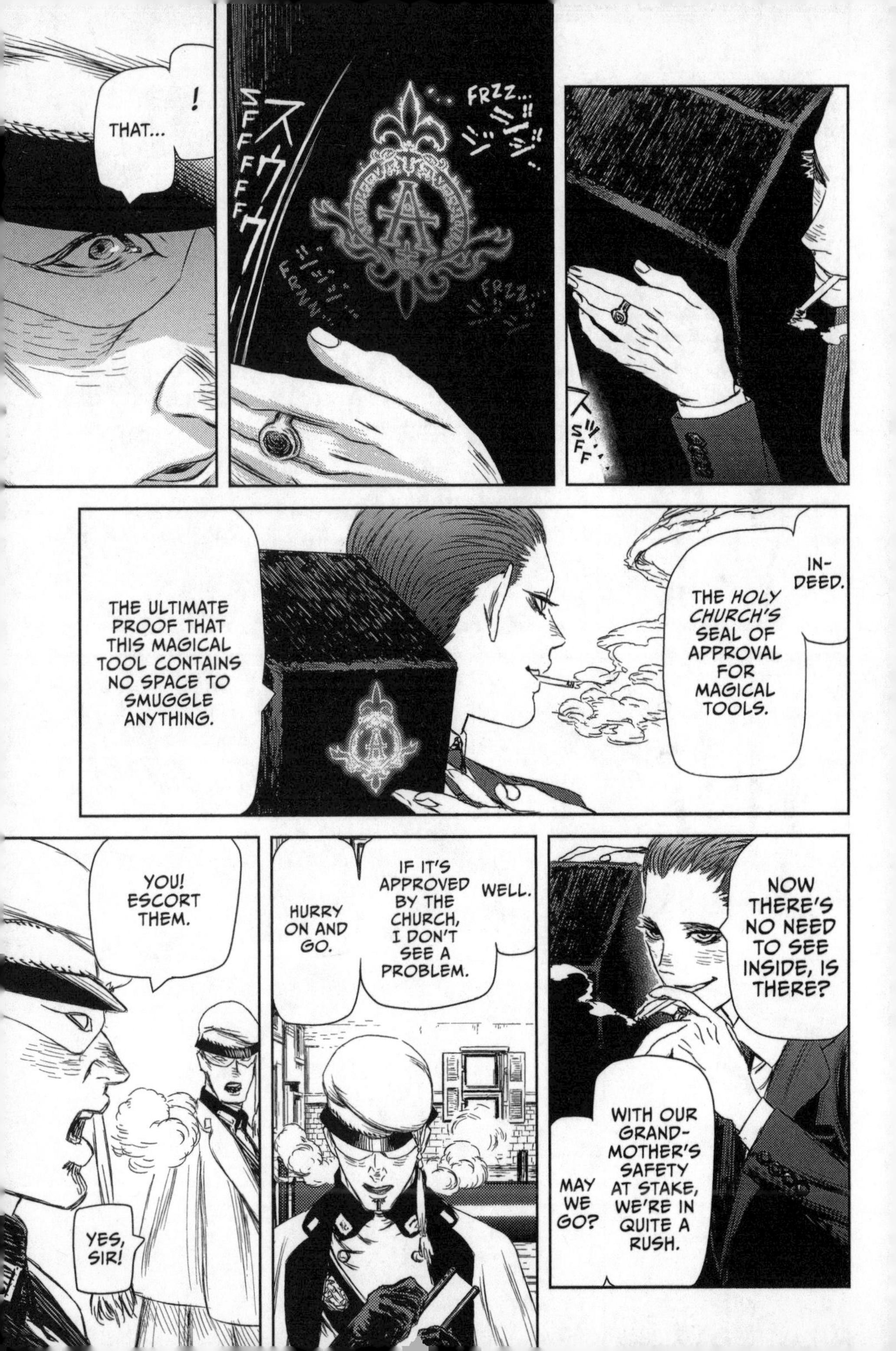
SFF
FRZZ...
SFFFFF
FRZZ
THAT... !
IN-DEED.
THE *HOLY CHURCH'S* SEAL OF APPROVAL FOR MAGICAL TOOLS.
THE ULTIMATE PROOF THAT THIS MAGICAL TOOL CONTAINS NO SPACE TO SMUGGLE ANYTHING.
NOW THERE'S NO NEED TO SEE INSIDE, IS THERE?
WITH OUR GRAND-MOTHER'S SAFETY AT STAKE, WE'RE IN QUITE A RUSH.
MAY WE GO?
WELL.
IF IT'S APPROVED BY THE CHURCH, I DON'T SEE A PROBLEM.
HURRY ON AND GO.
YOU! ESCORT THEM.
YES, SIR!

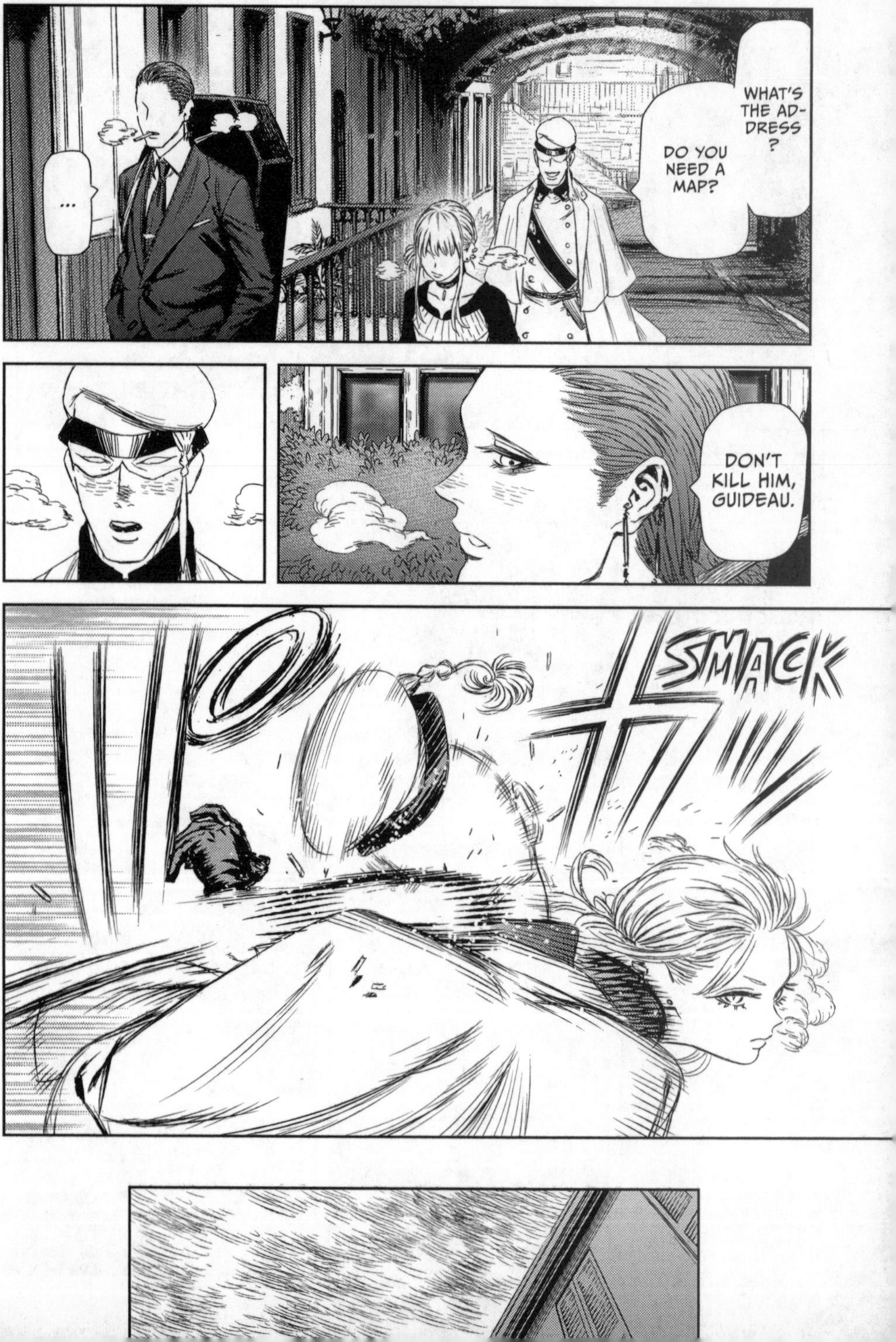
WHAT'S THE AD-DRESS?
DO YOU NEED A MAP?
...
DON'T KILL HIM, GUIDEAU.
SMACK

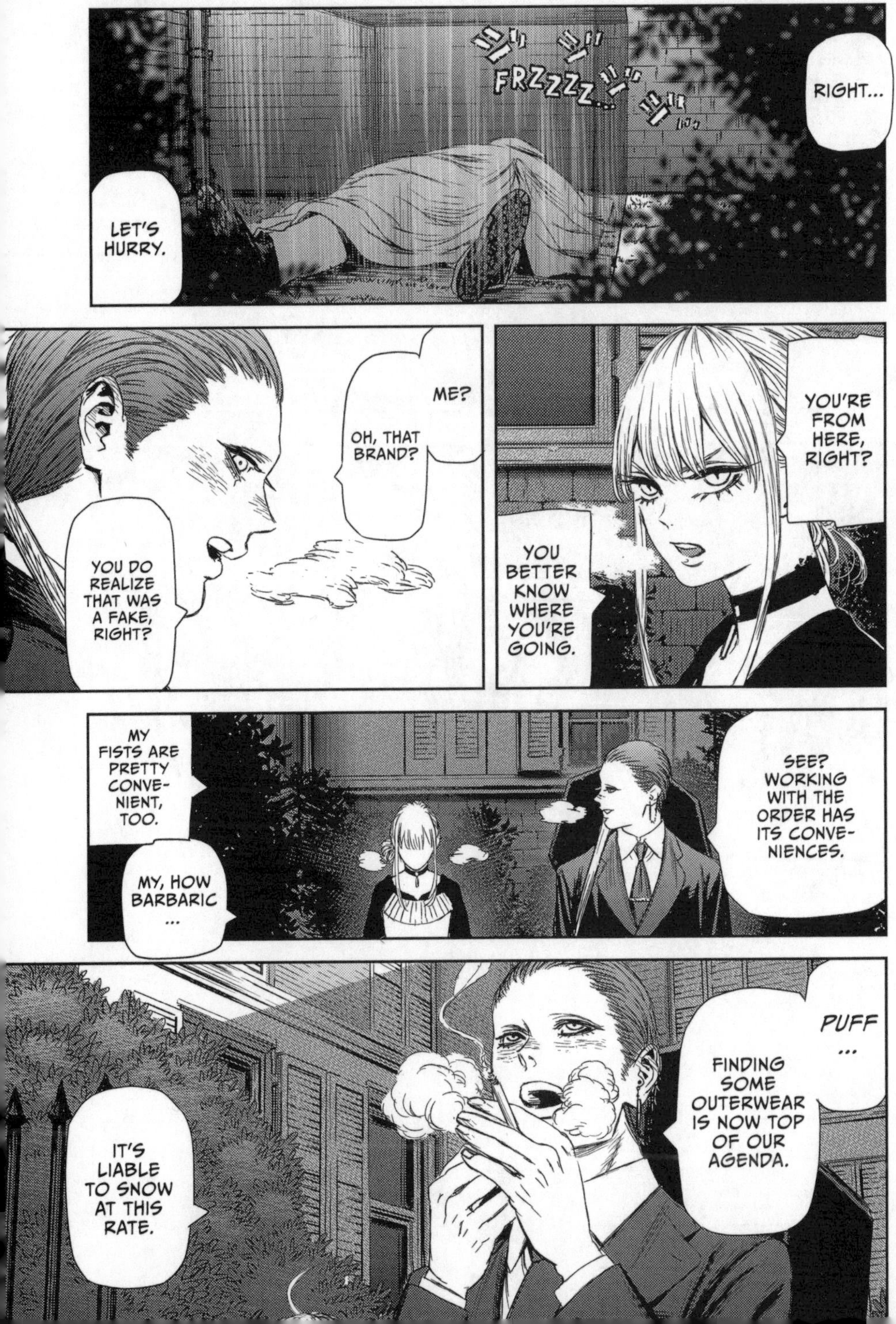
RIGHT...
FRZZZZ...
LET'S HURRY.
YOU'RE FROM HERE, RIGHT?
YOU BETTER KNOW WHERE YOU'RE GOING.
ME?
OH, THAT BRAND?
YOU DO REALIZE THAT WAS A FAKE, RIGHT?
SEE? WORKING WITH THE ORDER HAS ITS CONVENIENCES.
MY FISTS ARE PRETTY CONVENIENT, TOO.
MY, HOW BARBARIC...
PUFF...
FINDING SOME OUTERWEAR IS NOW TOP OF OUR AGENDA.
IT'S LIABLE TO SNOW AT THIS RATE.

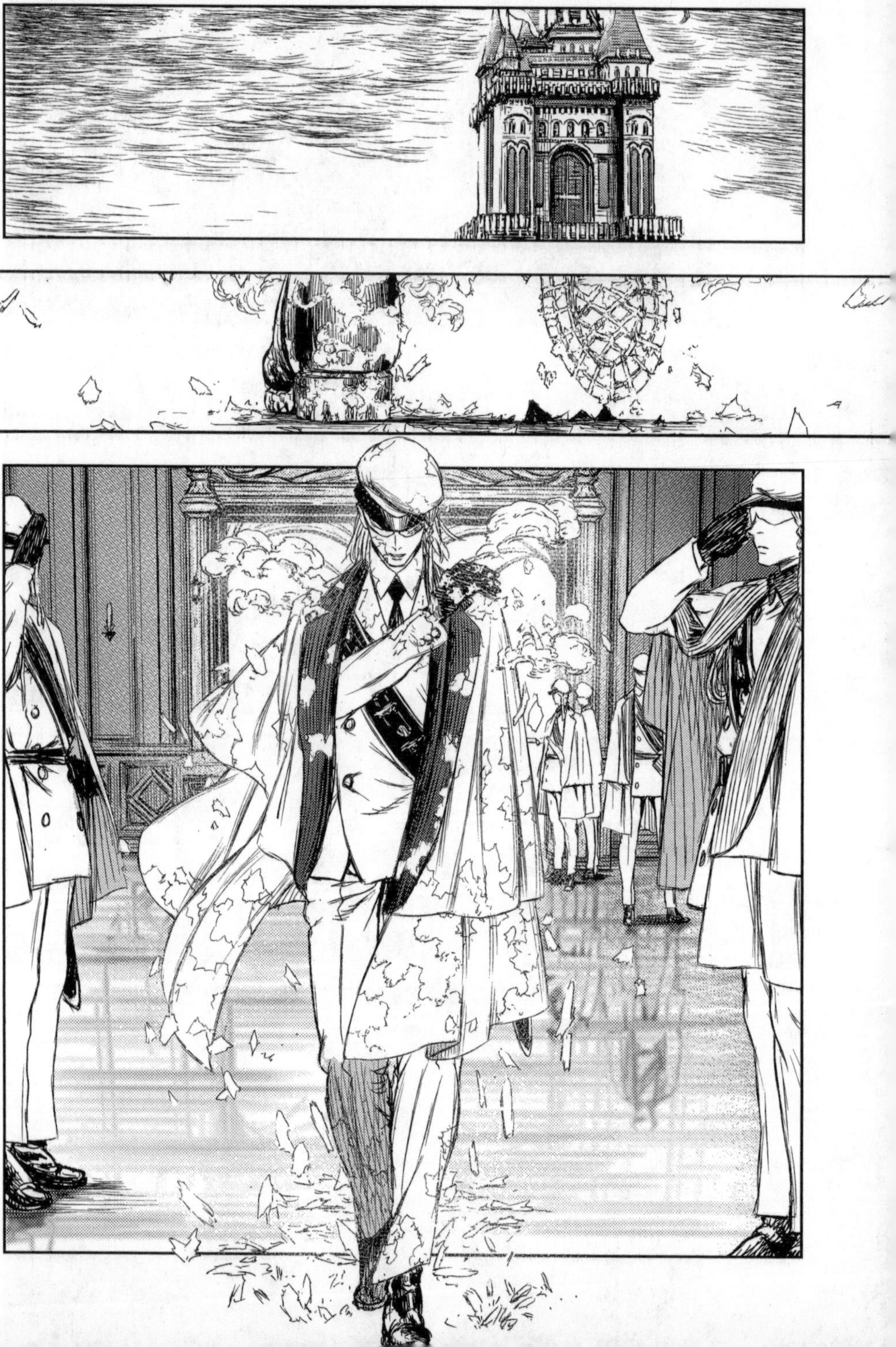

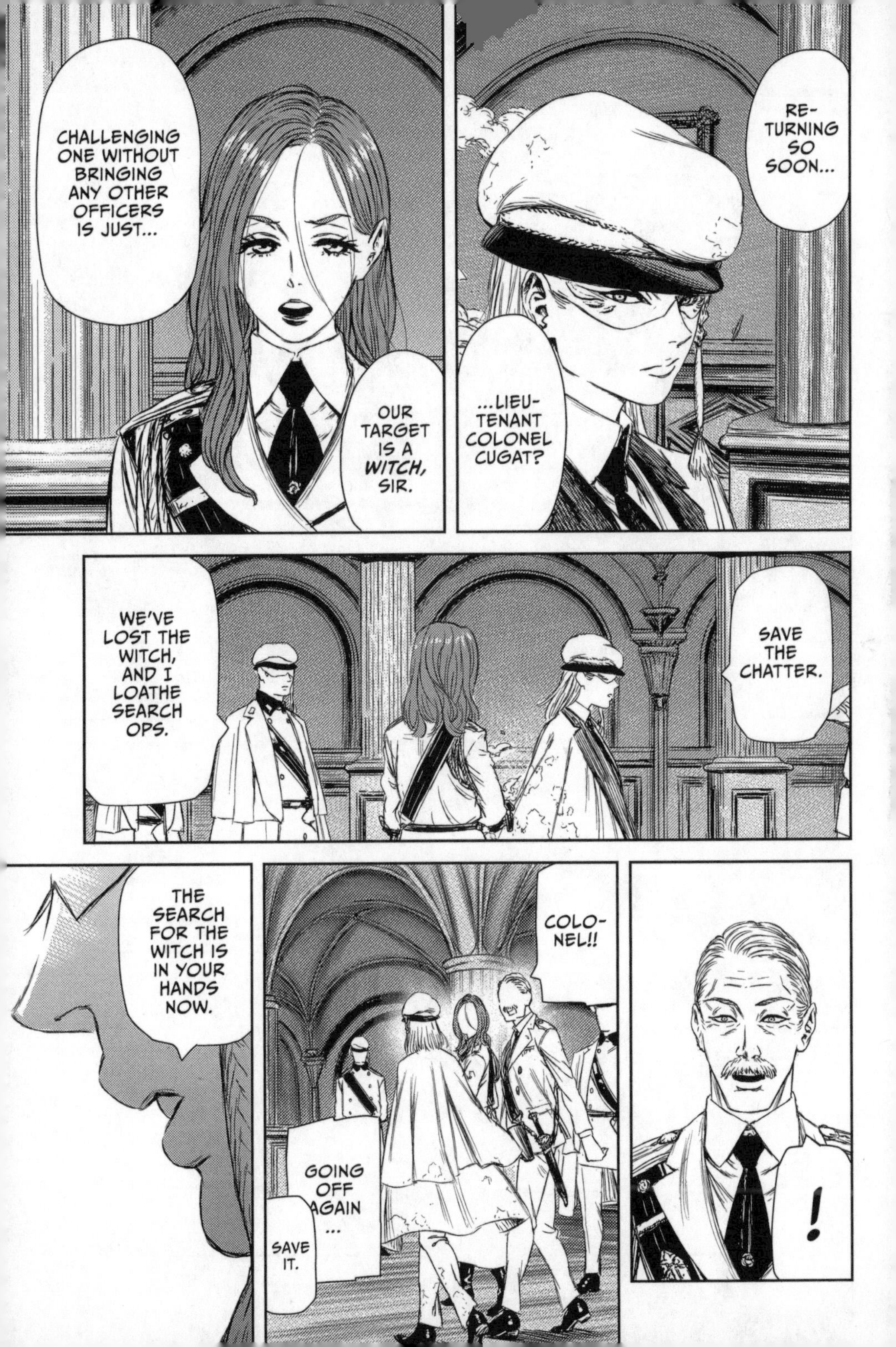
RE-TURNING SO SOON...
...LIEU-TENANT COLONEL CUGAT?
OUR TARGET IS A *WITCH,* SIR.
CHALLENGING ONE WITHOUT BRINGING ANY OTHER OFFICERS IS JUST...
SAVE THE CHATTER.
WE'VE LOST THE WITCH, AND I LOATHE SEARCH OPS.
!
COLO-NEL!!
GOING OFF AGAIN ...
SAVE IT.
THE SEARCH FOR THE WITCH IS IN YOUR HANDS NOW.

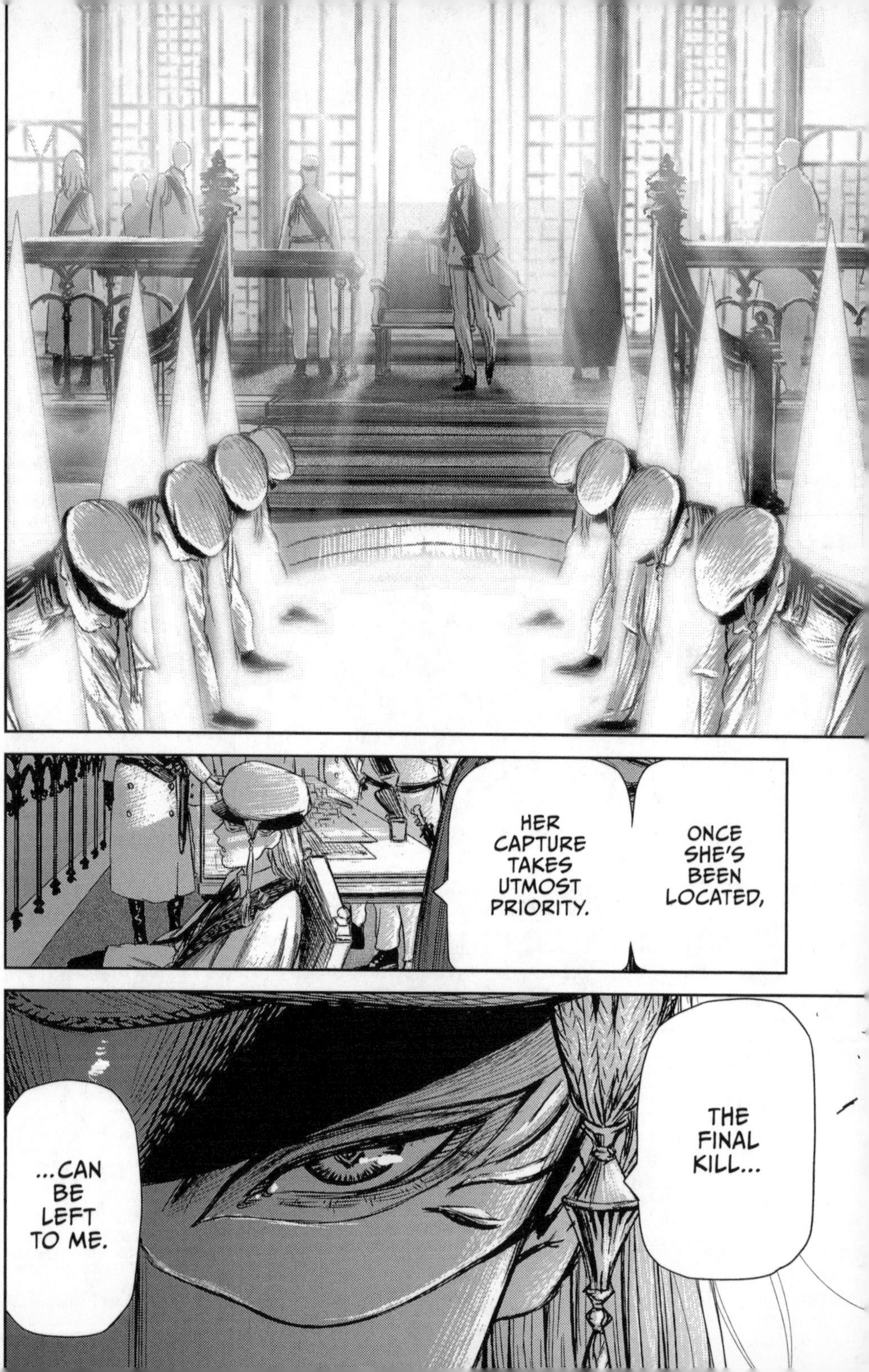
ONCE SHE'S BEEN LOCATED,
HER CAPTURE TAKES UTMOST PRIORITY.
THE FINAL KILL...
...CAN BE LEFT TO ME.

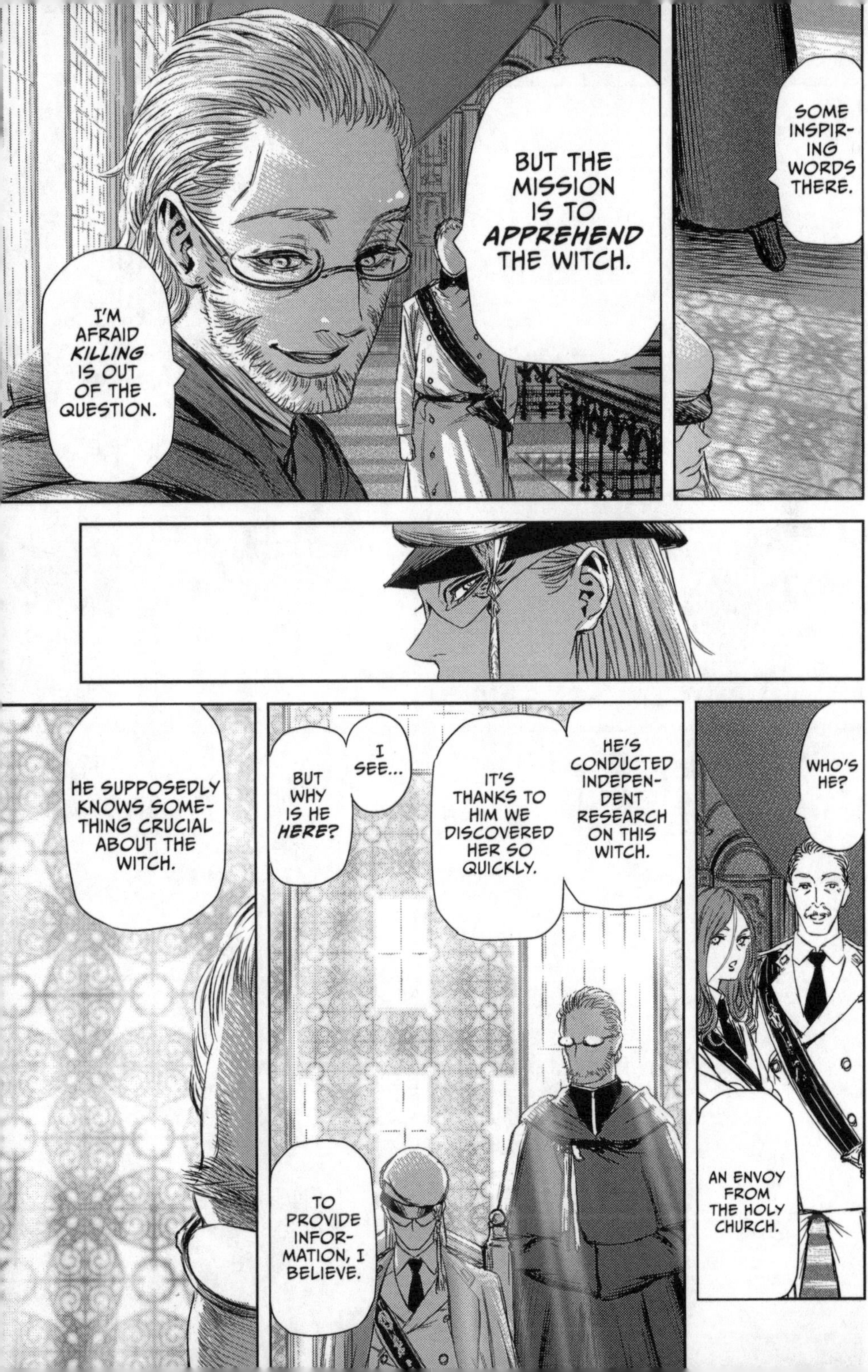
SOME INSPIRING WORDS THERE.
BUT THE MISSION IS TO *APPREHEND* THE WITCH.
I'M AFRAID *KILLING* IS OUT OF THE QUESTION.
WHO'S HE?
AN ENVOY FROM THE HOLY CHURCH.
HE'S CONDUCTED INDEPENDENT RESEARCH ON THIS WITCH.
IT'S THANKS TO HIM WE DISCOVERED HER SO QUICKLY.
I SEE...
BUT WHY IS HE *HERE*?
TO PROVIDE INFORMATION, I BELIEVE.
HE SUPPOSEDLY KNOWS SOMETHING CRUCIAL ABOUT THE WITCH.

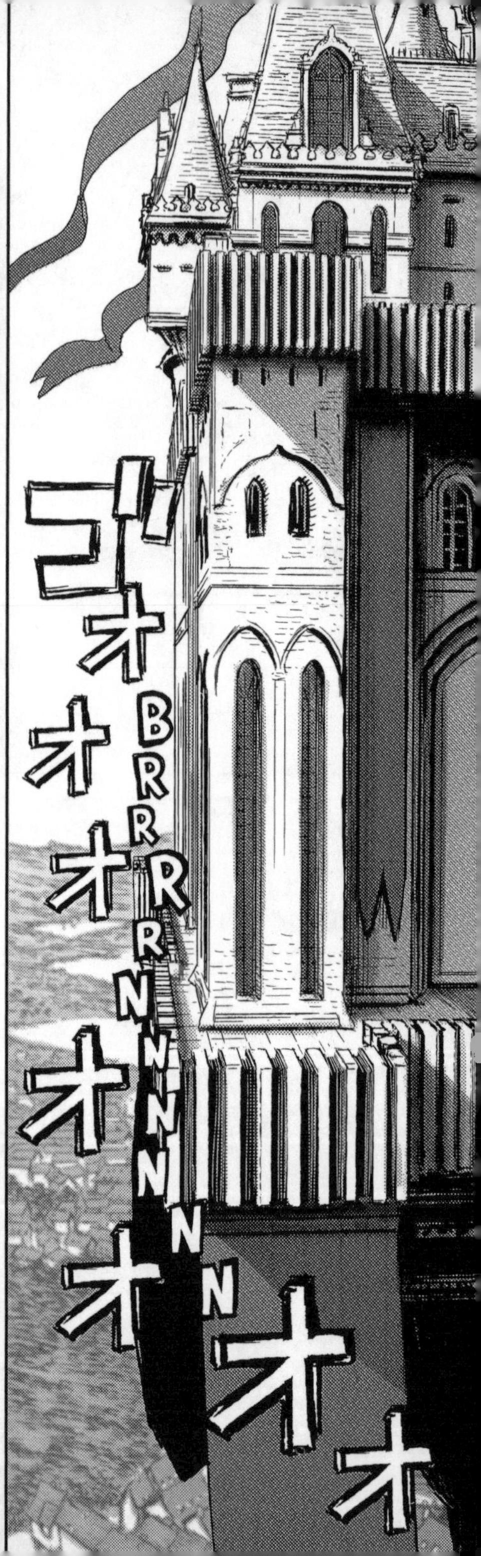
ゴオオオオオオオ
BRRRRNNNNNN

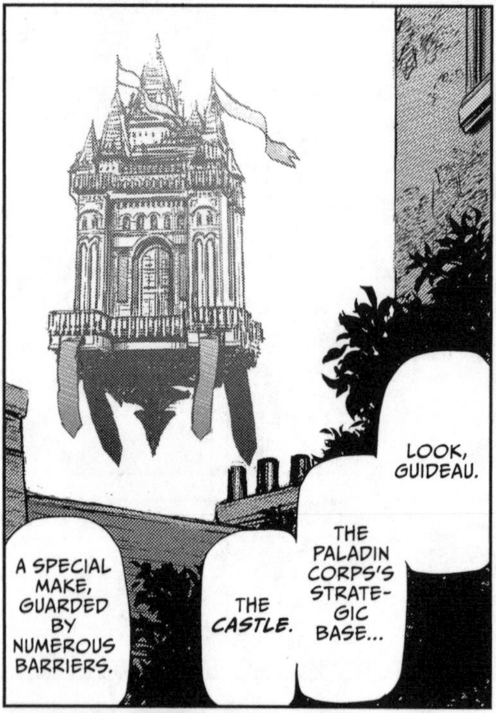
LOOK, GUIDEAU.
THE PALADIN CORPS'S STRATEGIC BASE...
THE *CASTLE*.
A SPECIAL MAKE, GUARDED BY NUMEROUS BARRIERS.

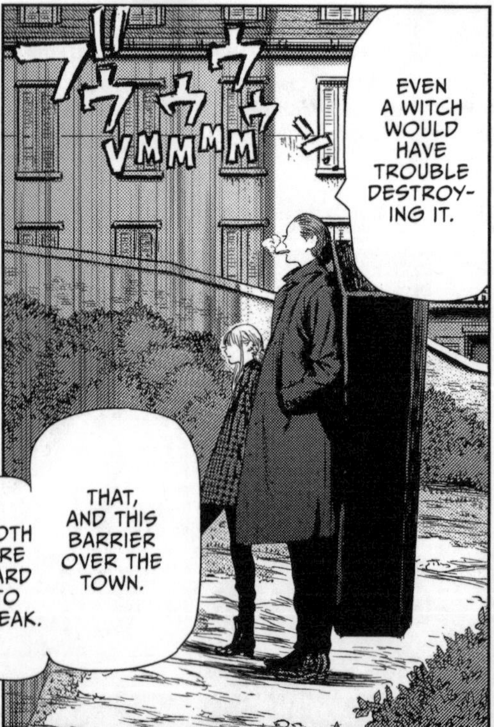
ブウウウウッ
VMMMM
EVEN A WITCH WOULD HAVE TROUBLE DESTROYING IT.
THAT, AND THIS BARRIER OVER THE TOWN.
BOTH ARE HARD TO BREAK.

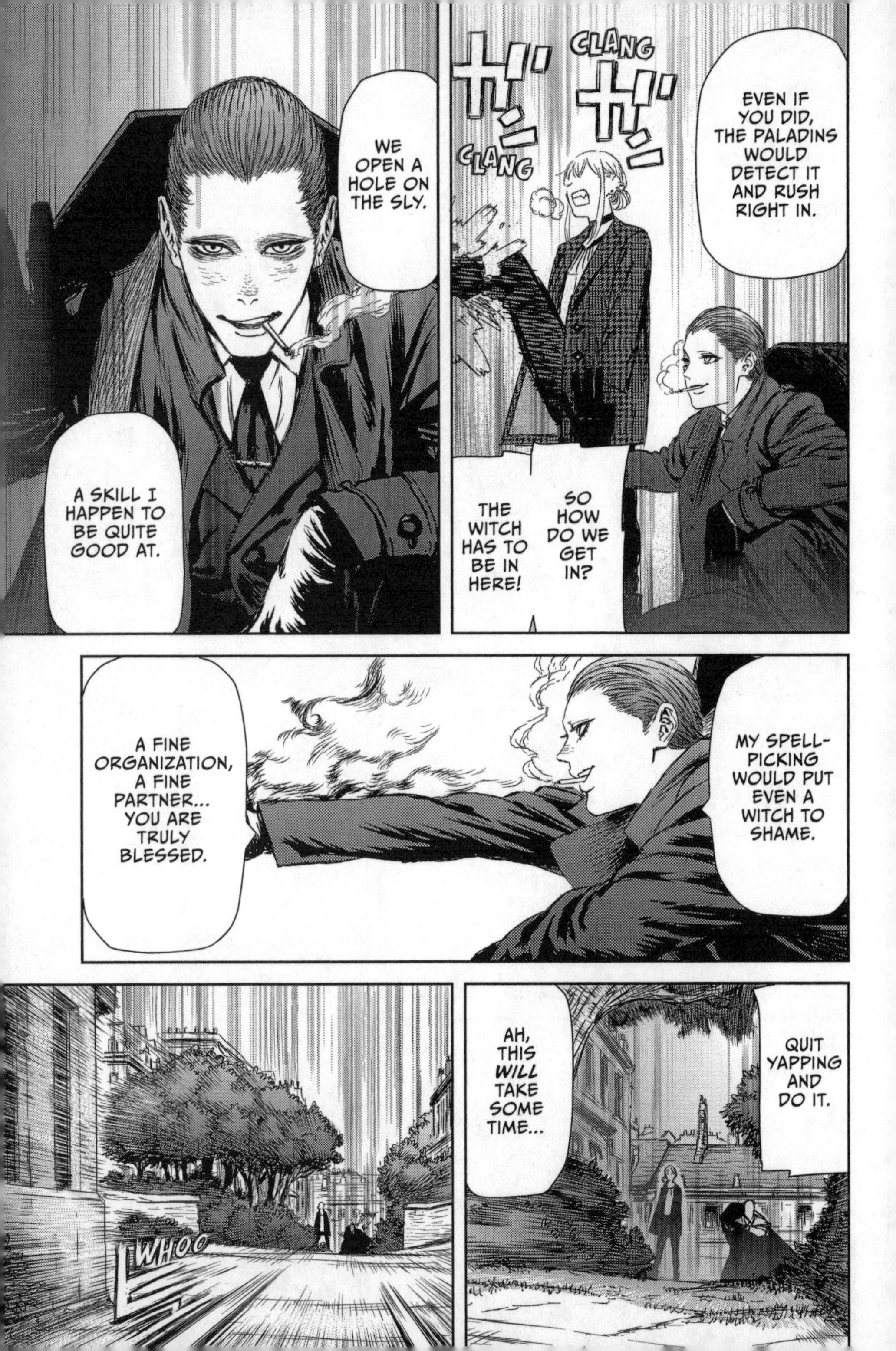
EVEN IF YOU DID, THE PALADINS WOULD DETECT IT AND RUSH RIGHT IN.
CLANG
CLANG
SO HOW DO WE GET IN?
THE WITCH HAS TO BE IN HERE!
WE OPEN A HOLE ON THE SLY.
A SKILL I HAPPEN TO BE QUITE GOOD AT.
MY SPELL-PICKING WOULD PUT EVEN A WITCH TO SHAME.
A FINE ORGANIZATION, A FINE PARTNER... YOU ARE TRULY BLESSED.
QUIT YAPPING AND DO IT.
AH, THIS *WILL* TAKE SOME TIME...
WHOO

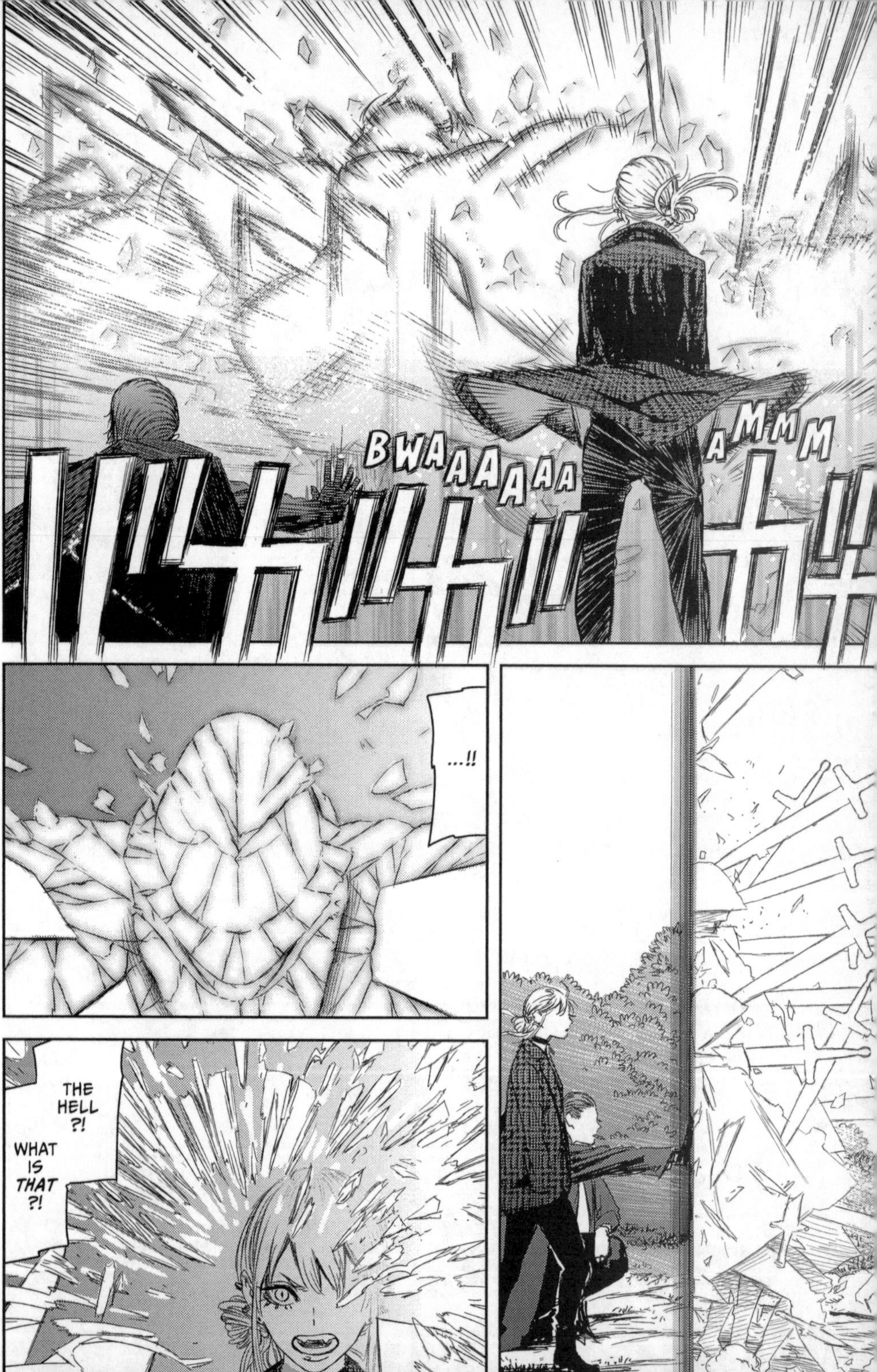
BWAAAAAAAAMMM
...!!
THE HELL ?!
WHAT IS *THAT* ?!

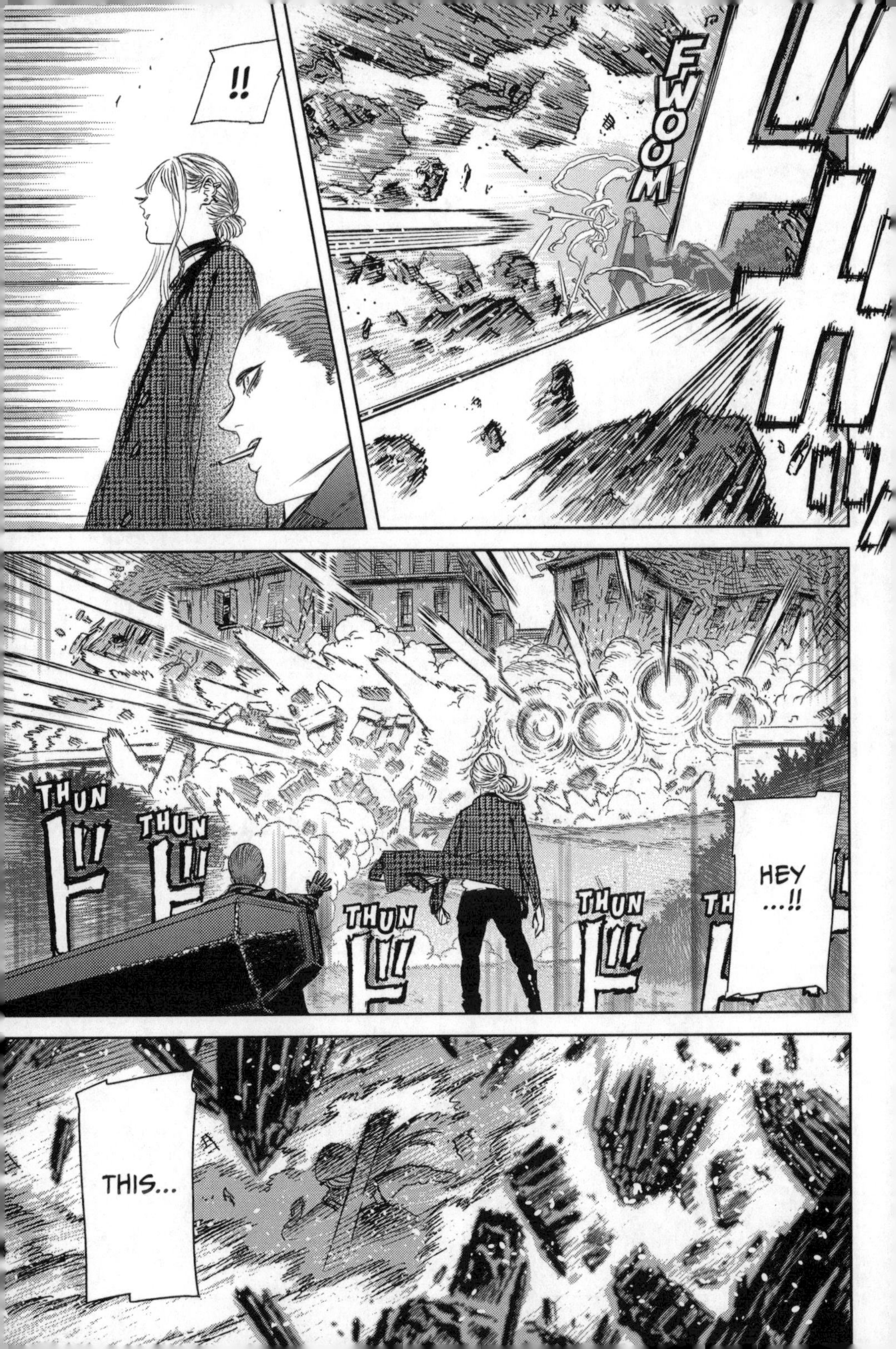
FWOOM
!!
HEY ...!!
THUN
THUN
THUN
THUN
THIS...

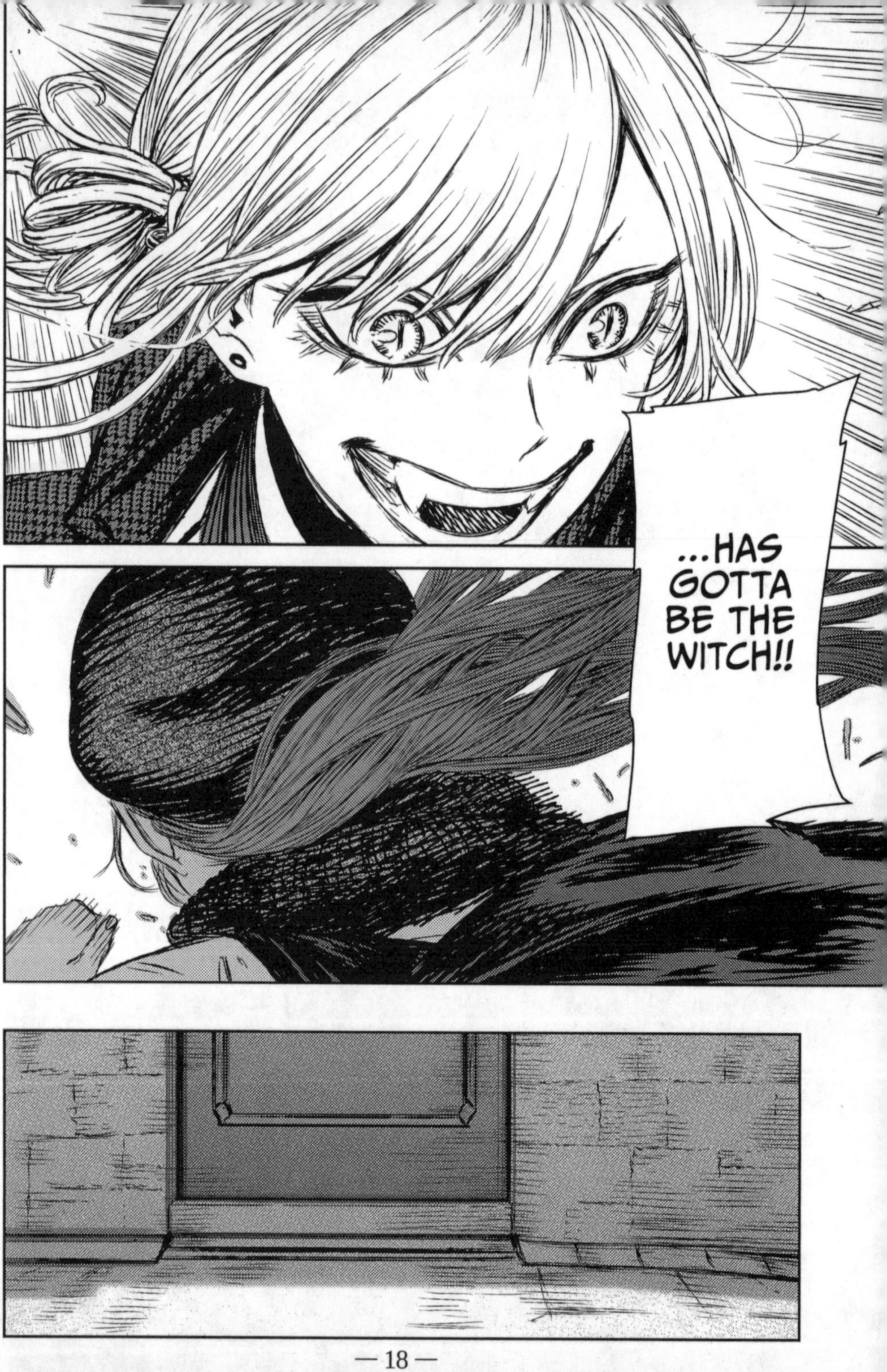
...HAS GOTTA BE THE WITCH!!

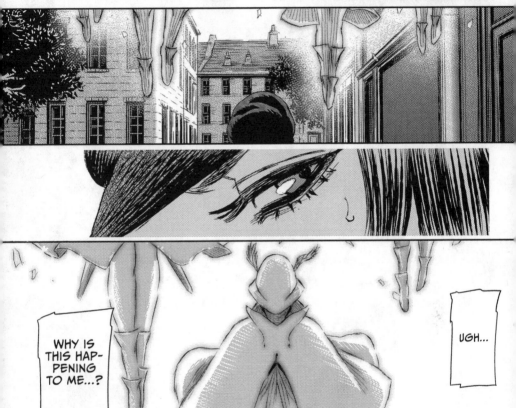

WHY IS THIS HAP- PENING TO ME...?

UGH...

I CAN'T DIE YET...!

I DON'T WANT TO DIE YET...

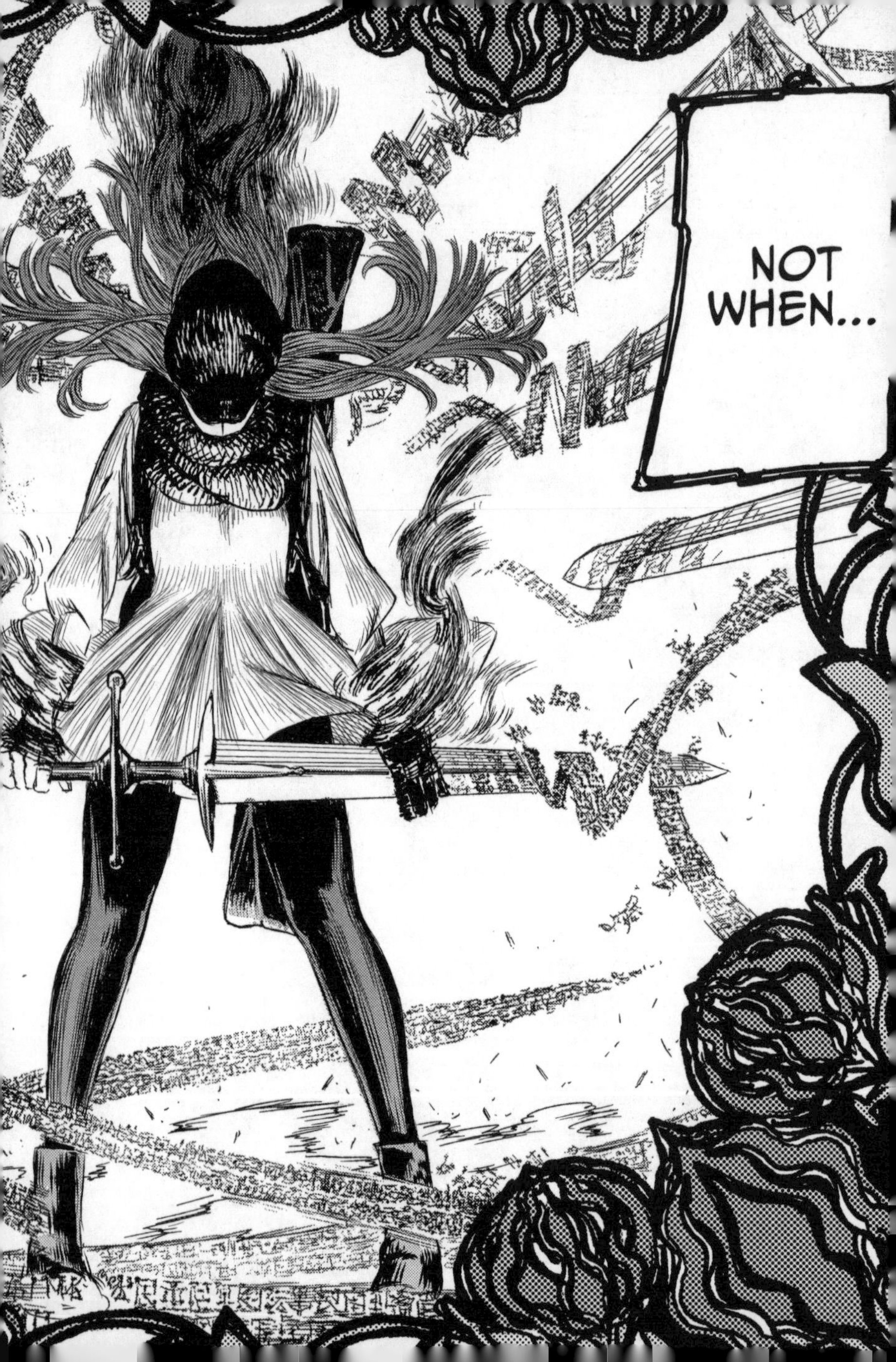
NOT WHEN...

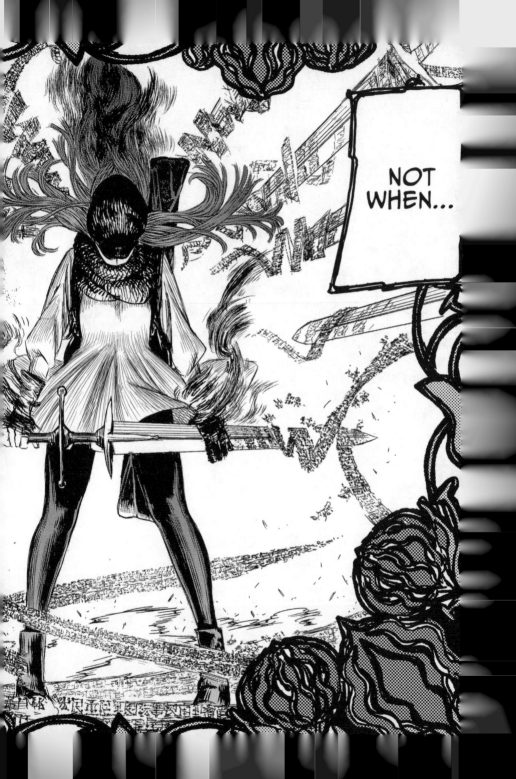

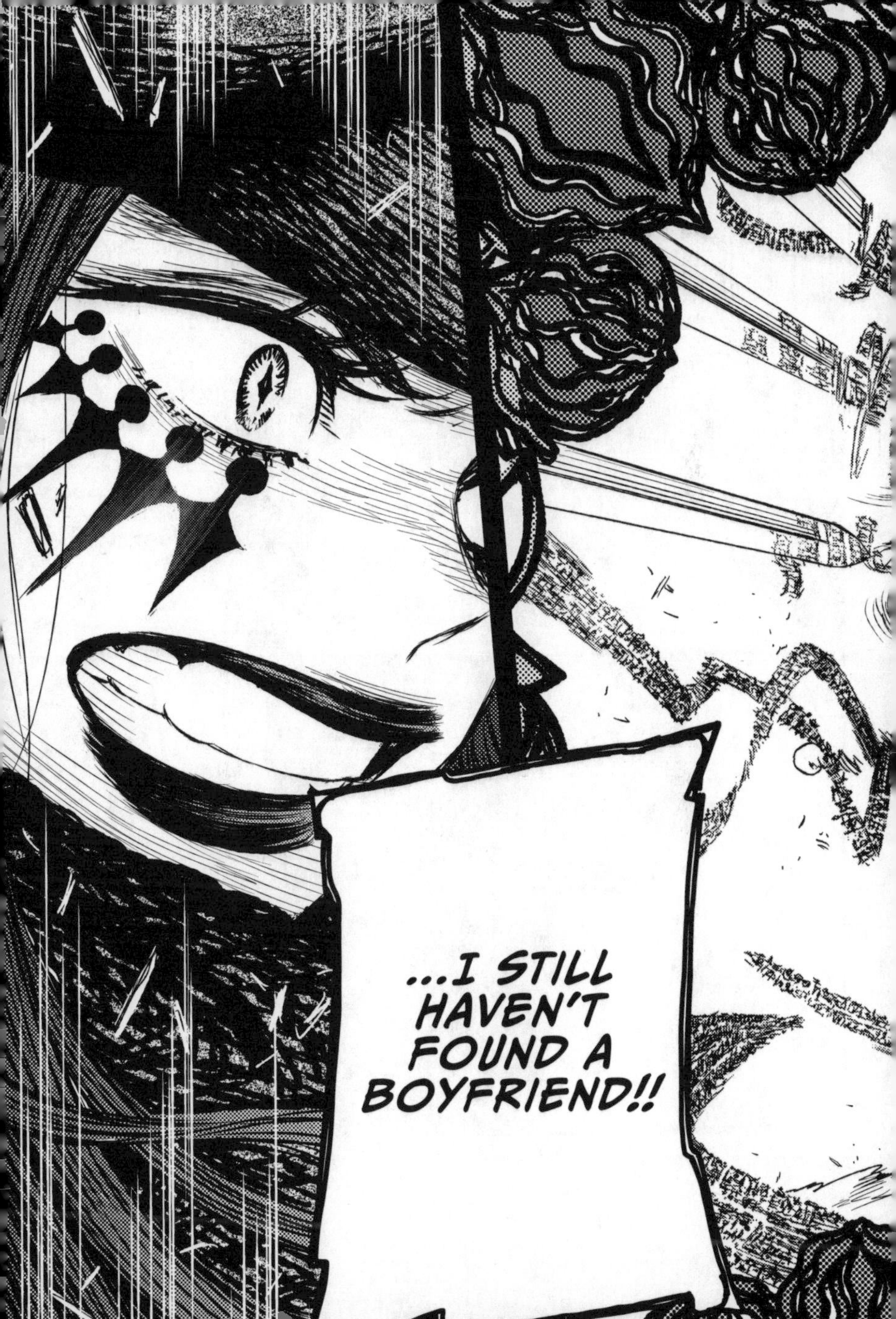
...I STILL HAVEN'T FOUND A BOYFRIEND!!

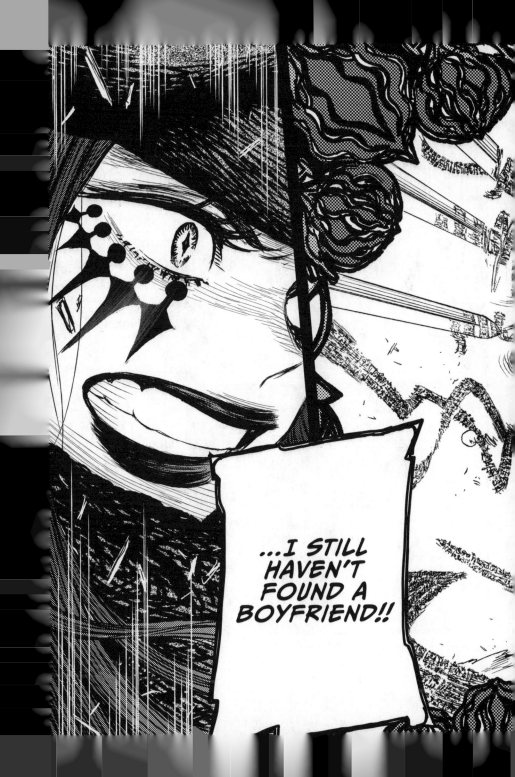

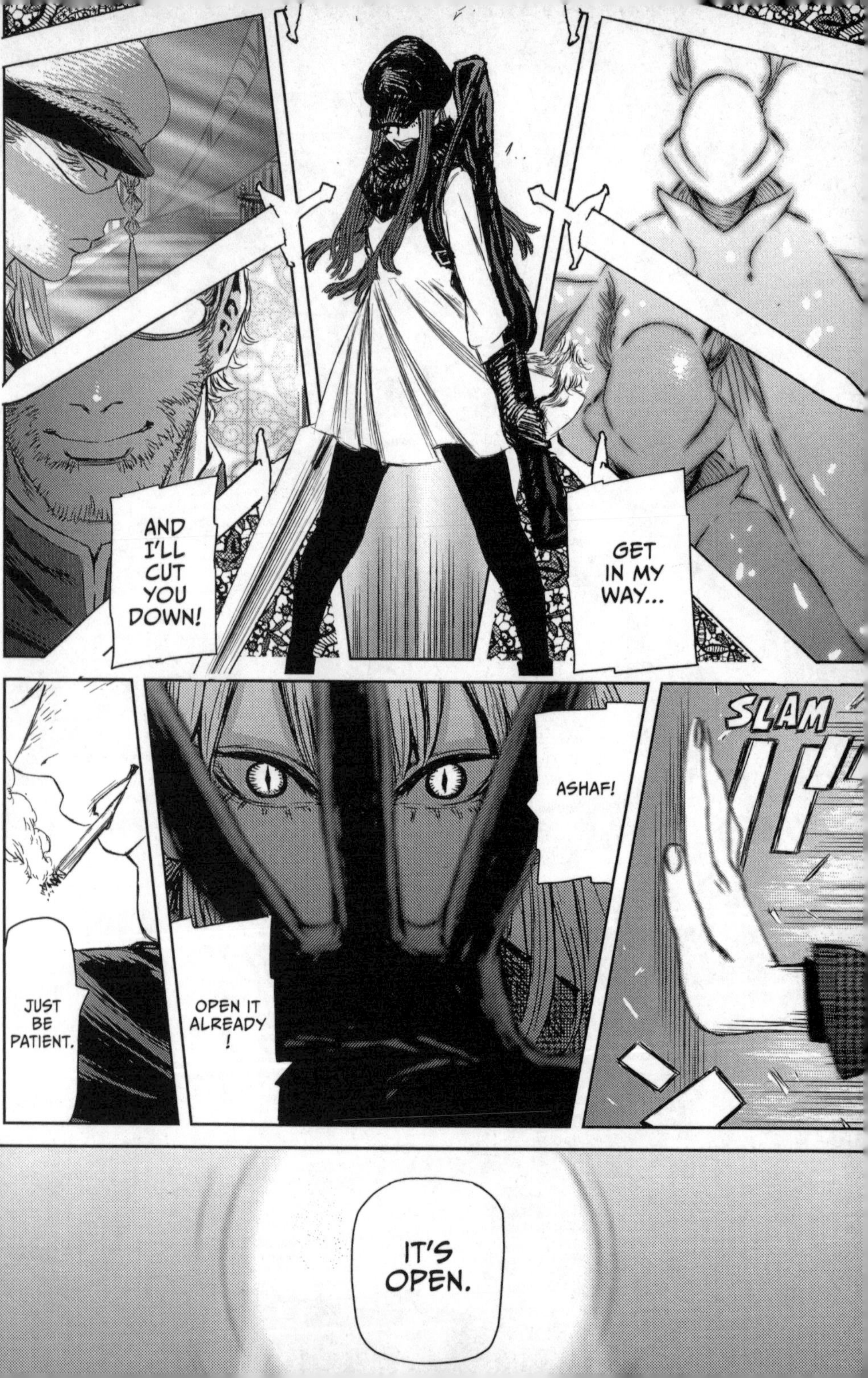
GET IN MY WAY...
AND I'LL CUT YOU DOWN!
SLAM
ASHAF!
OPEN IT ALREADY!
JUST BE PATIENT.
IT'S OPEN.

THE WITCH AND THE BEAST

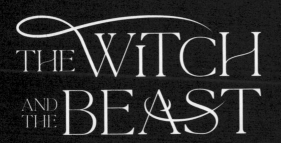

THE WITCH AND THE BEAST

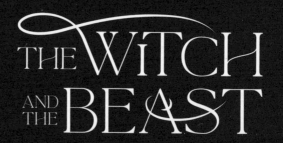

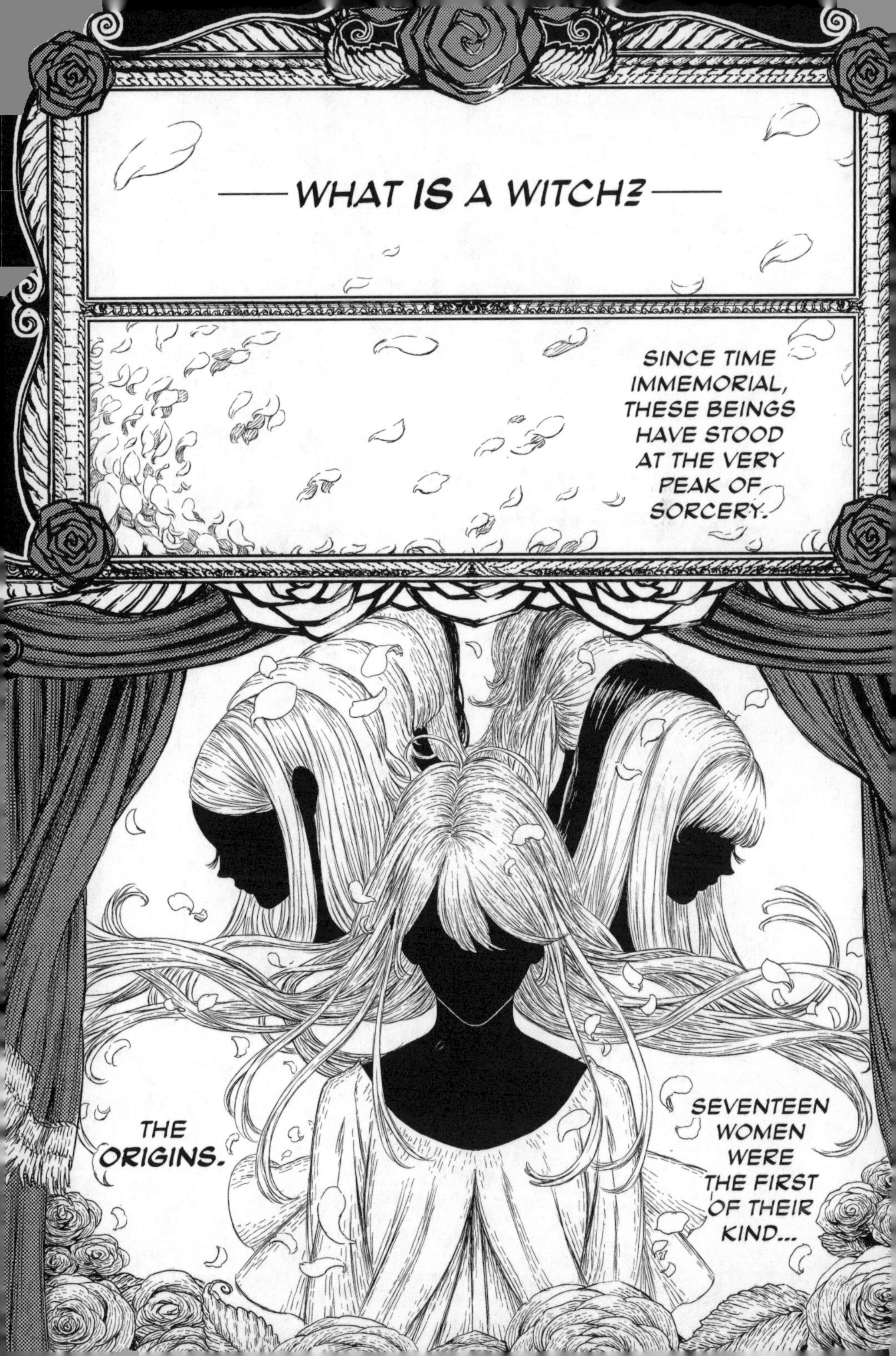
WHAT IS A WITCH?
SINCE TIME IMMEMORIAL, THESE BEINGS HAVE STOOD AT THE VERY PEAK OF SORCERY.
SEVENTEEN WOMEN WERE THE FIRST OF THEIR KIND...
THE ORIGINS.

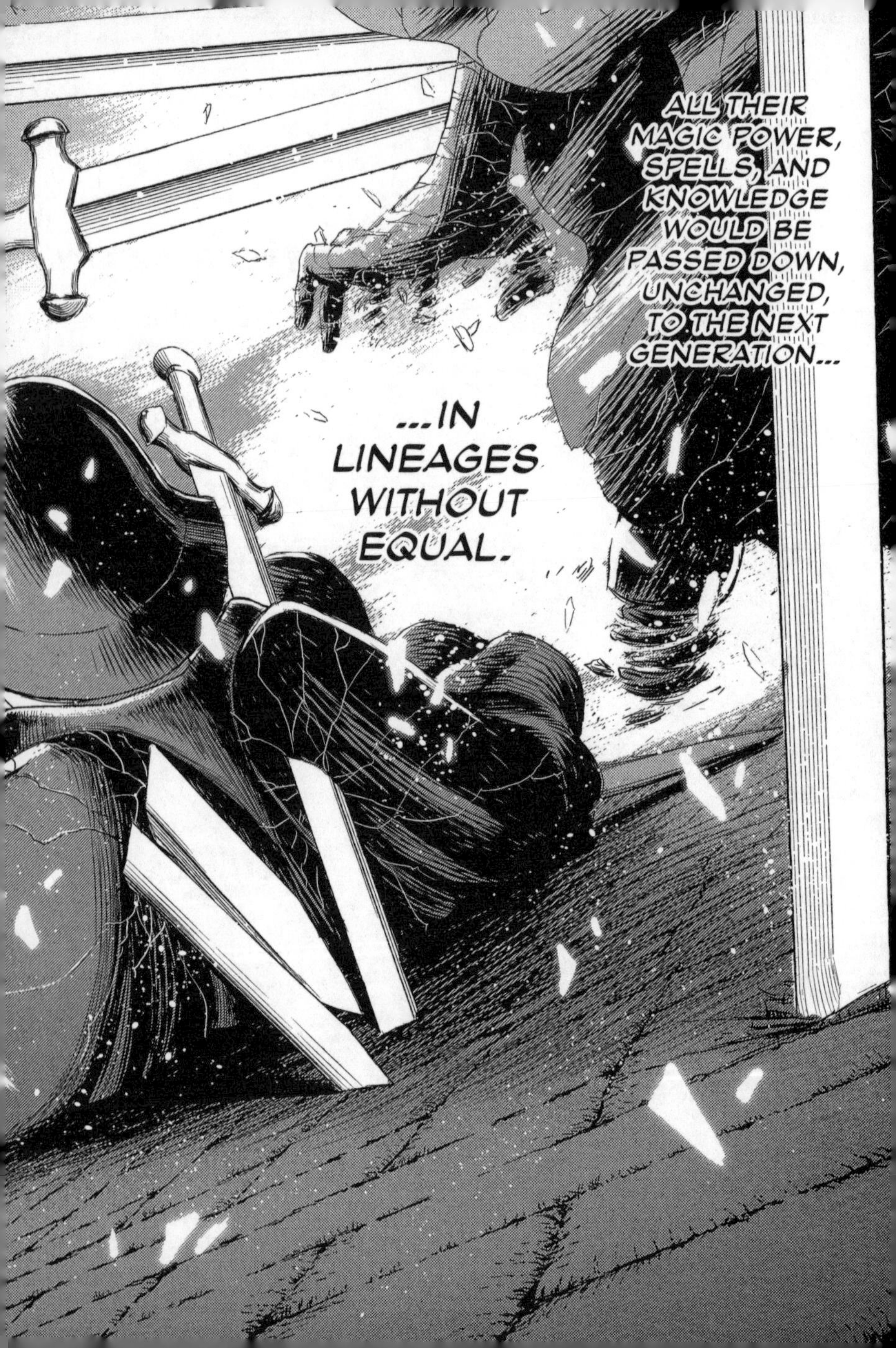
ALL THEIR MAGIC POWER, SPELLS, AND KNOWLEDGE WOULD BE PASSED DOWN, UNCHANGED, TO THE NEXT GENERATION...
...IN LINEAGES WITHOUT EQUAL.

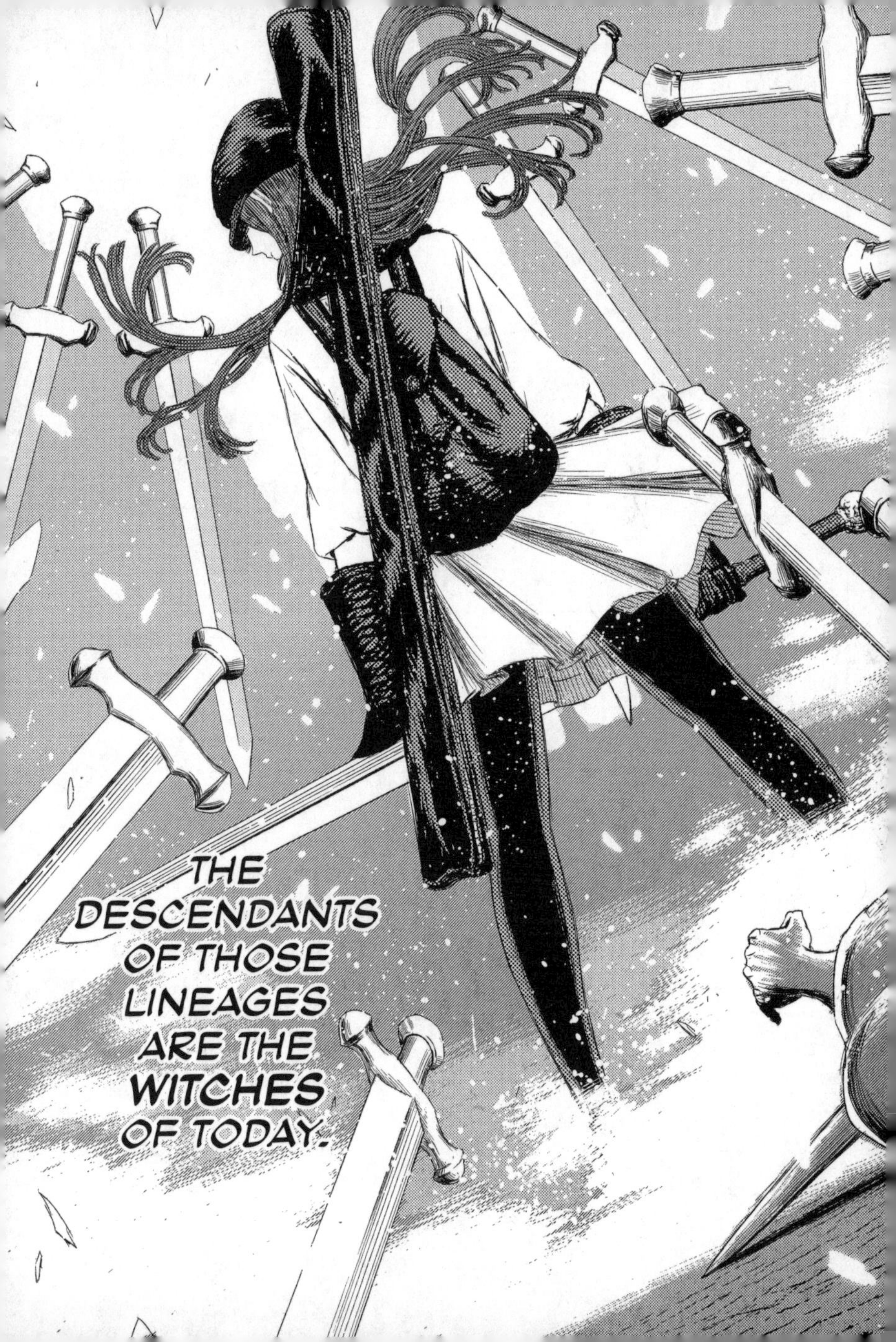
THE DESCENDANTS OF THOSE LINEAGES ARE THE WITCHES OF TODAY.

CHAPTER 12: THE WITCH AND THE DEMON SWORD—ACT III

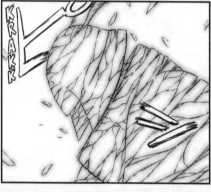

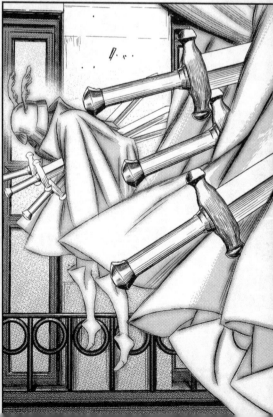

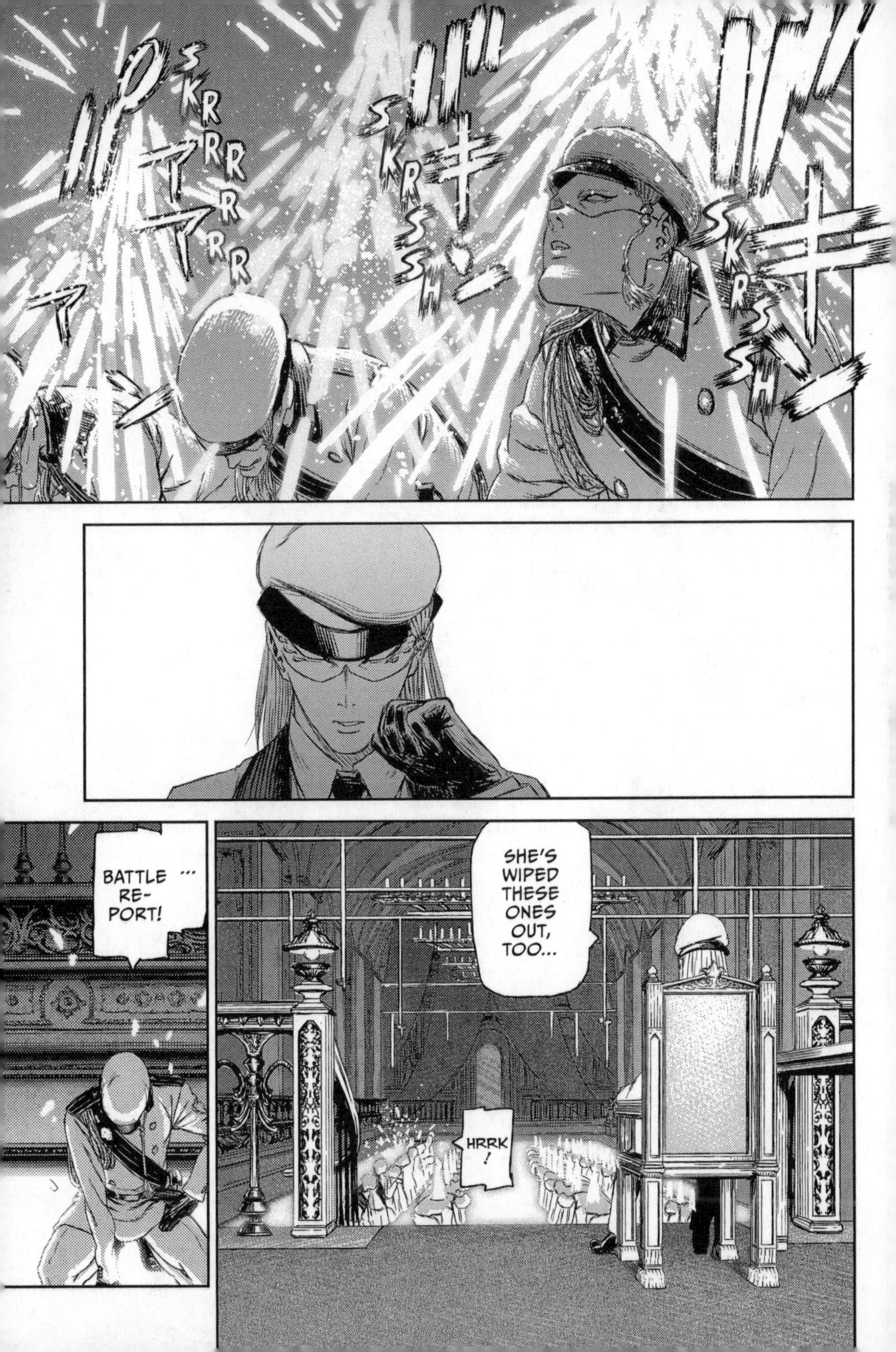
SKRSSH
SKRSSH
SKRRRRRR
SHE'S WIPED THESE ONES OUT, TOO...
HRRK!
BATTLE REPORT! ...

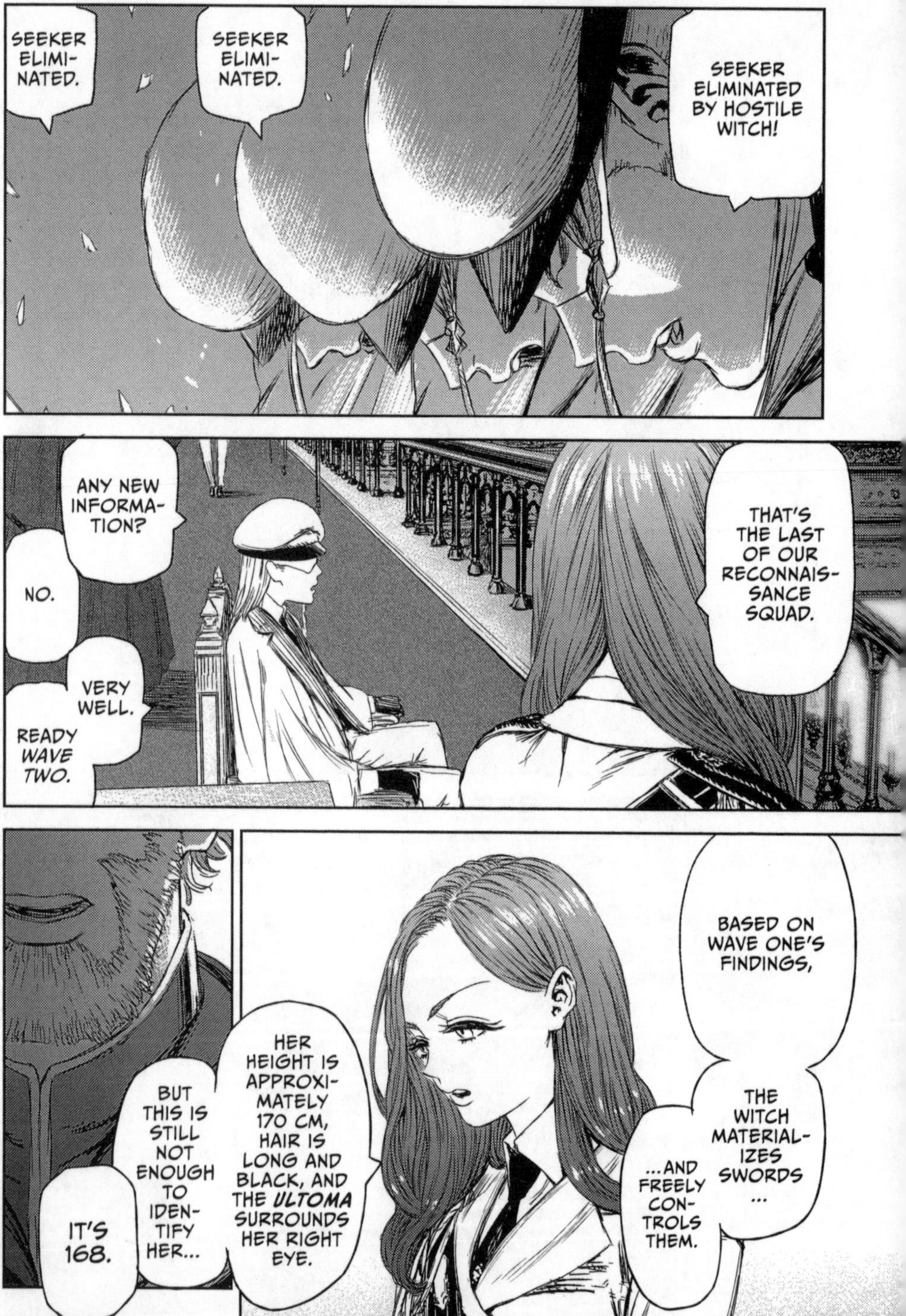
SEEKER ELIMINATED BY HOSTILE WITCH!
SEEKER ELIMINATED.
SEEKER ELIMINATED.
THAT'S THE LAST OF OUR RECONNAISSANCE SQUAD.
ANY NEW INFORMATION?
NO.
VERY WELL.
READY *WAVE TWO.*
BASED ON WAVE ONE'S FINDINGS,
THE WITCH MATERIALIZES SWORDS...
...AND FREELY CONTROLS THEM.
HER HEIGHT IS APPROXIMATELY 170 CM, HAIR IS LONG AND BLACK, AND THE *ULTOMA* SURROUNDS HER RIGHT EYE.
BUT THIS IS STILL NOT ENOUGH TO IDENTIFY HER...
IT'S 168.

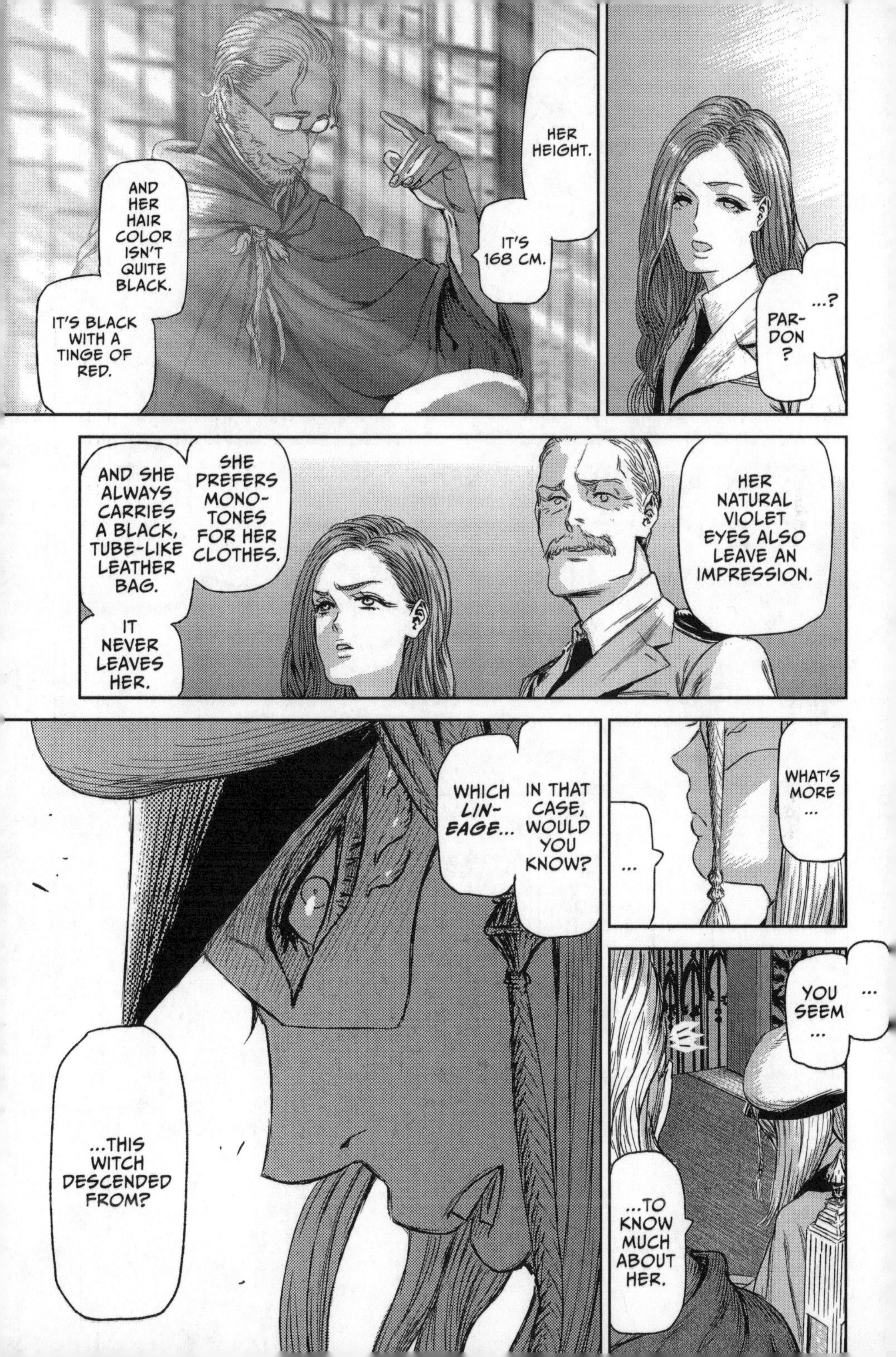
...?
PARDON?
HER HEIGHT.
IT'S 168 CM.
AND HER HAIR COLOR ISN'T QUITE BLACK.
IT'S BLACK WITH A TINGE OF RED.
HER NATURAL VIOLET EYES ALSO LEAVE AN IMPRESSION.
SHE PREFERS MONOTONES FOR HER CLOTHES.
AND SHE ALWAYS CARRIES A BLACK, TUBE-LIKE LEATHER BAG.
IT NEVER LEAVES HER.
WHAT'S MORE...
...
...
YOU SEEM...
...TO KNOW MUCH ABOUT HER.
IN THAT CASE, WOULD YOU KNOW?
WHICH *LINEAGE*...
...THIS WITCH DESCENDED FROM?

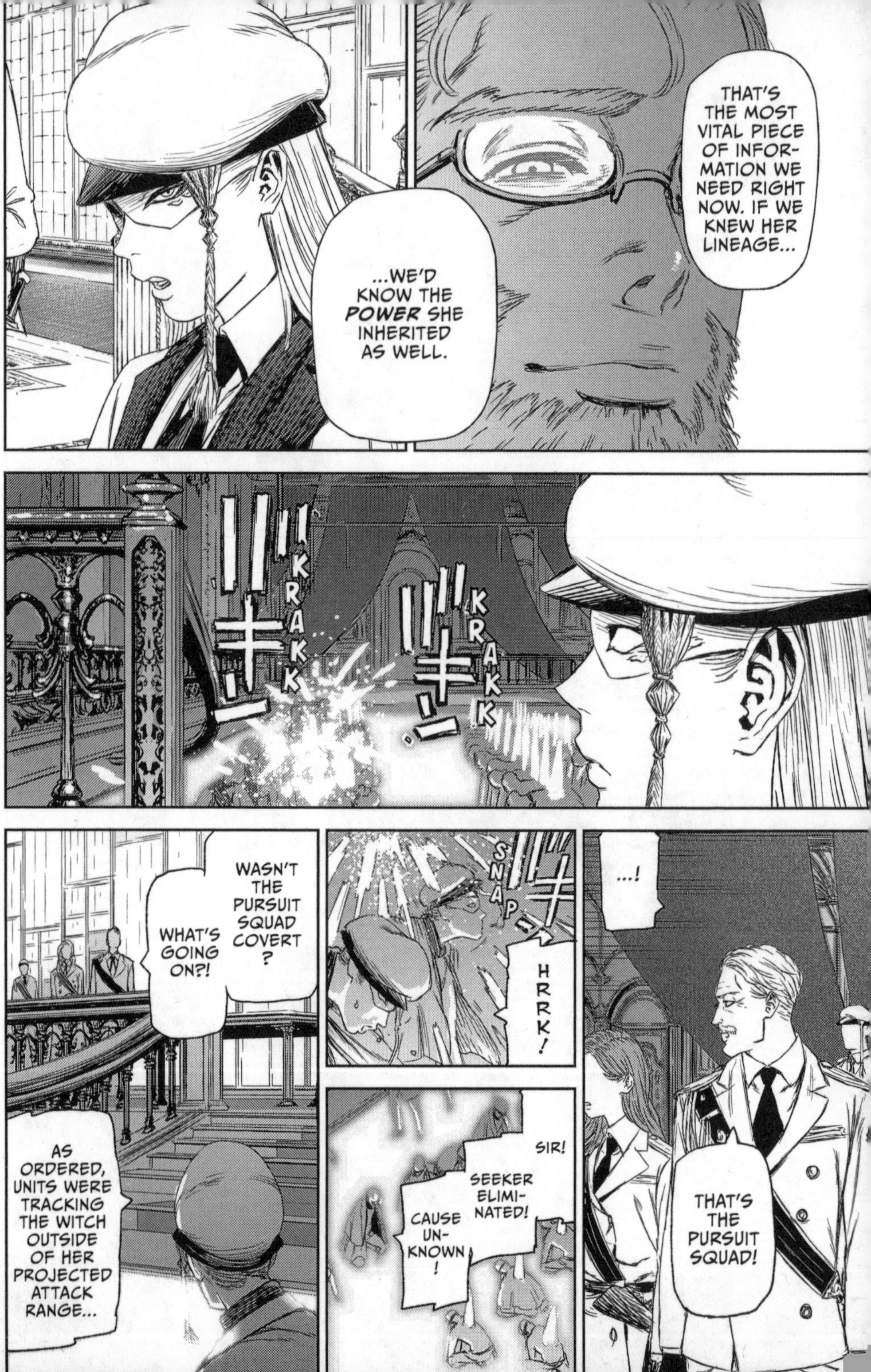
THAT'S THE MOST VITAL PIECE OF INFORMATION WE NEED RIGHT NOW. IF WE KNEW HER LINEAGE...
...WE'D KNOW THE *POWER* SHE INHERITED AS WELL.
KRAKK
KRAKK
...!
THAT'S THE PURSUIT SQUAD!
SNAP
HRRK!
SIR!
SEEKER ELIMINATED!
CAUSE UNKNOWN!
WASN'T THE PURSUIT SQUAD COVERT?
WHAT'S GOING ON?!
AS ORDERED, UNITS WERE TRACKING THE WITCH OUTSIDE OF HER PROJECTED ATTACK RANGE...

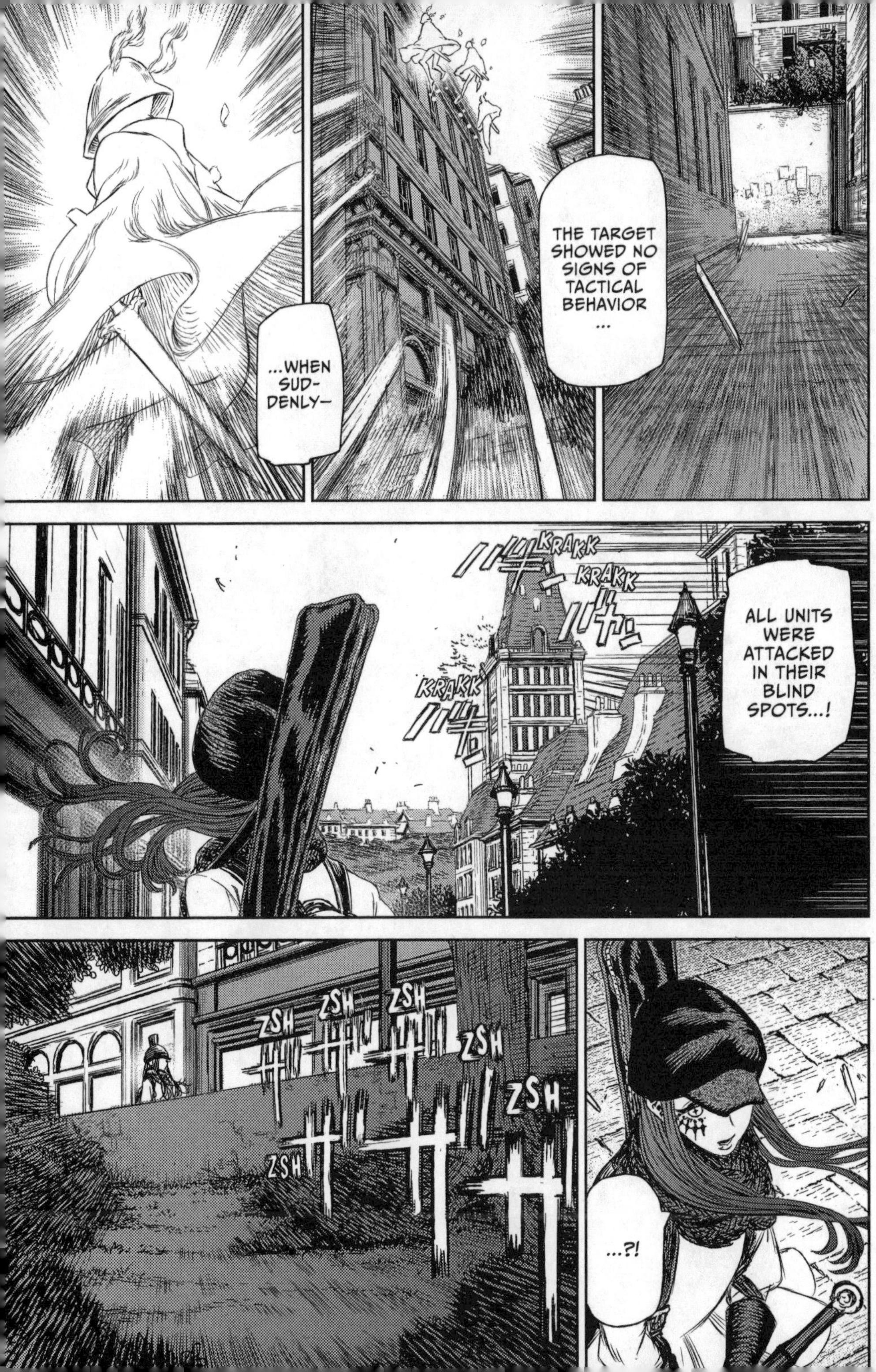
THE TARGET SHOWED NO SIGNS OF TACTICAL BEHAVIOR ...
...WHEN SUD-DENLY—
ALL UNITS WERE ATTACKED IN THEIR BLIND SPOTS...!
KRAKK
KRAKK
KRAKK
...?!
ZSH
ZSH
ZSH
ZSH
ZSH
ZSH

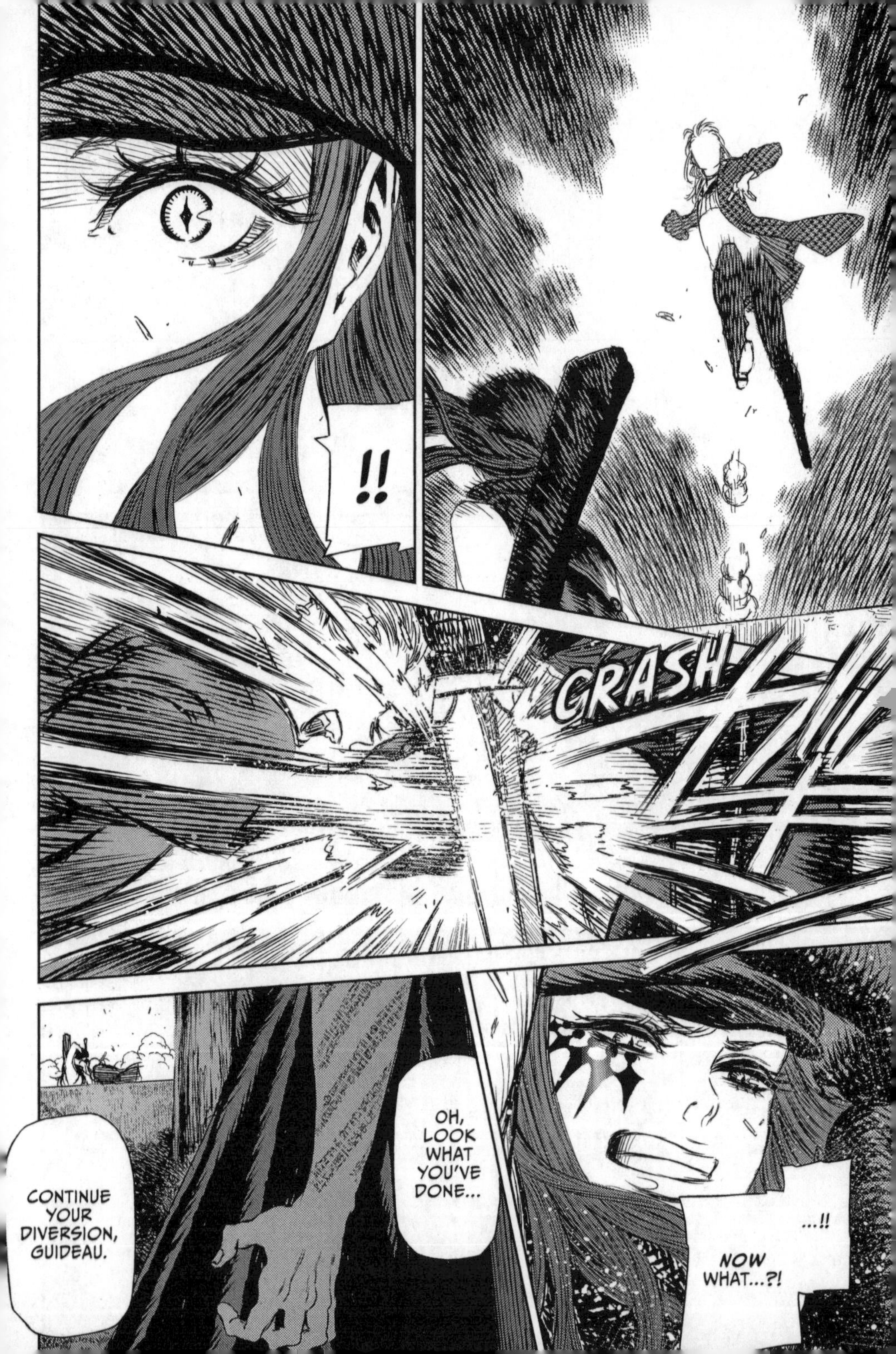

!!
CRASH
...!!
NOW WHAT...?!
OH, LOOK WHAT YOU'VE DONE...
CONTINUE YOUR DIVERSION, GUIDEAU.

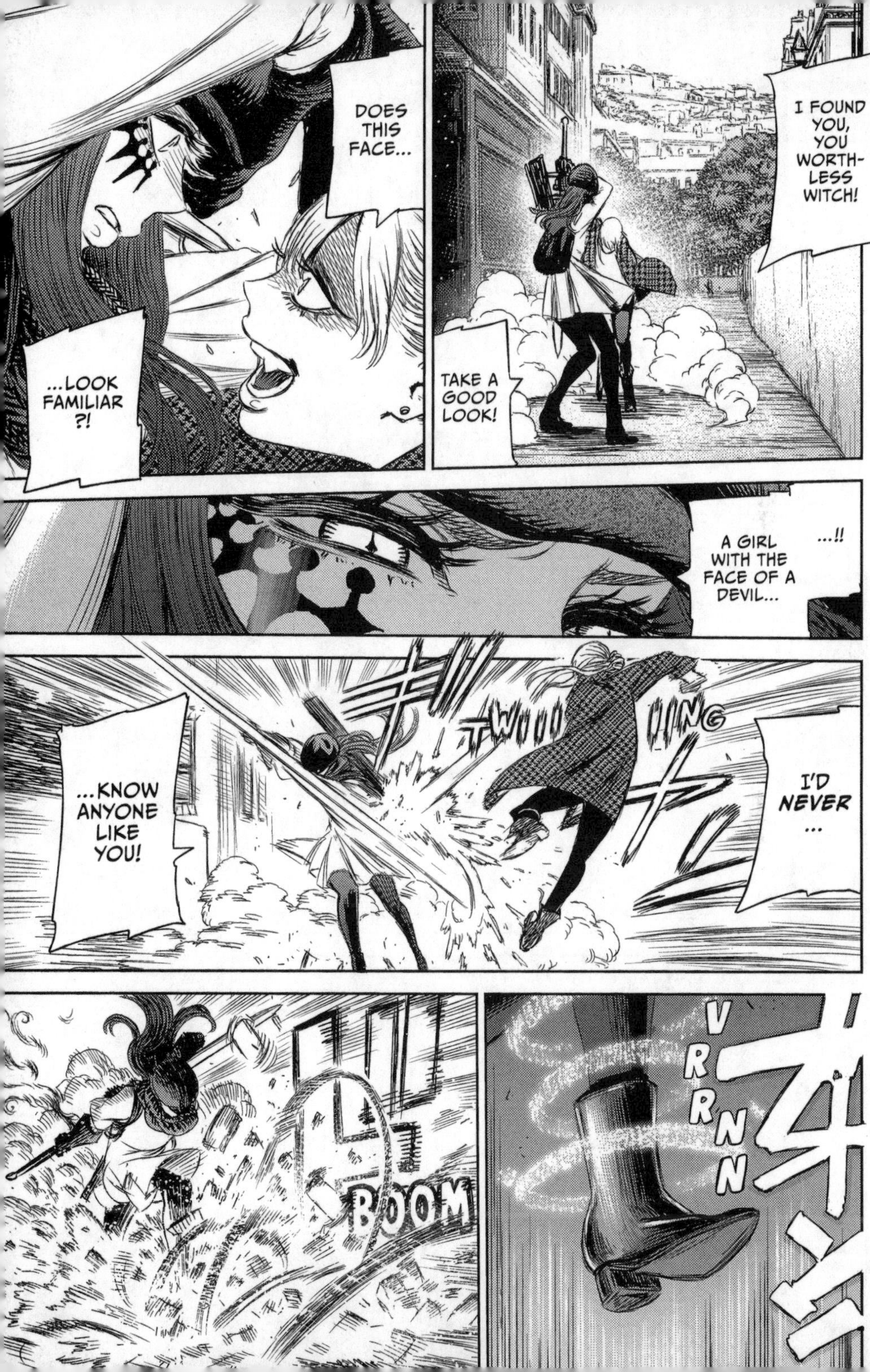

I FOUND YOU, YOU WORTHLESS WITCH!
TAKE A GOOD LOOK!
DOES THIS FACE...
...LOOK FAMILIAR ?!
...!!
A GIRL WITH THE FACE OF A DEVIL...
TWIIIING
I'D *NEVER* ...
...KNOW ANYONE LIKE YOU!
VRRNN
BOOM

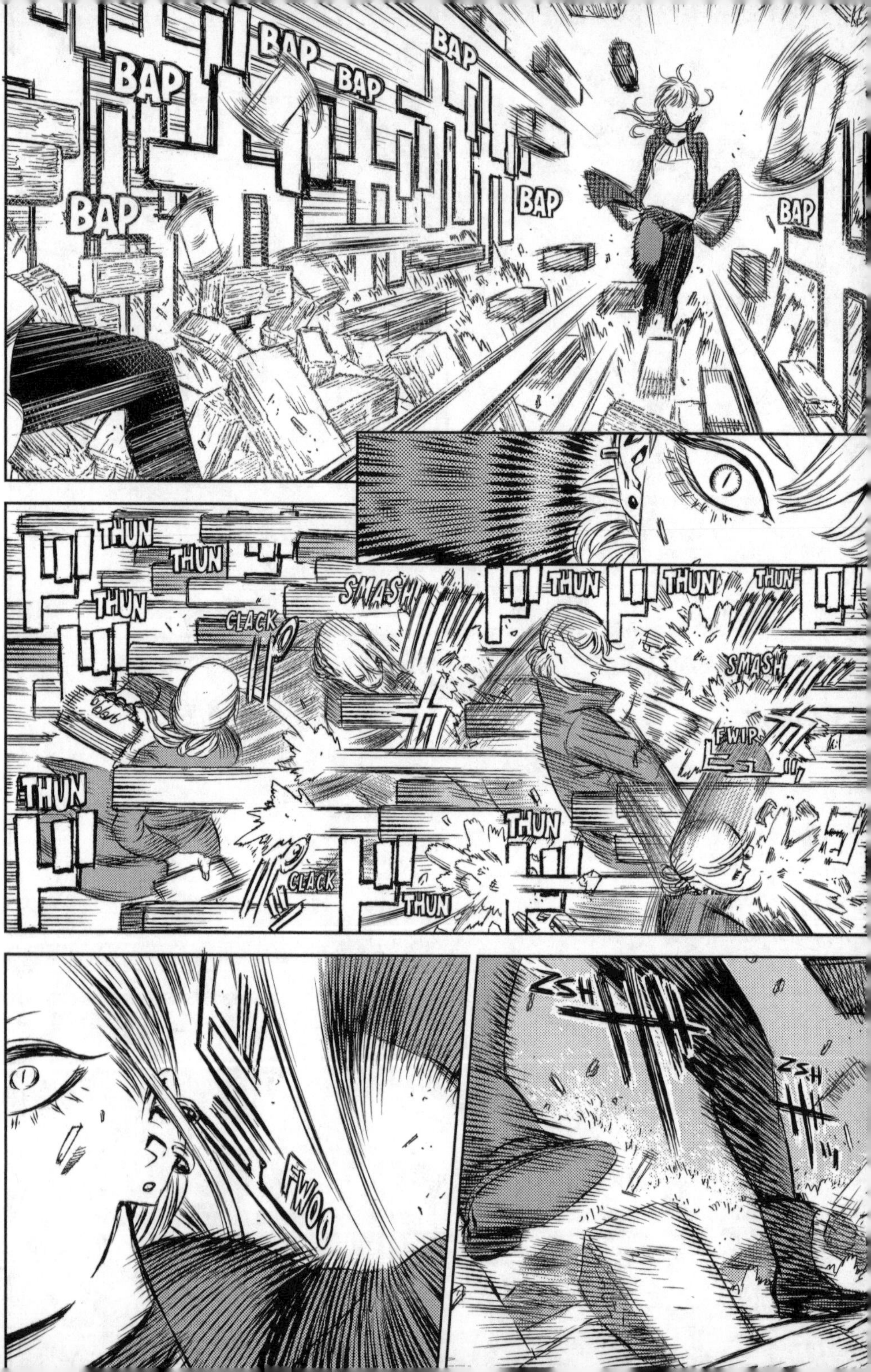
BAP
BAP
BAP
BAP
BAP
BAP
BAP
THUN
THUN
THUN
SMASH
FWIP
SMASH
CLACK
THUN
THUN
THUN
THUN
THUN
CLACK
THUN
ZSH
ZSH
FWOO

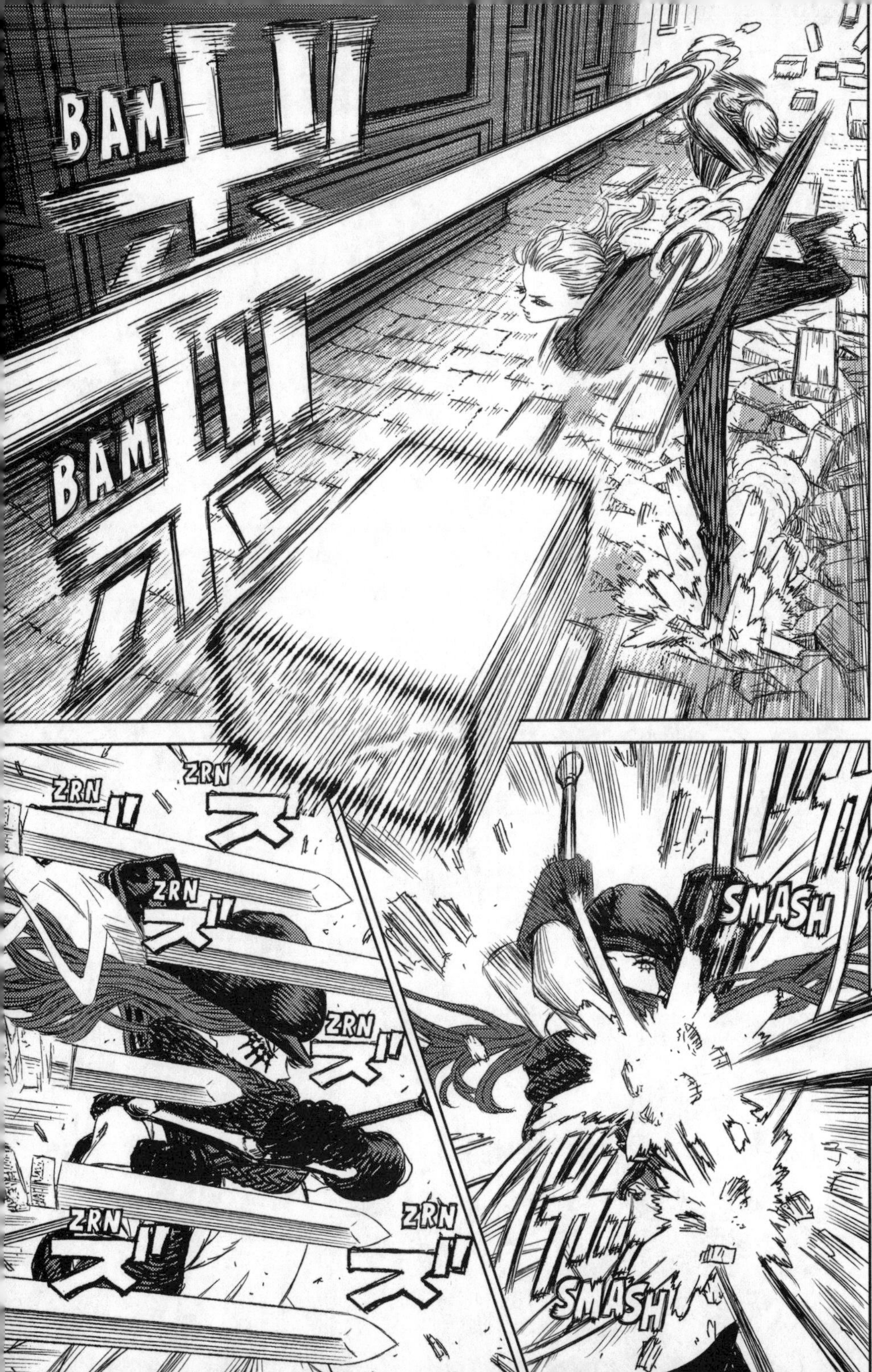
BAM
BAM
SMASH
SMASH
ZRN
ZRN
ZRN
ZRN
ZRN
ZRN

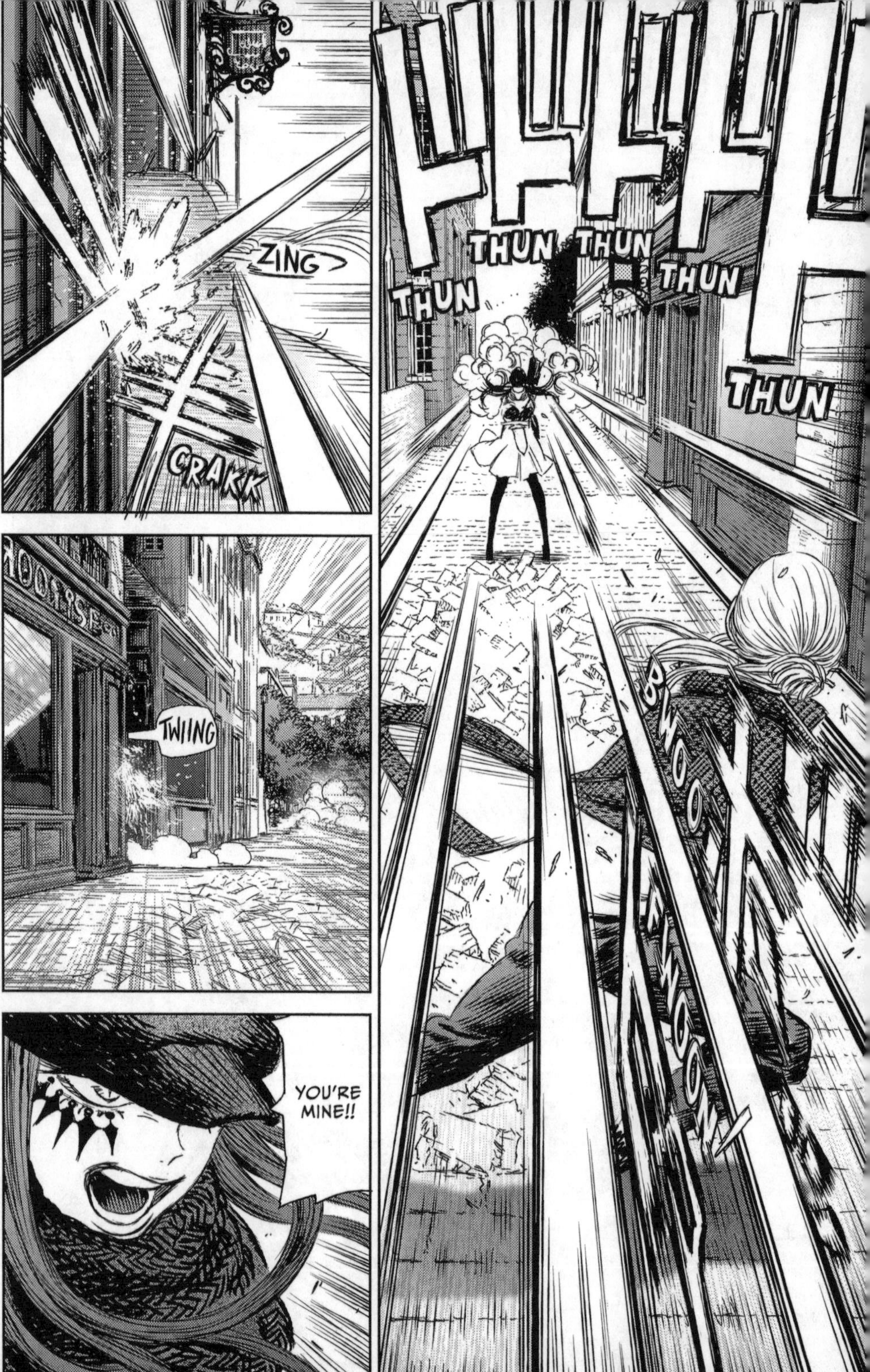
THUN
THUN
THUN
THUN
THUN
BWOO
BWOOOM
ZING
CRAKK
TWIING
YOU'RE MINE!!

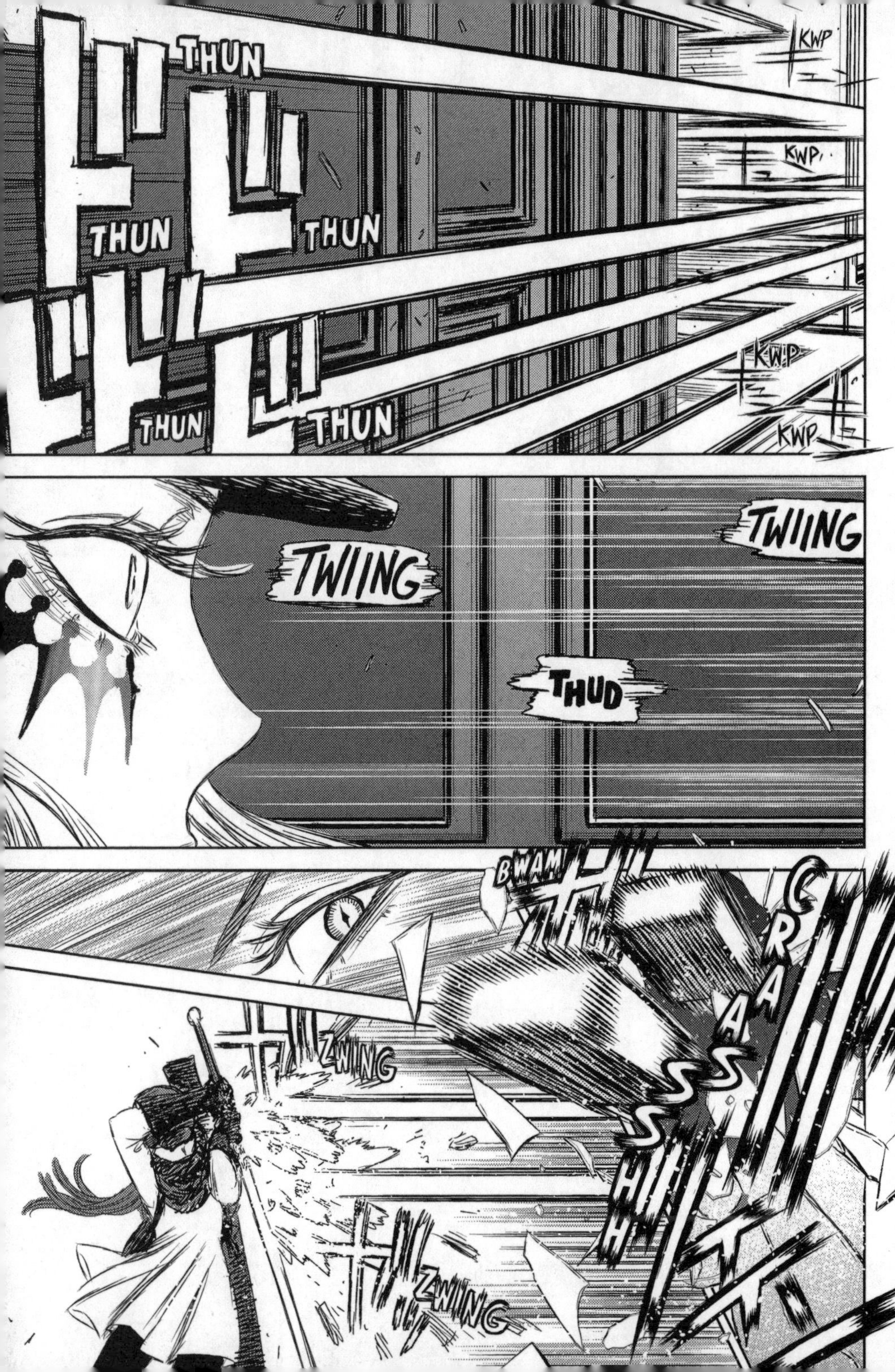
KWP
KWP
KWP
KWP
THUN
THUN
THUN
THUN
THUN
TWIING
THUD
TWIING
CRAASSHH
BWAM
ZWING
ZWING

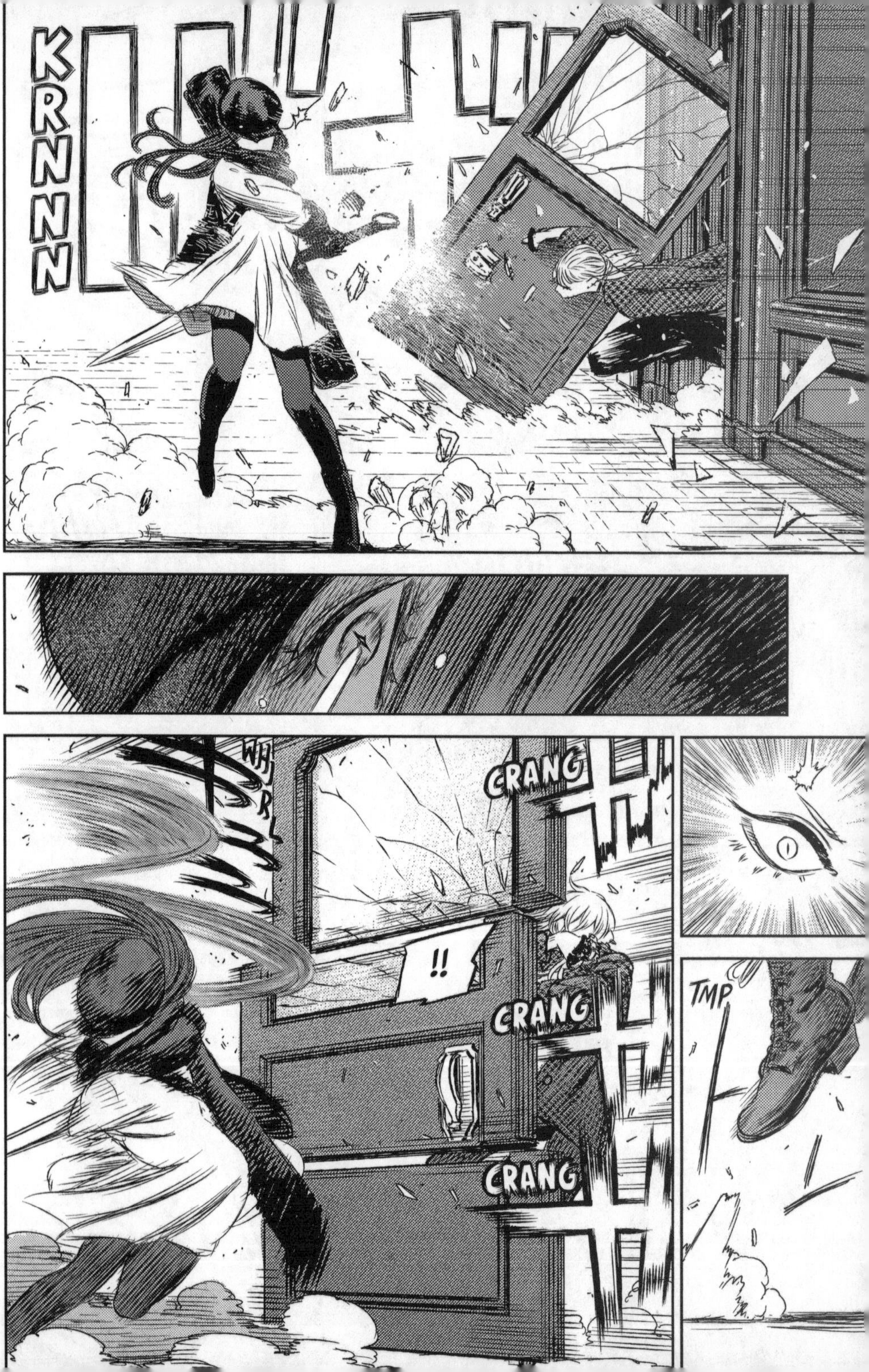
KRNNN
TMP
WHIRL
CRANG
!!
CRANG
CRANG

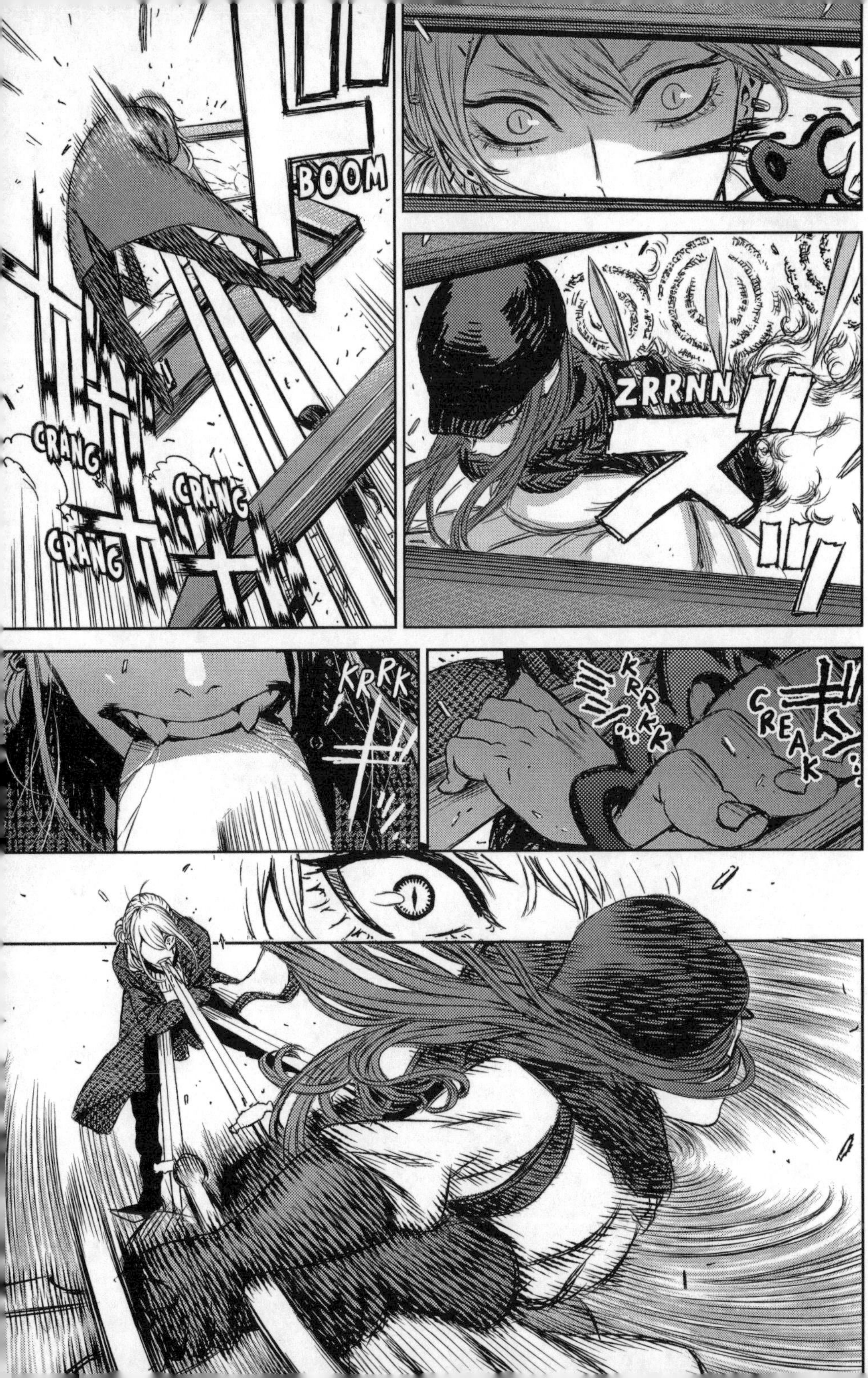
ZRRNN
BOOM
CRANG
CRANG
CRANG
CREAK
KRRKK
KRRK

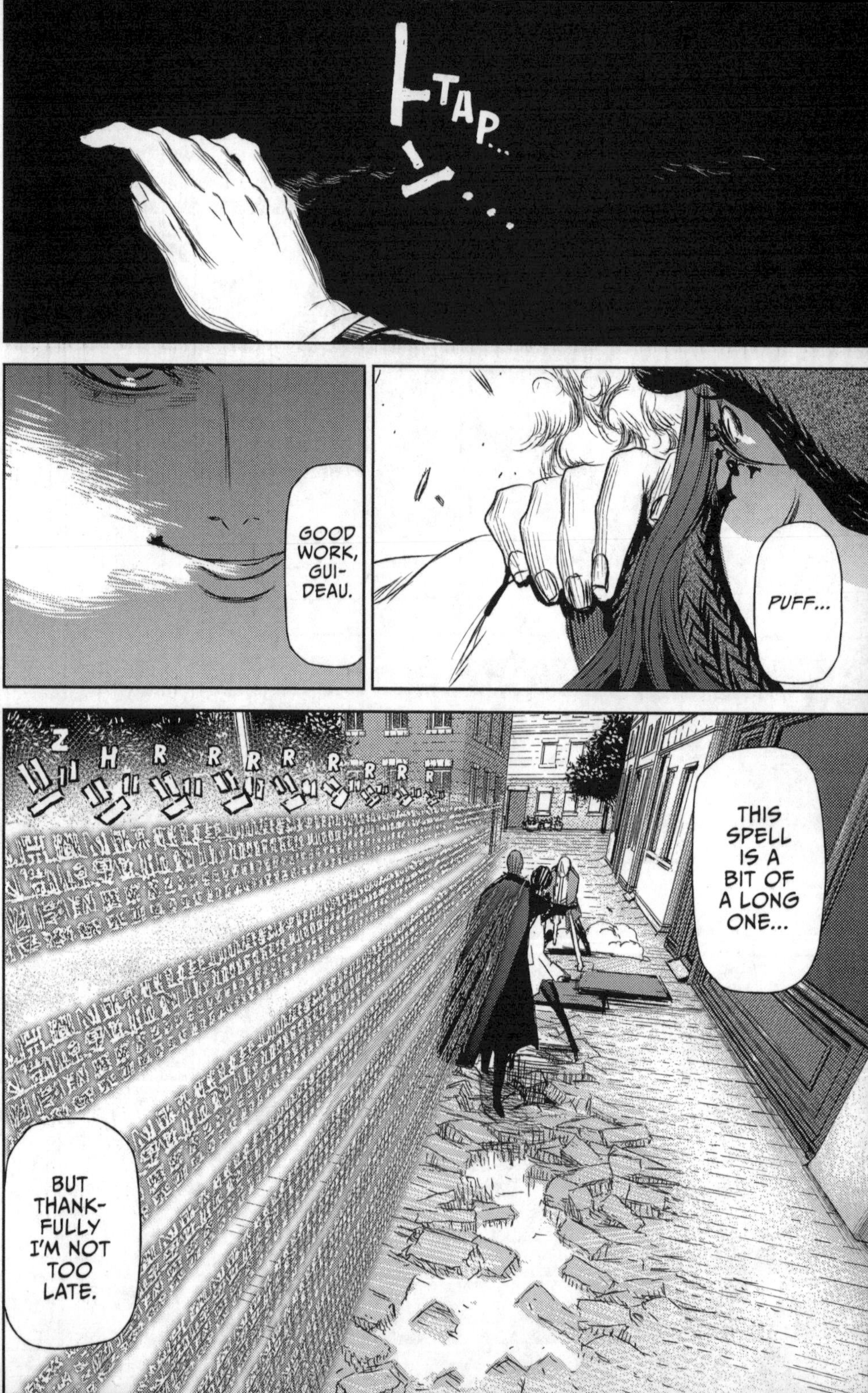
TAP...
PUFF...
GOOD WORK, GUIDEAU.
ZHRRRRRRRRR
THIS SPELL IS A BIT OF A LONG ONE...
BUT THANKFULLY I'M NOT TOO LATE.

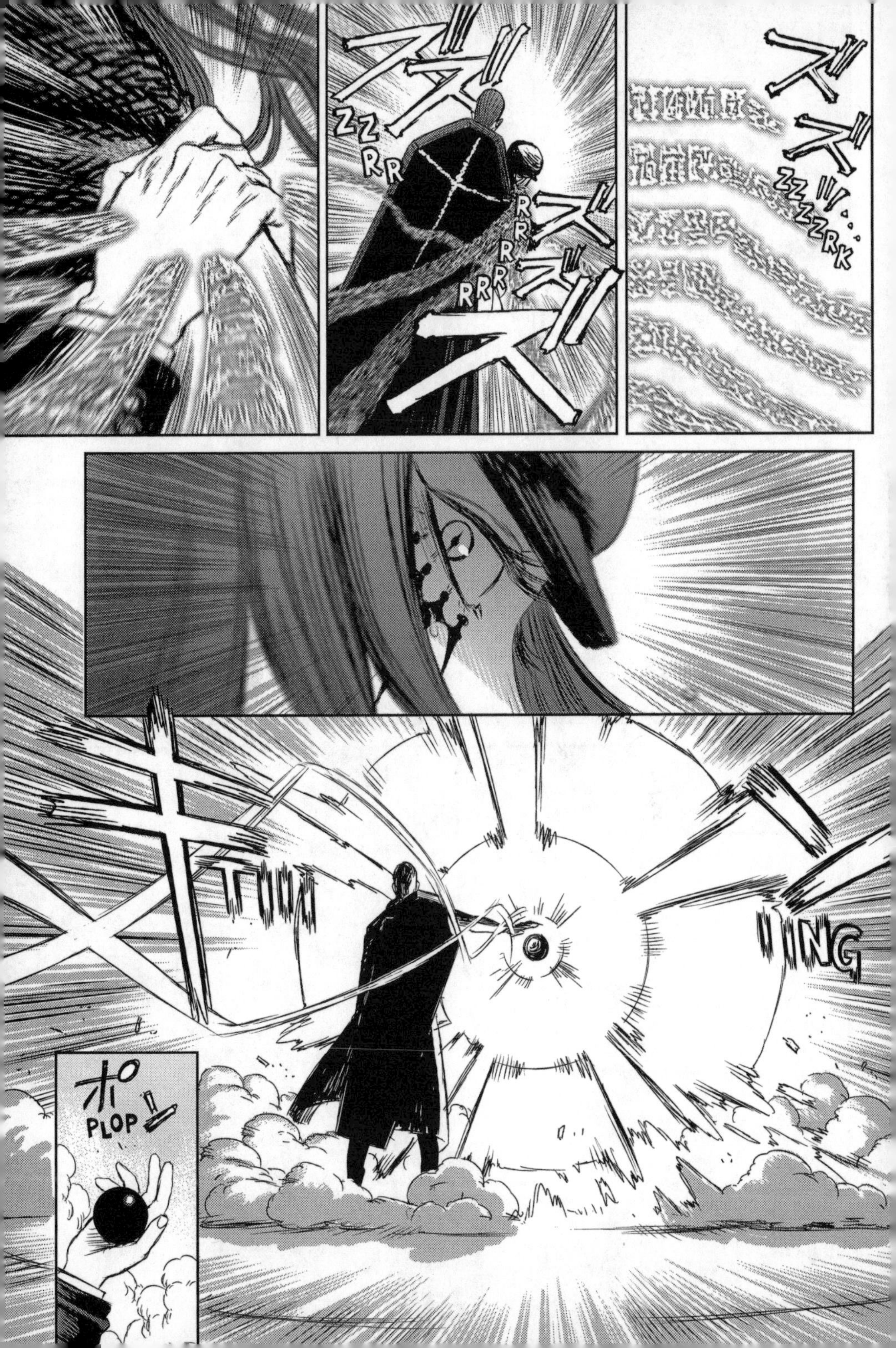
ZZZZZRK
ZZ RR
RRRRRR
TOOO
ING
PLOP

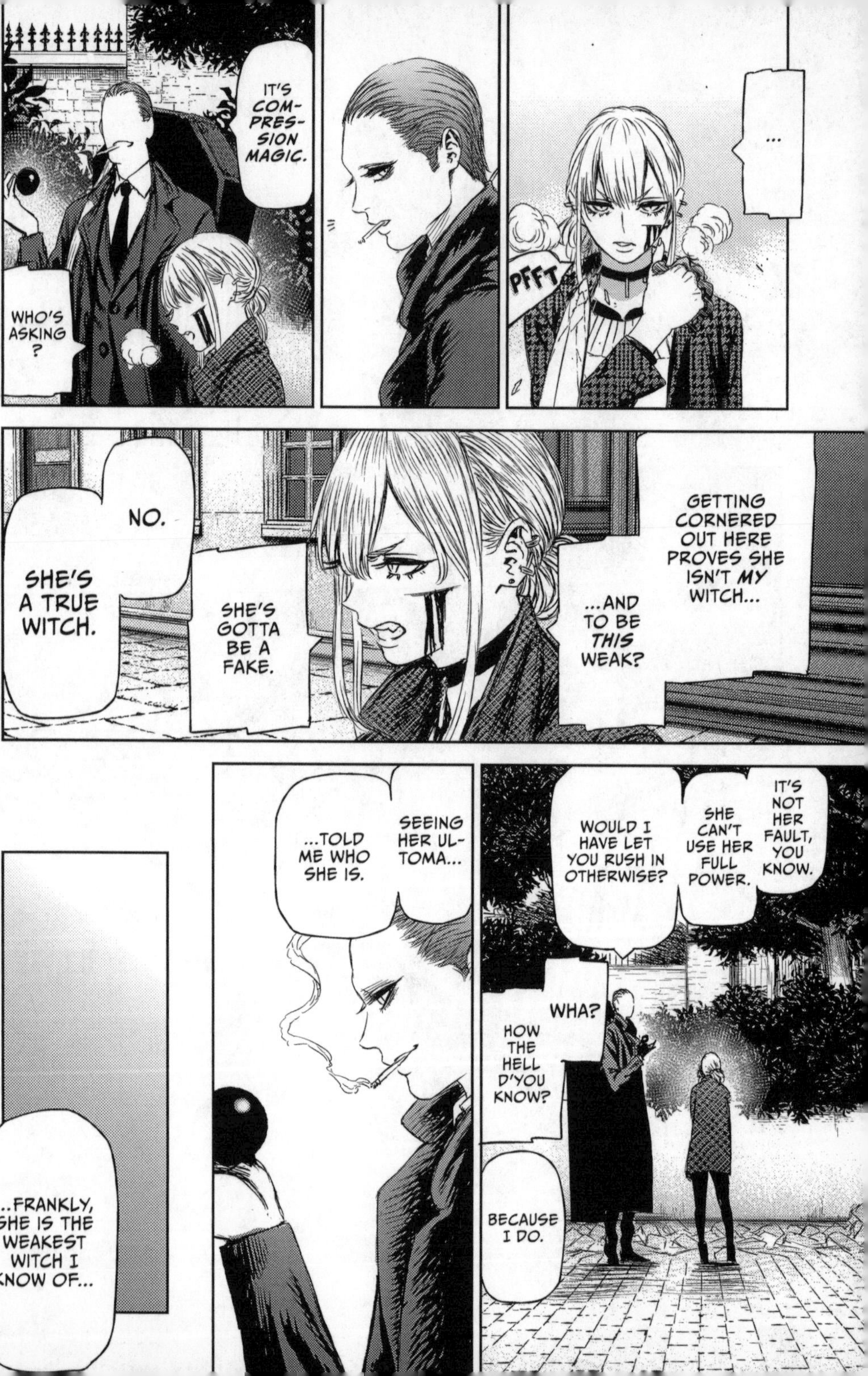
...
PFFT
IT'S COMPRESSION MAGIC.
WHO'S ASKING?
GETTING CORNERED OUT HERE PROVES SHE ISN'T *MY* WITCH...
...AND TO BE *THIS* WEAK?
SHE'S GOTTA BE A FAKE.
NO.
SHE'S A TRUE WITCH.
IT'S NOT HER FAULT, YOU KNOW.
SHE CAN'T USE HER FULL POWER.
WOULD I HAVE LET YOU RUSH IN OTHERWISE?
WHA?
HOW THE HELL D'YOU KNOW?
BECAUSE I DO.
SEEING HER ULTOMA...
...TOLD ME WHO SHE IS.
...FRANKLY, SHE IS THE WEAKEST WITCH I KNOW OF...

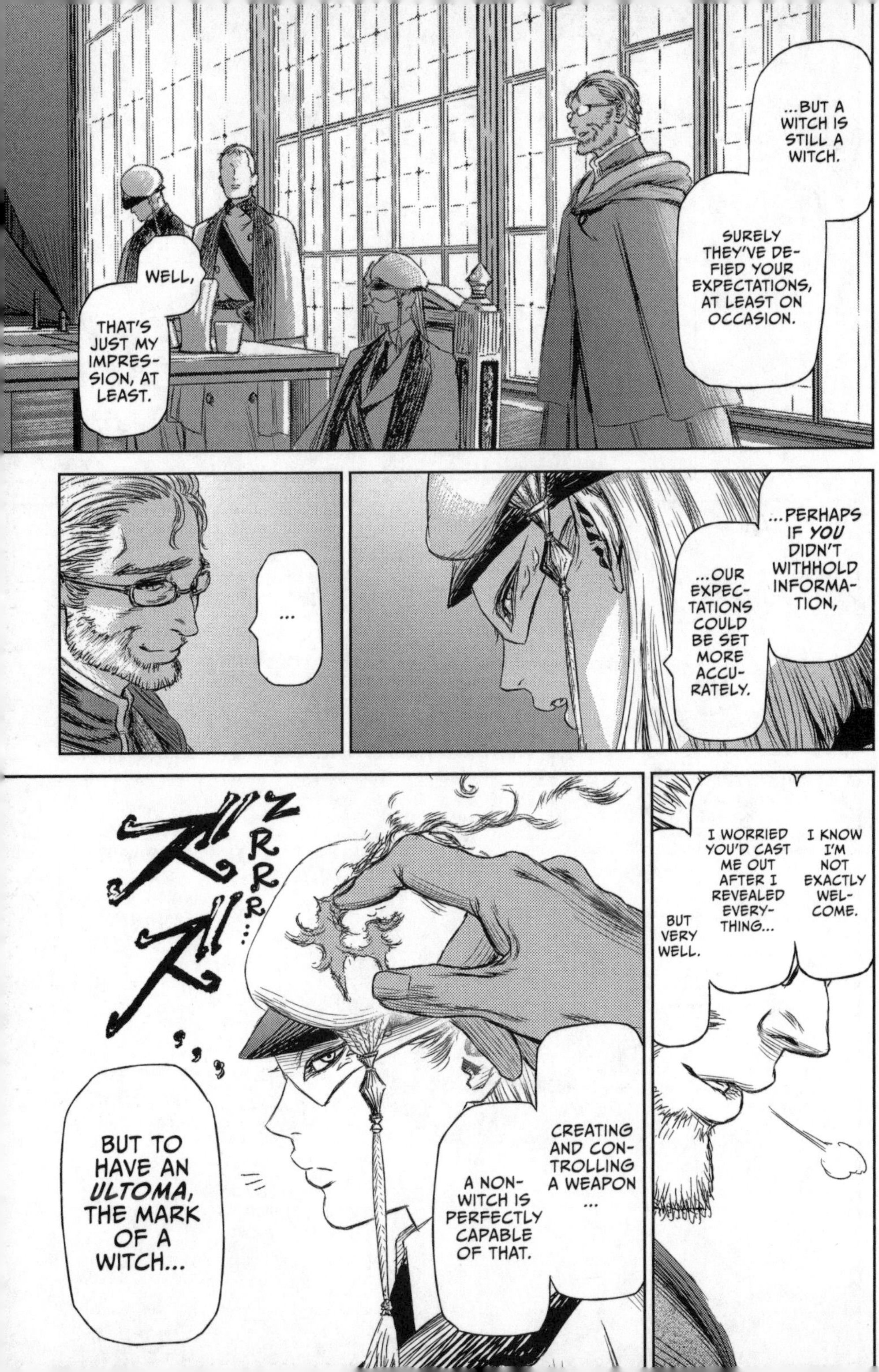
...BUT A WITCH IS STILL A WITCH.
SURELY THEY'VE DEFIED YOUR EXPECTATIONS, AT LEAST ON OCCASION.
WELL,
THAT'S JUST MY IMPRESSION, AT LEAST.
...PERHAPS IF *YOU* DIDN'T WITHHOLD INFORMATION,
...OUR EXPECTATIONS COULD BE SET MORE ACCURATELY.
...
I KNOW I'M NOT EXACTLY WELCOME.
I WORRIED YOU'D CAST ME OUT AFTER I REVEALED EVERYTHING...
BUT VERY WELL.
CREATING AND CONTROLLING A WEAPON...
A NON-WITCH IS PERFECTLY CAPABLE OF THAT.
ZRRRR...
BUT TO HAVE AN *ULTOMA*, THE MARK OF A WITCH...

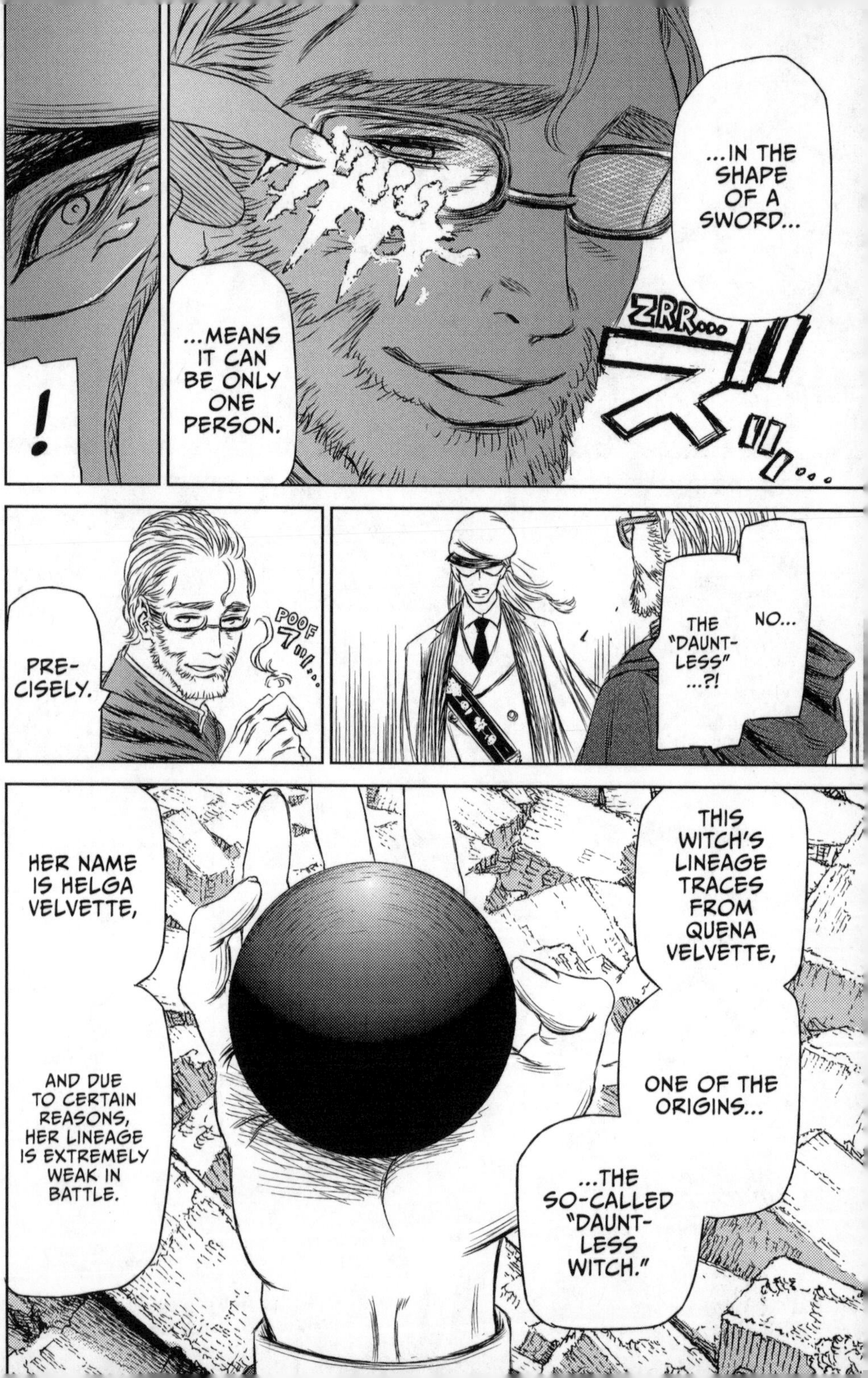
...IN THE SHAPE OF A SWORD...
ZRR...
...MEANS IT CAN BE ONLY ONE PERSON.
!
NO...
THE "DAUNTLESS" ...?!
POOF
PRECISELY.
HER NAME IS HELGA VELVETTE,
THIS WITCH'S LINEAGE TRACES FROM QUENA VELVETTE,
ONE OF THE ORIGINS...
...THE SO-CALLED "DAUNTLESS WITCH."
AND DUE TO CERTAIN REASONS, HER LINEAGE IS EXTREMELY WEAK IN BATTLE.

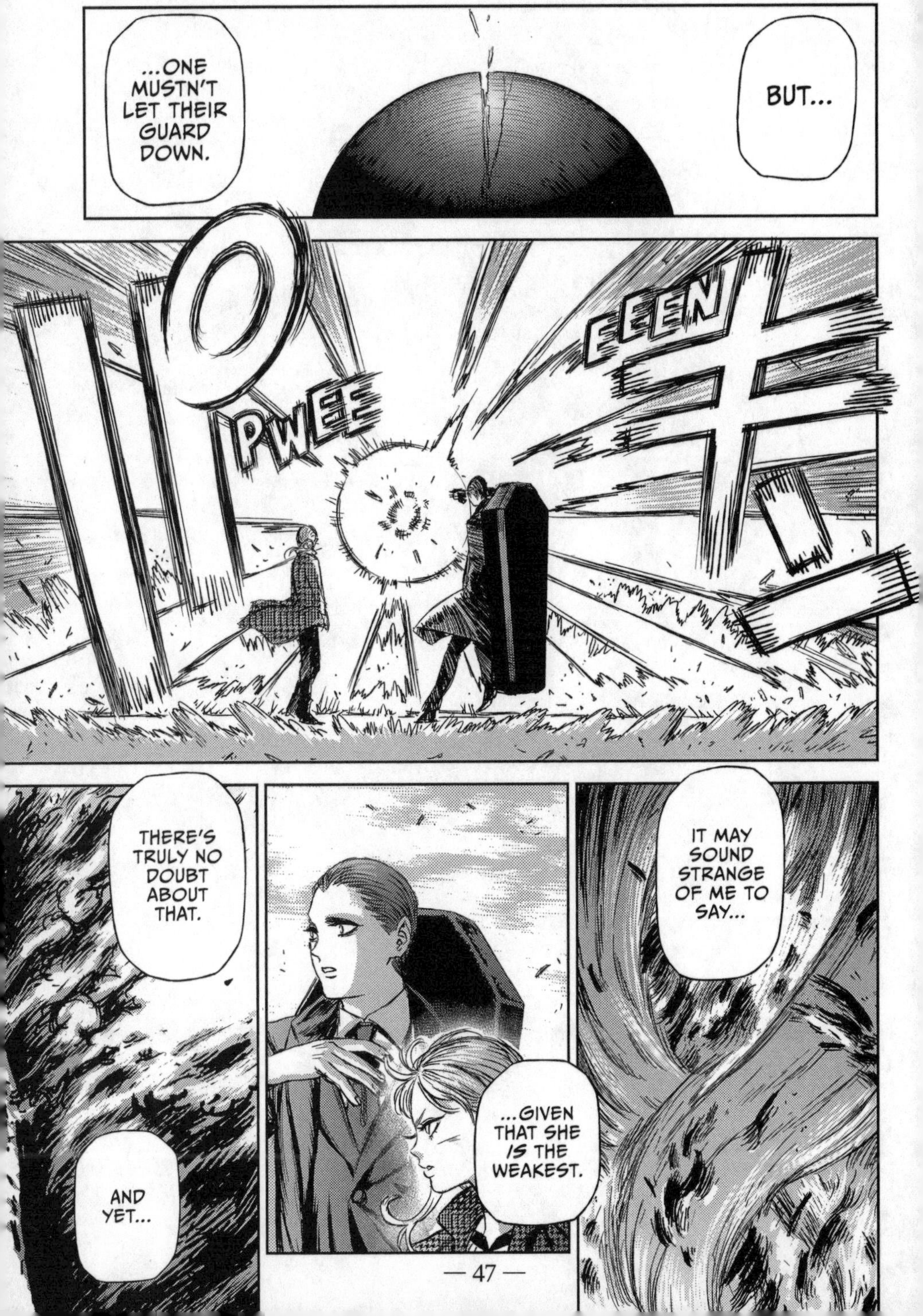
BUT...
...ONE MUSTN'T LET THEIR GUARD DOWN.
PWEE
EEEN
IT MAY SOUND STRANGE OF ME TO SAY...
...GIVEN THAT SHE *IS* THE WEAKEST.
THERE'S TRULY NO DOUBT ABOUT THAT.
AND YET...

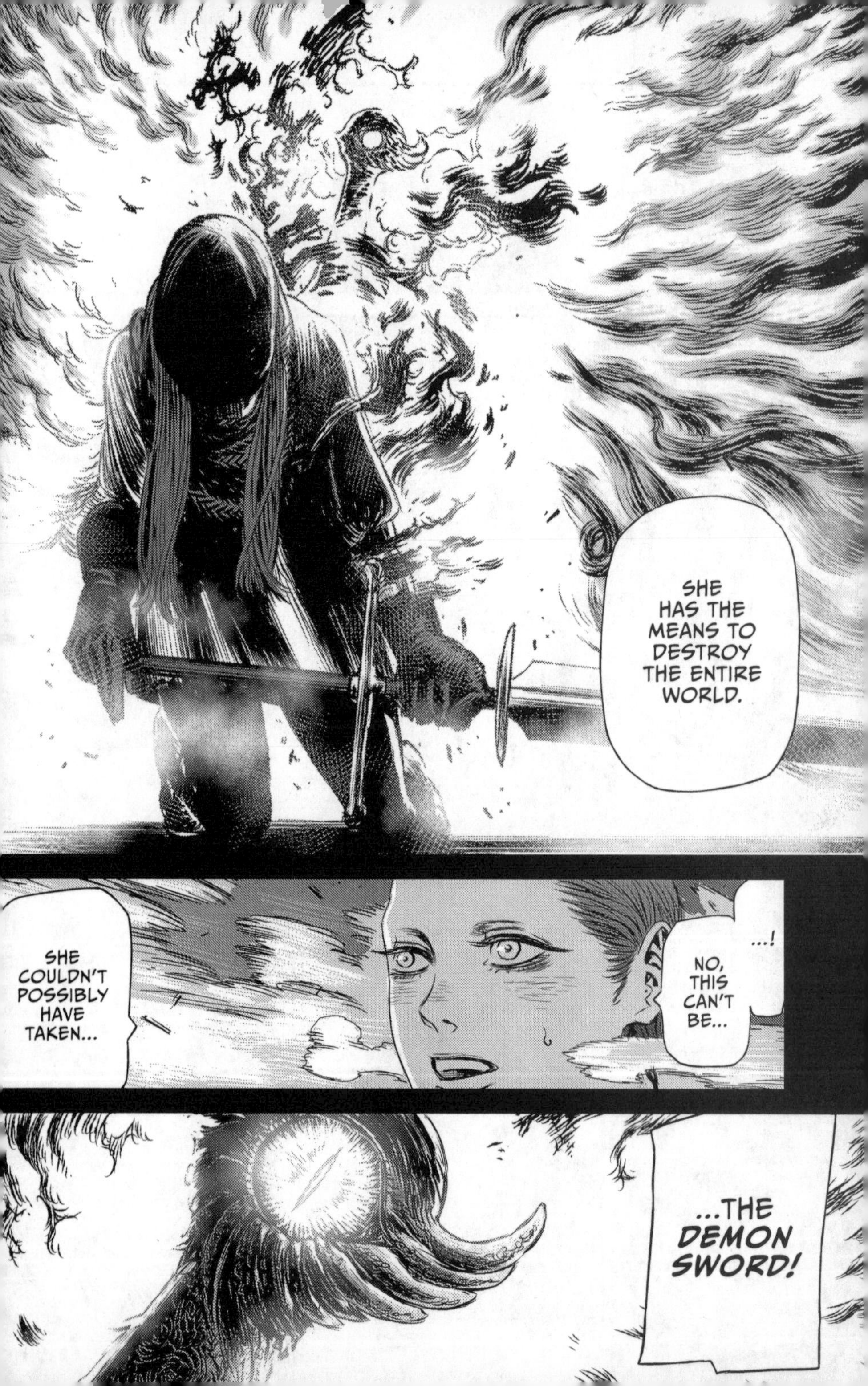
SHE HAS THE MEANS TO DESTROY THE ENTIRE WORLD.
...!
NO, THIS CAN'T BE...
SHE COULDN'T POSSIBLY HAVE TAKEN...
...THE *DEMON SWORD!*

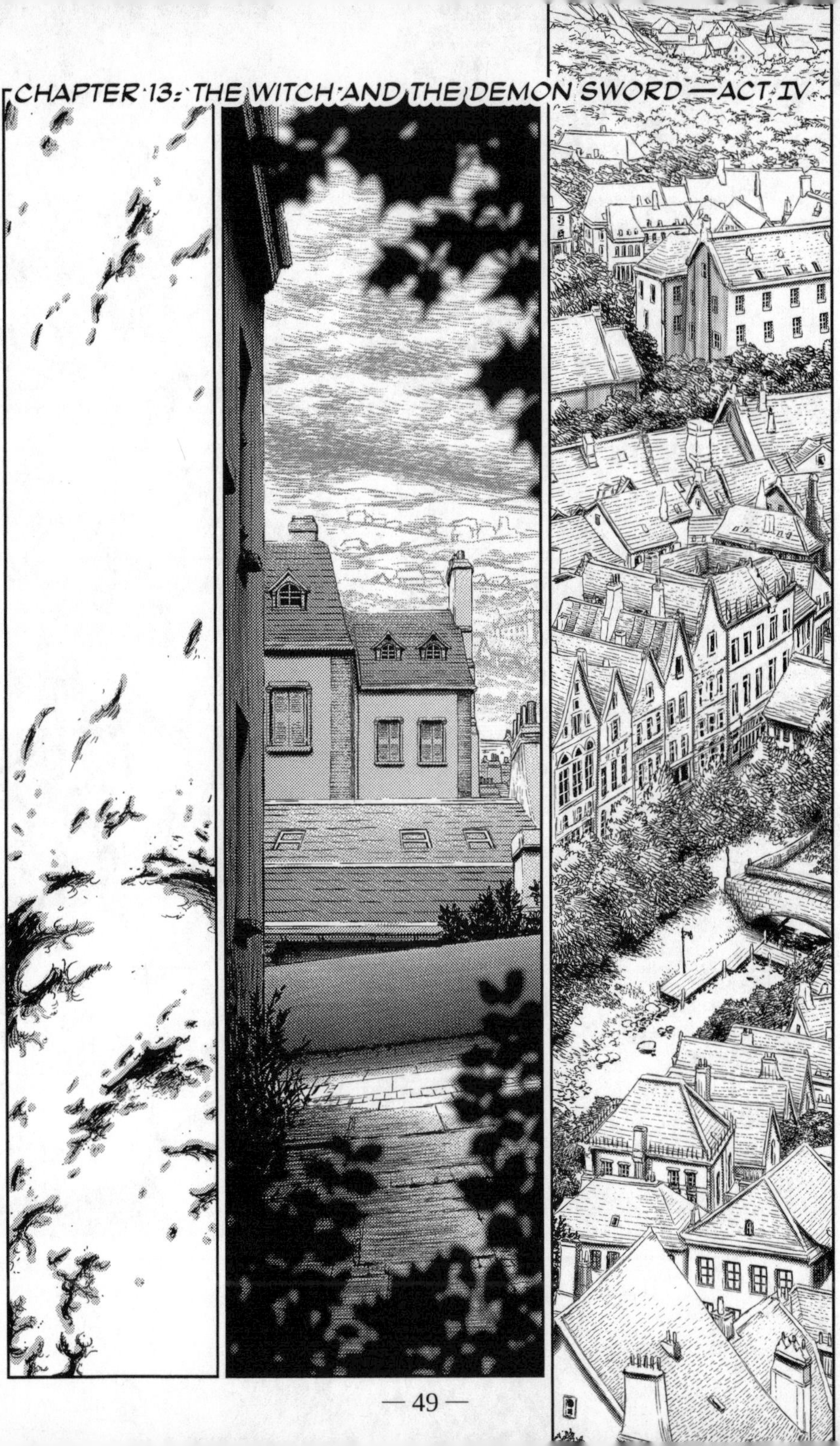
CHAPTER 13: THE WITCH AND THE DEMON SWORD—ACT IV

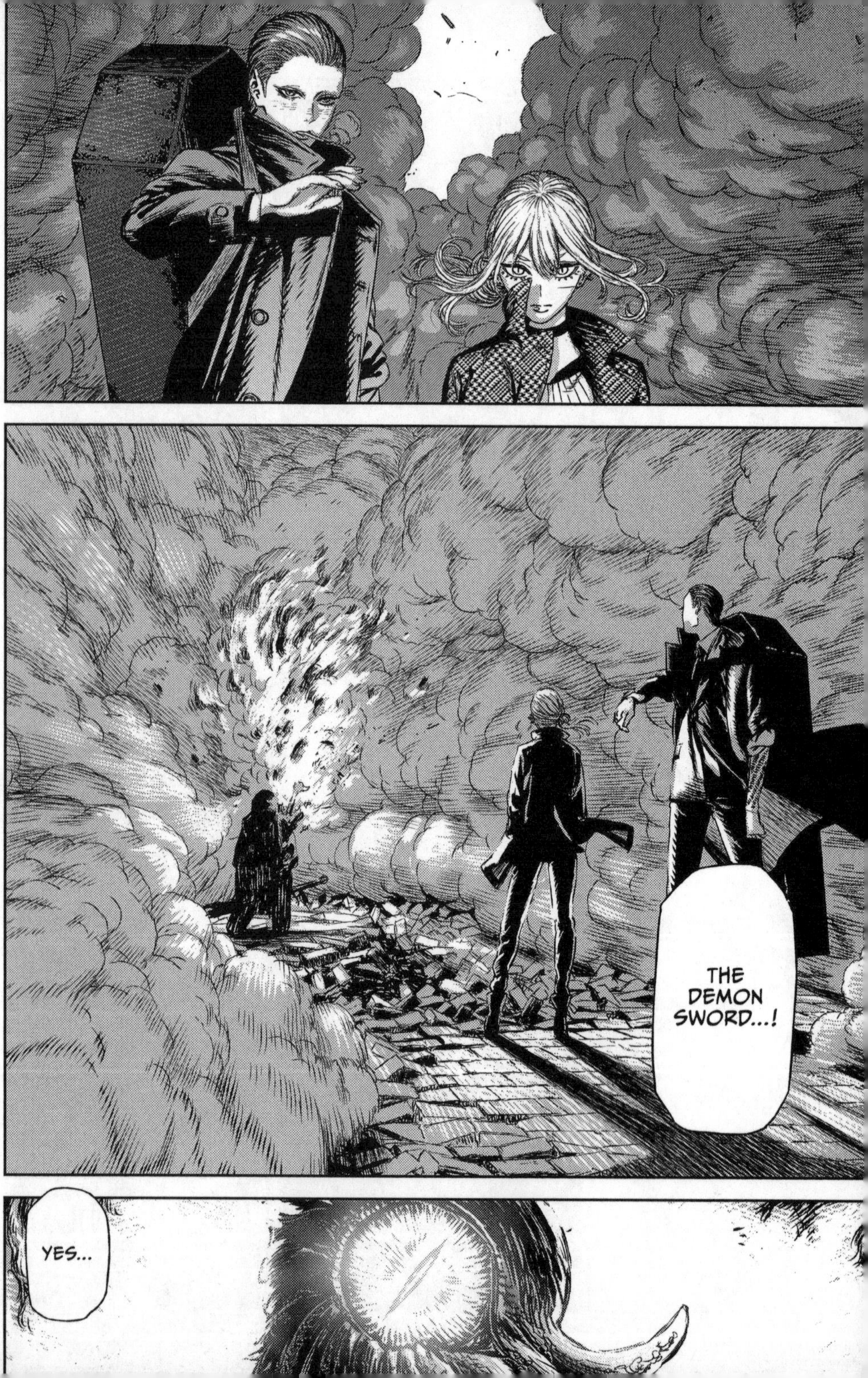
THE DEMON SWORD...!
YES...

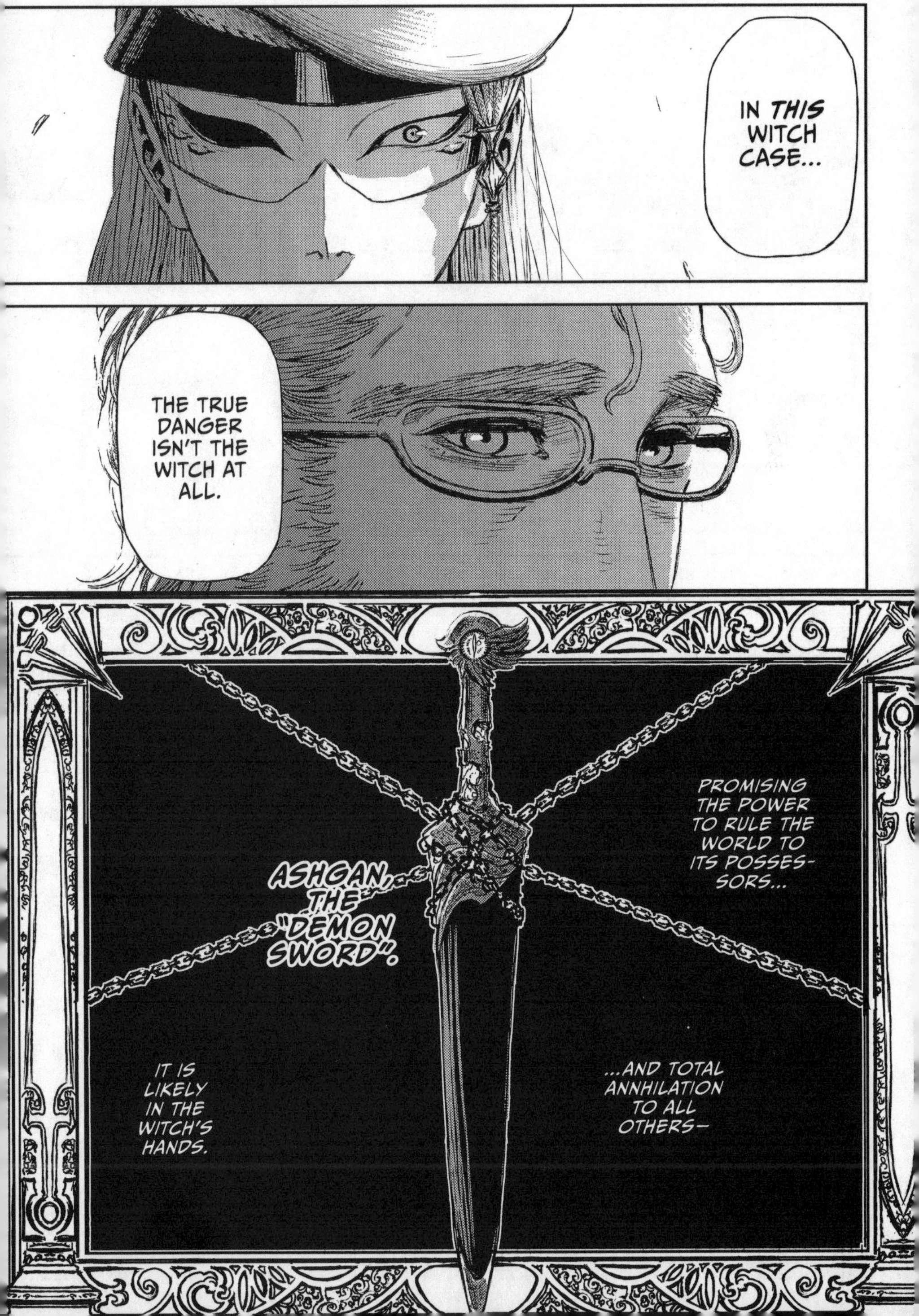
IN THIS WITCH CASE...
THE TRUE DANGER ISN'T THE WITCH AT ALL.
PROMISING THE POWER TO RULE THE WORLD TO ITS POSSES-SORS...
ASHGAN, THE "DEMON SWORD".
...AND TOTAL ANNHILATION TO ALL OTHERS–
IT IS LIKELY IN THE WITCH'S HANDS.

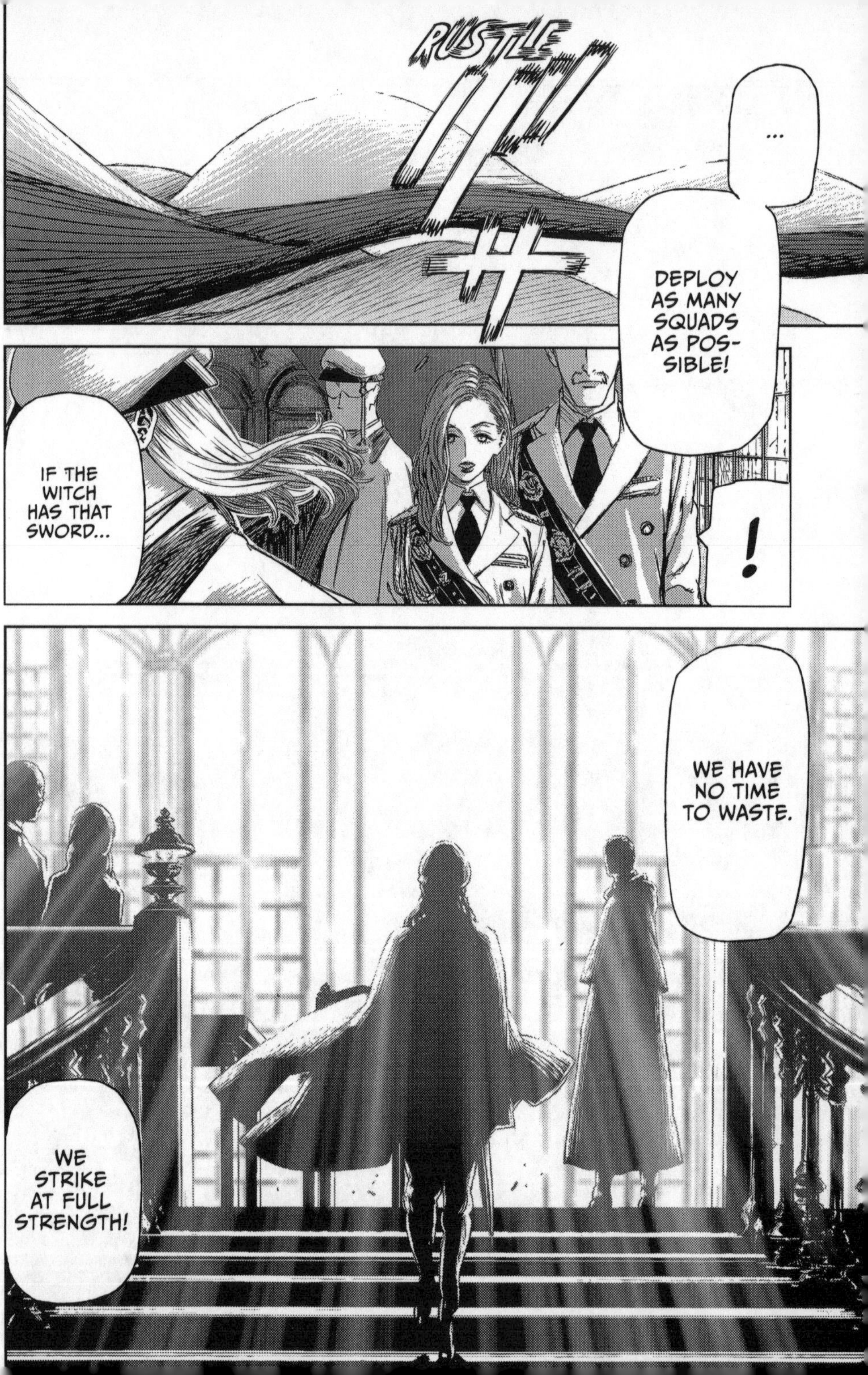
...
RUSTLE
DEPLOY AS MANY SQUADS AS POS- SIBLE!
!
IF THE WITCH HAS THAT SWORD...
WE HAVE NO TIME TO WASTE.
WE STRIKE AT FULL STRENGTH!

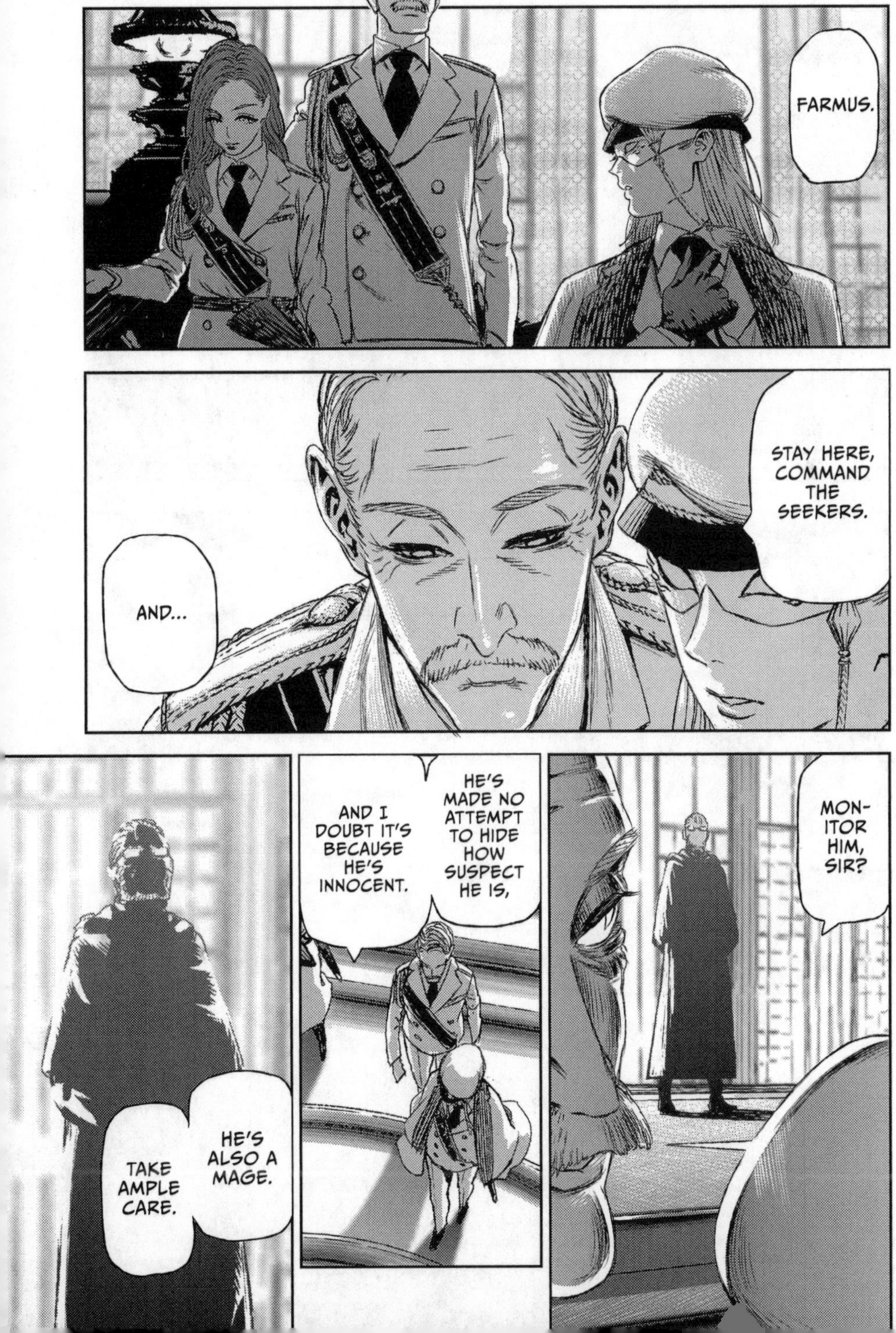
FARMUS.
STAY HERE, COMMAND THE SEEKERS.
AND...
MON-ITOR HIM, SIR?
HE'S MADE NO ATTEMPT TO HIDE HOW SUSPECT HE IS,
AND I DOUBT IT'S BECAUSE HE'S INNOCENT.
HE'S ALSO A MAGE.
TAKE AMPLE CARE.

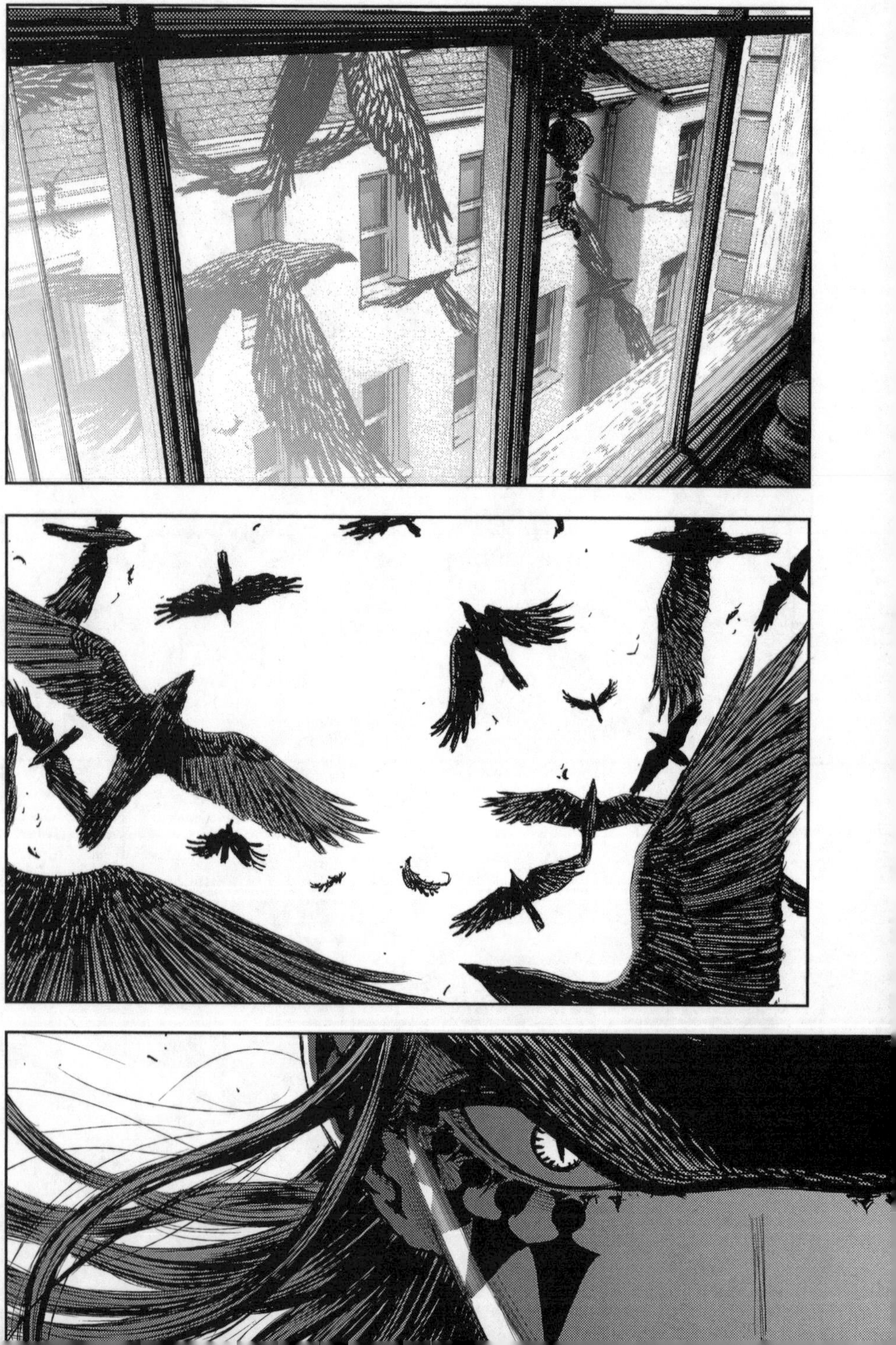

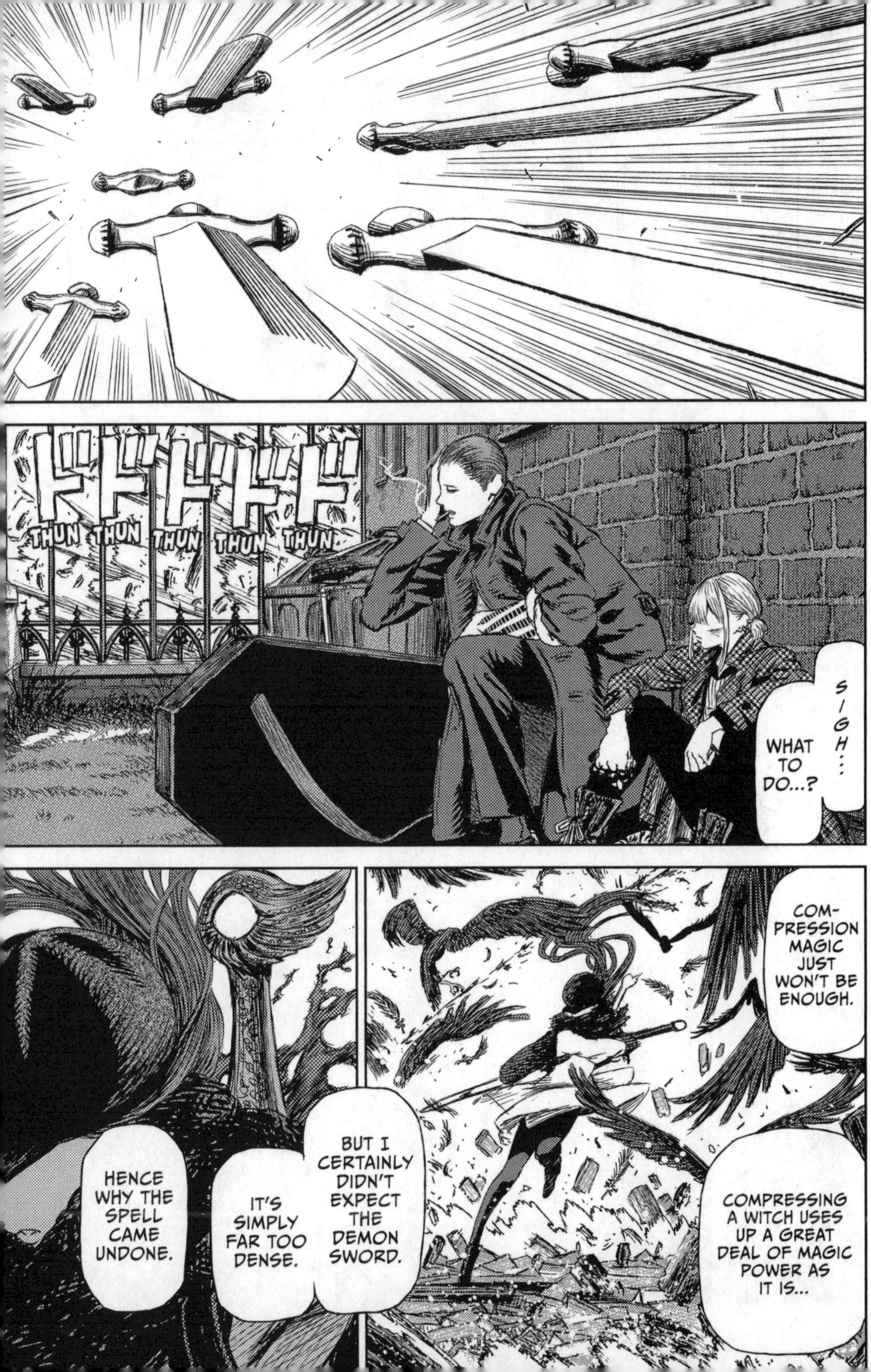
SIGH... WHAT TO DO...?
ドドドドド
THUN THUN THUN THUN THUN
COMPRESSION MAGIC JUST WON'T BE ENOUGH.
COMPRESSING A WITCH USES UP A GREAT DEAL OF MAGIC POWER AS IT IS...
BUT I CERTAINLY DIDN'T EXPECT THE DEMON SWORD.
IT'S SIMPLY FAR TOO DENSE.
HENCE WHY THE SPELL CAME UNDONE.

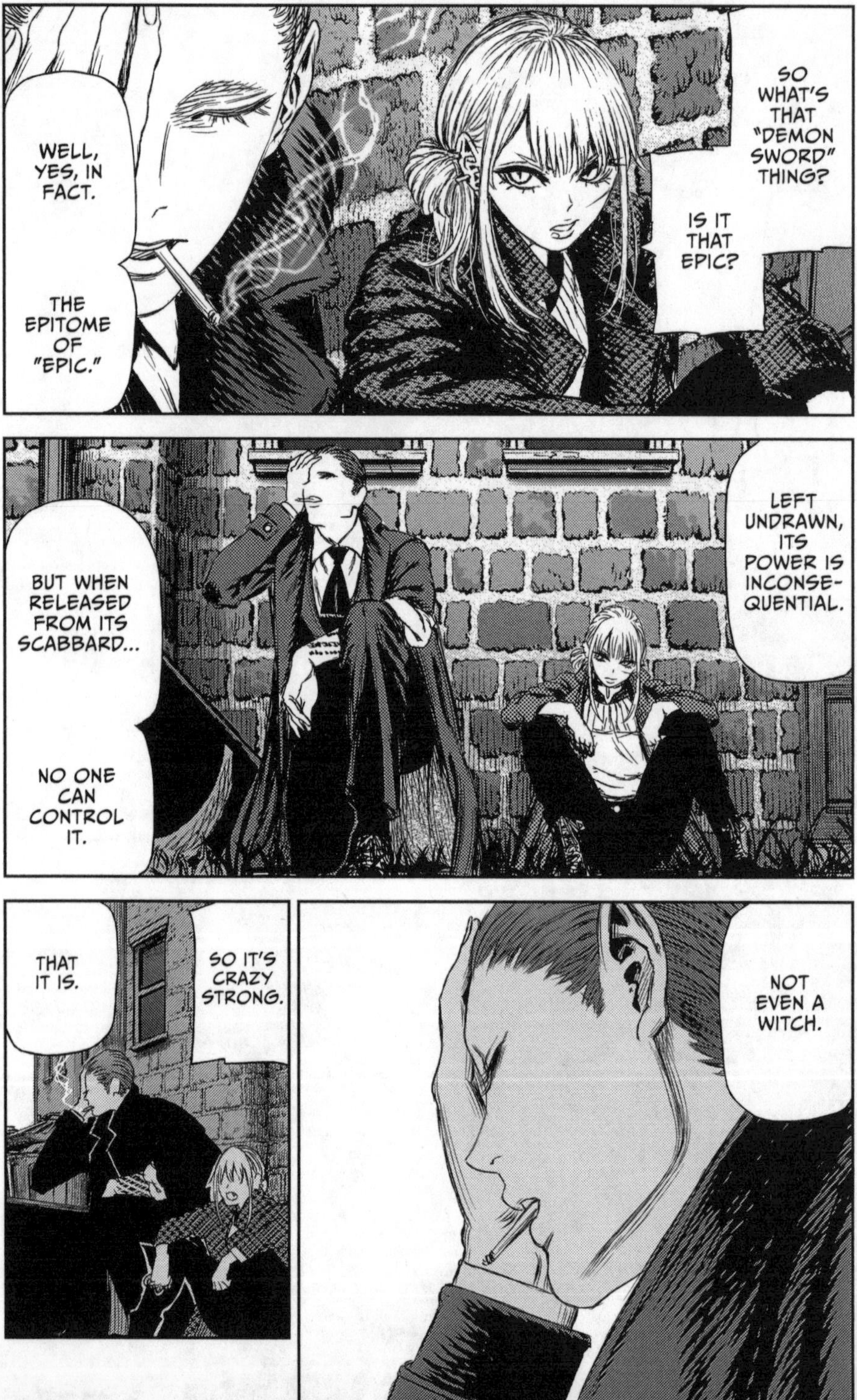
SO WHAT'S THAT "DEMON SWORD" THING?
IS IT THAT EPIC?
WELL, YES, IN FACT.
THE EPITOME OF "EPIC."
LEFT UNDRAWN, ITS POWER IS INCONSE-QUENTIAL.
BUT WHEN RELEASED FROM ITS SCABBARD...
NO ONE CAN CONTROL IT.
NOT EVEN A WITCH.
SO IT'S CRAZY STRONG.
THAT IT IS.

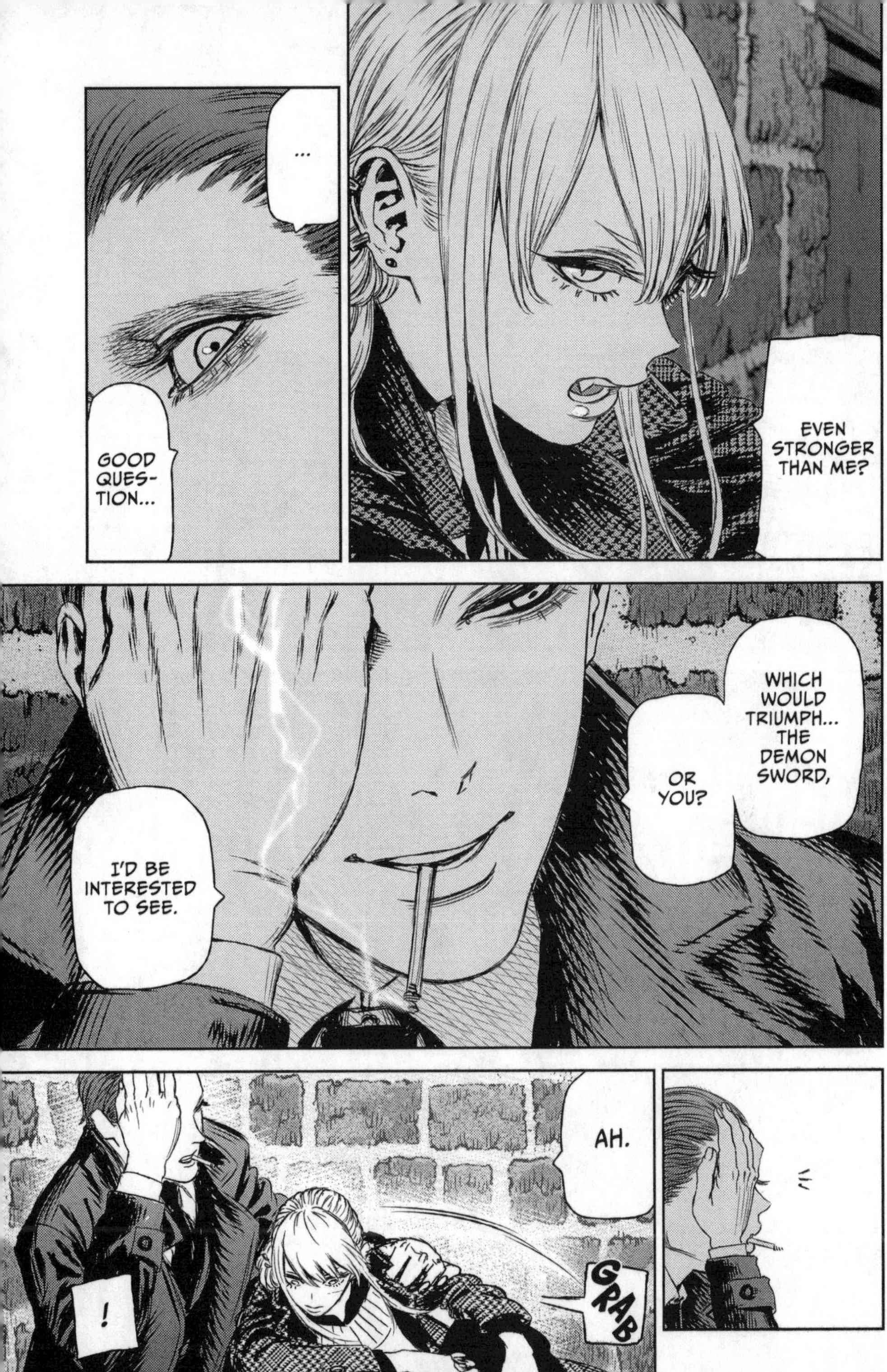
EVEN STRONGER THAN ME?
...
GOOD QUES-TION...
WHICH WOULD TRIUMPH... THE DEMON SWORD,
OR YOU?
I'D BE INTERESTED TO SEE.
AH.
GRAB
!

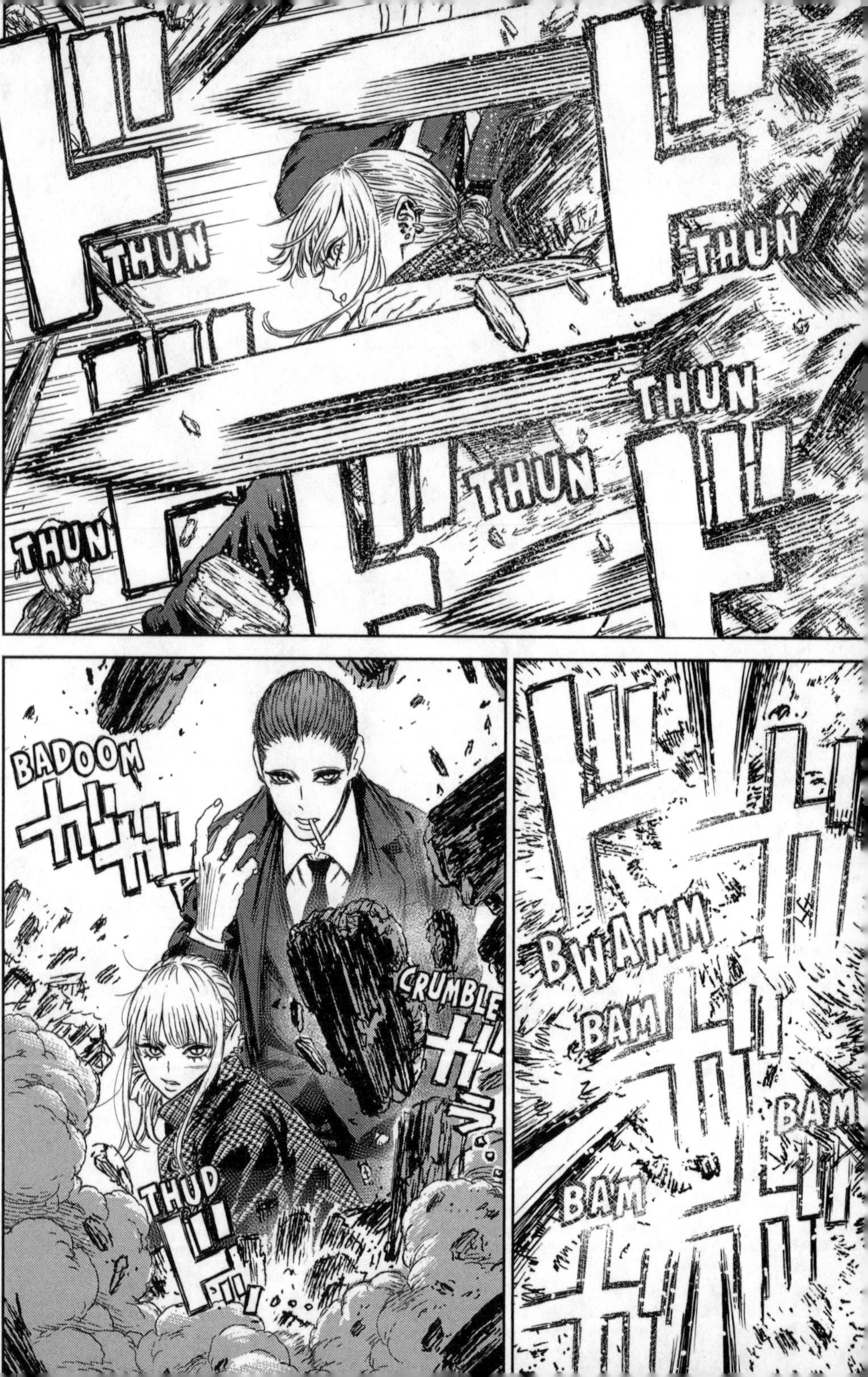
THUN
THUN
THUN
THUN
THUN
BWAMM
BAM
BAM
BAM
BADOOM
CRUMBLE
THUD

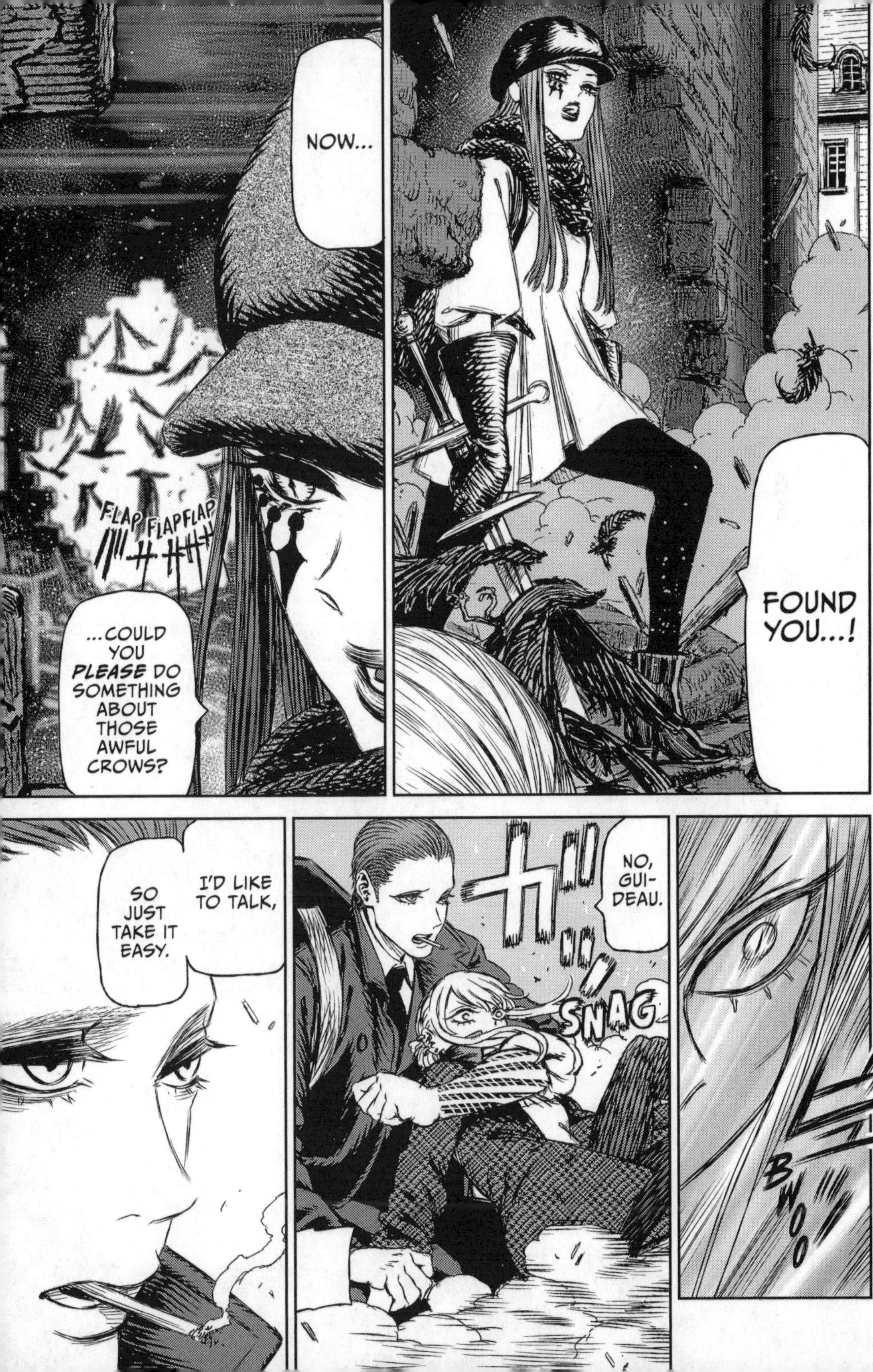
NOW...
FOUND YOU...!
FLAP FLAPFLAP
...COULD YOU *PLEASE* DO SOMETHING ABOUT THOSE AWFUL CROWS?
NO, GUI-DEAU.
SNAG
I'D LIKE TO TALK,
SO JUST TAKE IT EASY.
BWOO

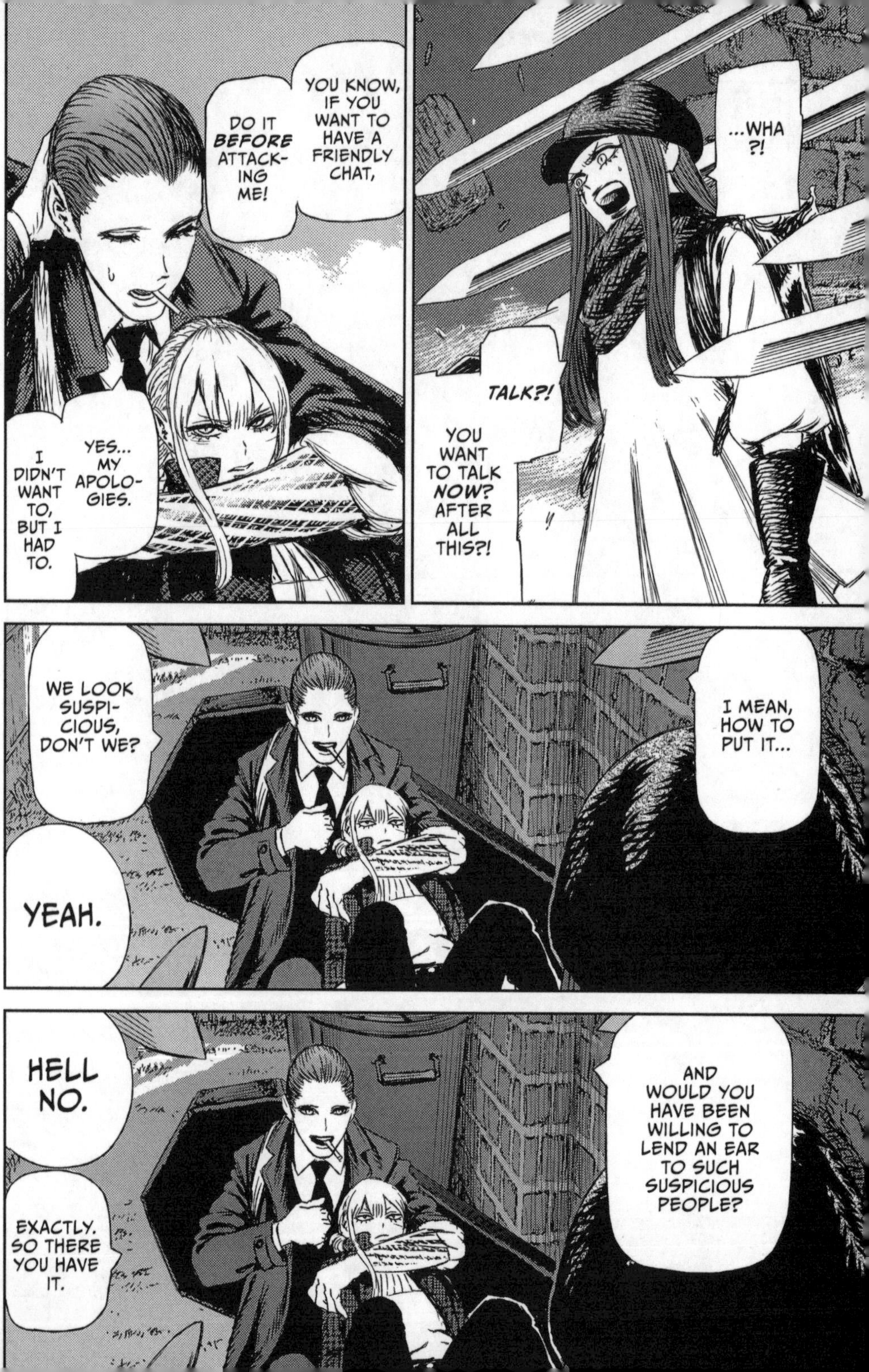
...WHA?!
TALK?!
YOU WANT TO TALK *NOW*? AFTER ALL THIS?!
YOU KNOW, IF YOU WANT TO HAVE A FRIENDLY CHAT,
DO IT *BEFORE* ATTACKING ME!
YES... MY APOLOGIES.
I DIDN'T WANT TO, BUT I HAD TO.
I MEAN, HOW TO PUT IT...
WE LOOK SUSPICIOUS, DON'T WE?
YEAH.
AND WOULD YOU HAVE BEEN WILLING TO LEND AN EAR TO SUCH SUSPICIOUS PEOPLE?
HELL NO.
EXACTLY. SO THERE YOU HAVE IT.

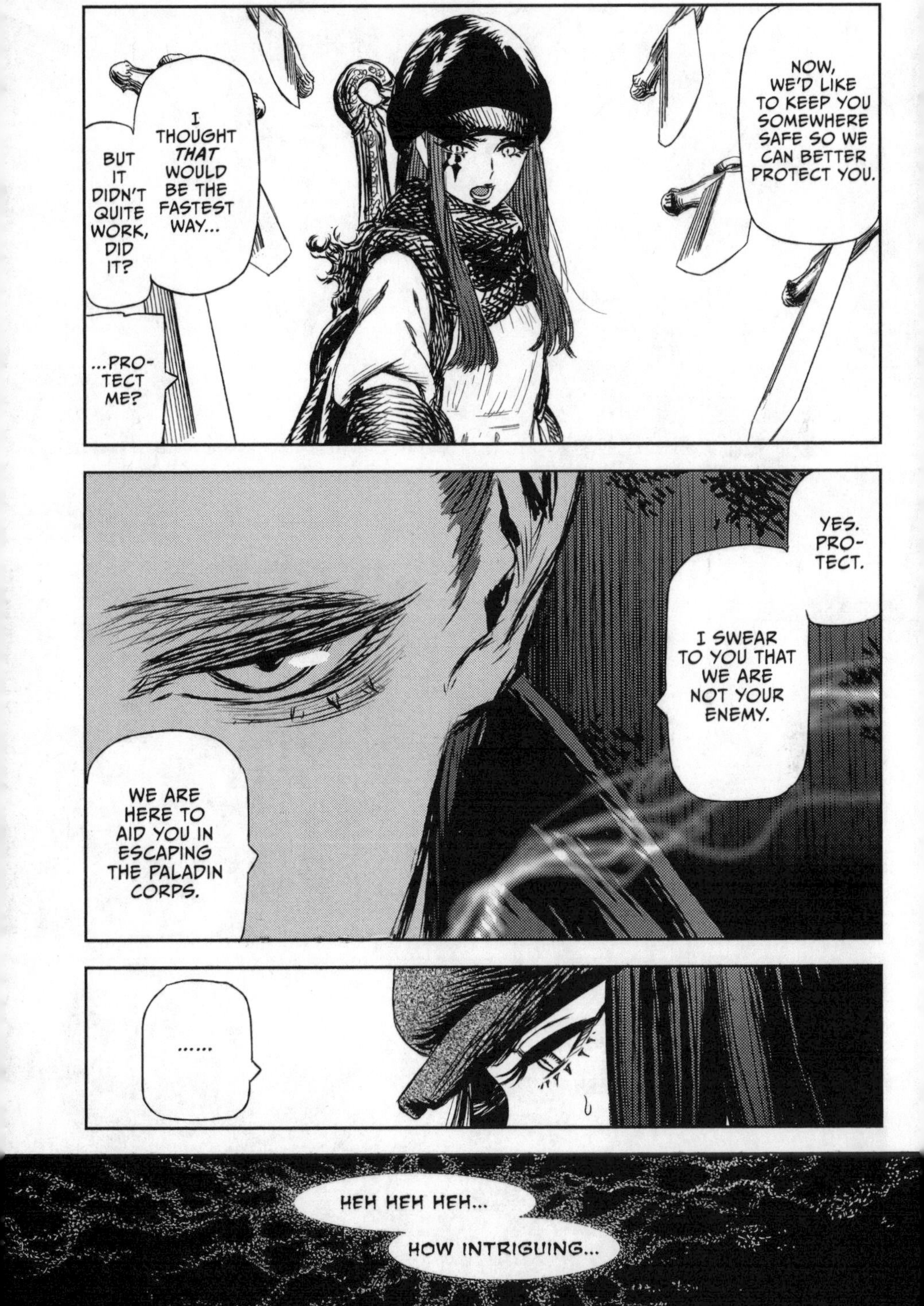

NOW, WE'D LIKE TO KEEP YOU SOMEWHERE SAFE SO WE CAN BETTER PROTECT YOU.
I THOUGHT *THAT* WOULD BE THE FASTEST WAY...
BUT IT DIDN'T QUITE WORK, DID IT?
...PRO-TECT ME?
YES. PRO-TECT.
I SWEAR TO YOU THAT WE ARE NOT YOUR ENEMY.
WE ARE HERE TO AID YOU IN ESCAPING THE PALADIN CORPS.
......
HEH HEH HEH...
HOW INTRIGUING...

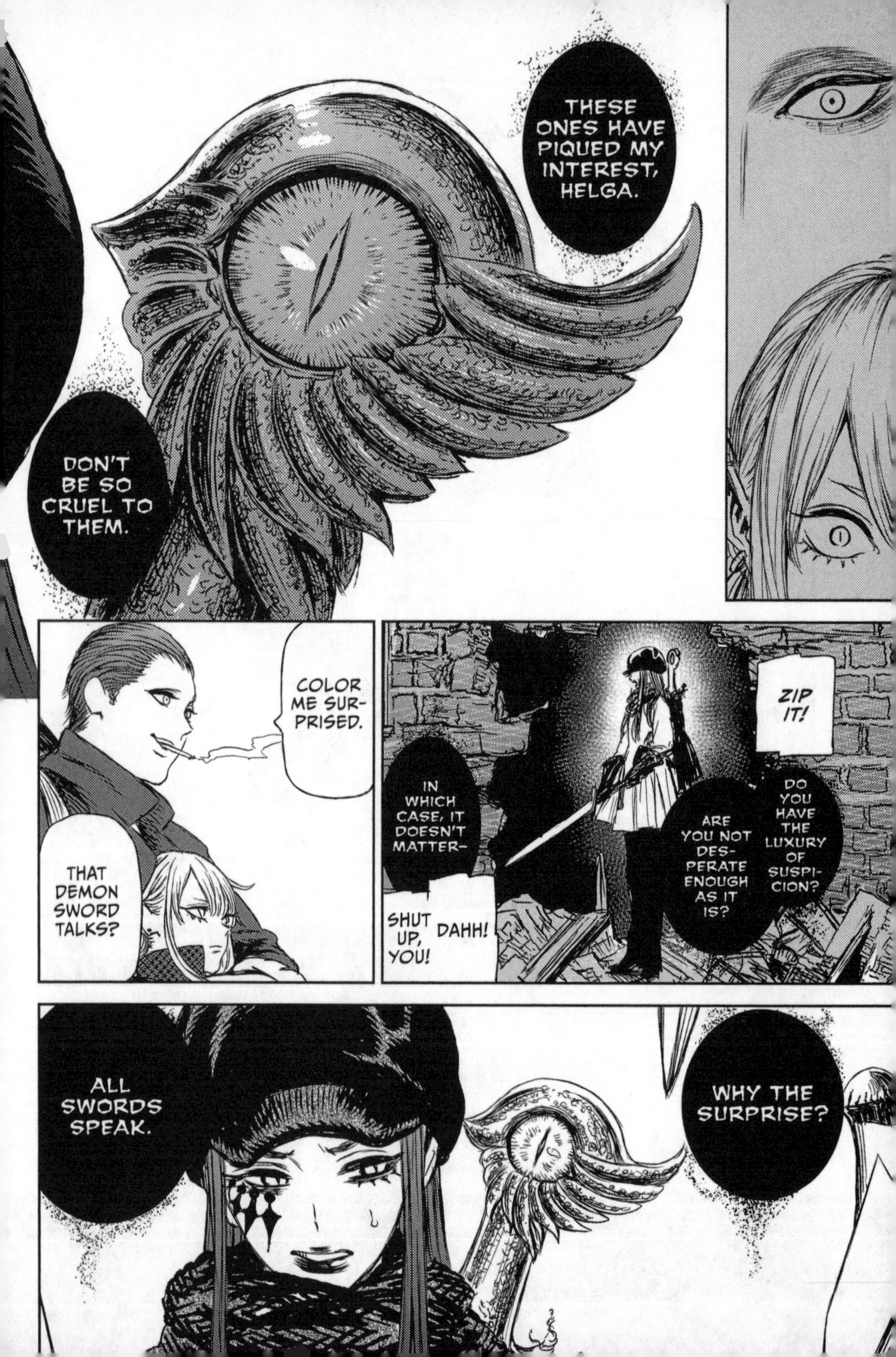
THESE ONES HAVE PIQUED MY INTEREST, HELGA.
DON'T BE SO CRUEL TO THEM.
ZIP IT!
DO YOU HAVE THE LUXURY OF SUSPICION?
ARE YOU NOT DESPERATE ENOUGH AS IT IS?
IN WHICH CASE, IT DOESN'T MATTER–
DAHH!
SHUT UP, YOU!
COLOR ME SURPRISED.
THAT DEMON SWORD TALKS?
WHY THE SURPRISE?
ALL SWORDS SPEAK.

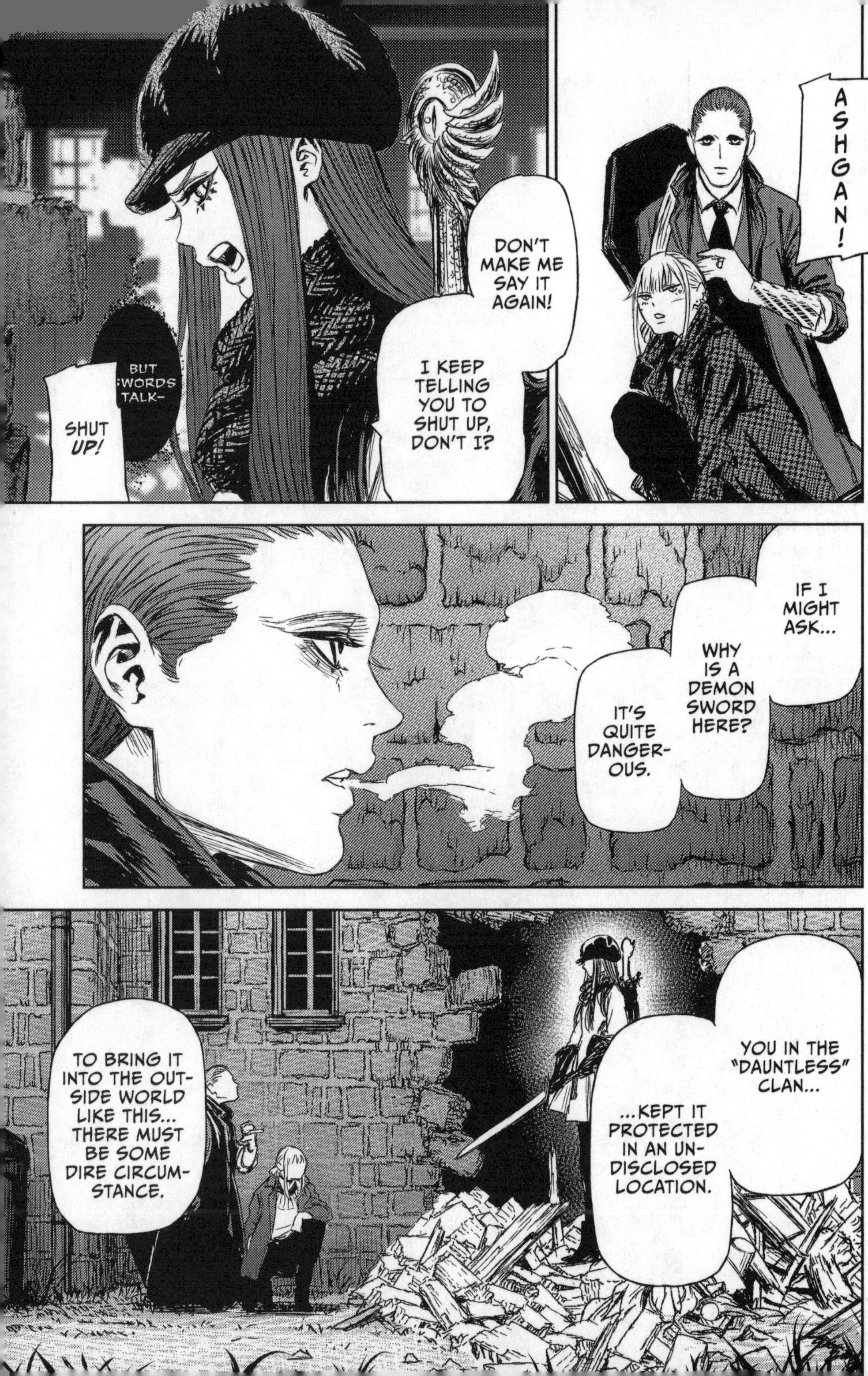
ASHGAN!
BUT SWORDS TALK–
SHUT UP!
I KEEP TELLING YOU TO SHUT UP, DON'T I?
DON'T MAKE ME SAY IT AGAIN!
IF I MIGHT ASK...
WHY IS A DEMON SWORD HERE?
IT'S QUITE DANGER-OUS.
YOU IN THE "DAUNTLESS" CLAN...
...KEPT IT PROTECTED IN AN UN-DISCLOSED LOCATION.
TO BRING IT INTO THE OUT-SIDE WORLD LIKE THIS... THERE MUST BE SOME DIRE CIRCUM-STANCE.

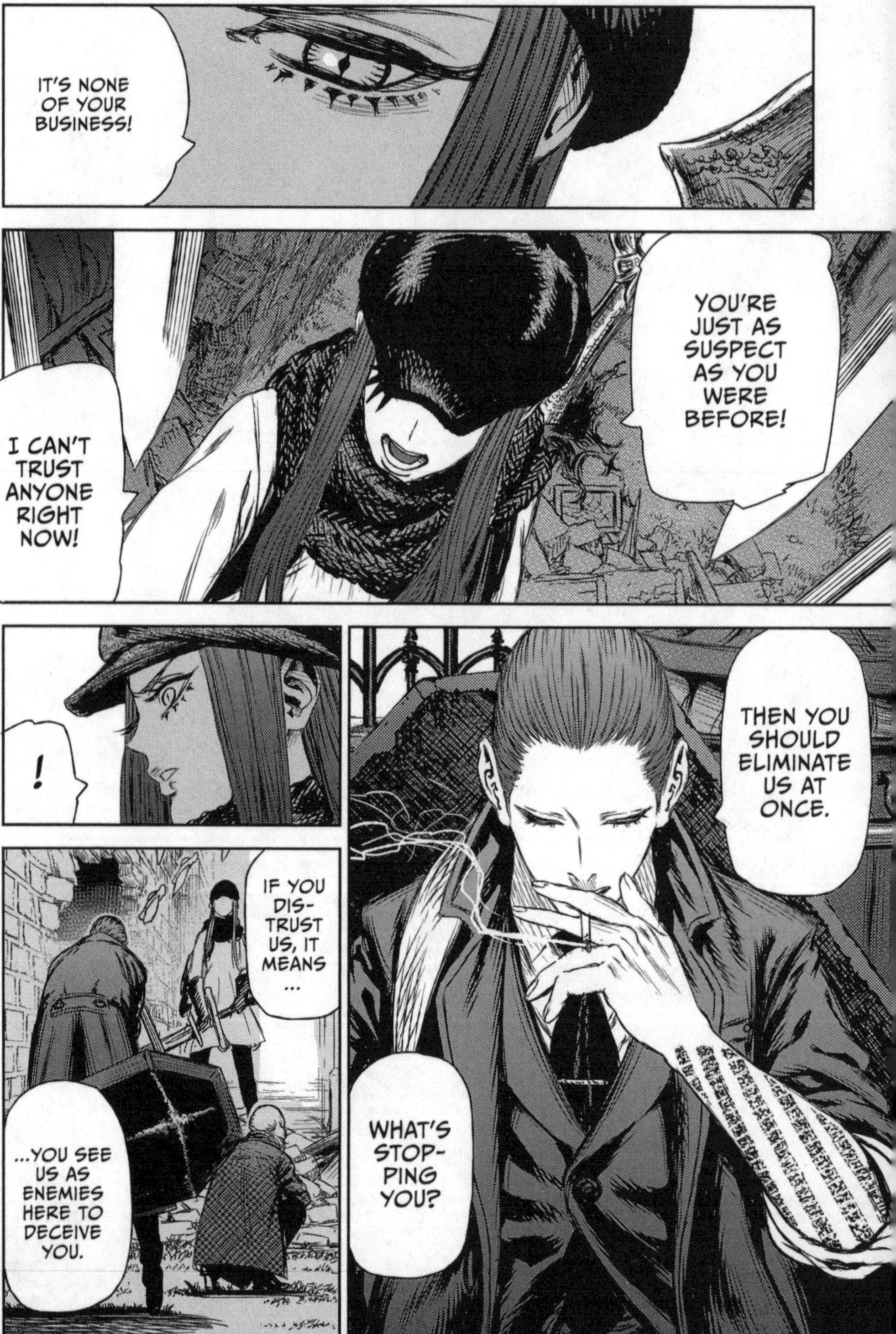
IT'S NONE OF YOUR BUSINESS!
YOU'RE JUST AS SUSPECT AS YOU WERE BEFORE!
I CAN'T TRUST ANYONE RIGHT NOW!
THEN YOU SHOULD ELIMINATE US AT ONCE.
WHAT'S STOP-PING YOU?
!
IF YOU DIS-TRUST US, IT MEANS ...
...YOU SEE US AS ENEMIES HERE TO DECEIVE YOU.

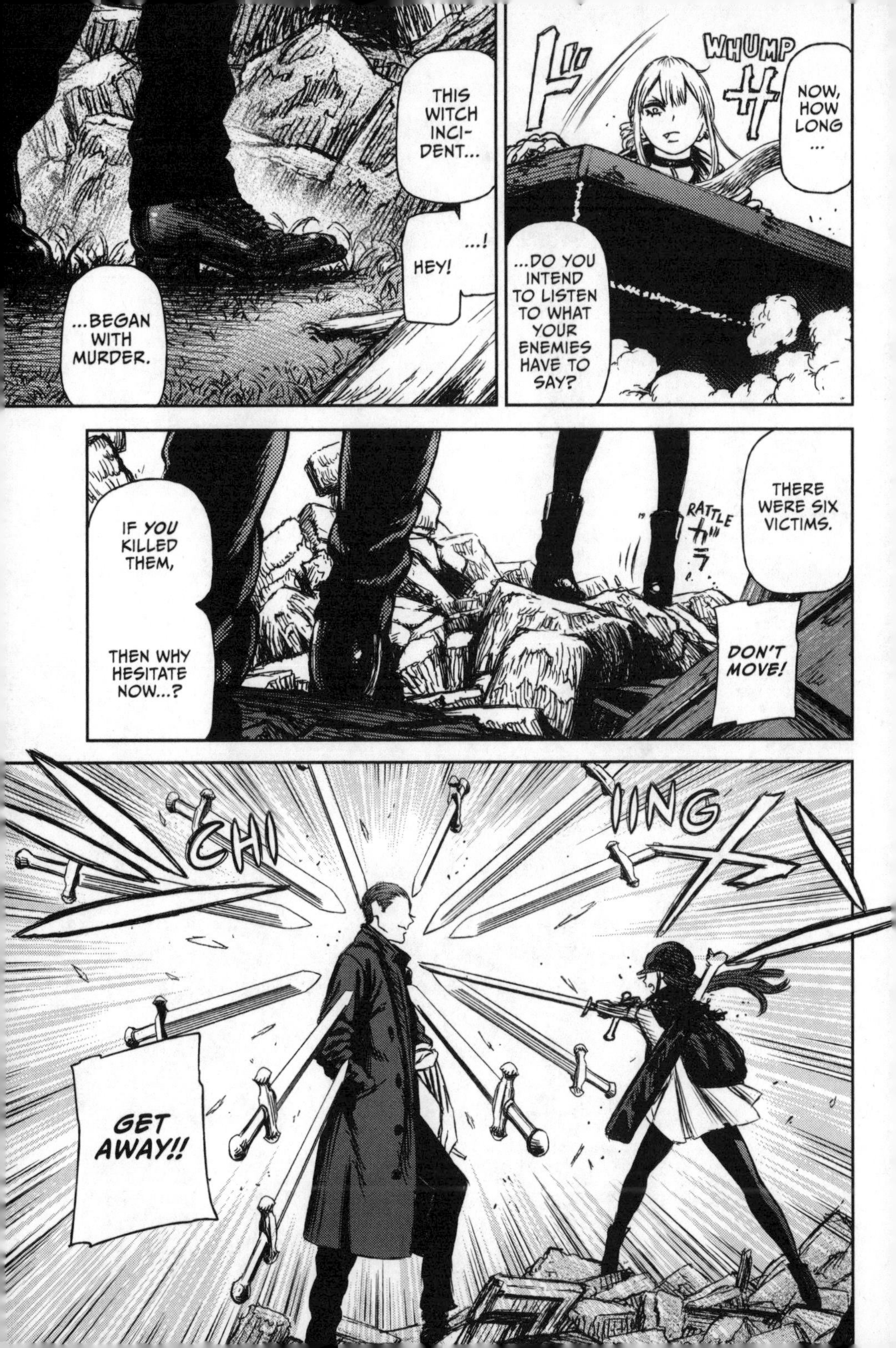
WHUMP
NOW, HOW LONG ...
...DO YOU INTEND TO LISTEN TO WHAT YOUR ENEMIES HAVE TO SAY?
THIS WITCH INCIDENT...
...! HEY!
...BEGAN WITH MURDER.
THERE WERE SIX VICTIMS.
RATTLE
DON'T MOVE!
IF *YOU* KILLED THEM,
THEN WHY HESITATE NOW...?
CHI
IING
GET AWAY!!

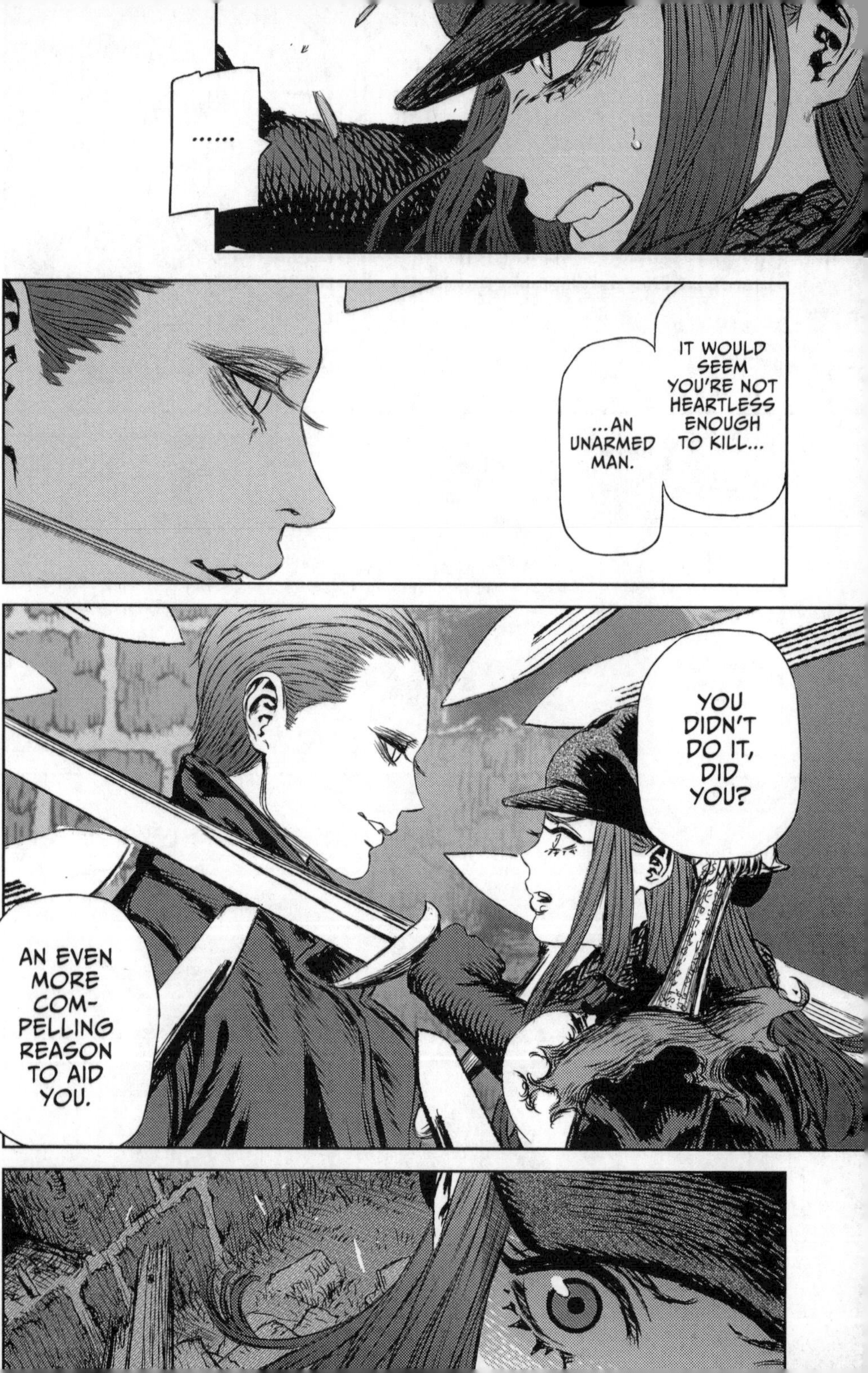
......
IT WOULD SEEM YOU'RE NOT HEARTLESS ENOUGH TO KILL...
...AN UNARMED MAN.
YOU DIDN'T DO IT, DID YOU?
AN EVEN MORE COM-PELLING REASON TO AID YOU.

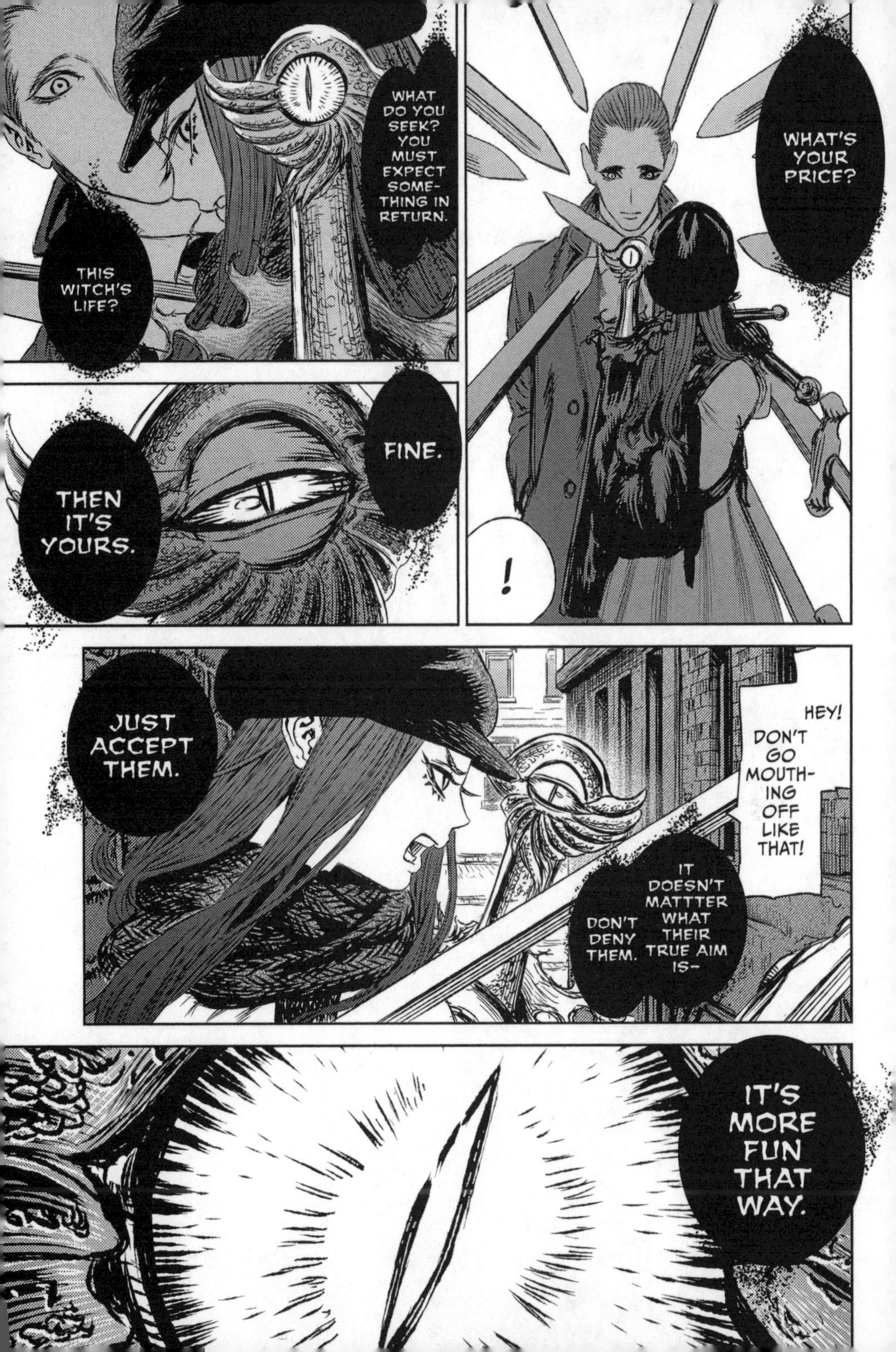
WHAT'S YOUR PRICE?
!
WHAT DO YOU SEEK? YOU MUST EXPECT SOME-THING IN RETURN.
THIS WITCH'S LIFE?
FINE.
THEN IT'S YOURS.
HEY! DON'T GO MOUTH-ING OFF LIKE THAT!
IT DOESN'T MATTTER WHAT THEIR TRUE AIM IS–
DON'T DENY THEM.
JUST ACCEPT THEM.
IT'S MORE FUN THAT WAY.

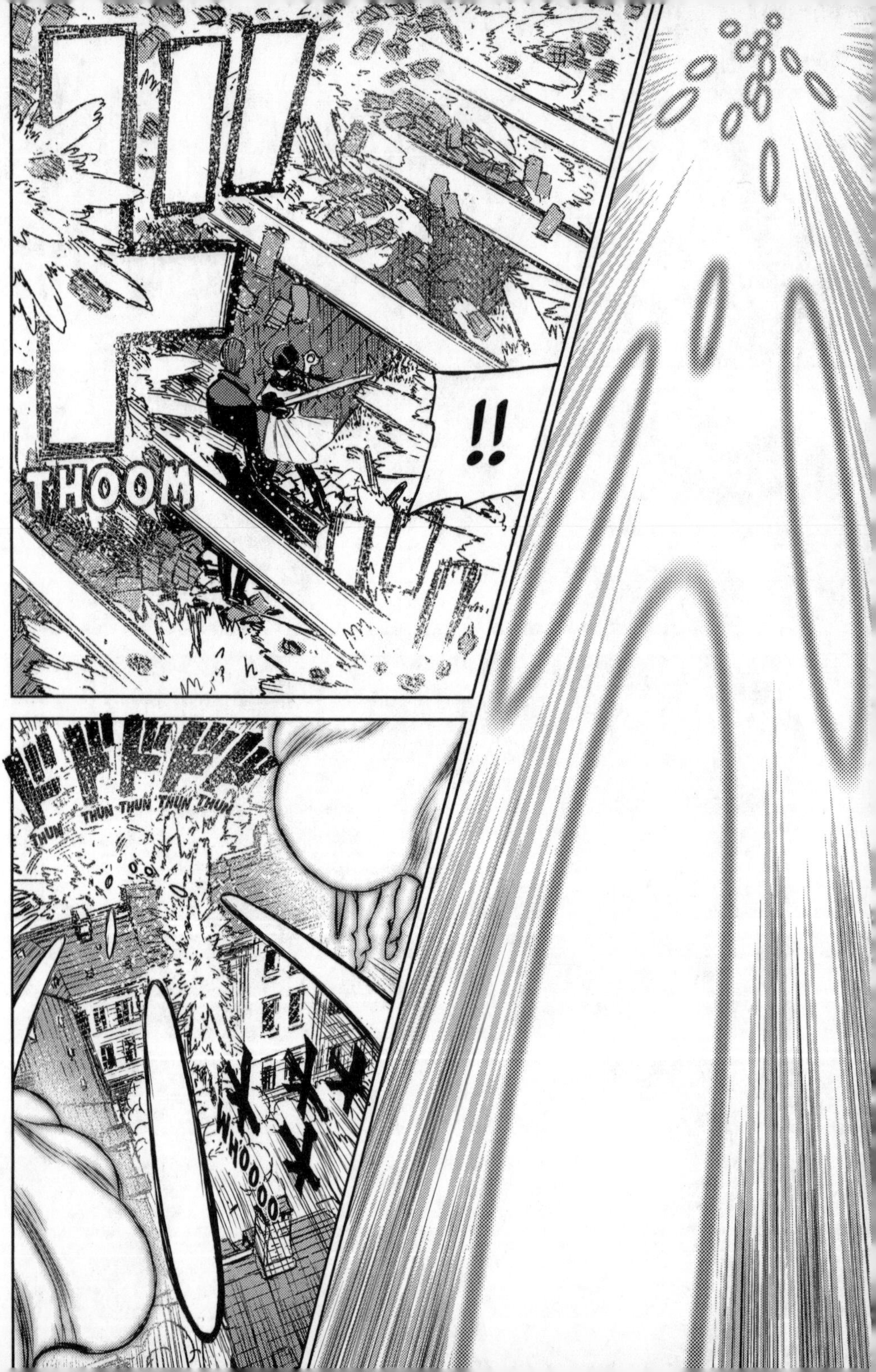
THOOM
!!
THUN THUN THUN THUN THUN
WHOOOOO

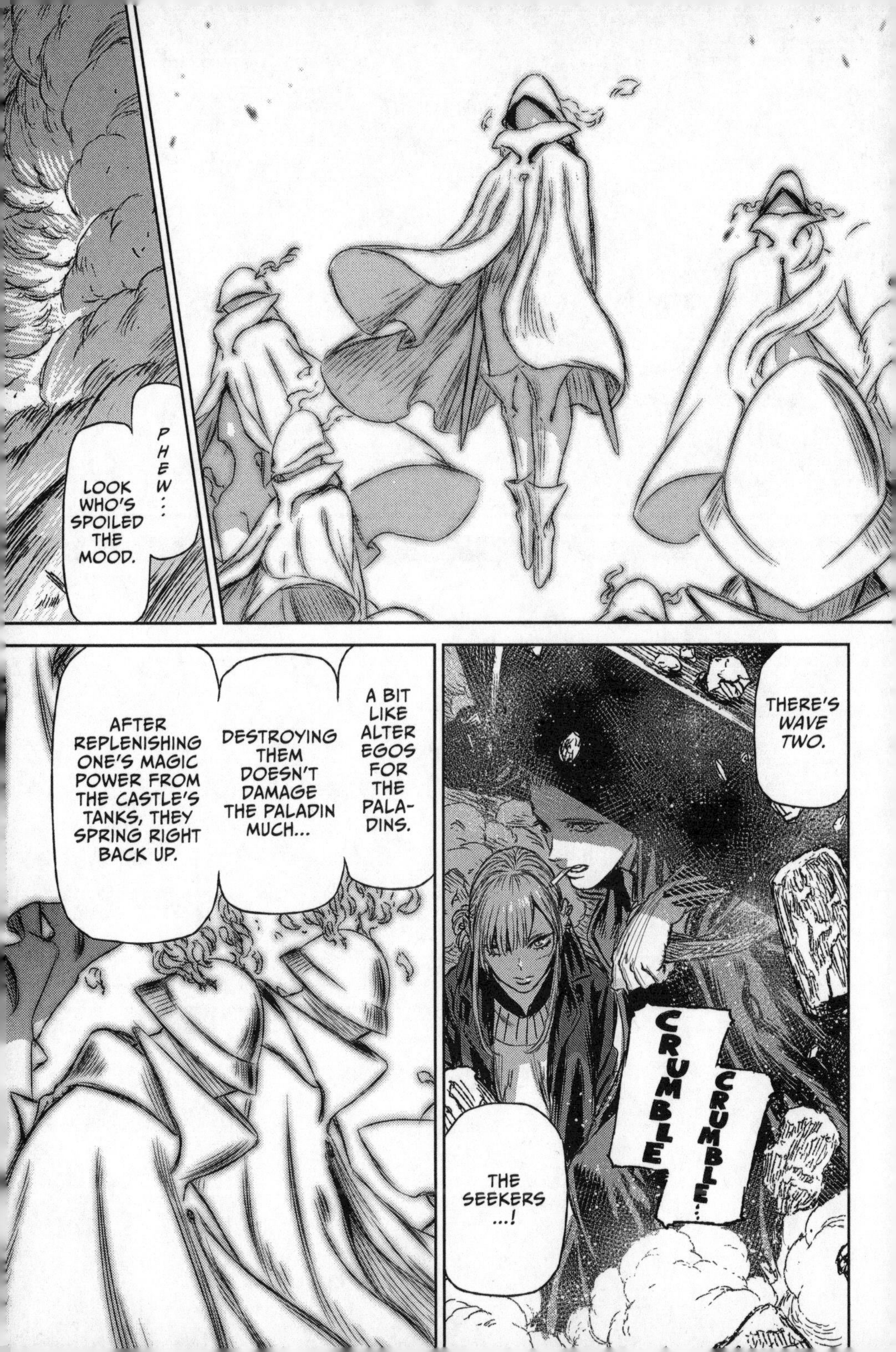
PHEW...
LOOK WHO'S SPOILED THE MOOD.
THERE'S WAVE TWO.
CRUMBLE
CRUMBLE...
THE SEEKERS ...!
A BIT LIKE ALTER EGOS FOR THE PALADINS.
DESTROYING THEM DOESN'T DAMAGE THE PALADIN MUCH...
AFTER REPLENISHING ONE'S MAGIC POWER FROM THE CASTLE'S TANKS, THEY SPRING RIGHT BACK UP.

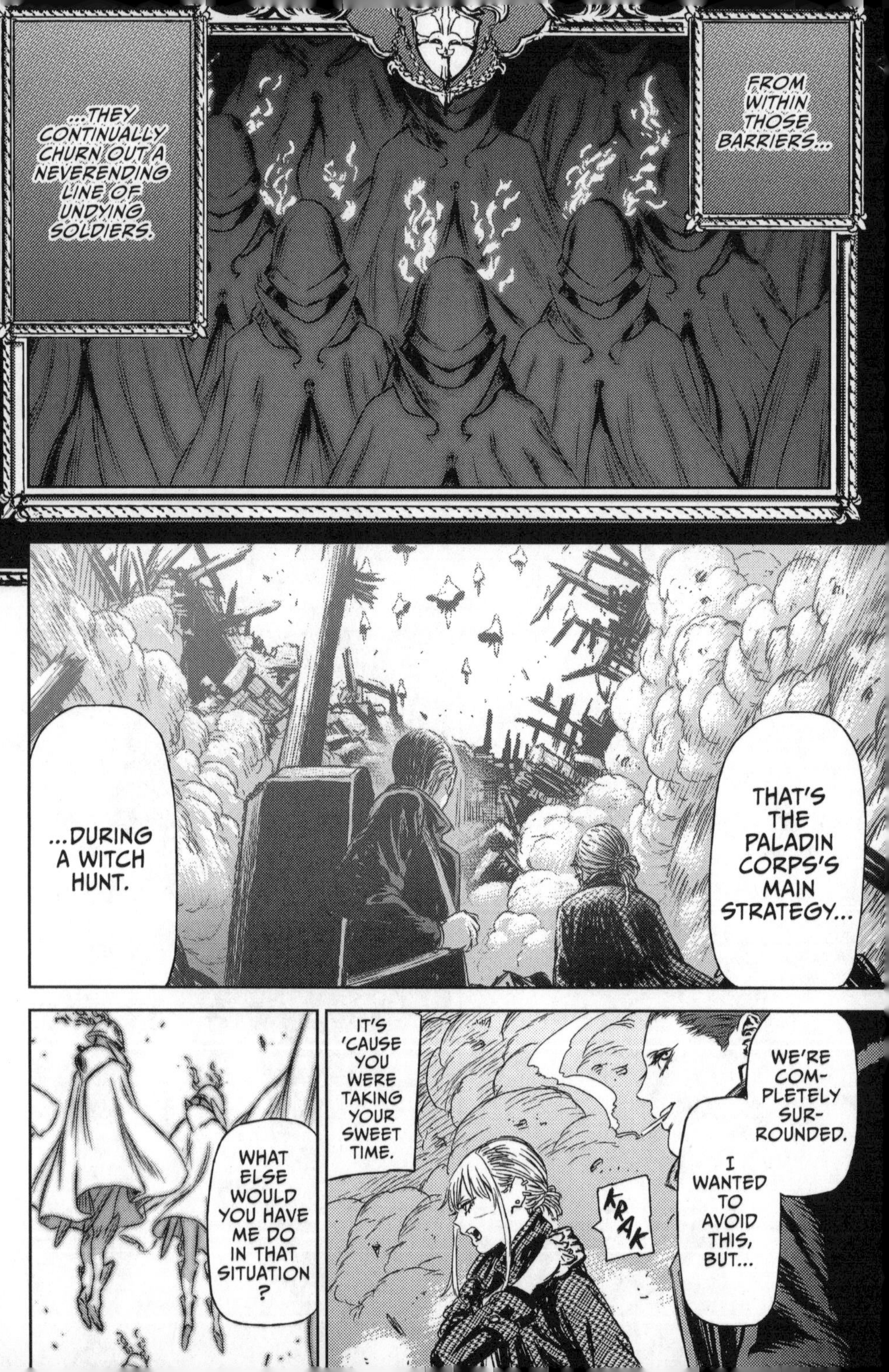
FROM WITHIN THOSE BARRIERS...
...THEY CONTINUALLY CHURN OUT A NEVERENDING LINE OF UNDYING SOLDIERS.
THAT'S THE PALADIN CORPS'S MAIN STRATEGY...
...DURING A WITCH HUNT.
WE'RE COM-PLETELY SUR-ROUNDED.
I WANTED TO AVOID THIS, BUT...
KRAK
IT'S 'CAUSE YOU WERE TAKING YOUR SWEET TIME.
WHAT ELSE WOULD YOU HAVE ME DO IN THAT SITUATION?

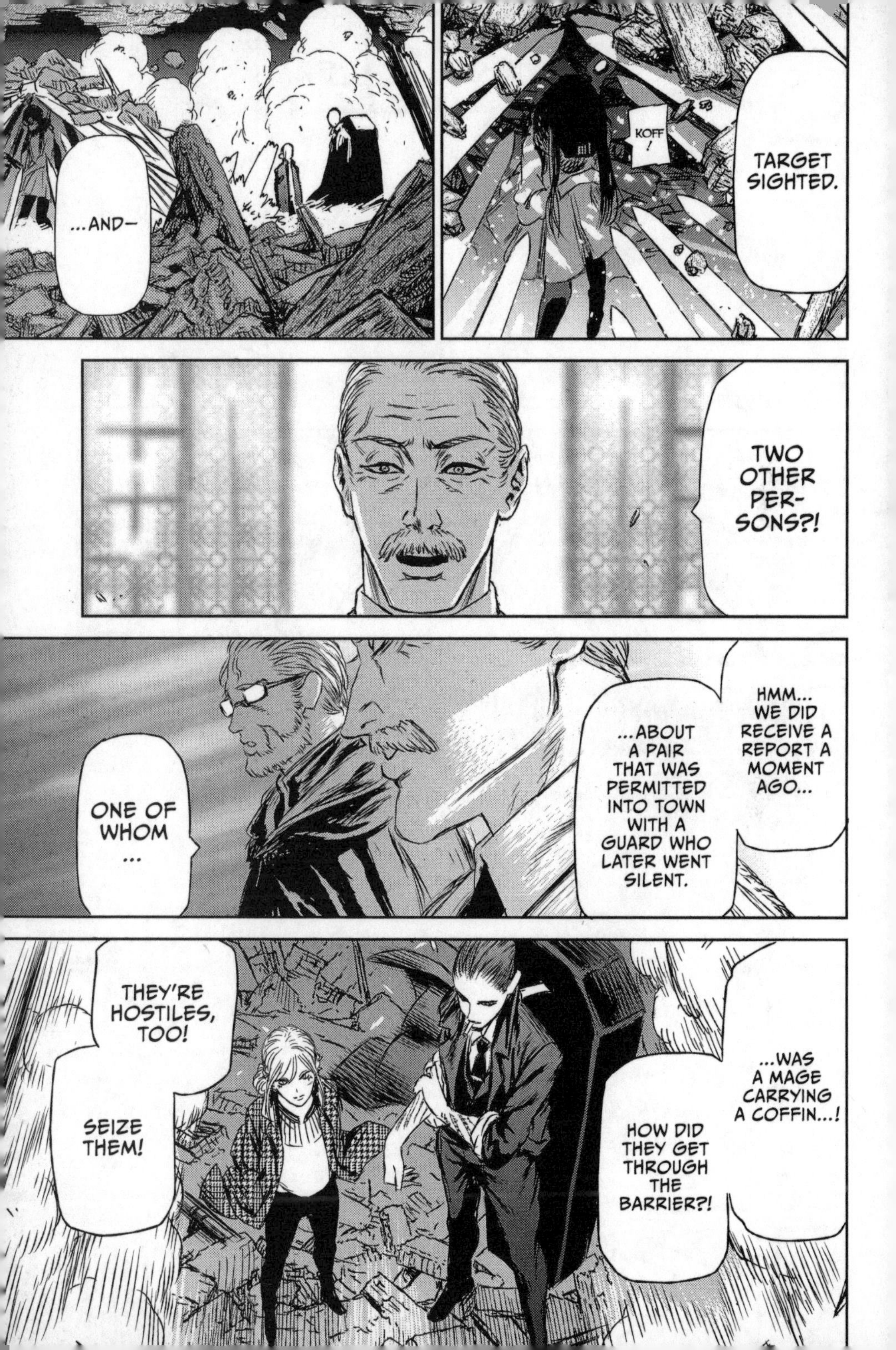
TARGET SIGHTED.
KOFF!
...AND—
TWO OTHER PERSONS?!
HMM... WE DID RECEIVE A REPORT A MOMENT AGO...
...ABOUT A PAIR THAT WAS PERMITTED INTO TOWN WITH A GUARD WHO LATER WENT SILENT.
ONE OF WHOM ...
...WAS A MAGE CARRYING A COFFIN...!
HOW DID THEY GET THROUGH THE BARRIER?!
THEY'RE HOSTILES, TOO!
SEIZE THEM!

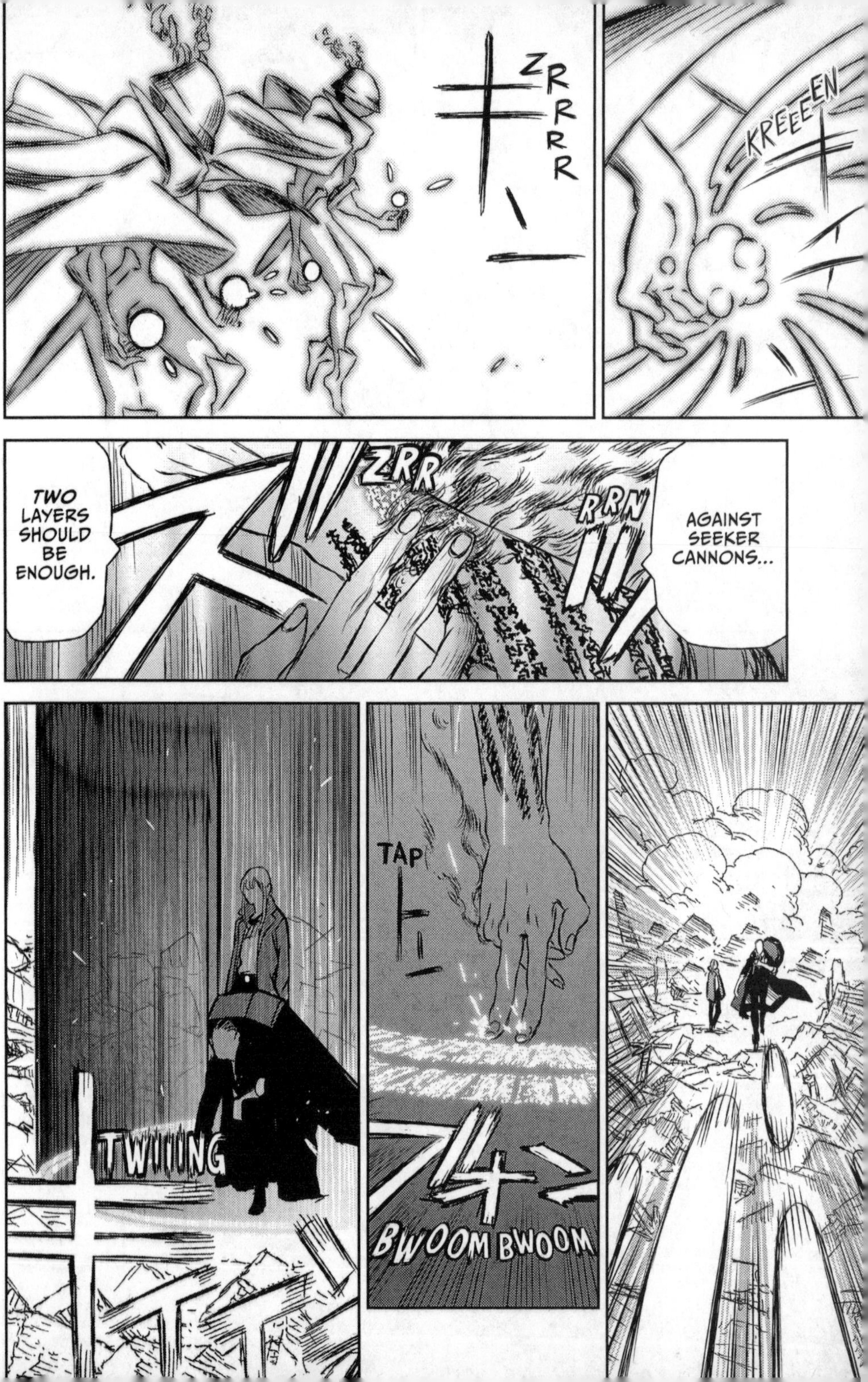
KREEEEEN
ZRRRRR
AGAINST SEEKER CANNONS...
ZRR RRN
TWO LAYERS SHOULD BE ENOUGH.
TAP
BWOOM BWOOM
TWIIING

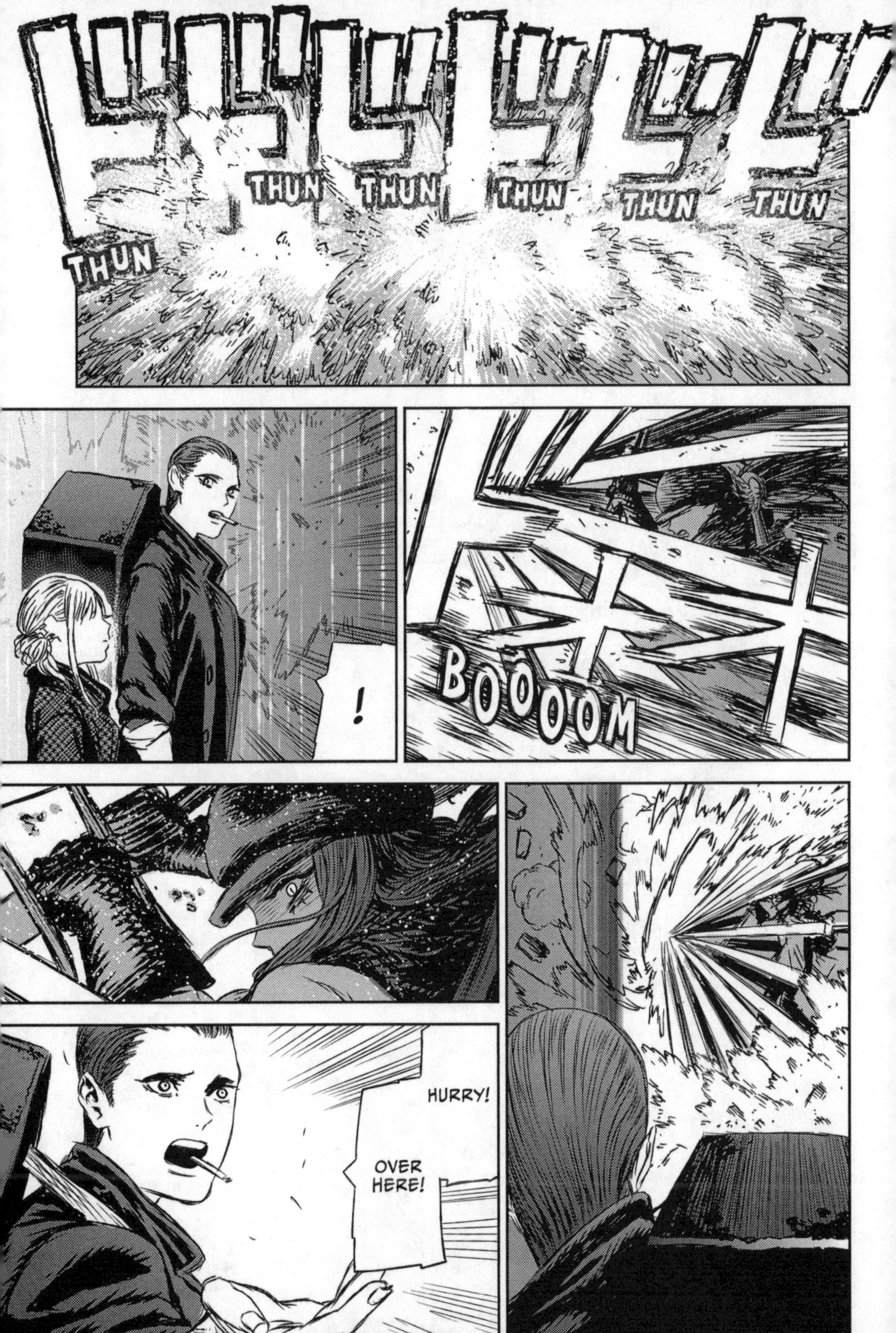
THUN
THUN
THUN
THUN
THUN
THUN
BOOOOM
!
HURRY!
OVER HERE!

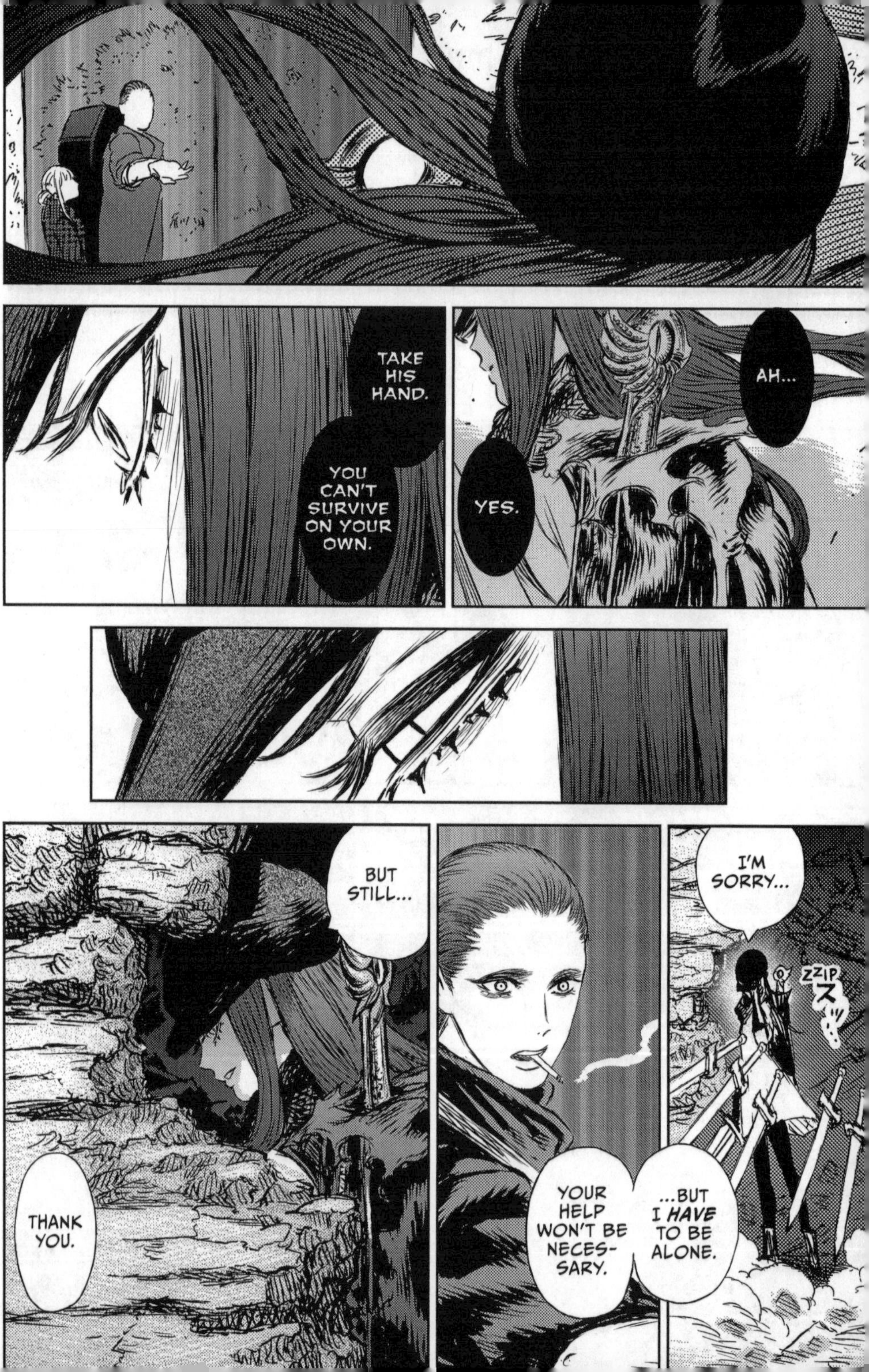
AH...
YES.
TAKE HIS HAND.
YOU CAN'T SURVIVE ON YOUR OWN.
I'M SORRY...
ZZIP
スッ...
...BUT I *HAVE* TO BE ALONE.
YOUR HELP WON'T BE NECES-SARY.
BUT STILL...
THANK YOU.

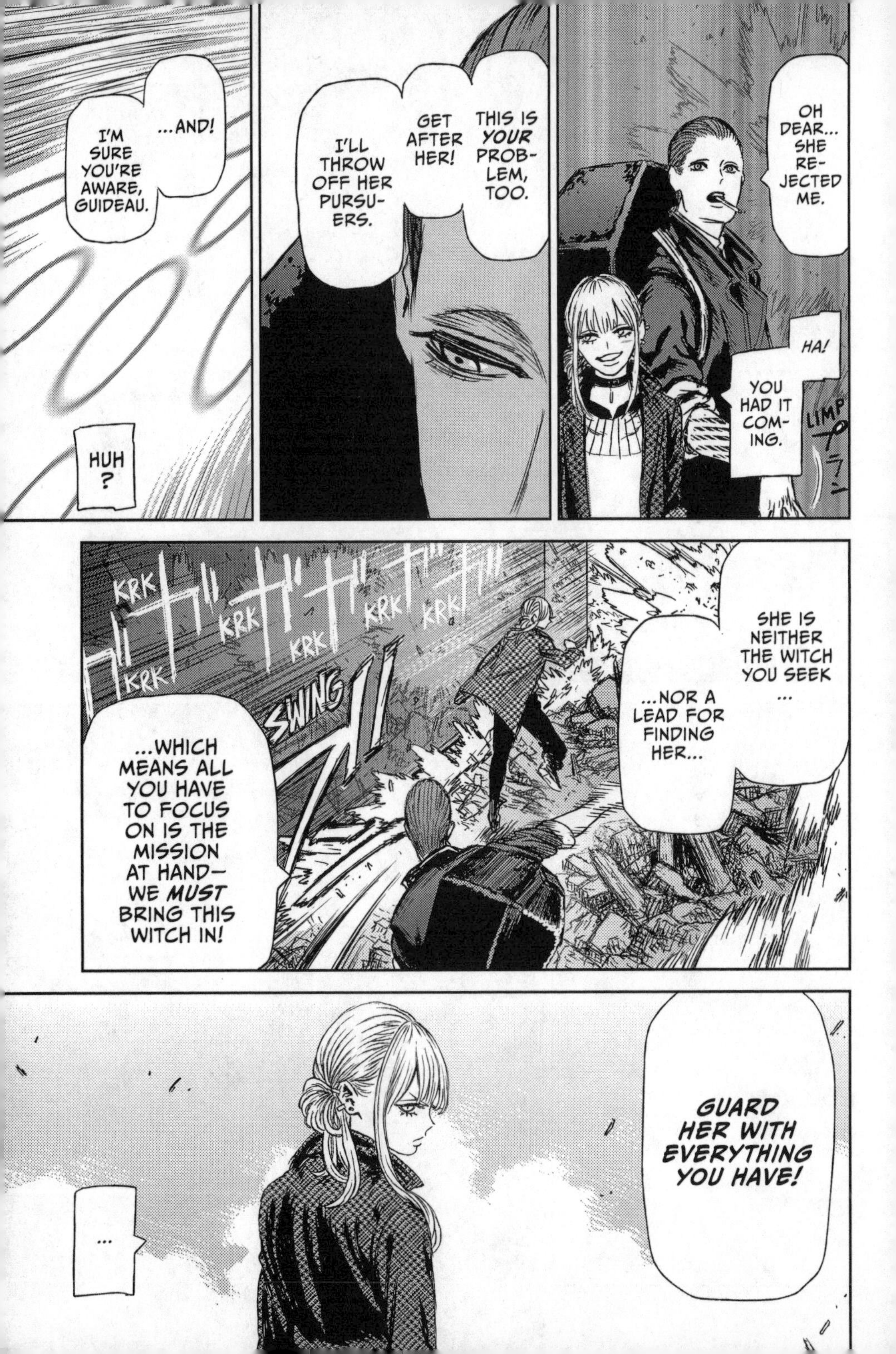
OH DEAR... SHE REJECTED ME.
HA!
YOU HAD IT COMING.
LIMP
THIS IS YOUR PROBLEM, TOO.
GET AFTER HER!
I'LL THROW OFF HER PURSUERS.
...AND!
I'M SURE YOU'RE AWARE, GUIDEAU.
HUH?
SHE IS NEITHER THE WITCH YOU SEEK...
...NOR A LEAD FOR FINDING HER...
KRK KRK KRK KRK KRK KRK
SWING
...WHICH MEANS ALL YOU HAVE TO FOCUS ON IS THE MISSION AT HAND— WE MUST BRING THIS WITCH IN!
GUARD HER WITH EVERYTHING YOU HAVE!
...

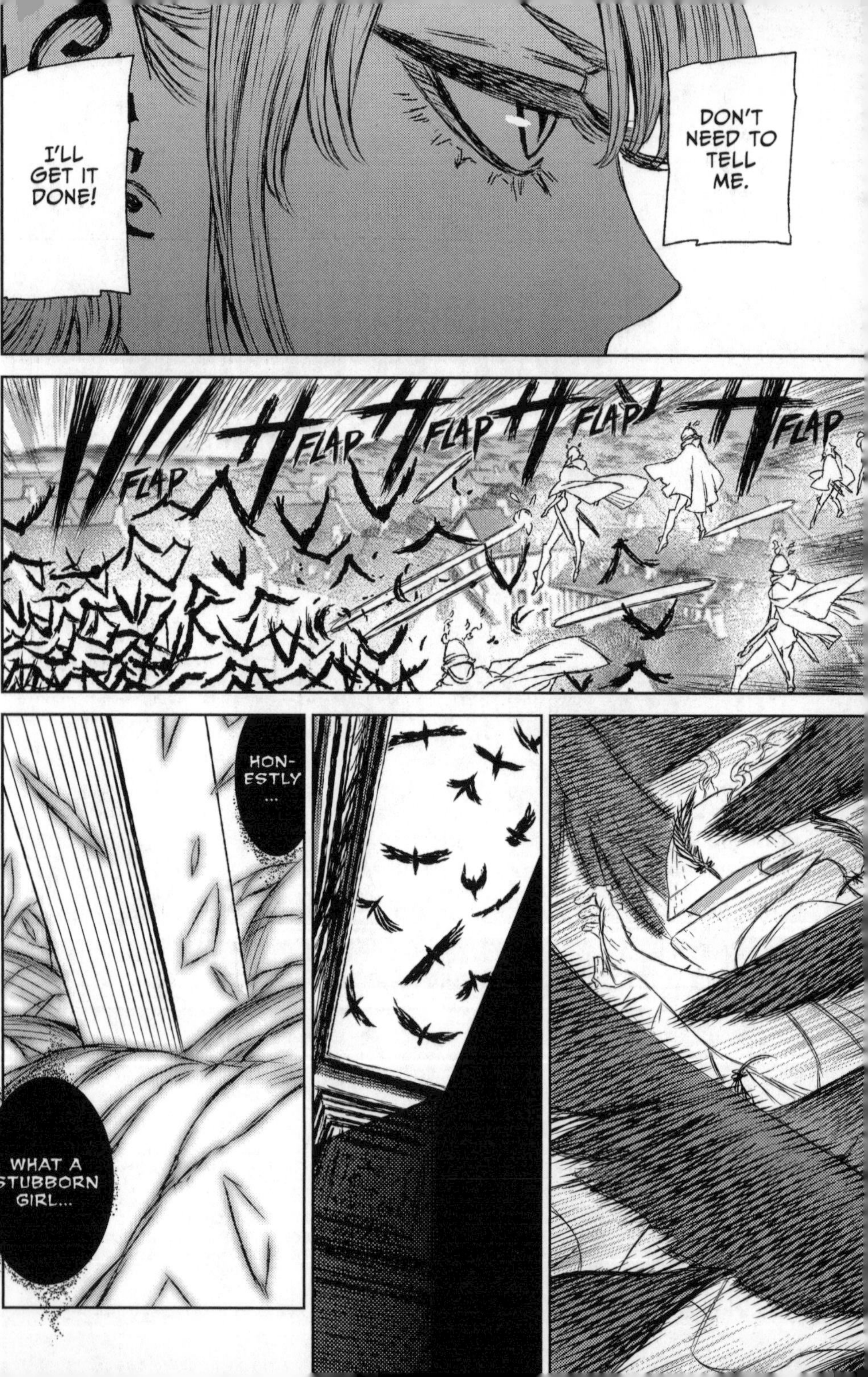
DON'T NEED TO TELL ME.
I'LL GET IT DONE!
FLAP
FLAP
FLAP
FLAP
FLAP
HON-ESTLY...
WHAT A STUBBORN GIRL...

IT'S ADMIRABLE, IN A WAY.

NOW, JUST HOW LONG...

...CAN YOU WITHSTAND THIS SOLITUDE?

SHUT UP!!

...BE RID OF YOU...

CRKK

IF I COULD JUST...

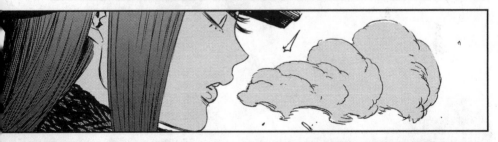

I SEE NOW...

...AH.

THIS COLD...

WHOO

...!

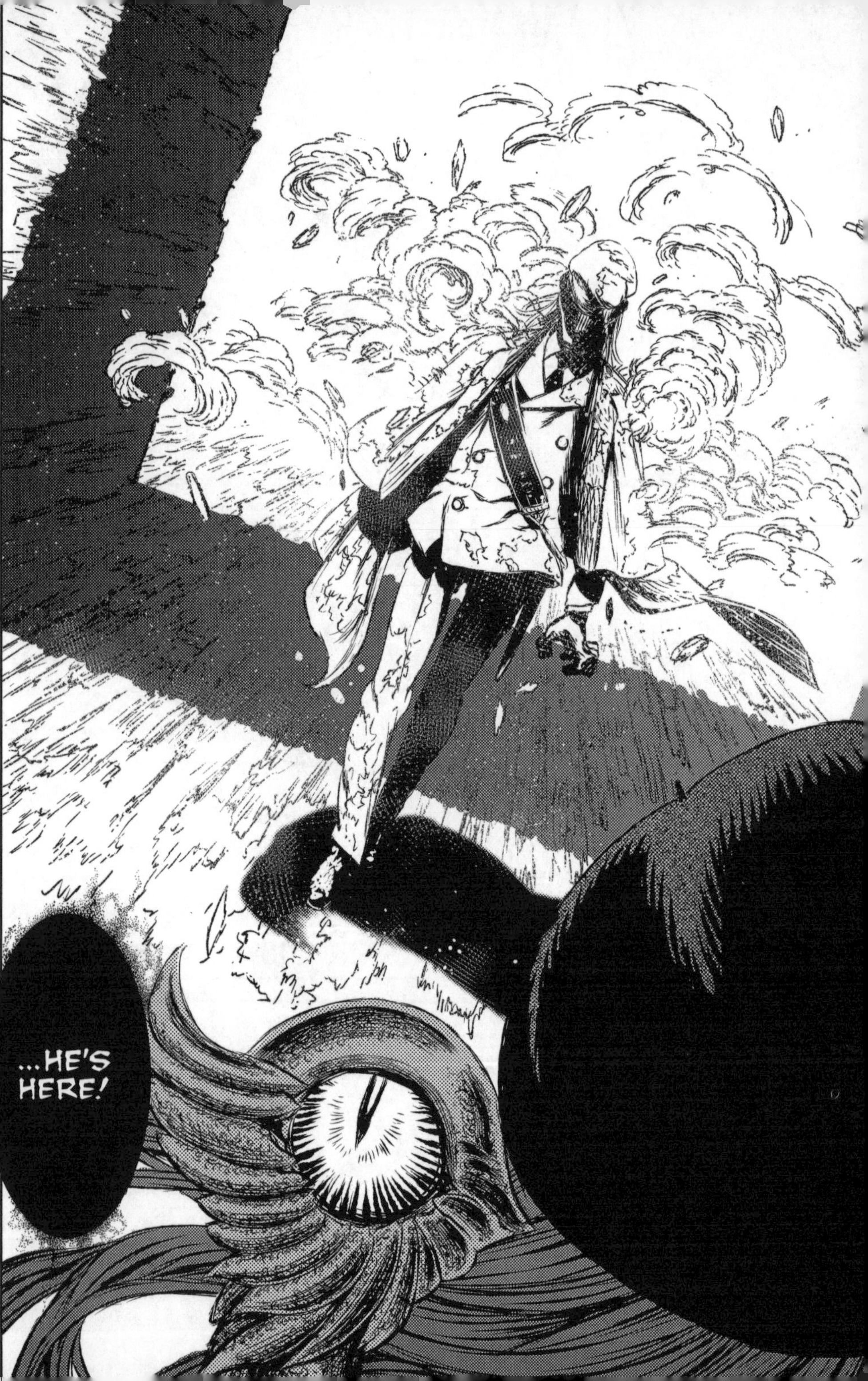
...HE'S HERE!

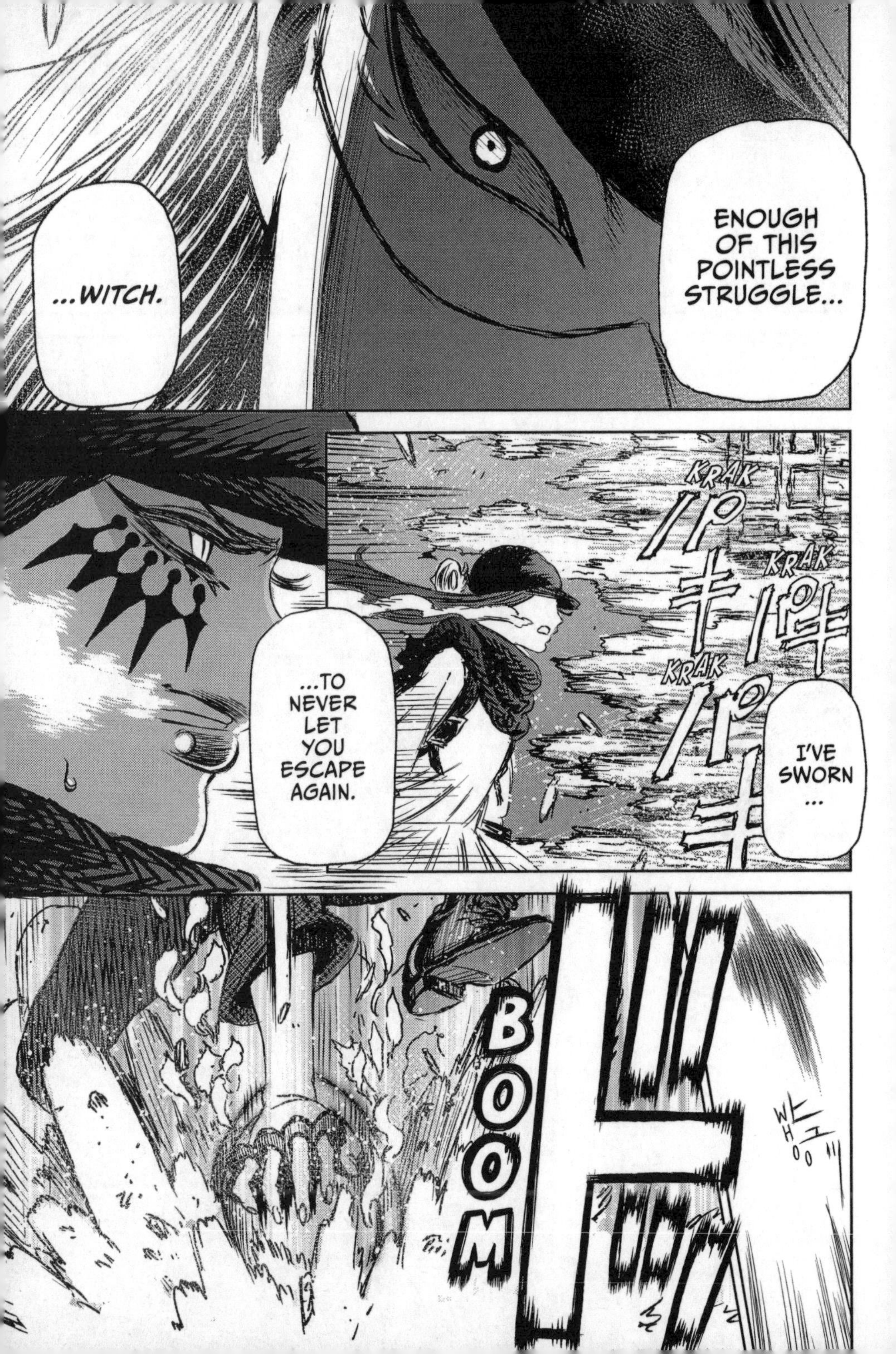

ENOUGH OF THIS POINTLESS STRUGGLE...
...WITCH.
KRAK
KRAK
KRAK
I'VE SWORN ...
...TO NEVER LET YOU ESCAPE AGAIN.
WHOO
BOOM

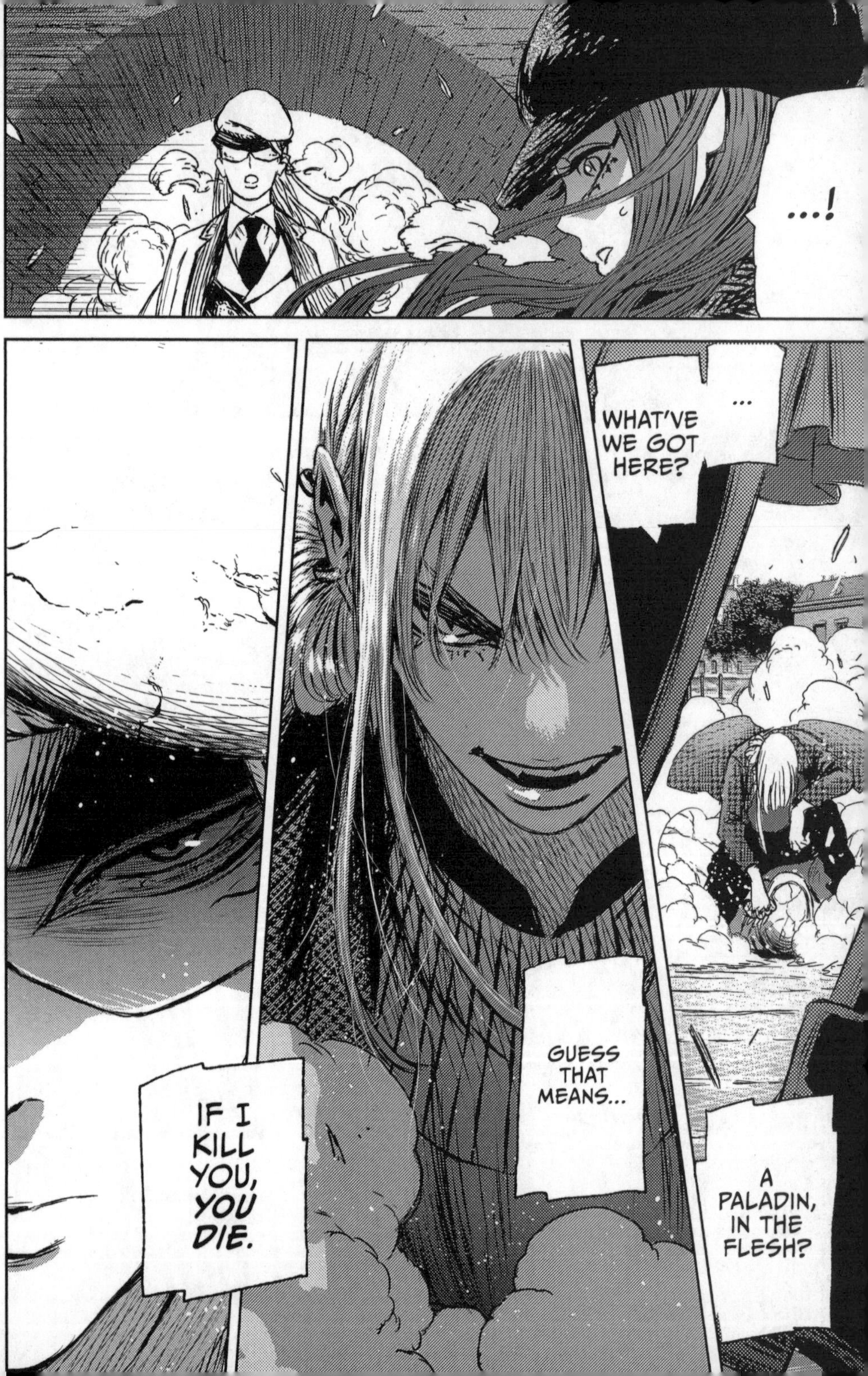
...!
...
WHAT'VE WE GOT HERE?
A PALADIN, IN THE FLESH?
GUESS THAT MEANS...
IF I KILL YOU, YOU DIE.

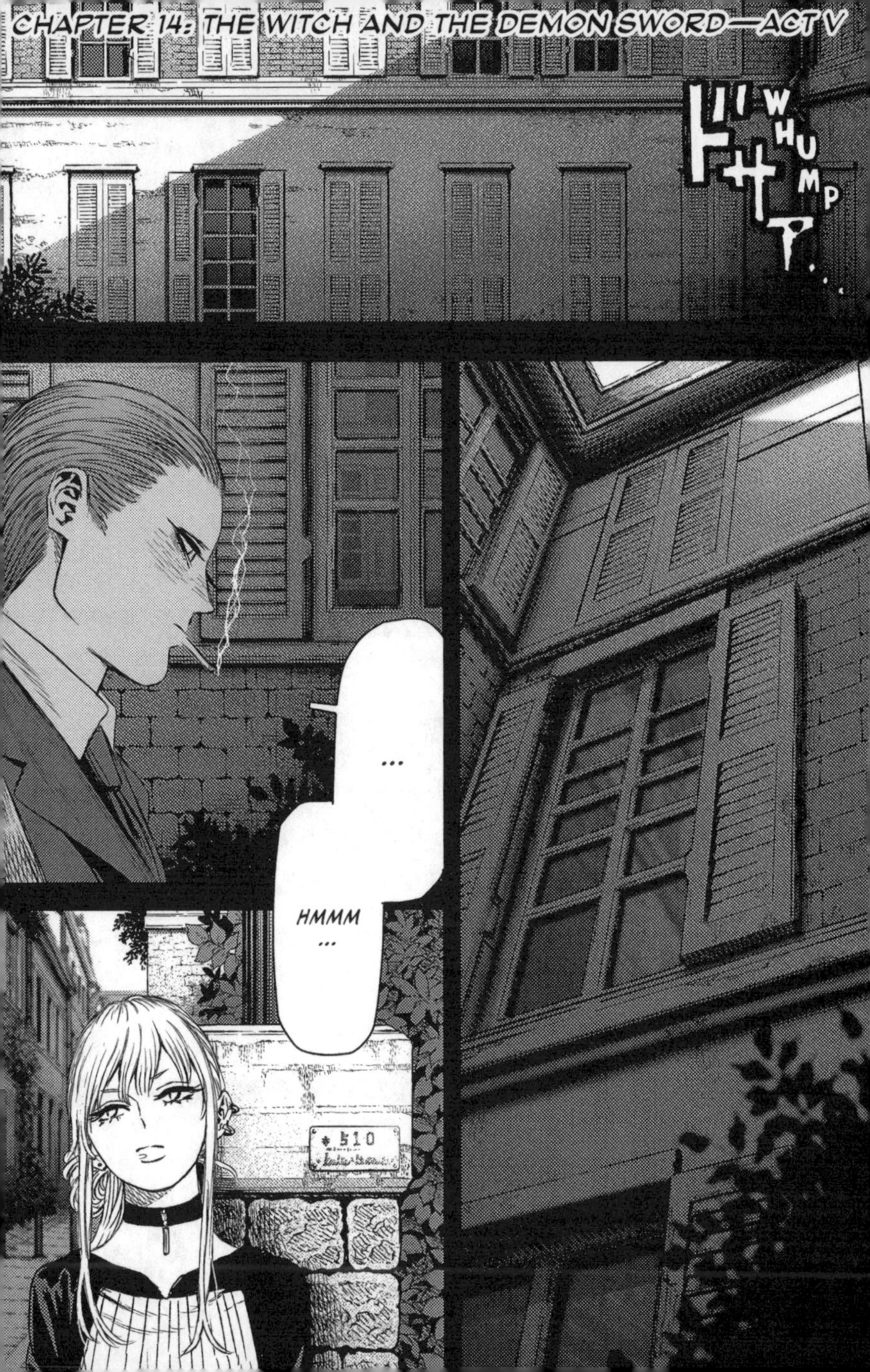
CHAPTER 14: THE WITCH AND THE DEMON SWORD—ACT V
ドサァ...
WHUMP
...
HMMM ...

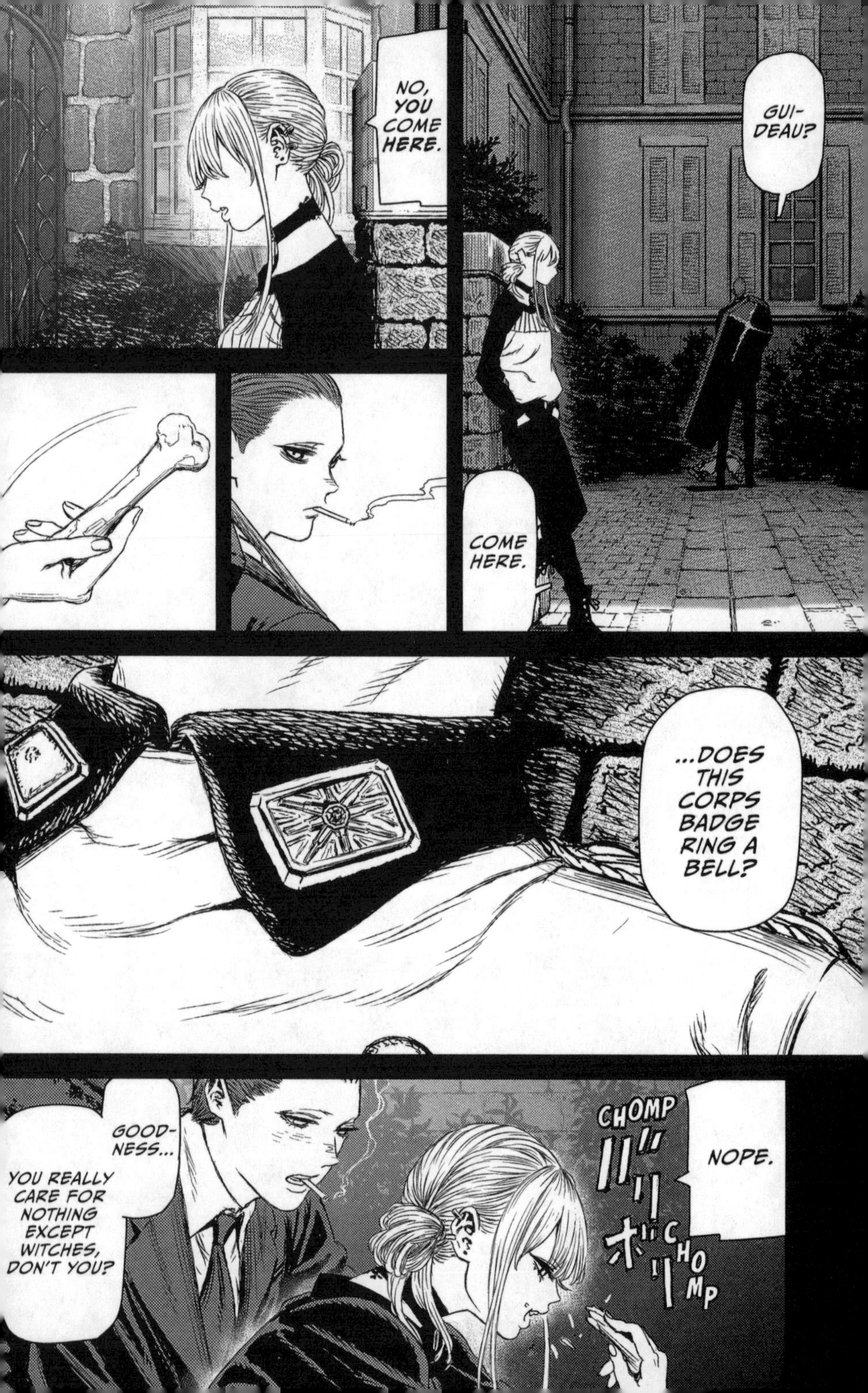
GUI-DEAU?
COME HERE.
NO, YOU COME HERE.
...DOES THIS CORPS BADGE RING A BELL?
NOPE.
CHOMP
CHOMP
GOODNESS...
YOU REALLY CARE FOR NOTHING EXCEPT WITCHES, DON'T YOU?

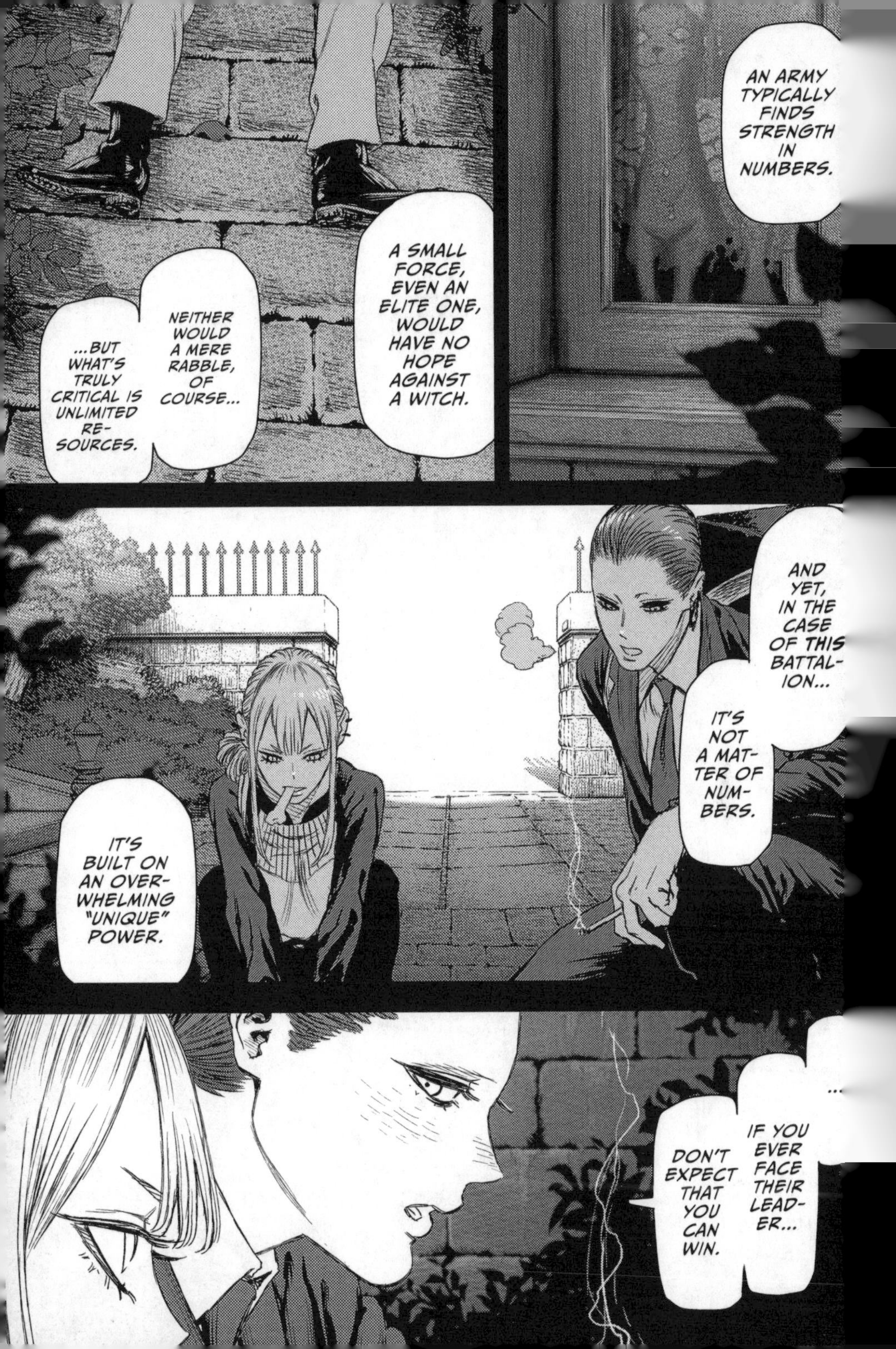
AN ARMY TYPICALLY FINDS STRENGTH IN NUMBERS.
A SMALL FORCE, EVEN AN ELITE ONE, WOULD HAVE NO HOPE AGAINST A WITCH.
NEITHER WOULD A MERE RABBLE, OF COURSE...
...BUT WHAT'S TRULY CRITICAL IS UNLIMITED RE-SOURCES.
AND YET, IN THE CASE OF THIS BATTAL-ION...
IT'S NOT A MAT-TER OF NUM-BERS.
IT'S BUILT ON AN OVER-WHELMING "UNIQUE" POWER.
...
IF YOU EVER FACE THEIR LEAD-ER...
DON'T EXPECT THAT YOU CAN WIN.

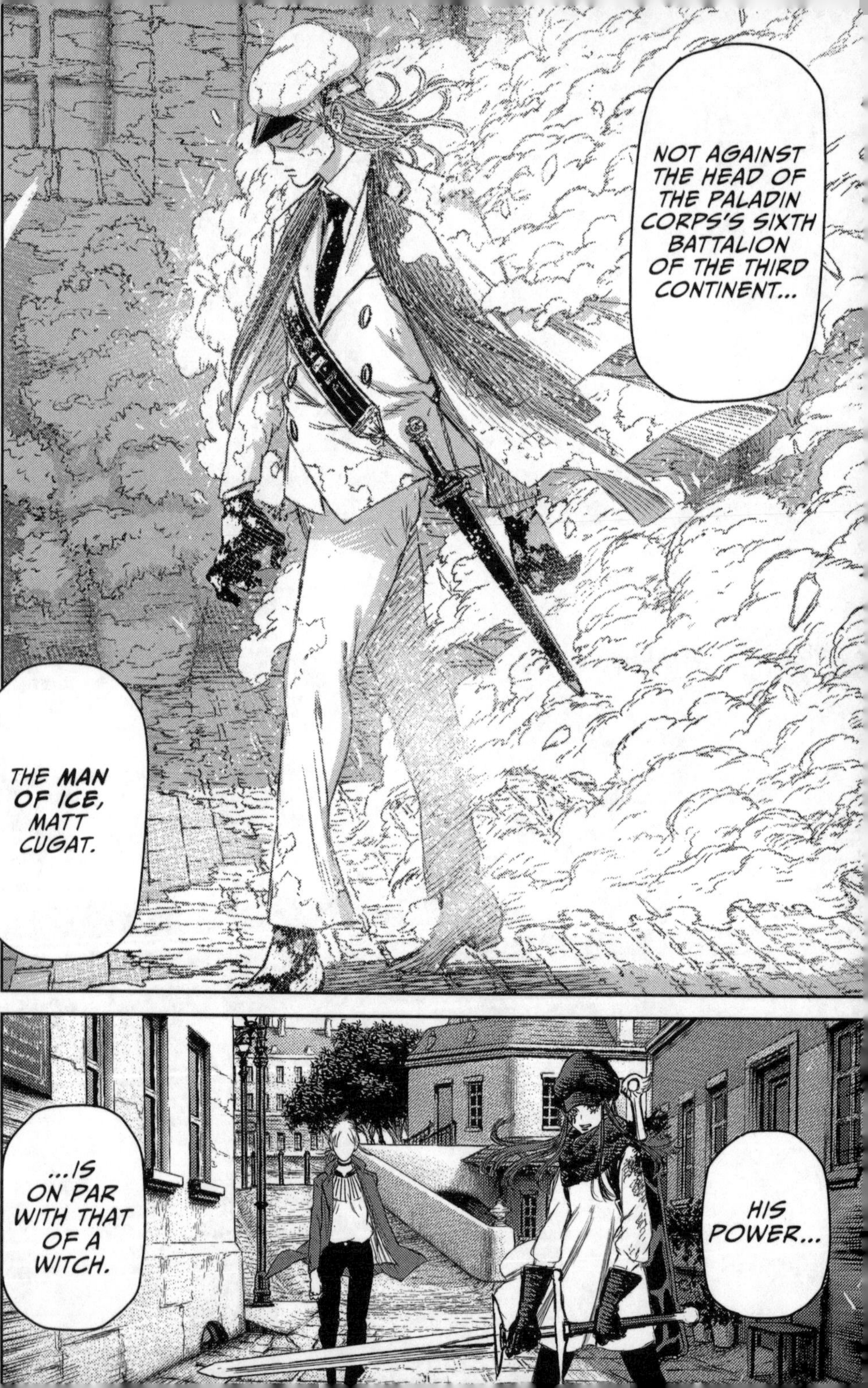
NOT AGAINST THE HEAD OF THE PALADIN CORPS'S SIXTH BATTALION OF THE THIRD CONTINENT...
THE MAN OF ICE, MATT CUGAT.
HIS POWER...
...IS ON PAR WITH THAT OF A WITCH.

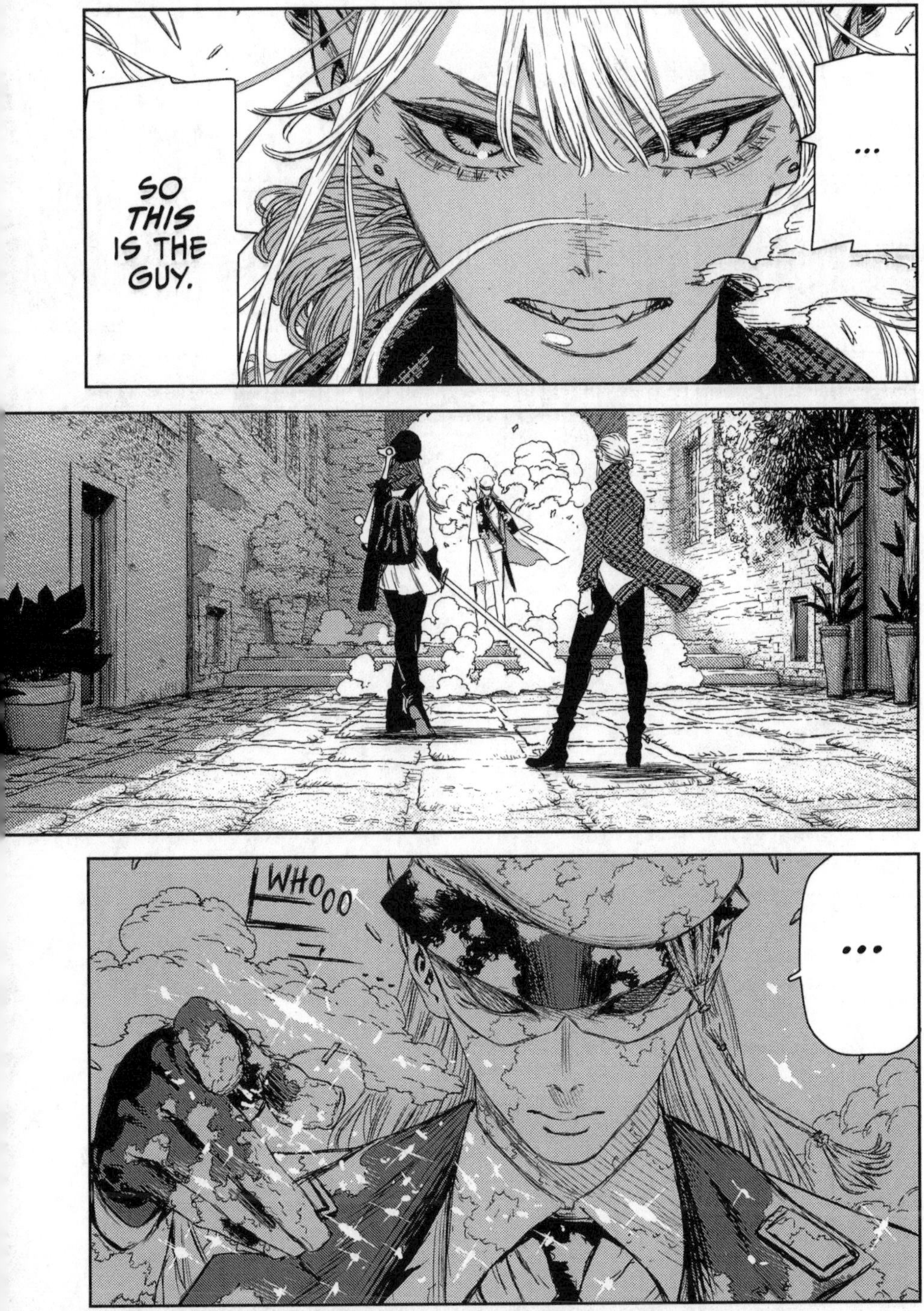
...
SO THIS IS THE GUY.
...
WHOOO

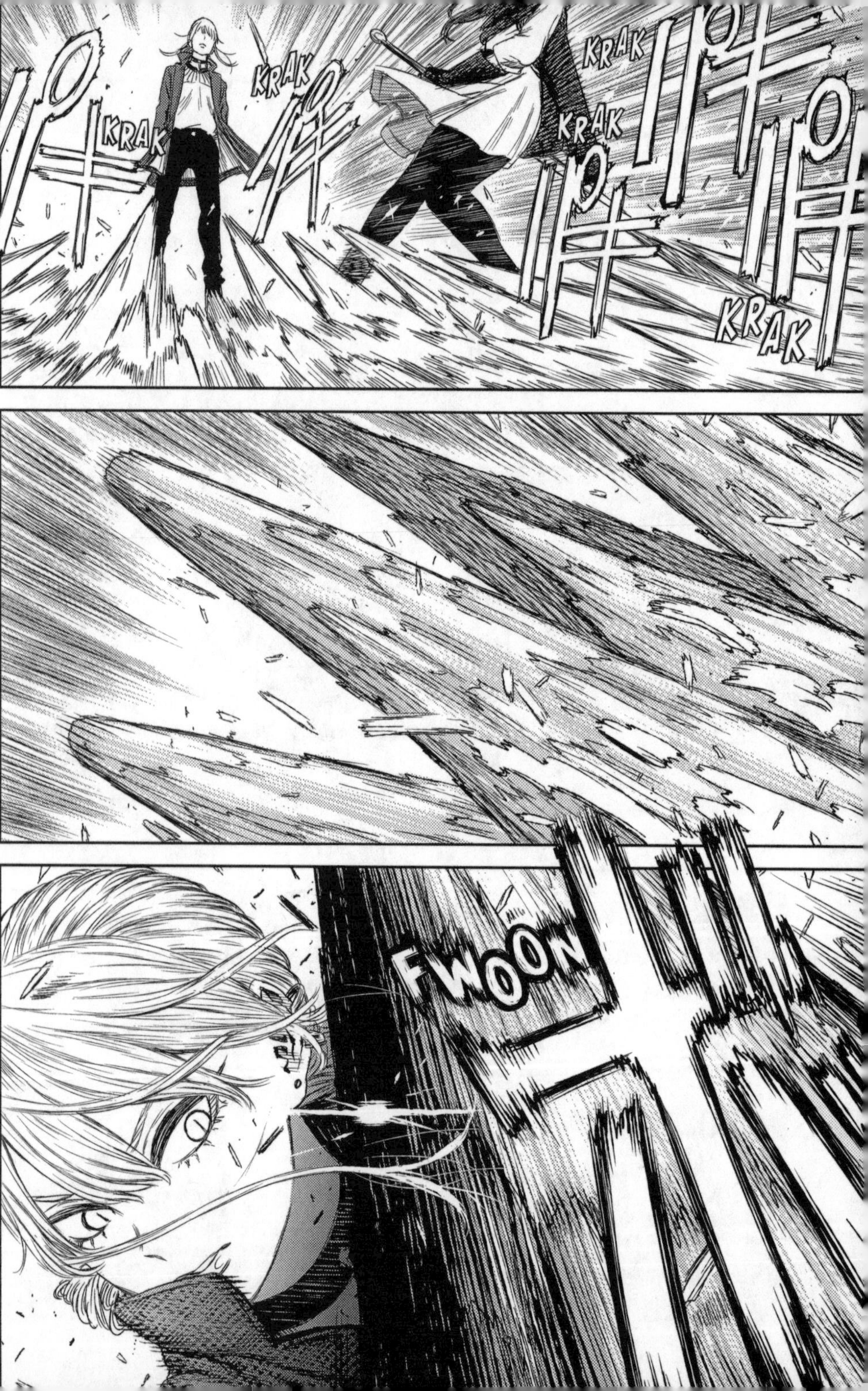
KRAK
KRAK
KRAK
KRAK
KRAK
FWOON

SMASH!!

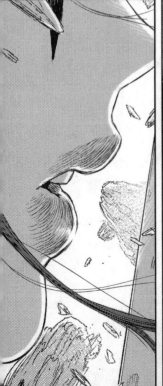

...LIKE THIS?

DON'T EXPECT THAT YOU CAN WIN.

SO WE DON'T STAND A CHANCE...

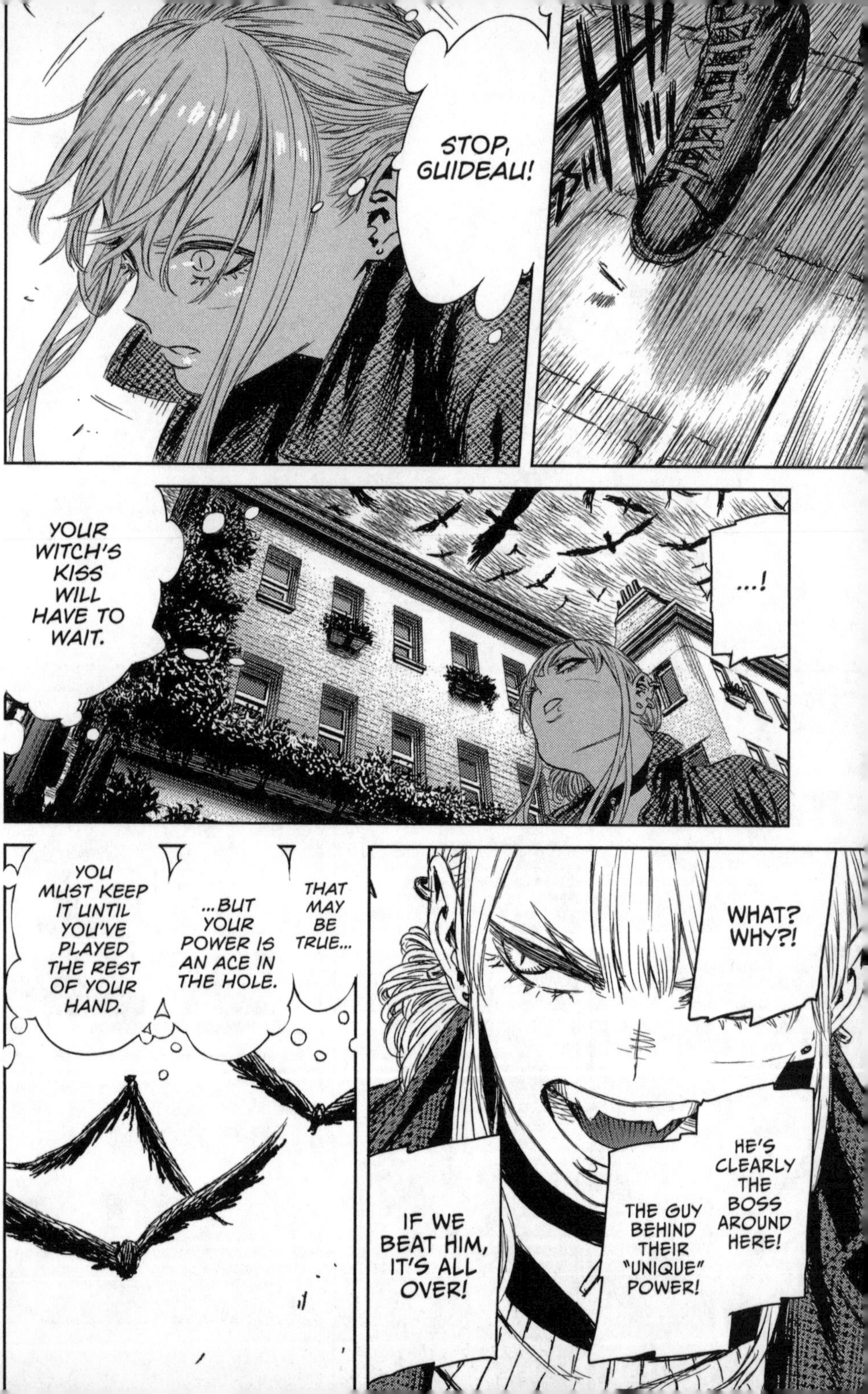
STOP, GUIDEAU!
...!
YOUR WITCH'S KISS WILL HAVE TO WAIT.
WHAT? WHY?!
HE'S CLEARLY THE BOSS AROUND HERE!
THE GUY BEHIND THEIR "UNIQUE" POWER!
IF WE BEAT HIM, IT'S ALL OVER!
THAT MAY BE TRUE...
...BUT YOUR POWER IS AN ACE IN THE HOLE.
YOU MUST KEEP IT UNTIL YOU'VE PLAYED THE REST OF YOUR HAND.

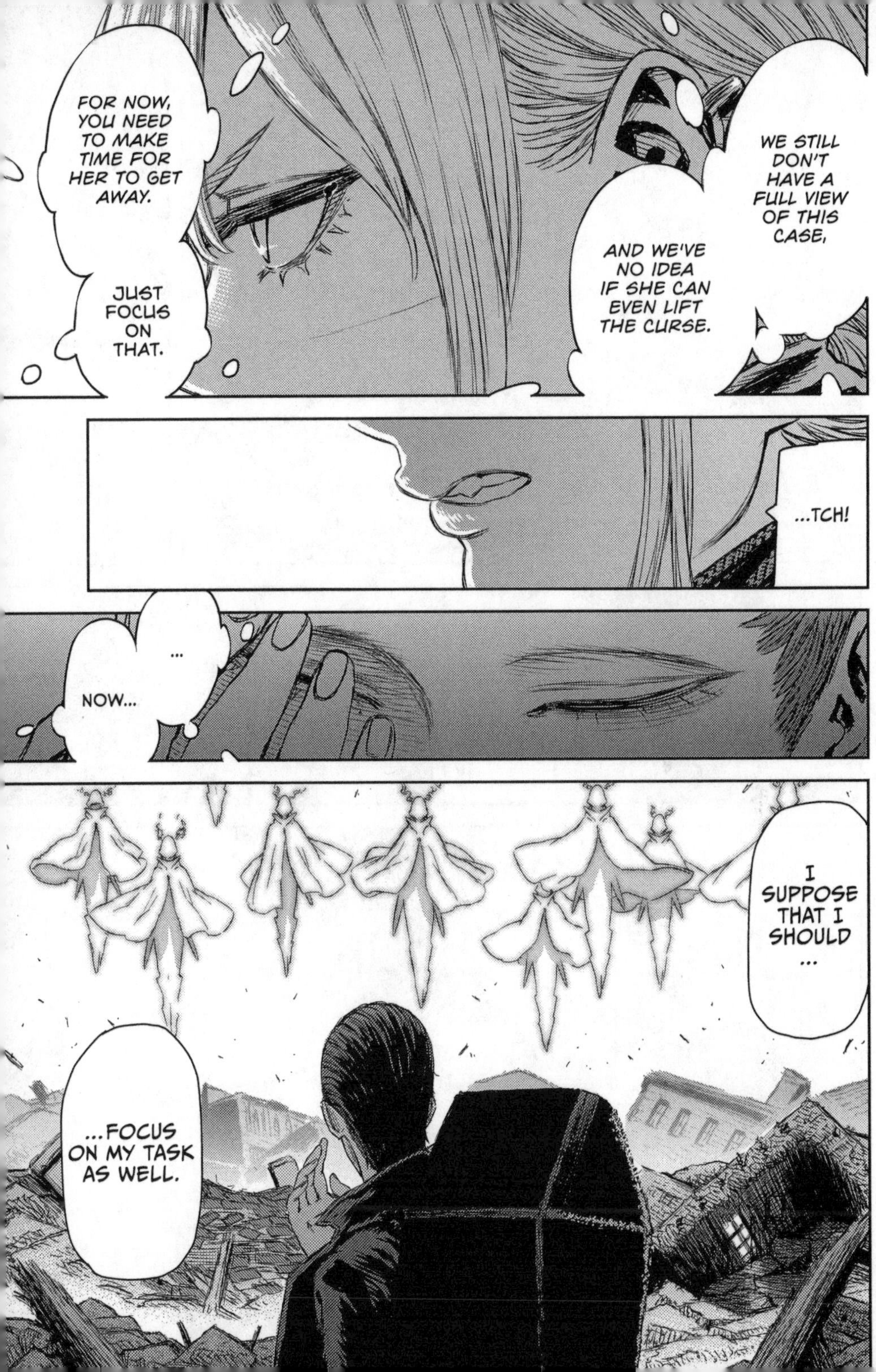
WE STILL DON'T HAVE A FULL VIEW OF THIS CASE,
AND WE'VE NO IDEA IF SHE CAN EVEN LIFT THE CURSE.
FOR NOW, YOU NEED TO MAKE TIME FOR HER TO GET AWAY.
JUST FOCUS ON THAT.
...TCH!
...
NOW...
I SUPPOSE THAT I SHOULD ...
...FOCUS ON MY TASK AS WELL.

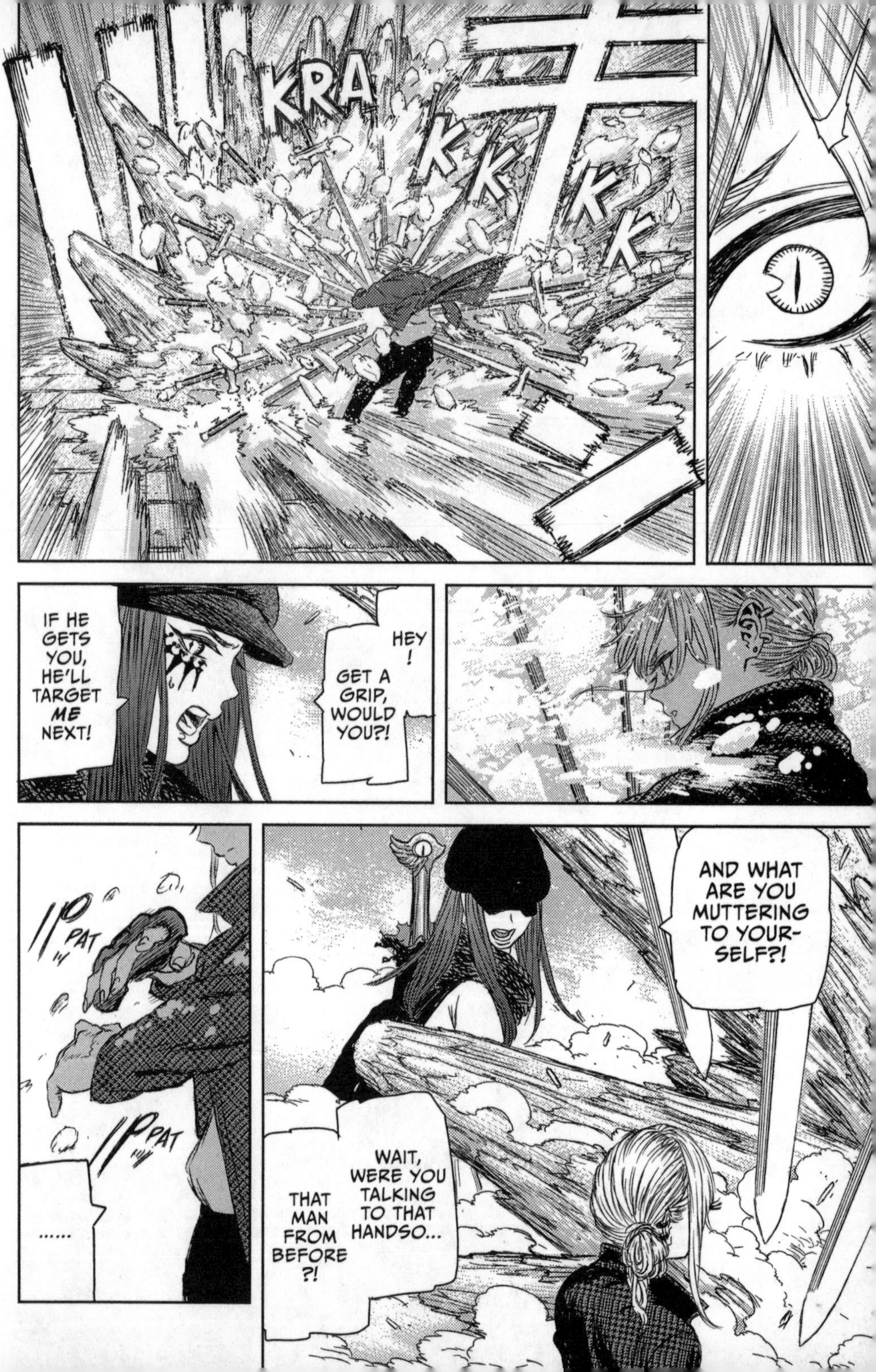
KRAKKKK
HEY! GET A GRIP, WOULD YOU?!
IF HE GETS YOU, HE'LL TARGET *ME* NEXT!
AND WHAT ARE YOU MUTTERING TO YOURSELF?!
WAIT, WERE YOU TALKING TO THAT HANDSO...
THAT MAN FROM BEFORE?!
PAT
PAT
......

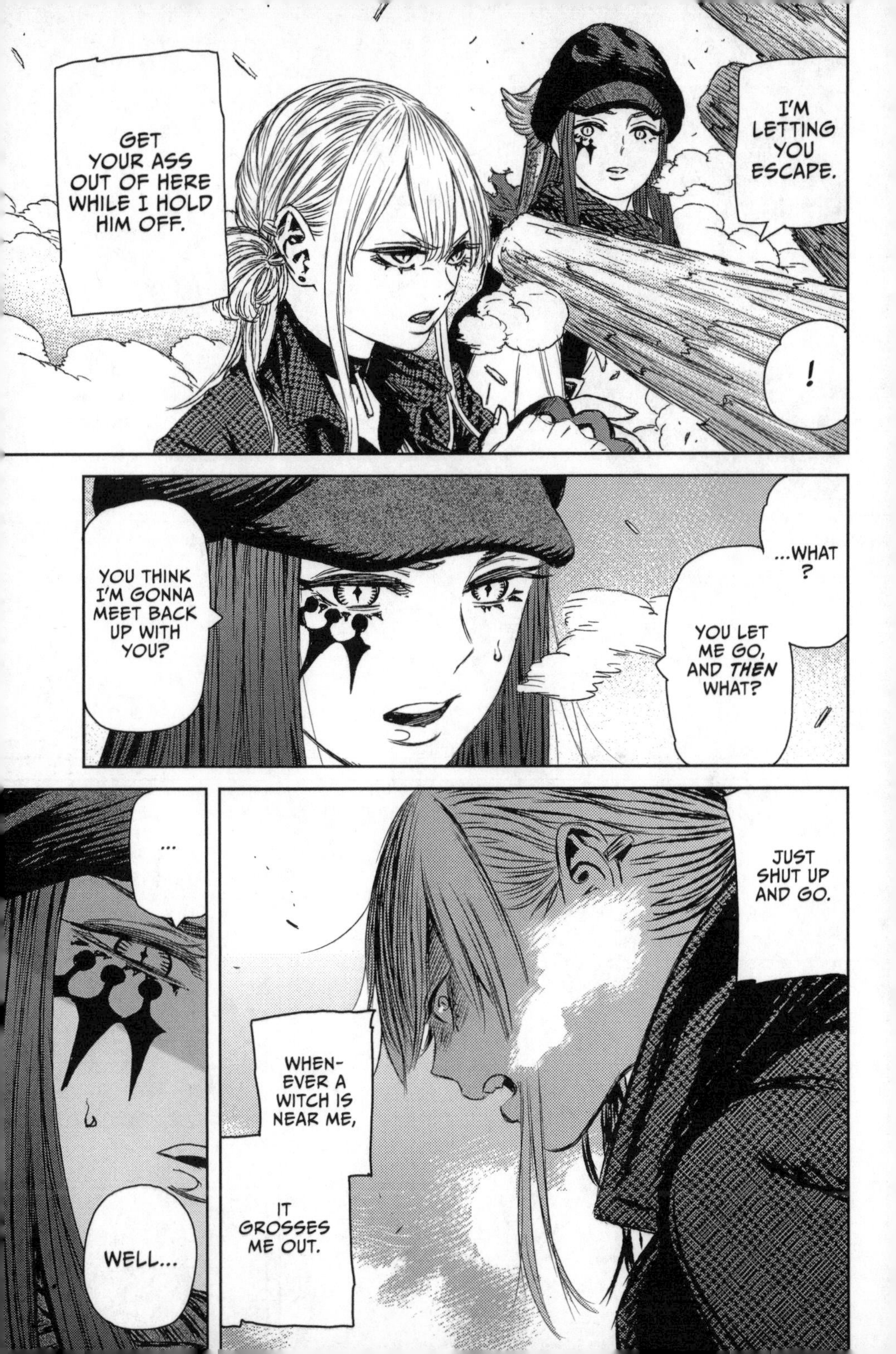
I'M LETTING YOU ESCAPE.
!
GET YOUR ASS OUT OF HERE WHILE I HOLD HIM OFF.
...WHAT?
YOU LET ME GO, AND *THEN* WHAT?
YOU THINK I'M GONNA MEET BACK UP WITH YOU?
JUST SHUT UP AND GO.
WHEN-EVER A WITCH IS NEAR ME,
IT GROSSES ME OUT.
...
WELL...

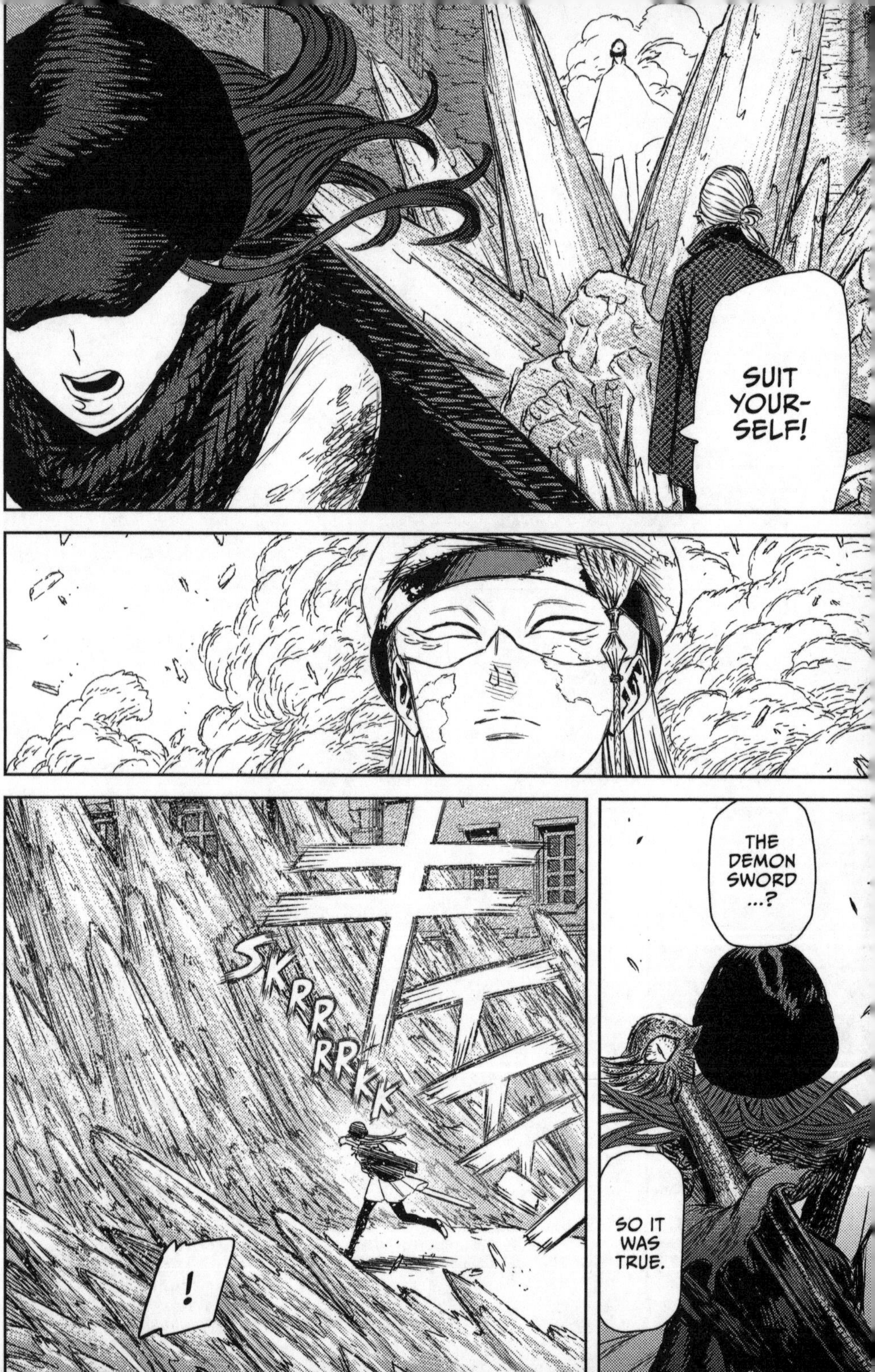
SUIT YOUR-SELF!
THE DEMON SWORD ...?
SO IT WAS TRUE.
SKRRRRKK
!

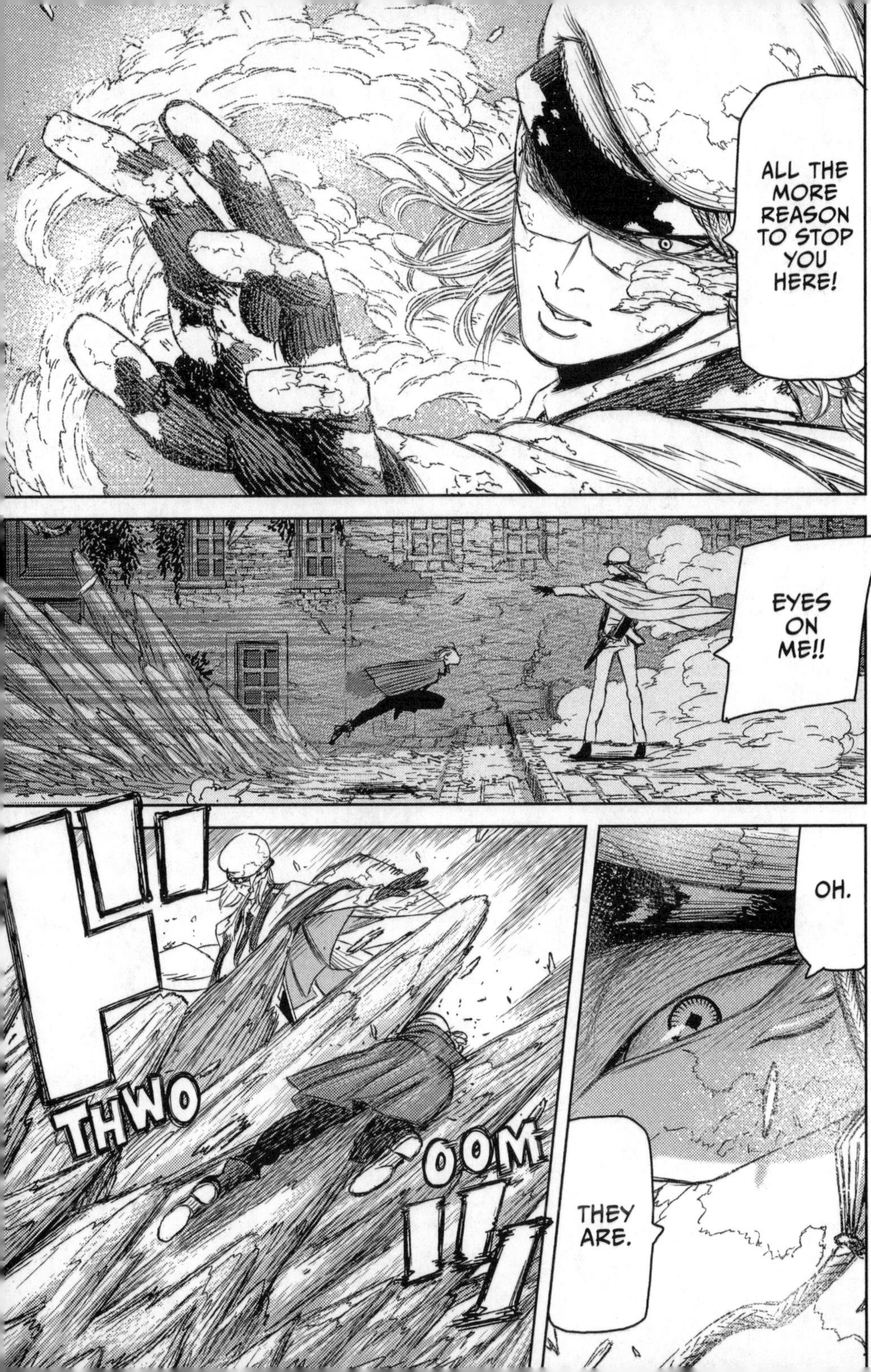
ALL THE MORE REASON TO STOP YOU HERE!
EYES ON ME!!
OH.
THEY ARE.
THWOOOM!!

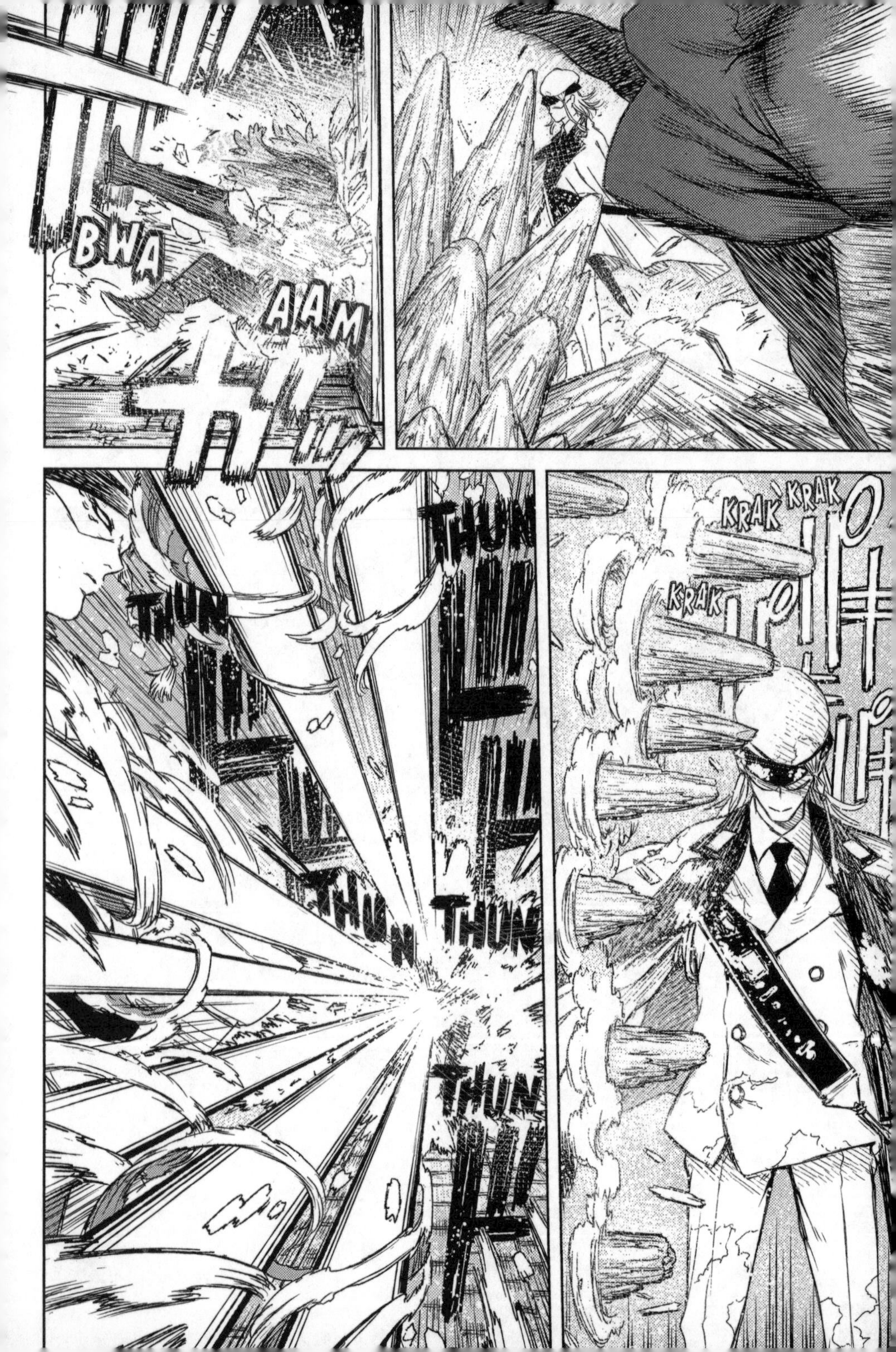
BWA
AAM
KRAK KRAK
KRAK
THUN
THUN
THUN
THUN
THUN

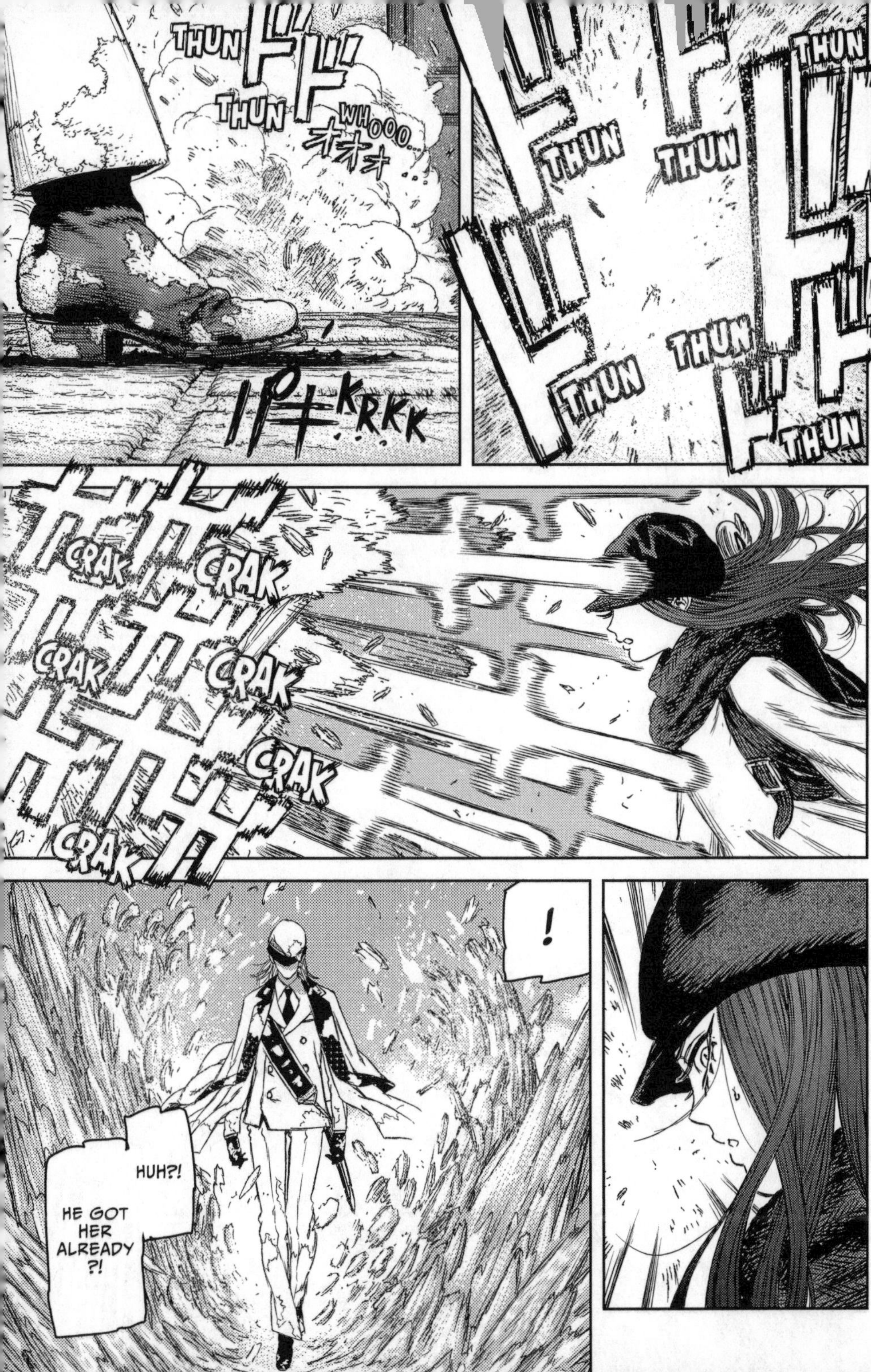
THUN
THUN
THUN
THUN
THUN
THUN
THUN
THUN
WHOOO...
KRKK
CRAK
CRAK
CRAK
CRAK
CRAK
CRAK
!
HUH?!
HE GOT HER ALREADY?!

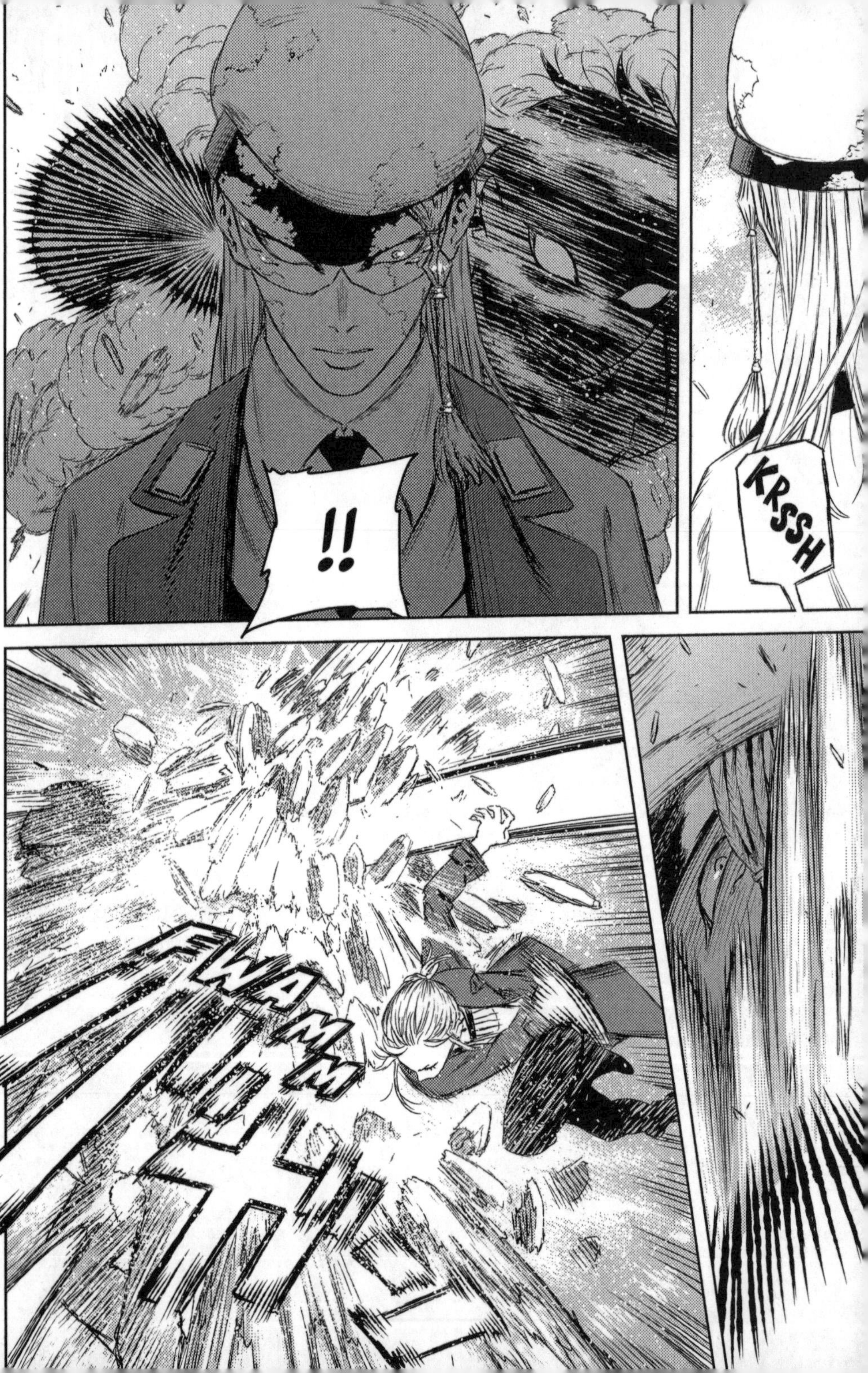
KRSSH
!!
FWAMM

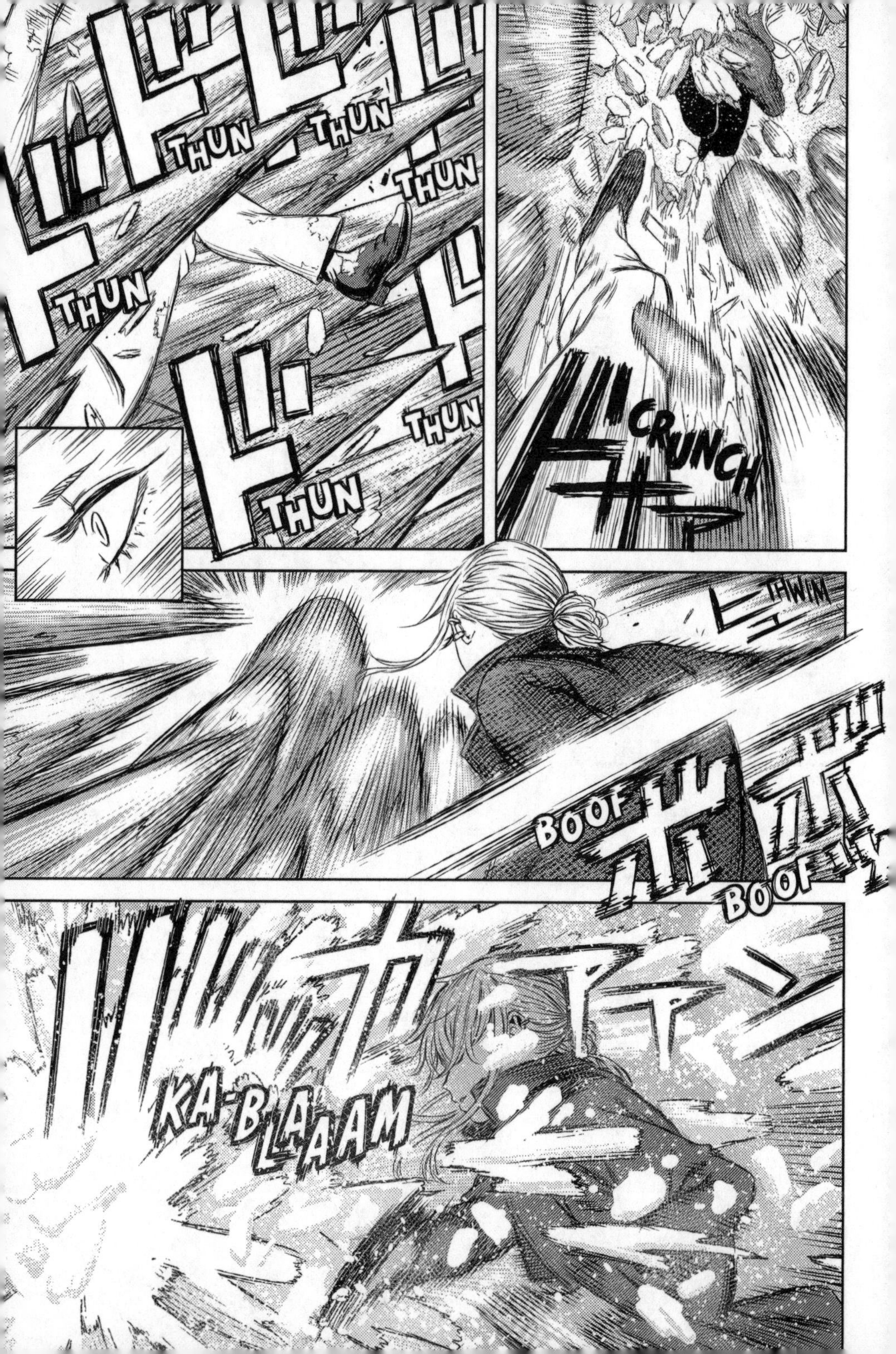
CRUNCH
THUN
THUN
THUN
THUN
THUN
THUN
THWIM
BOOF
BOOF
KA-BLAAM

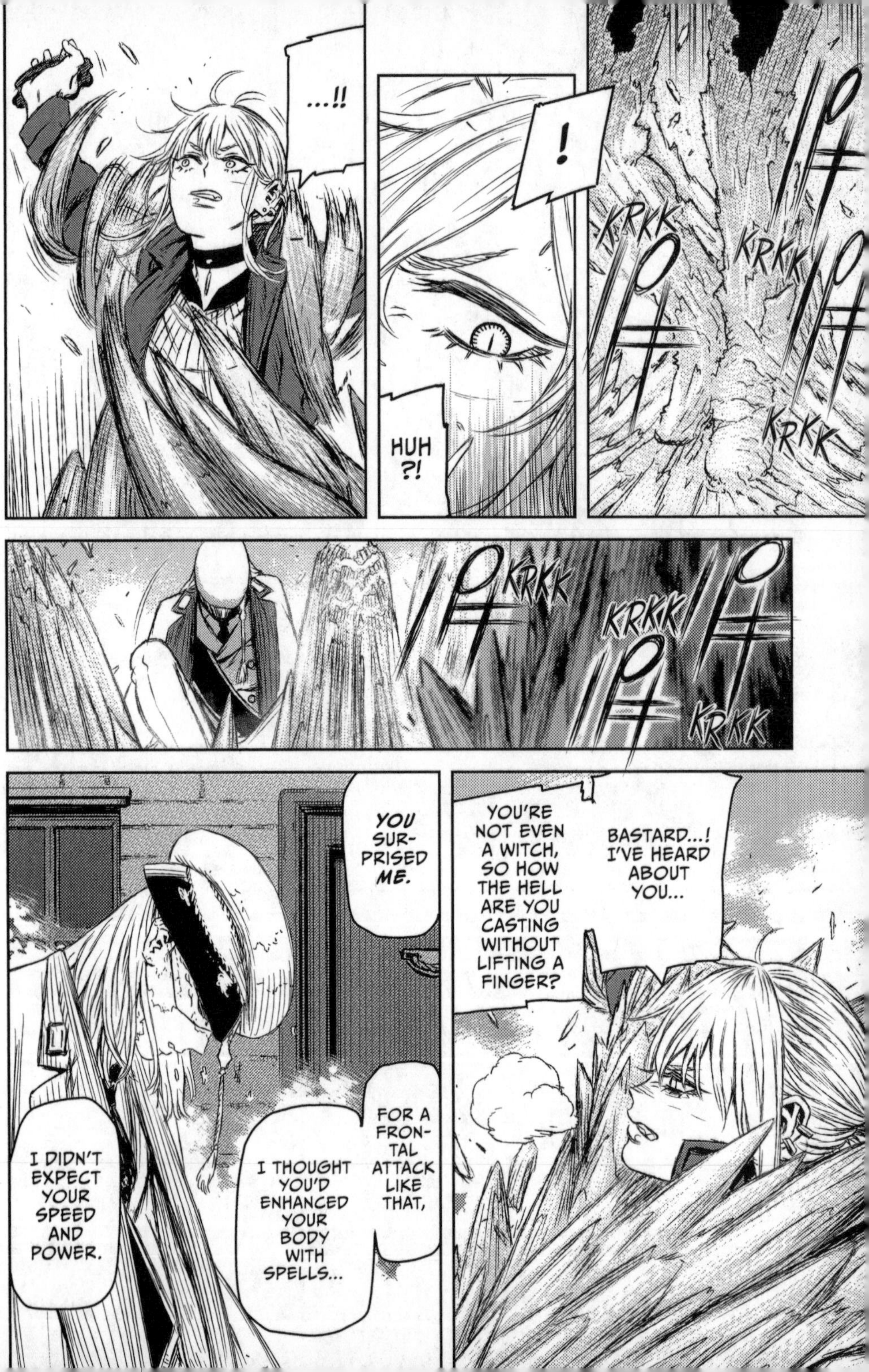
KRKK
KRKK
KRKK
!
HUH ?!
...!!
KRKK
KRKK
KRKK
KRKK
BASTARD...! I'VE HEARD ABOUT YOU...
YOU'RE NOT EVEN A WITCH, SO HOW THE HELL ARE YOU CASTING WITHOUT LIFTING A FINGER?
YOU SURPRISED ME.
FOR A FRONTAL ATTACK LIKE THAT,
I THOUGHT YOU'D ENHANCED YOUR BODY WITH SPELLS...
I DIDN'T EXPECT YOUR SPEED AND POWER.

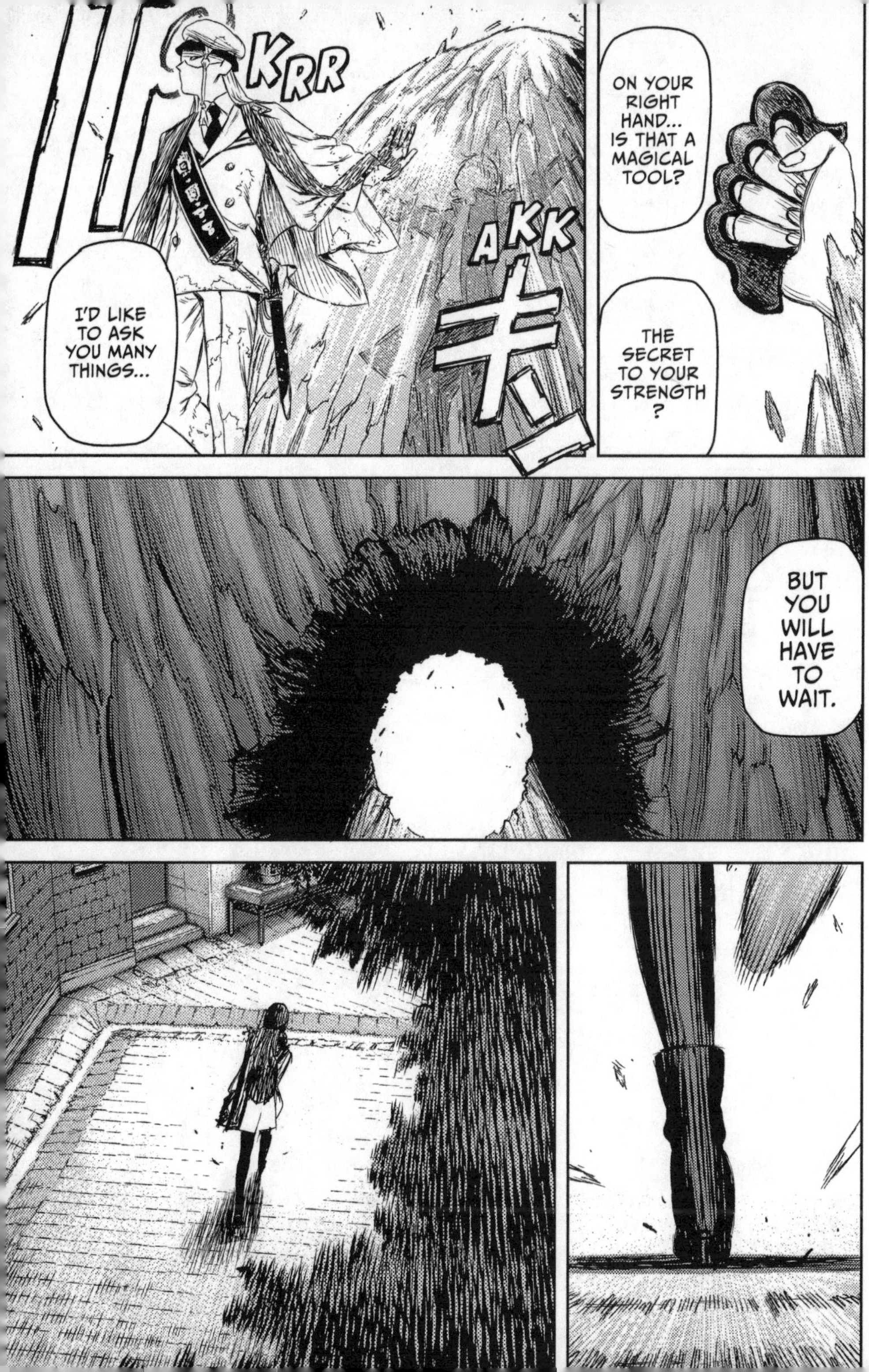
ON YOUR RIGHT HAND... IS THAT A MAGICAL TOOL?
THE SECRET TO YOUR STRENGTH?
KRR
AKK
I'D LIKE TO ASK YOU MANY THINGS...
BUT YOU WILL HAVE TO WAIT.

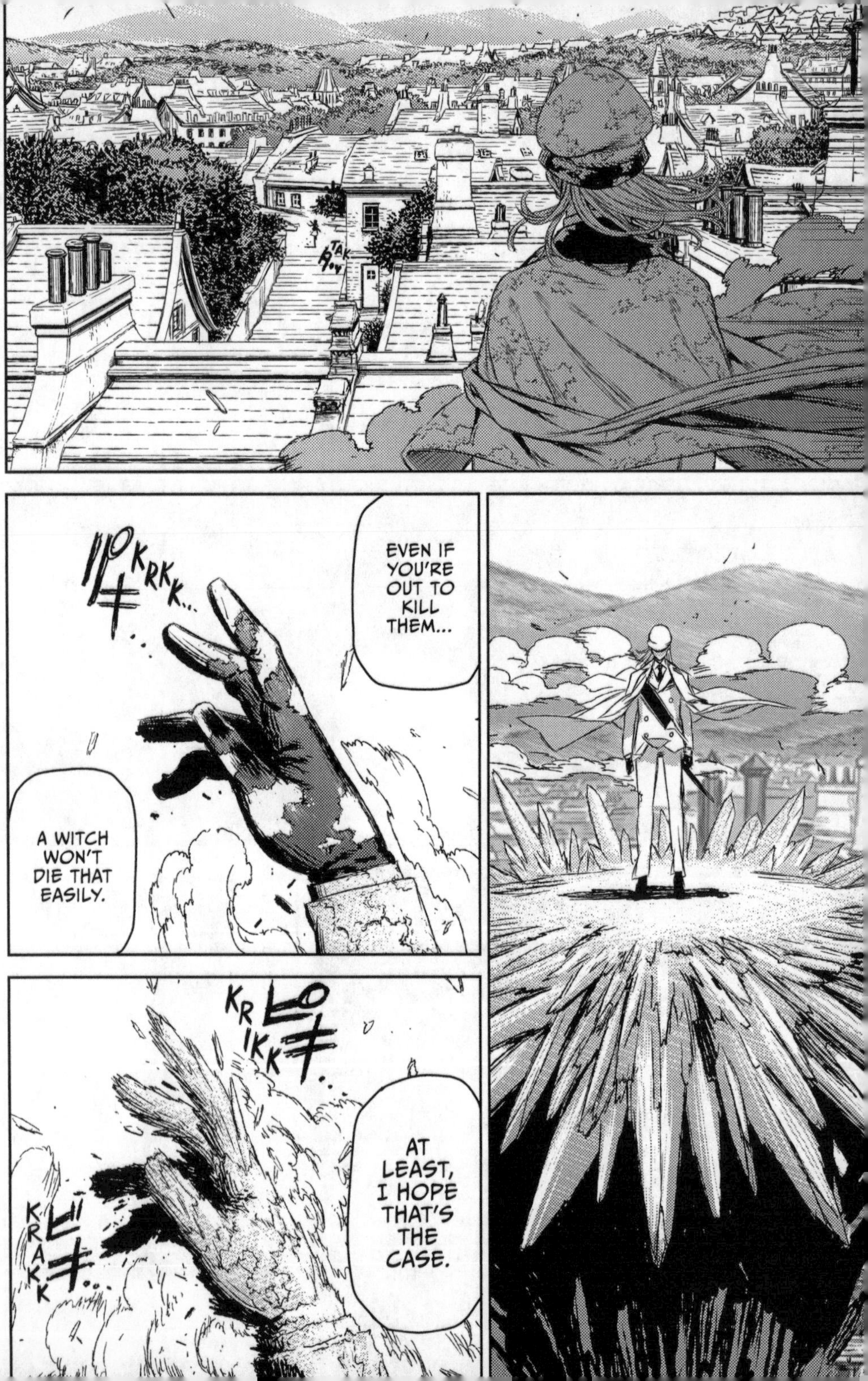
TAK
EVEN IF YOU'RE OUT TO KILL THEM...
KRKK...
A WITCH WON'T DIE THAT EASILY.
KRIKK...
AT LEAST, I HOPE THAT'S THE CASE.
KRAKK...

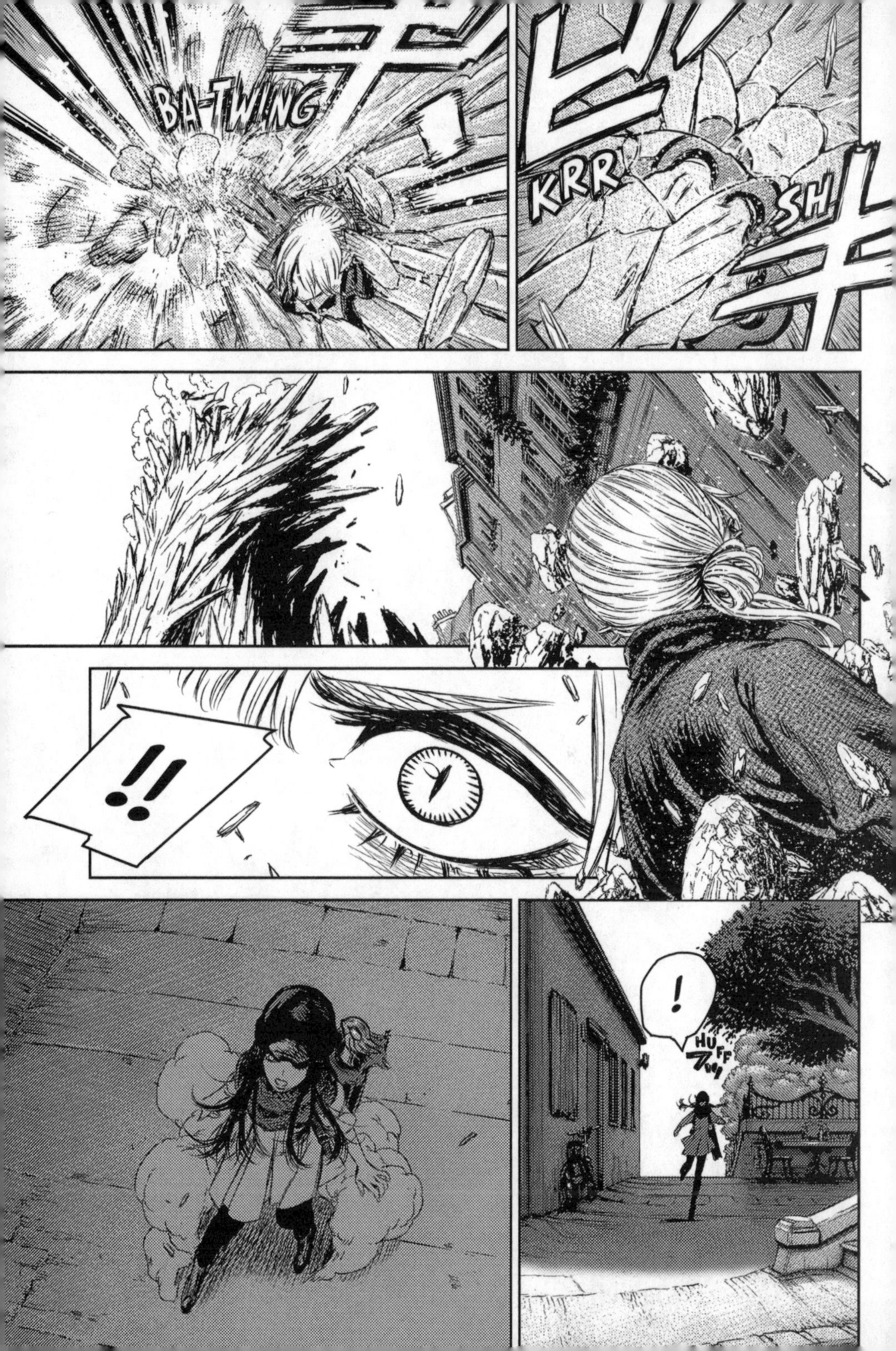
KRR
SH
BA-TWING
!!
!
HUFF

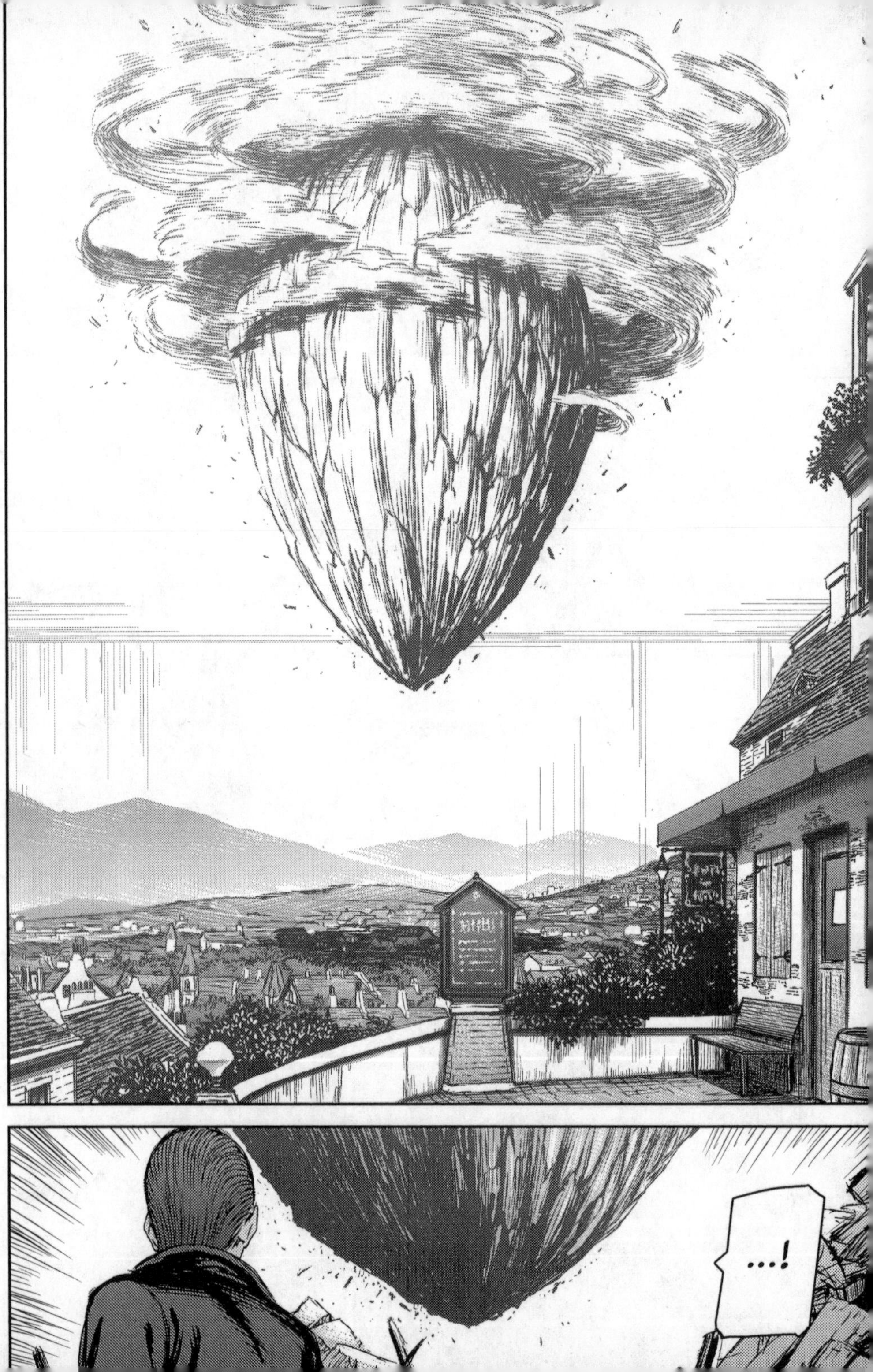
...!

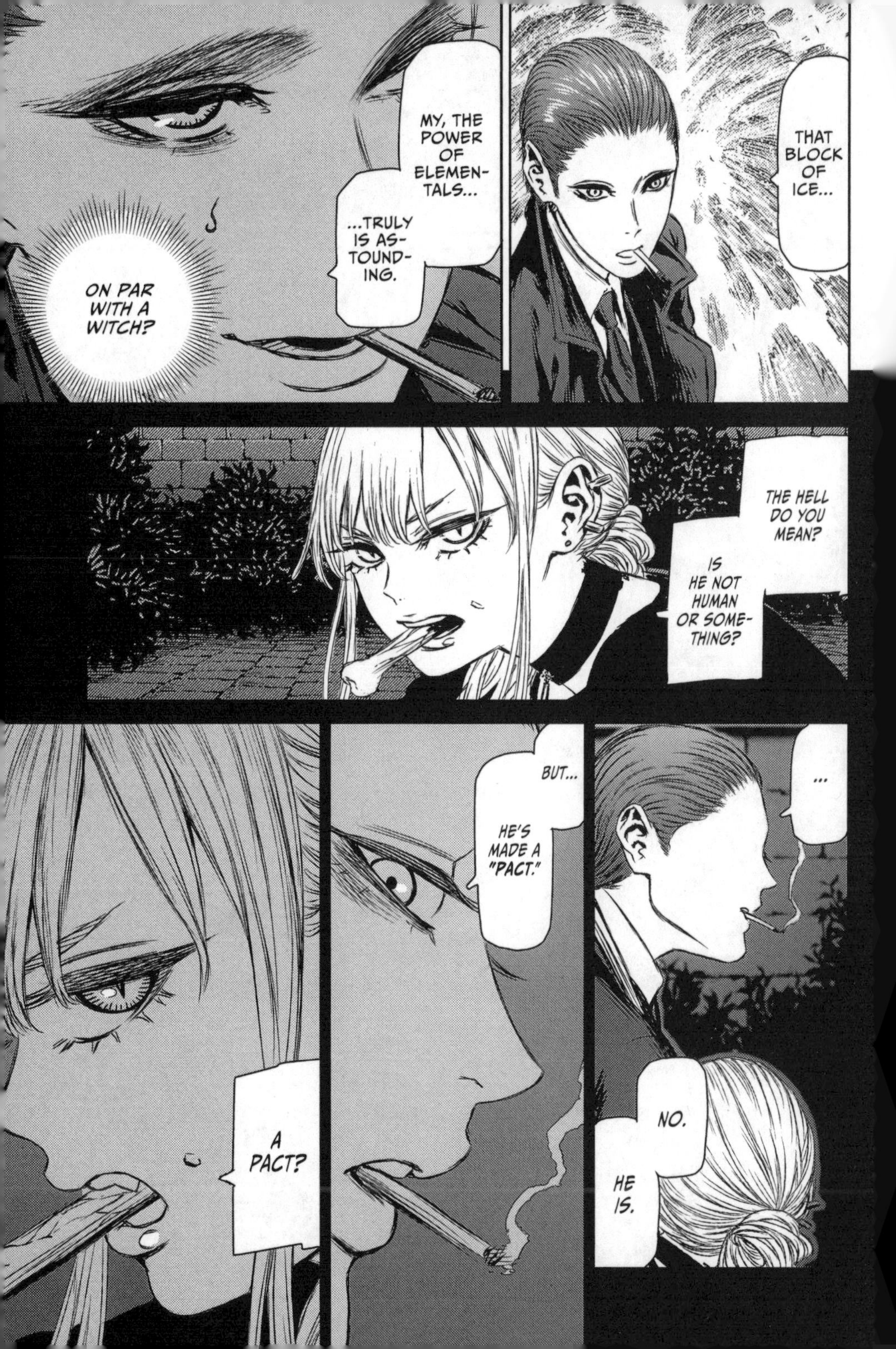
THAT BLOCK OF ICE...
MY, THE POWER OF ELEMENTALS...
...TRULY IS ASTOUNDING.
ON PAR WITH A WITCH?
THE HELL DO YOU MEAN?
IS HE NOT HUMAN OR SOMETHING?
...
NO.
HE IS.
BUT...
HE'S MADE A "PACT."
A PACT?

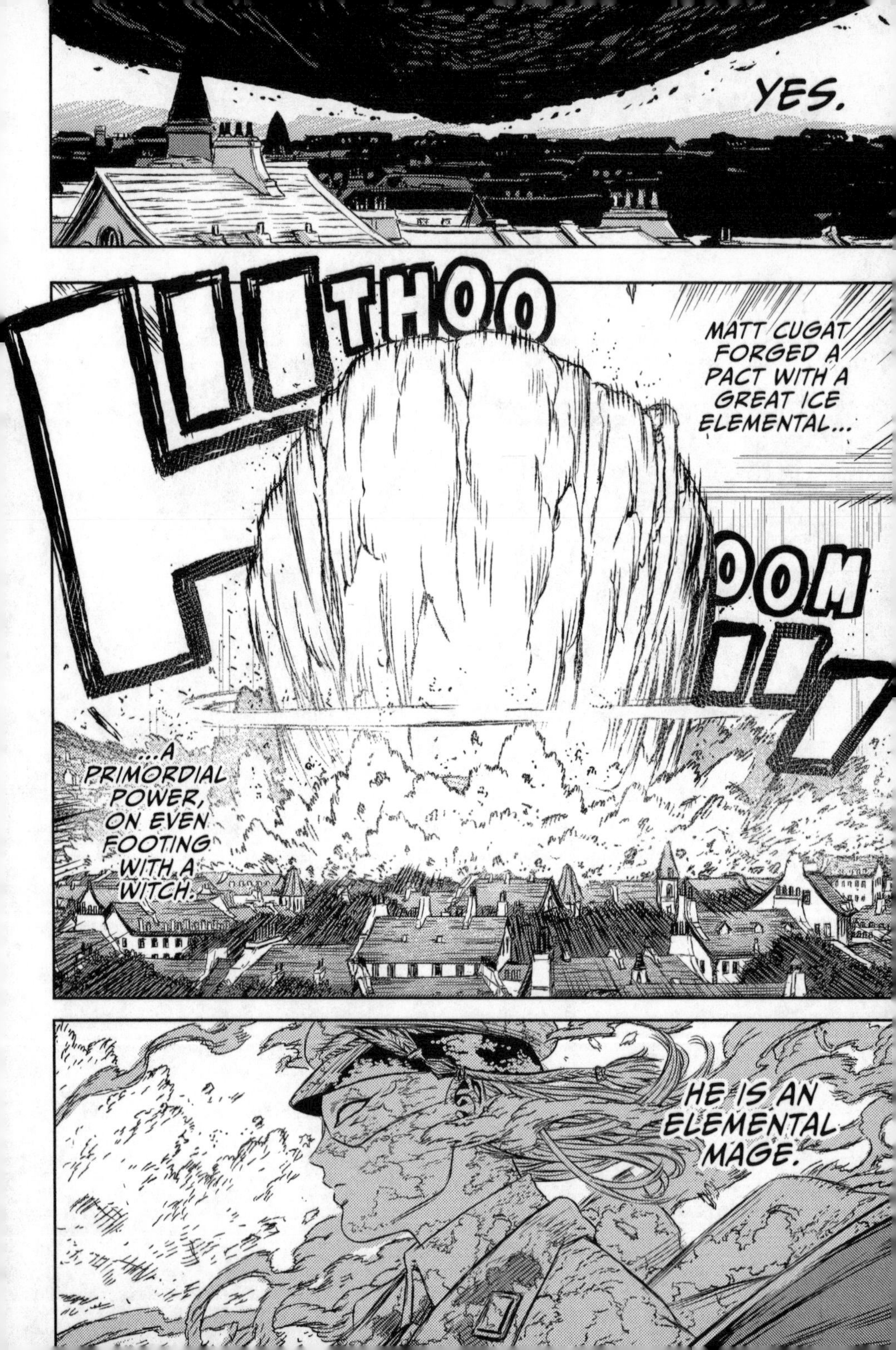
YES.
MATT CUGAT FORGED A PACT WITH A GREAT ICE ELEMENTAL...
THOOOOM
...A PRIMORDIAL POWER, ON EVEN FOOTING WITH A WITCH.
HE IS AN ELEMENTAL MAGE.

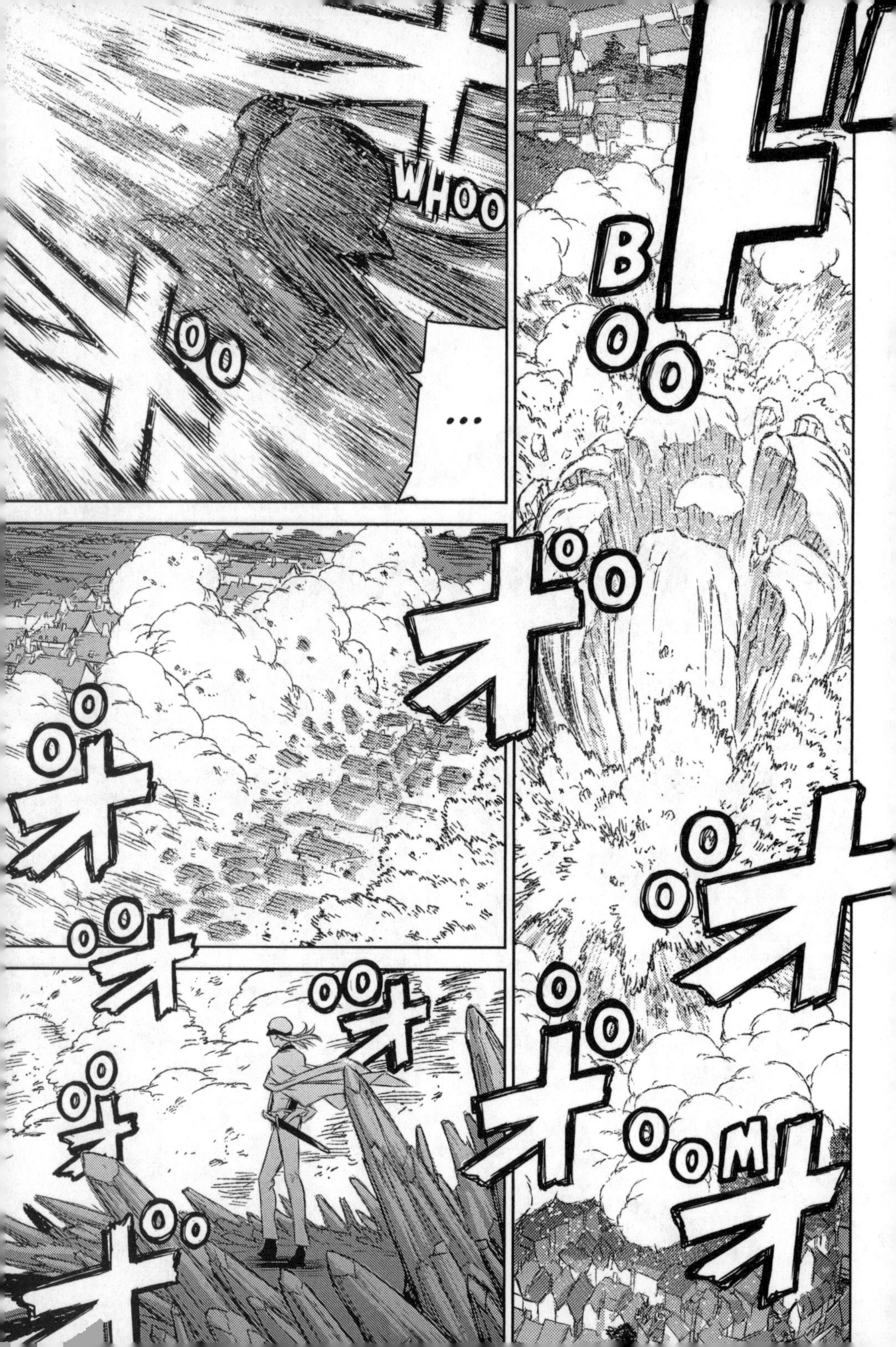
BOO
OOM
WHOOO
OO
...

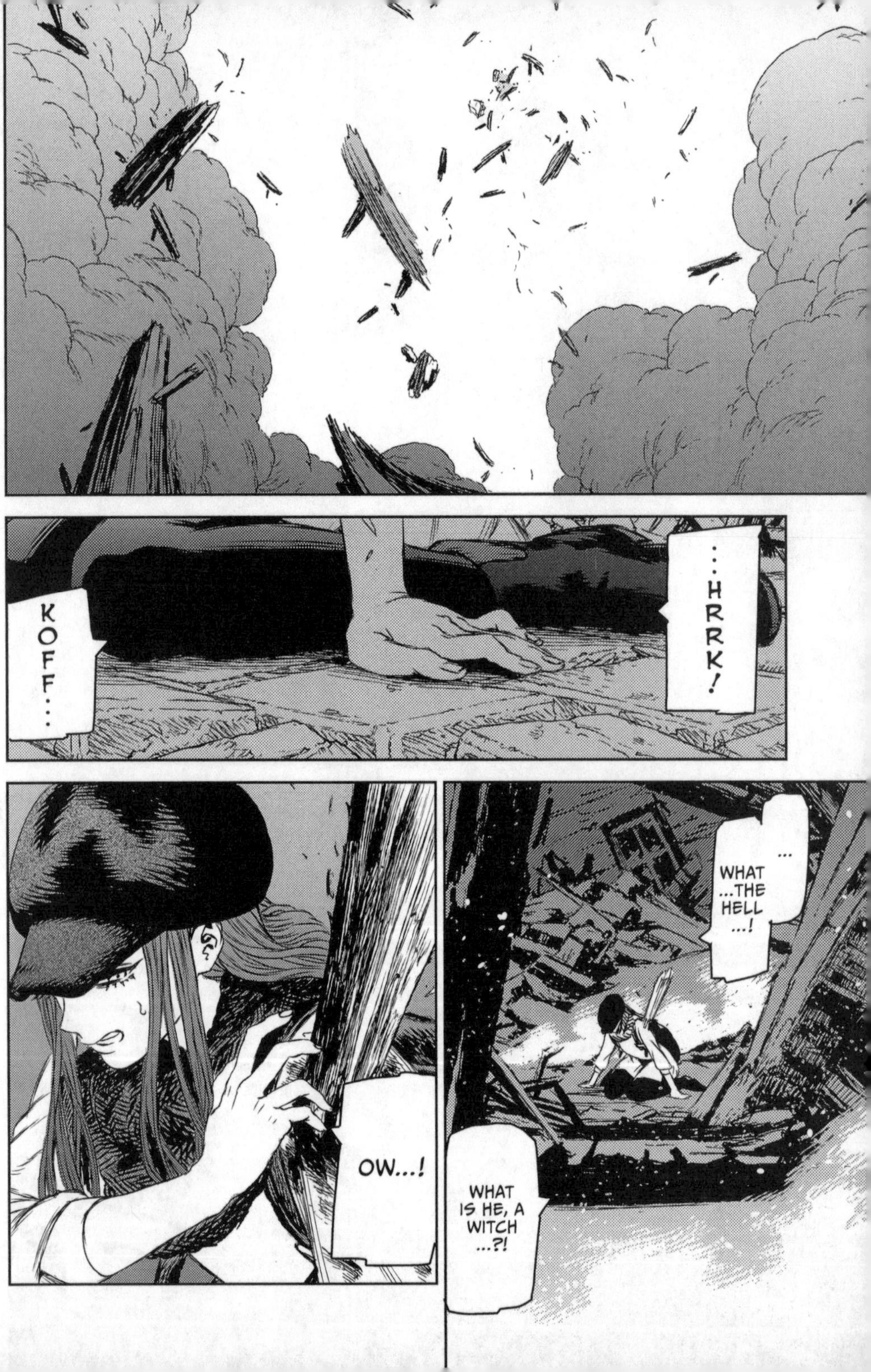
...HRRK!
KOFF...
... WHAT ...THE HELL ...!
WHAT IS HE, A WITCH ...?!
OW...!

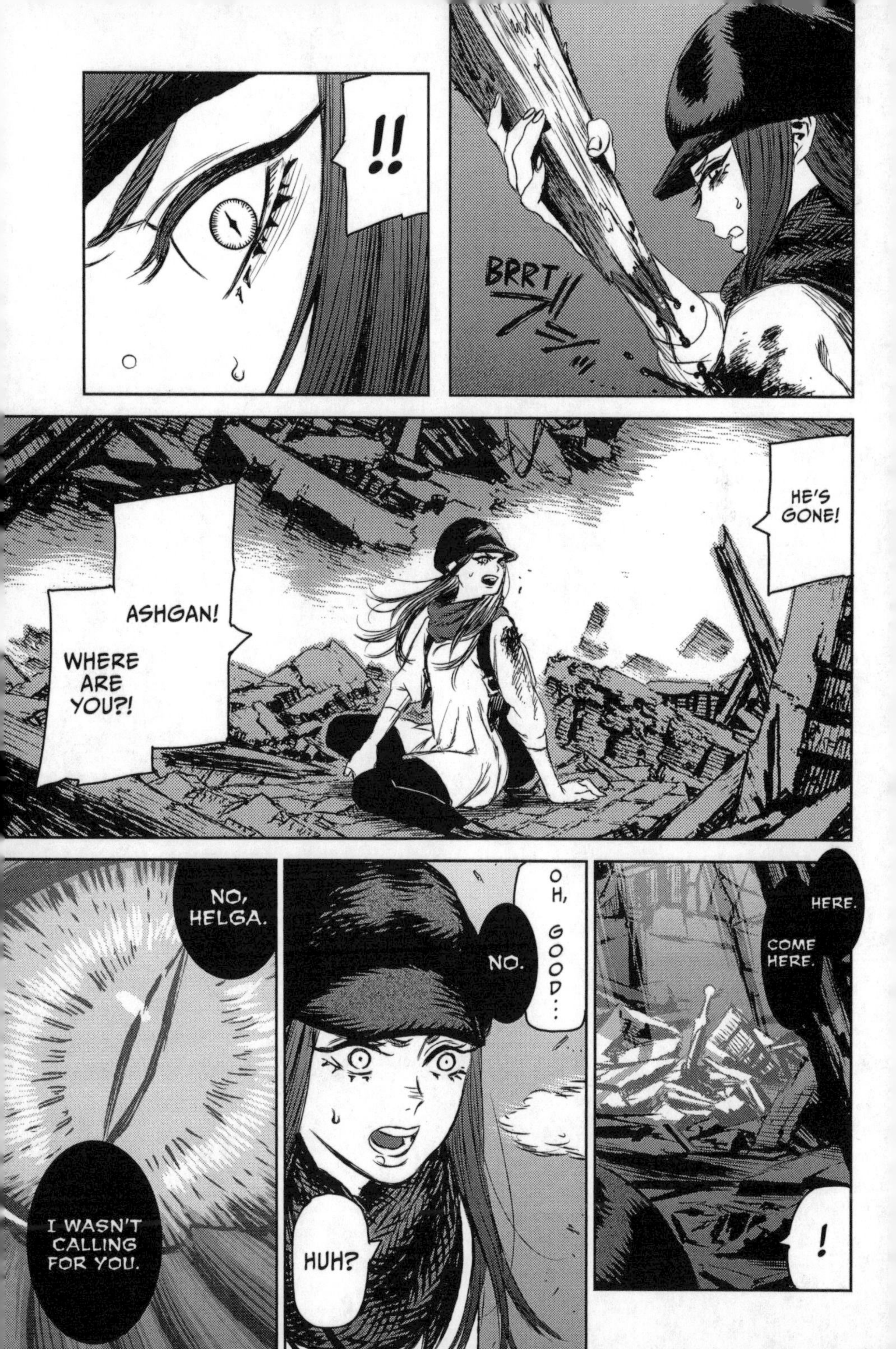
BRRT
!!
HE'S GONE!
ASHGAN!
WHERE ARE YOU?!
HERE.
COME HERE.
!
OH, GOOD...
NO.
HUH?
NO, HELGA.
I WASN'T CALLING FOR YOU.

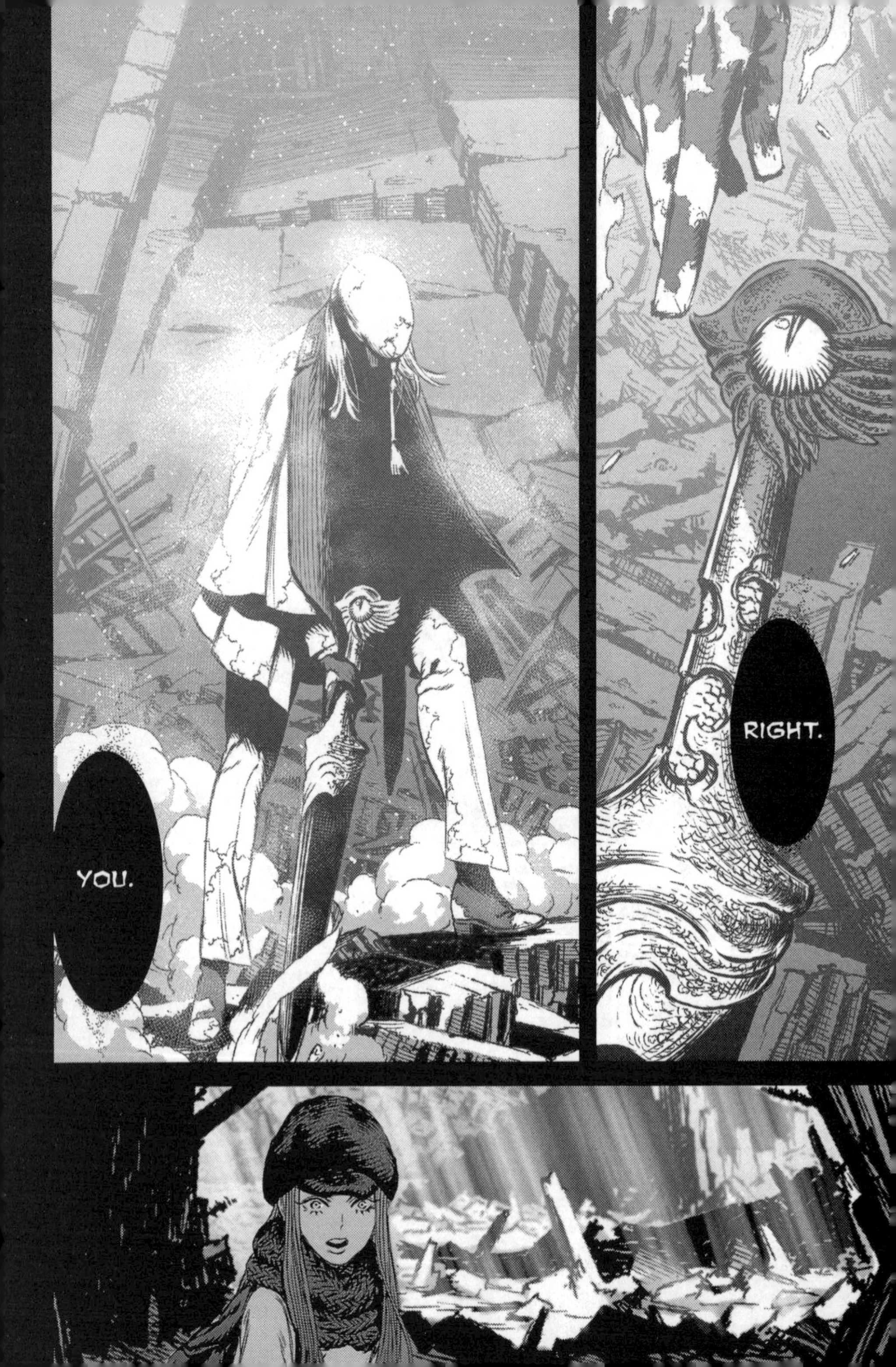
RIGHT.
YOU.

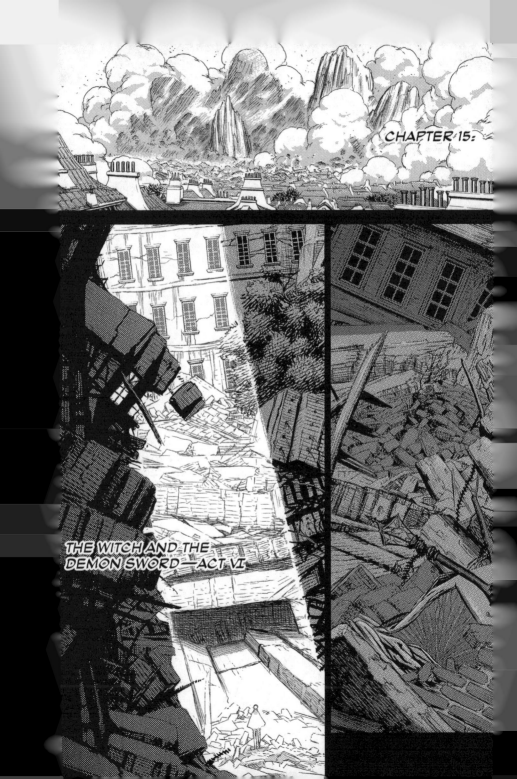

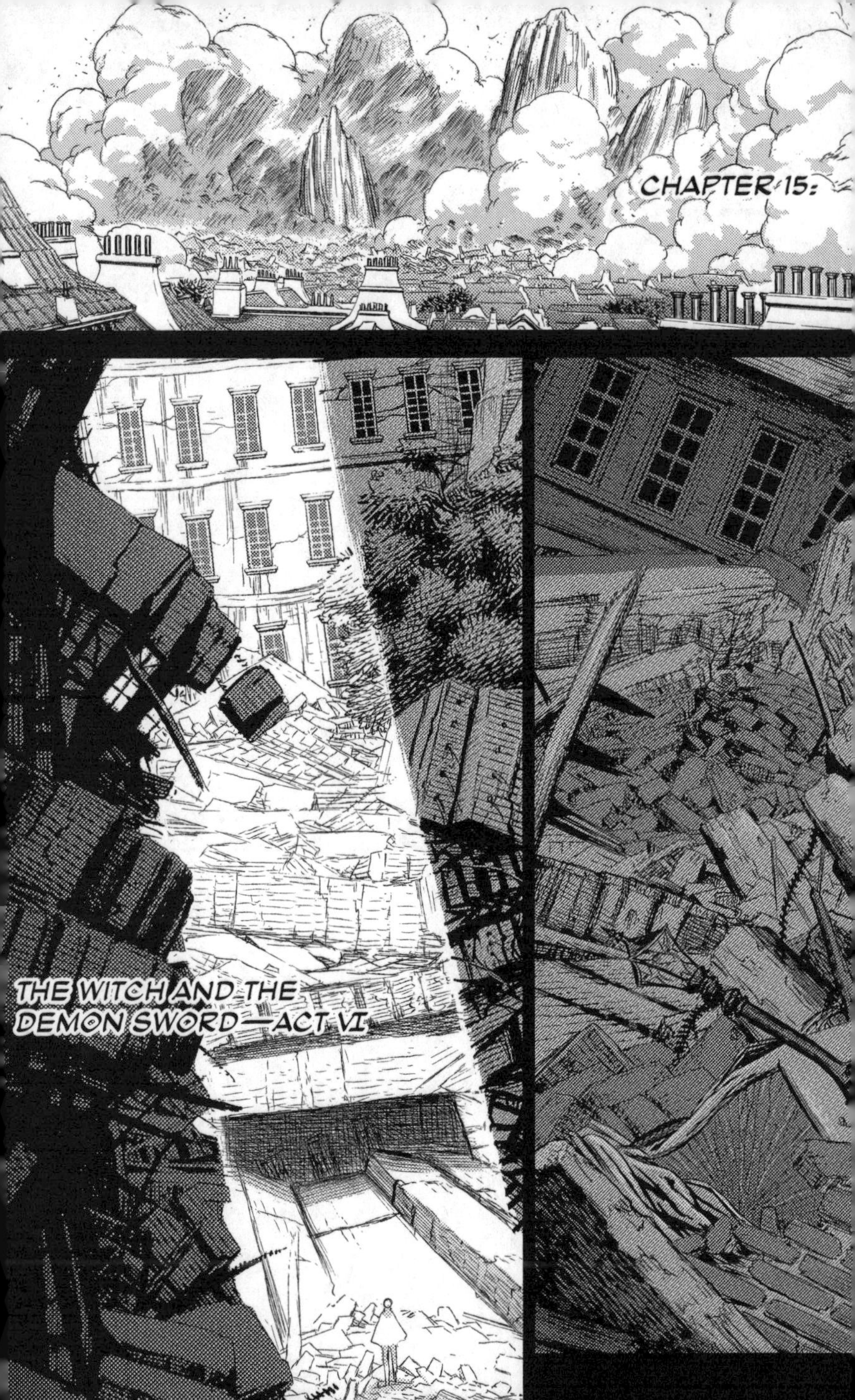
CHAPTER 15:
THE WITCH AND THE DEMON SWORD—ACT VI

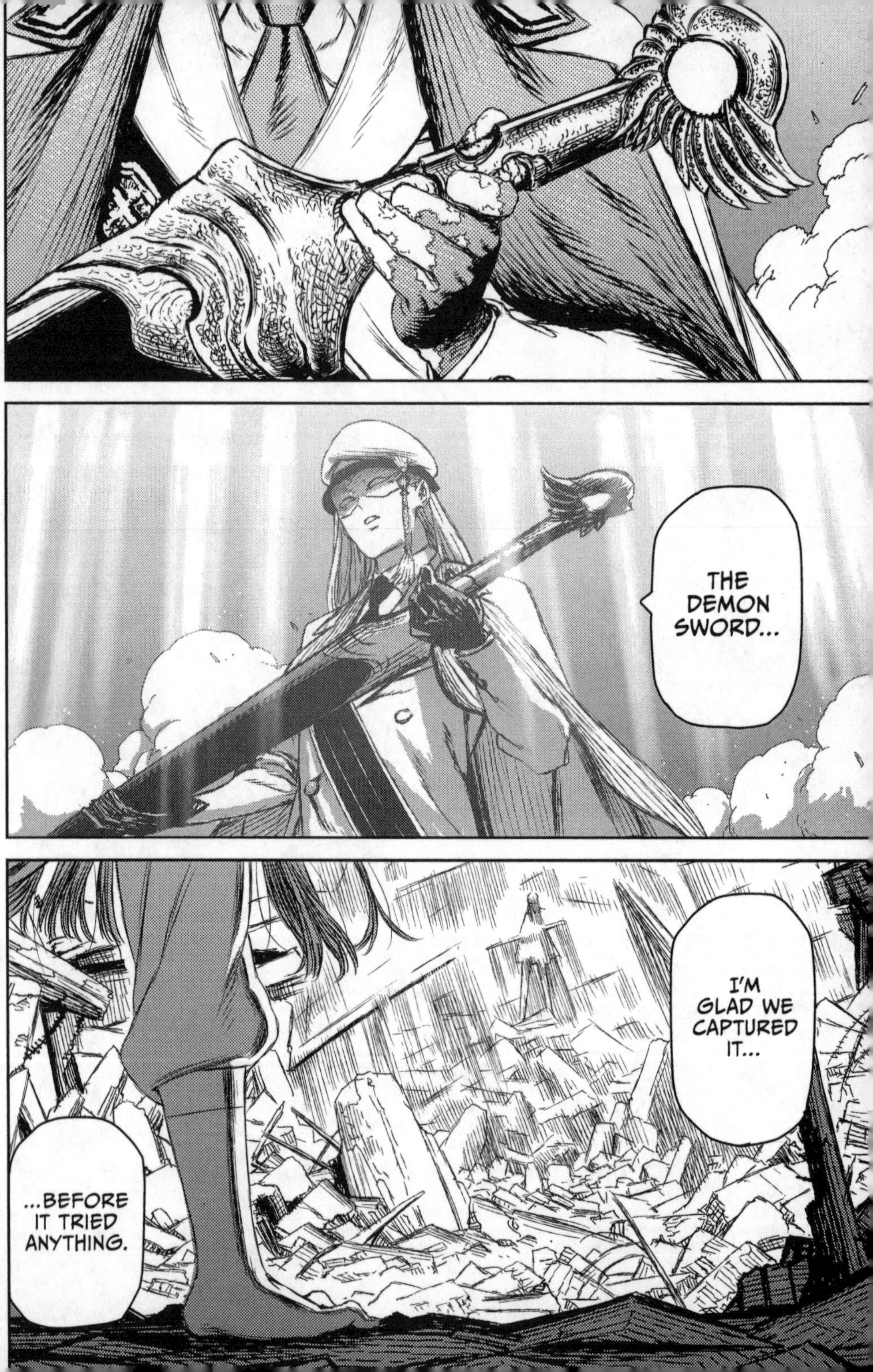
THE DEMON SWORD...
I'M GLAD WE CAPTURED IT...
...BEFORE IT TRIED ANYTHING.

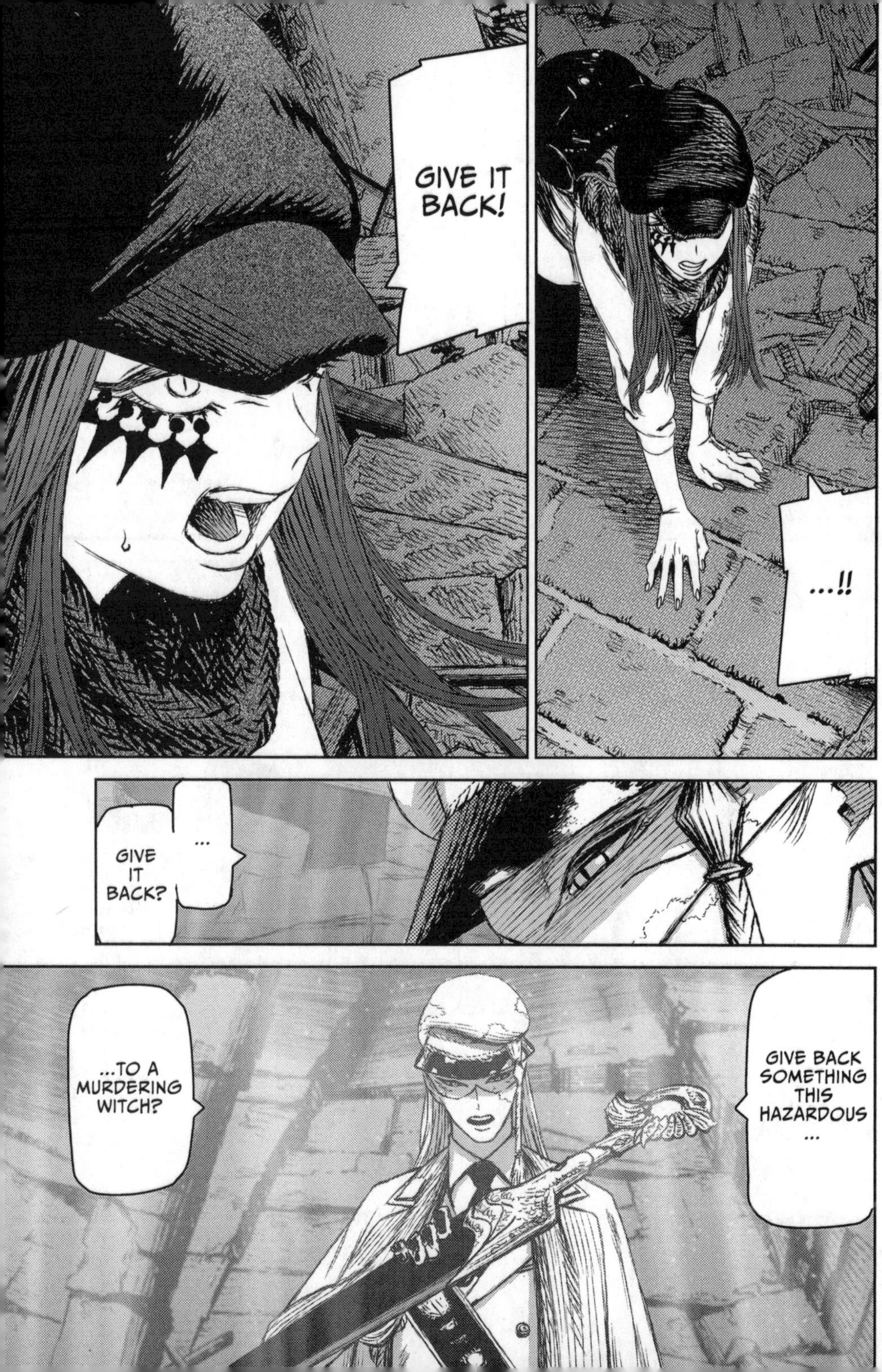
...!!
GIVE IT BACK!
...
GIVE IT BACK?
GIVE BACK SOMETHING THIS HAZARDOUS...
...TO A MURDERING WITCH?

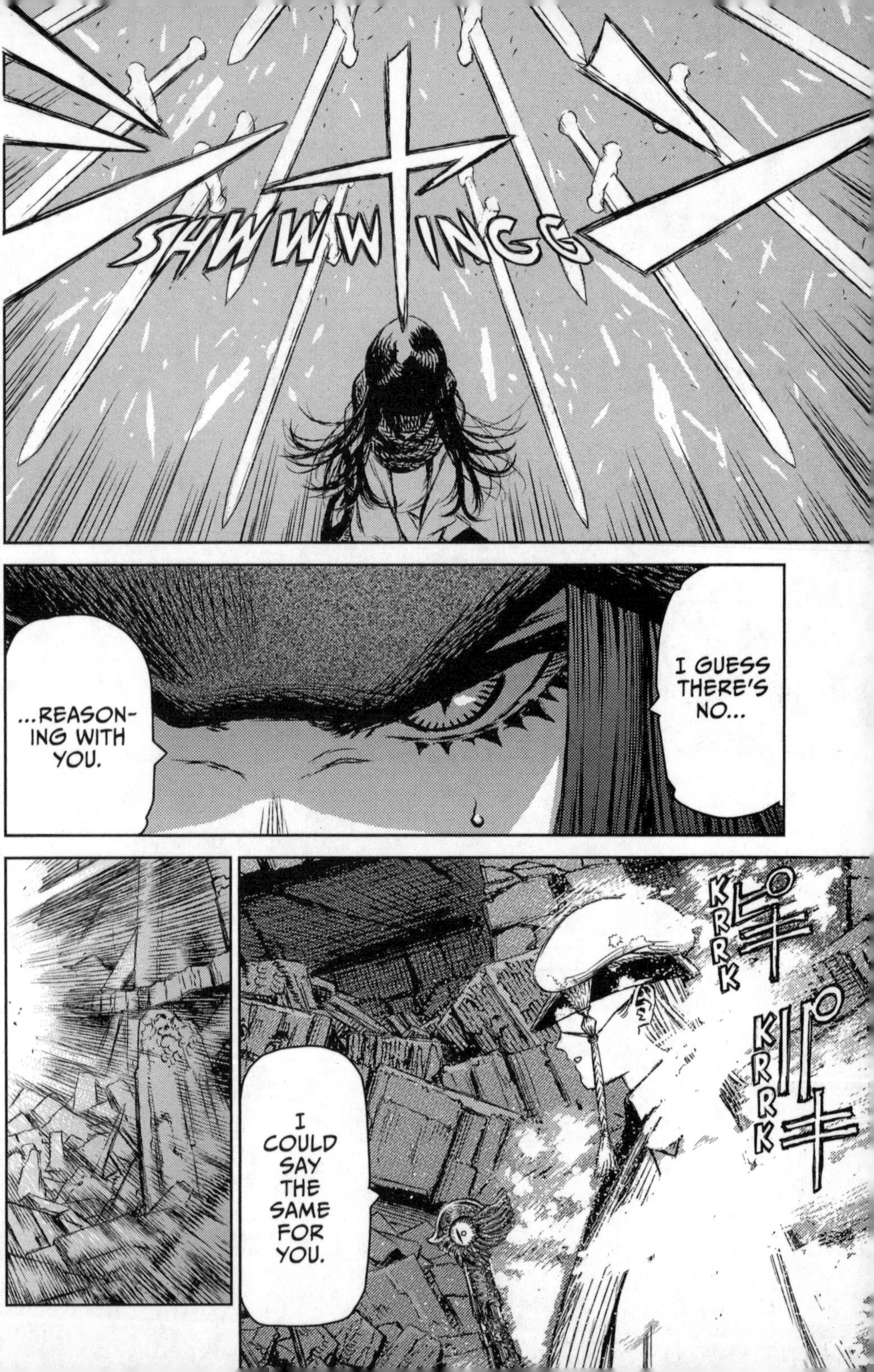
SHWWWINGG
I GUESS THERE'S NO...
...REASONING WITH YOU.
KRRK
KRRK
I COULD SAY THE SAME FOR YOU.

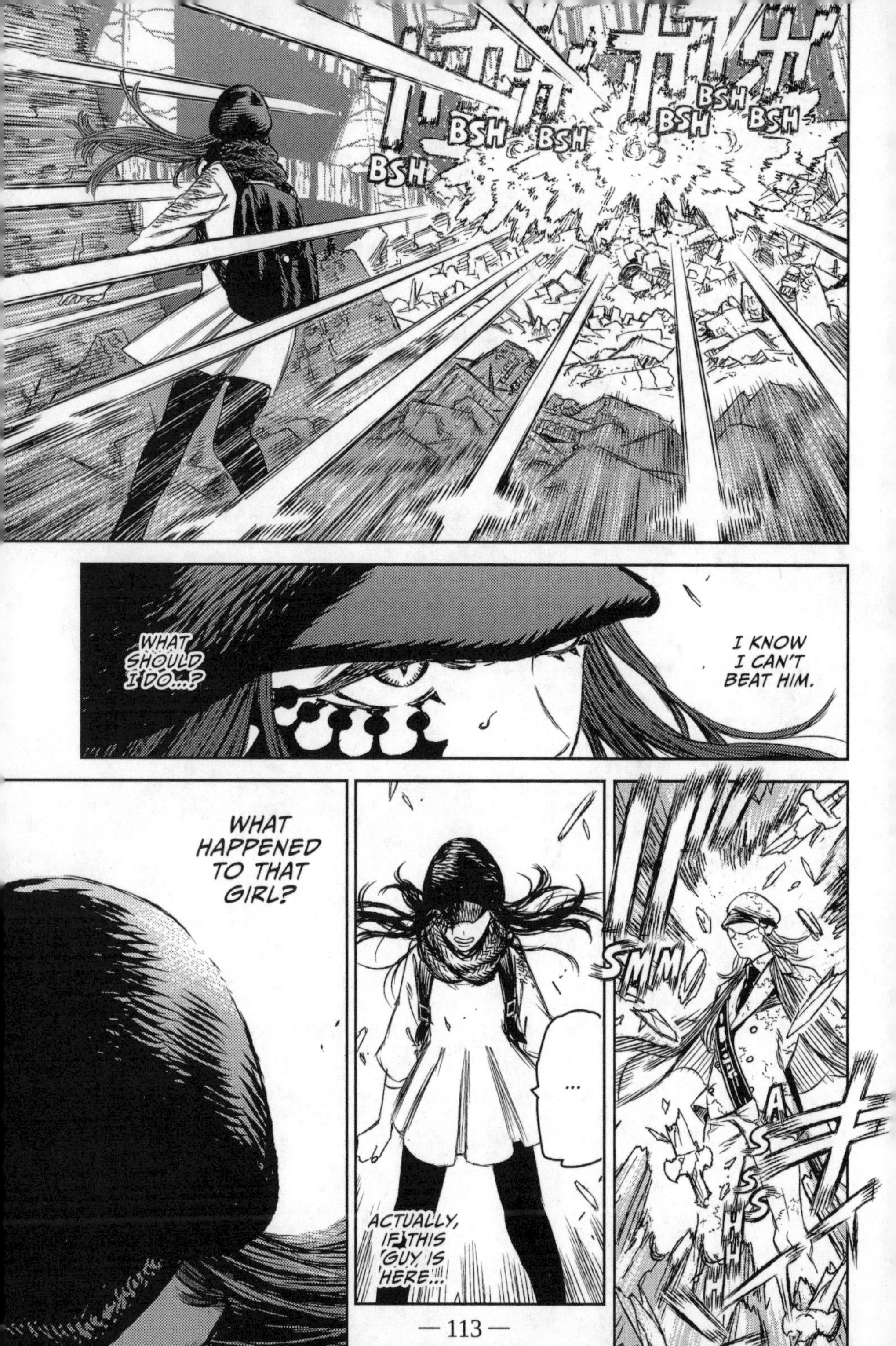
BSH
BSH
BSH
BSH
BSH
BSH
I KNOW I CAN'T BEAT HIM.
WHAT SHOULD I DO...?
SMM
ASSSHH
...
ACTUALLY, IF THIS GUY IS HERE...
WHAT HAPPENED TO THAT GIRL?

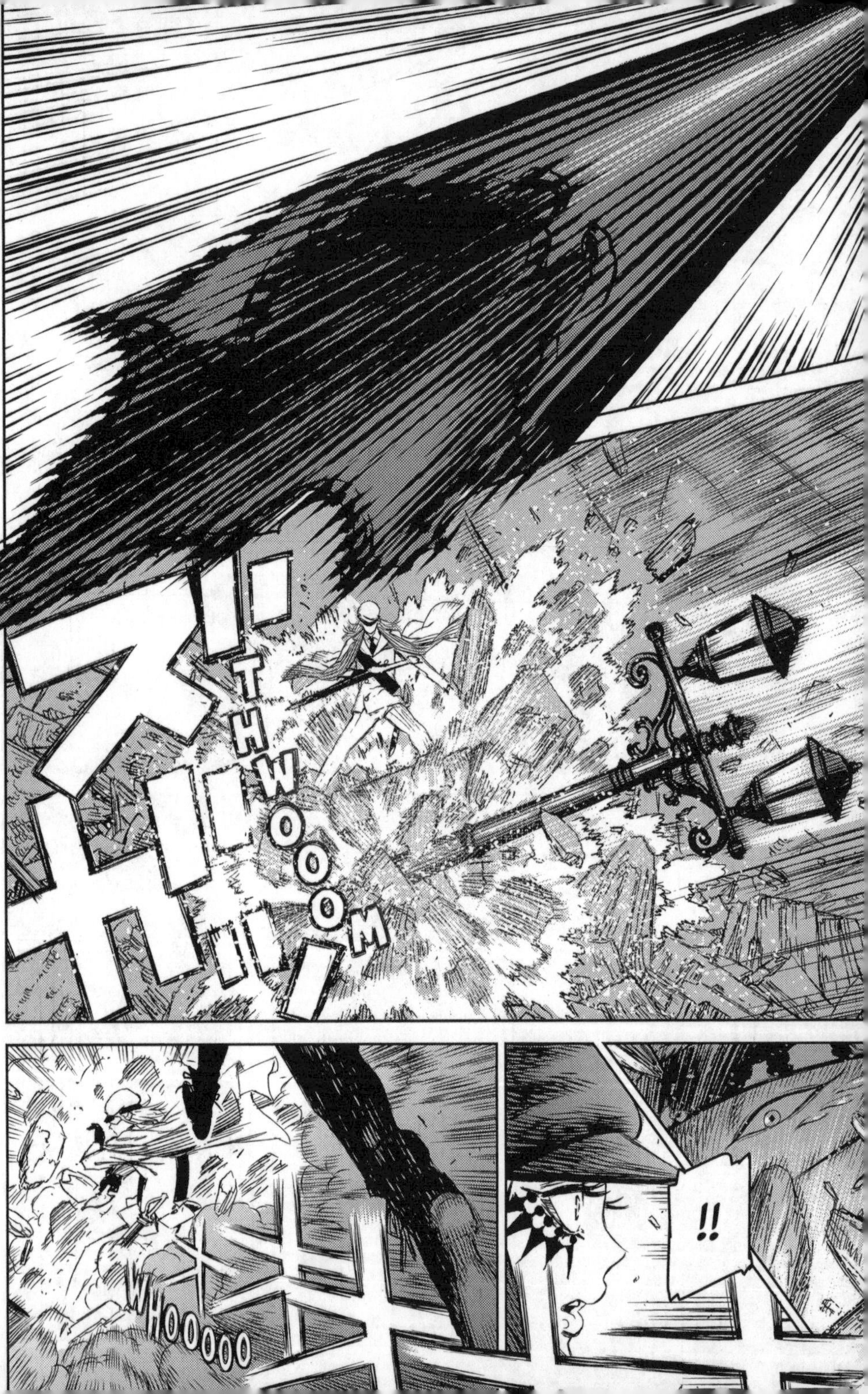
THWOOOM
!!
WHOOOOO

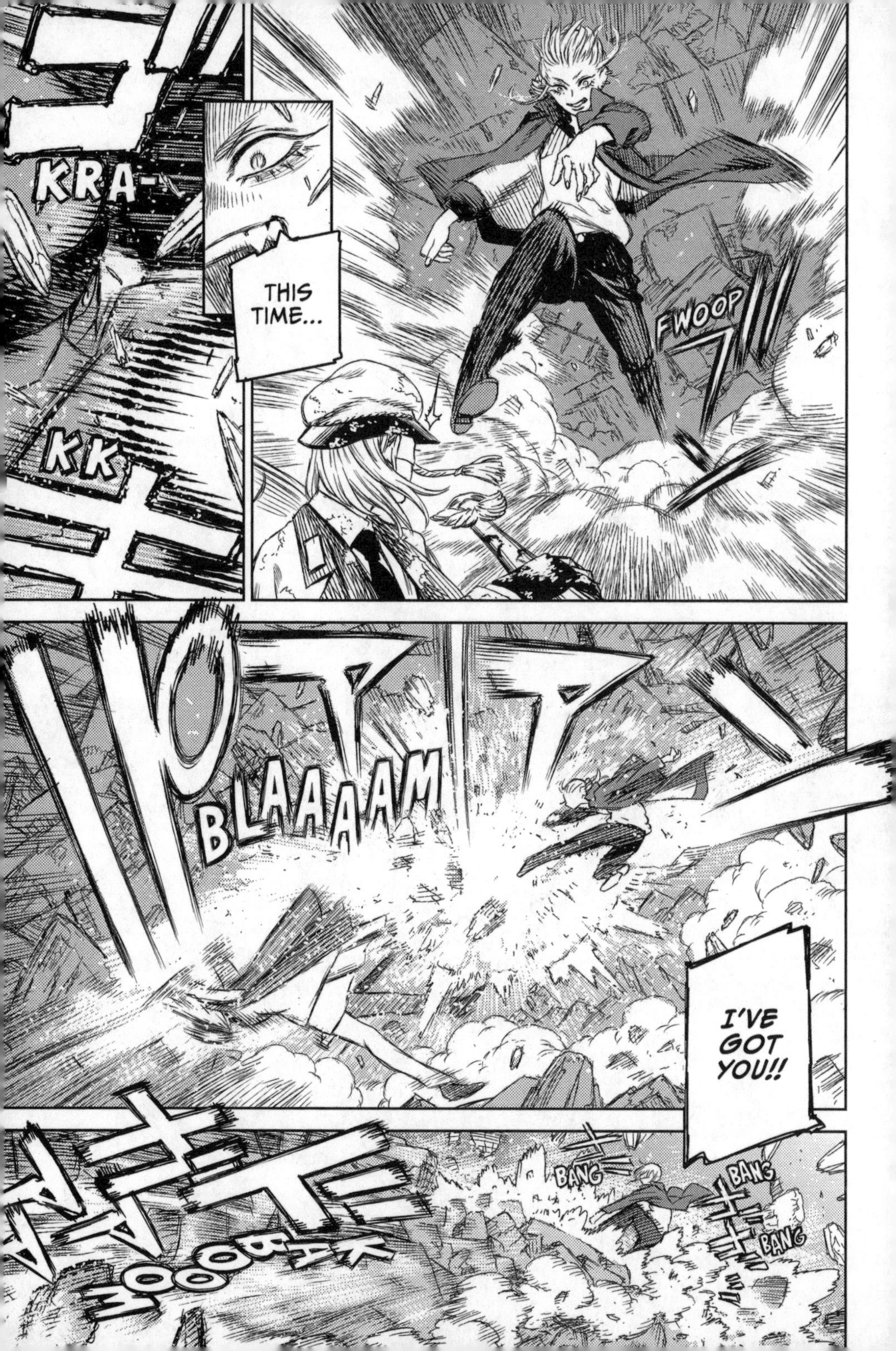

FWOOP
THIS TIME...
KRA-
KK
BLAAAAM
I'VE GOT YOU!!
BANG
BANG
BANG
KA-BOOOM

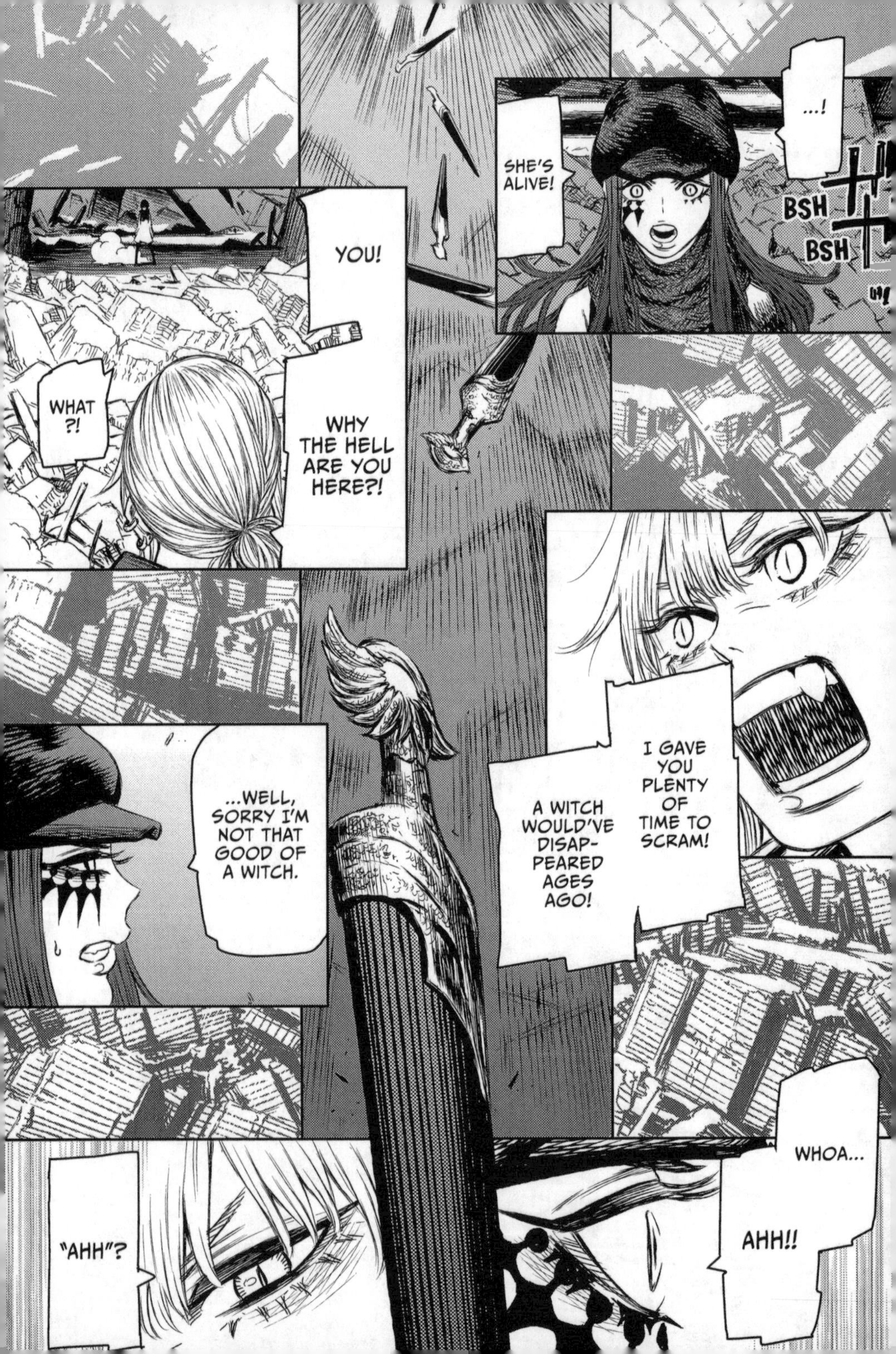
...!
BSH
BSH
SHE'S ALIVE!
YOU!
WHY THE HELL ARE YOU HERE?!
WHAT ?!
I GAVE YOU PLENTY OF TIME TO SCRAM!
A WITCH WOULD'VE DISAP-PEARED AGES AGO!
...WELL, SORRY I'M NOT THAT GOOD OF A WITCH.
WHOA...
AHH!!
"AHH"?

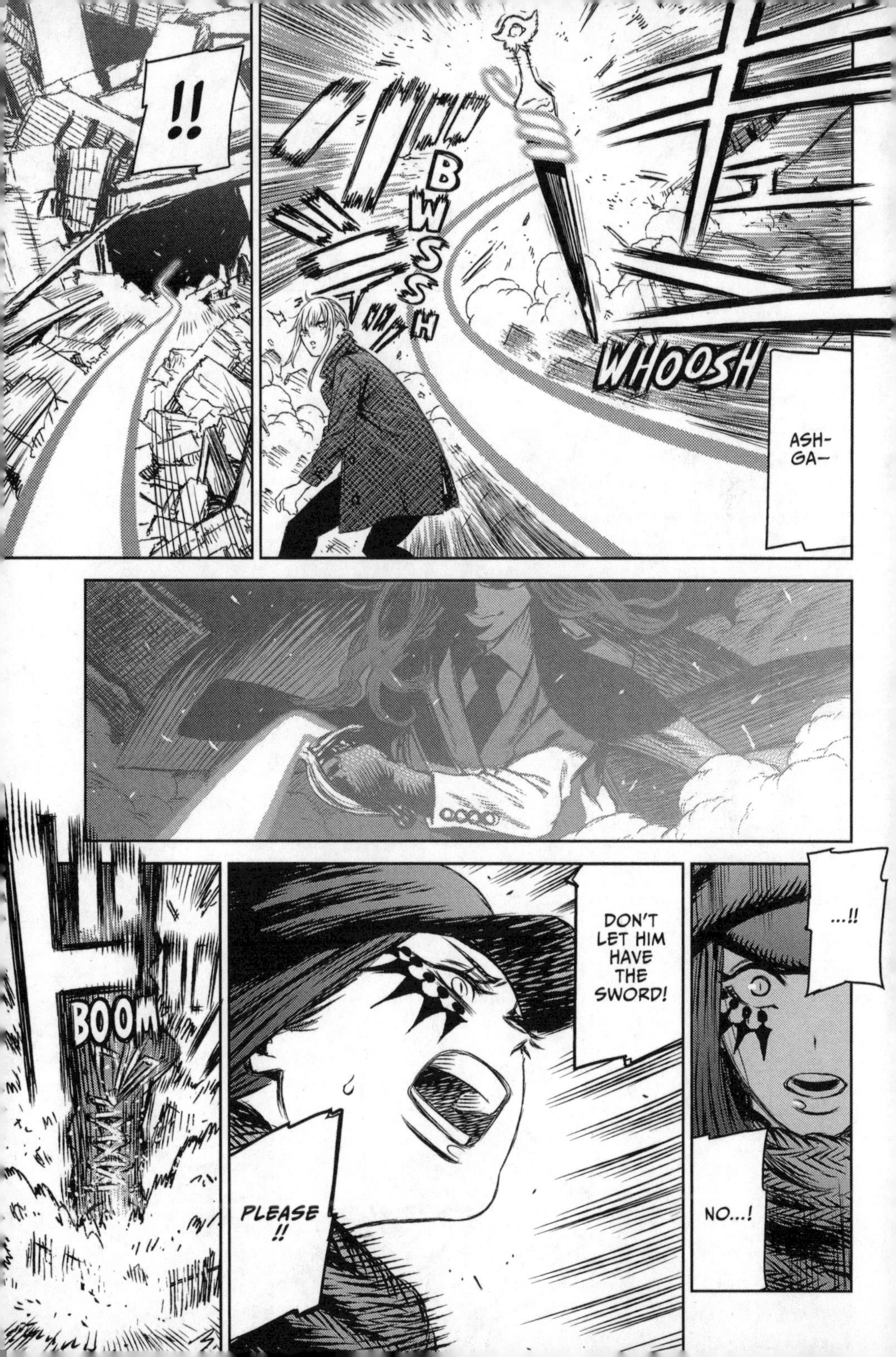
WHOOSH
ASH-GA—
BWSSH
!!
...!!
NO...!
DON'T LET HIM HAVE THE SWORD!
PLEASE !!
BOOM

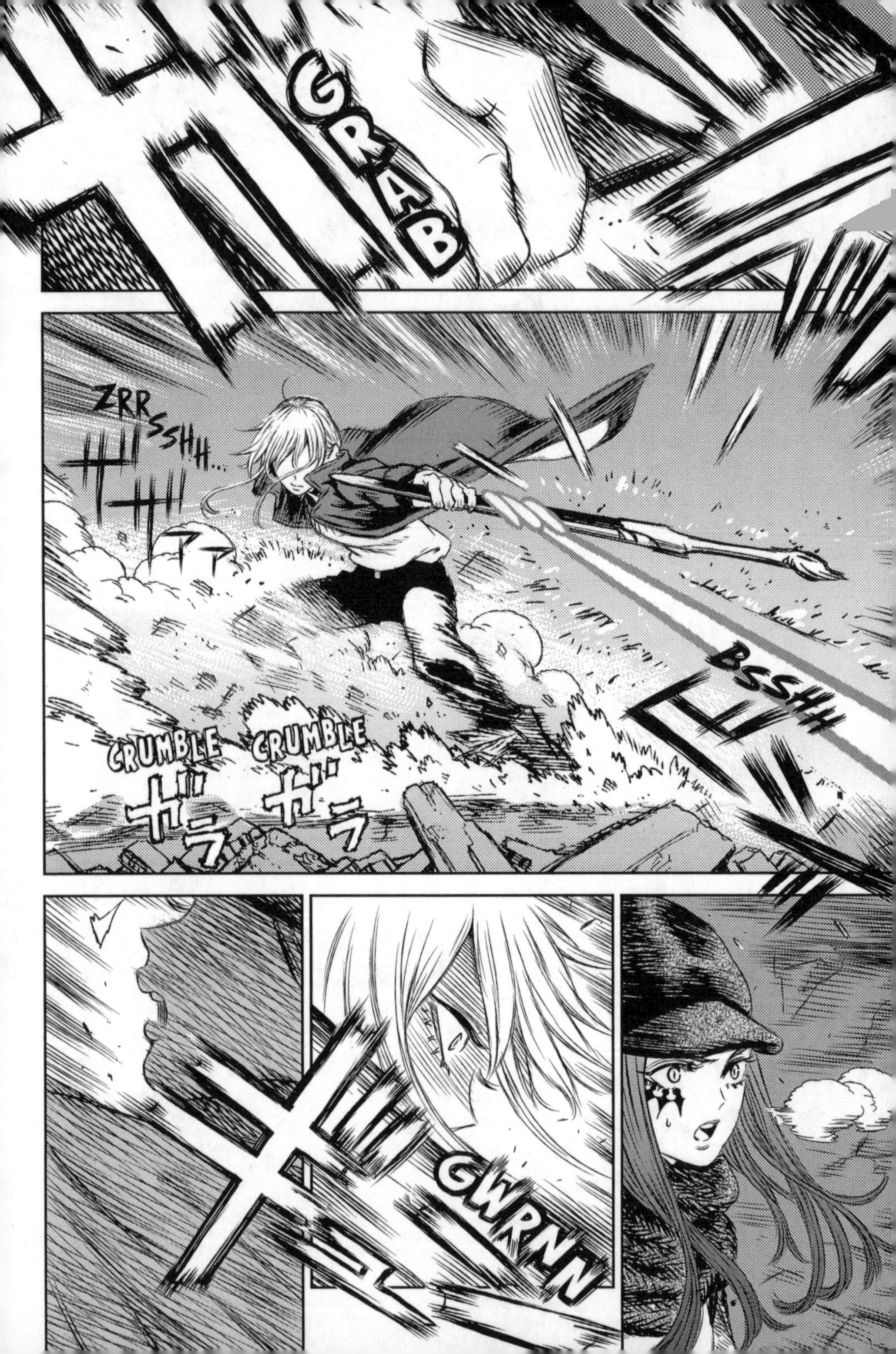
GRAB
ZRRSSHH...
BSSHH
CRUMBLE CRUMBLE
ガラ ガラ
GWRNN

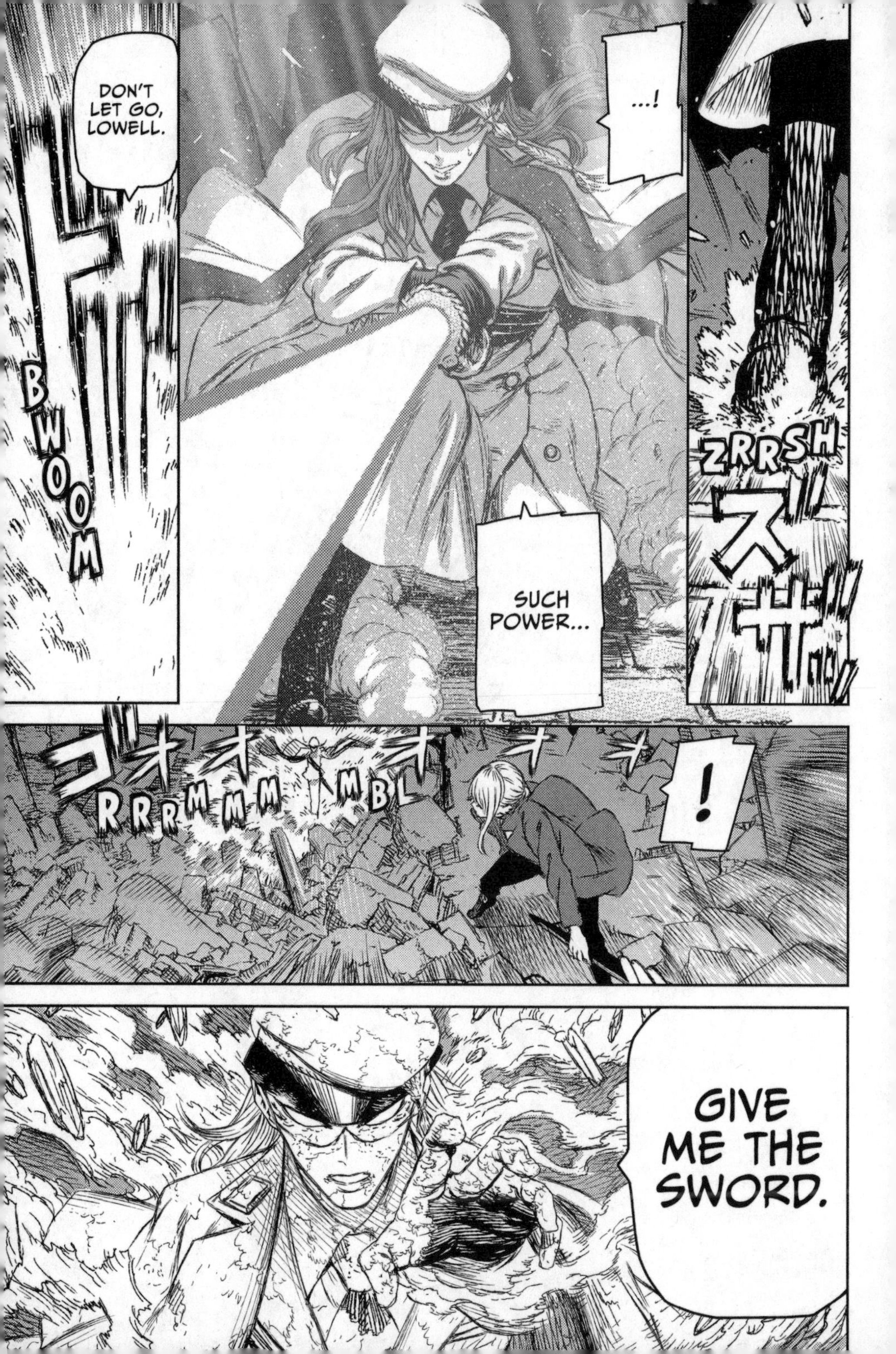
ZRRSH
...!
SUCH POWER...
DON'T LET GO, LOWELL.
BWOOM
!
RRRMMMMMBL
GIVE ME THE SWORD.

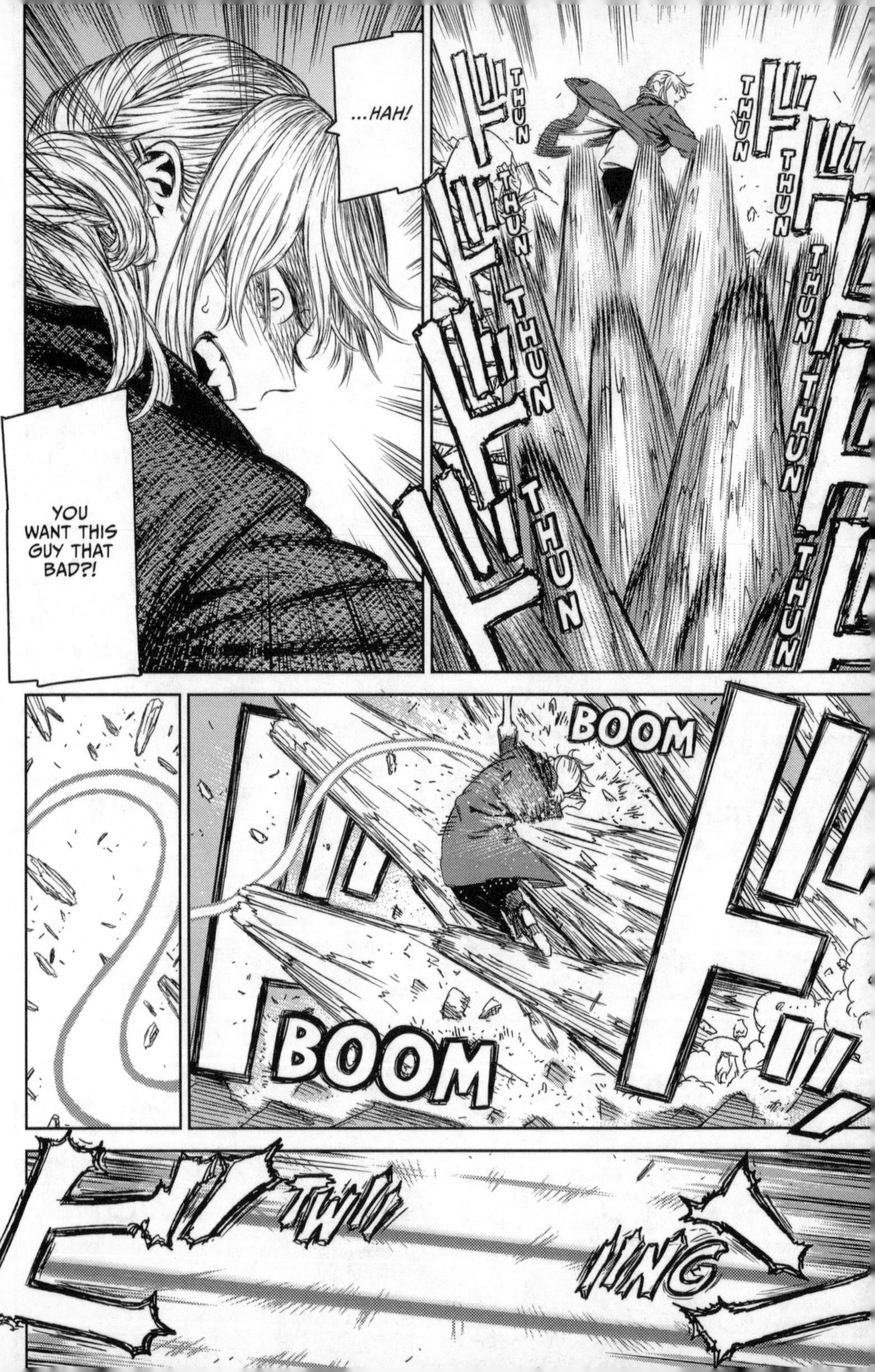

THUN
THUN
THUN
THUN
THUN
THUN
THUN
THUN
THUN
...HAH!
YOU WANT THIS GUY THAT BAD?!
BOOM
BOOM
TWII
ING

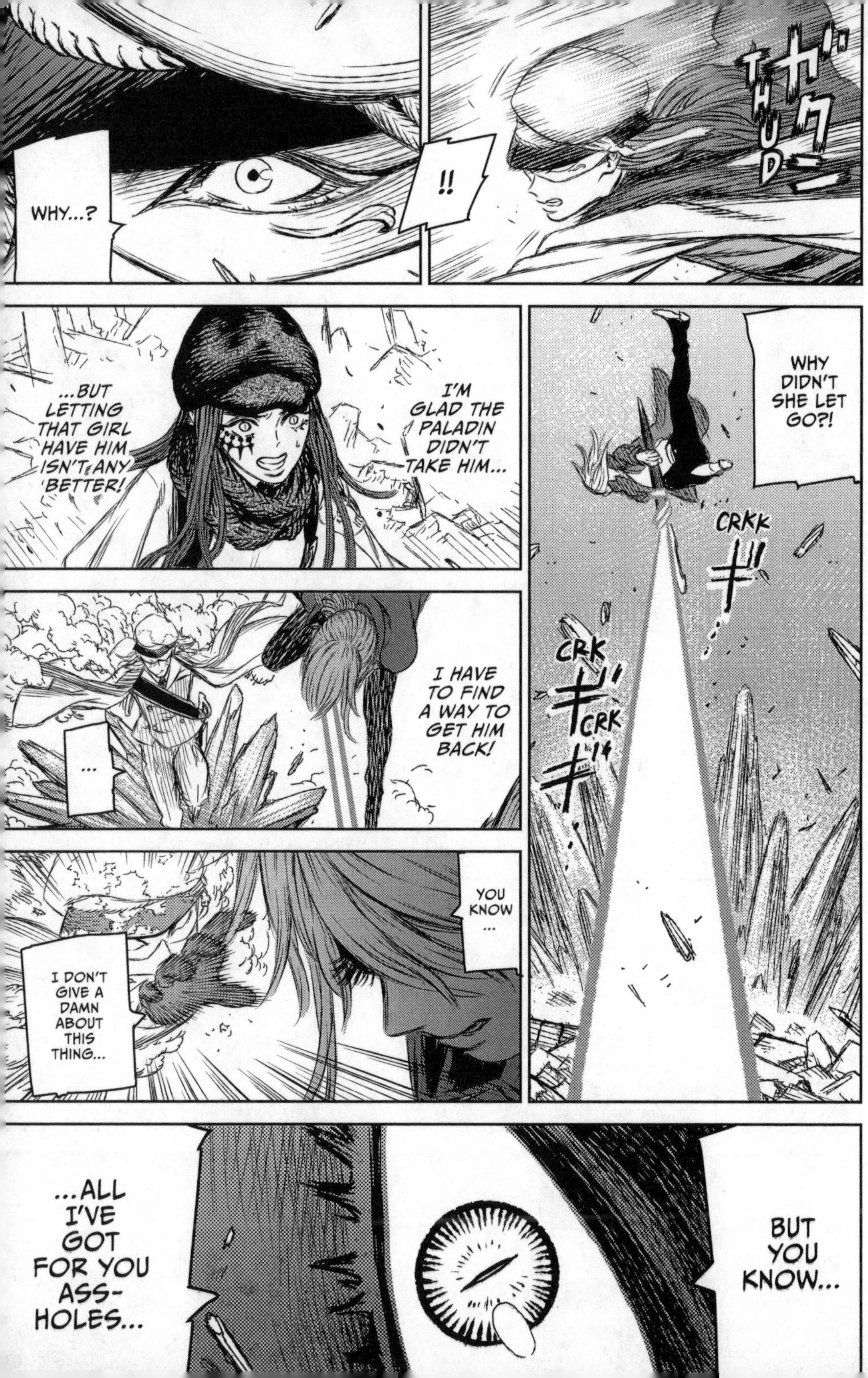
THUD
!!
WHY...?
WHY DIDN'T SHE LET GO?!
CRKK
CRK
CRK
I'M GLAD THE PALADIN DIDN'T TAKE HIM...
...BUT LETTING THAT GIRL HAVE HIM ISN'T ANY BETTER!
I HAVE TO FIND A WAY TO GET HIM BACK!
...
YOU KNOW ...
I DON'T GIVE A DAMN ABOUT THIS THING...
BUT YOU KNOW...
...ALL I'VE GOT FOR YOU ASS-HOLES...

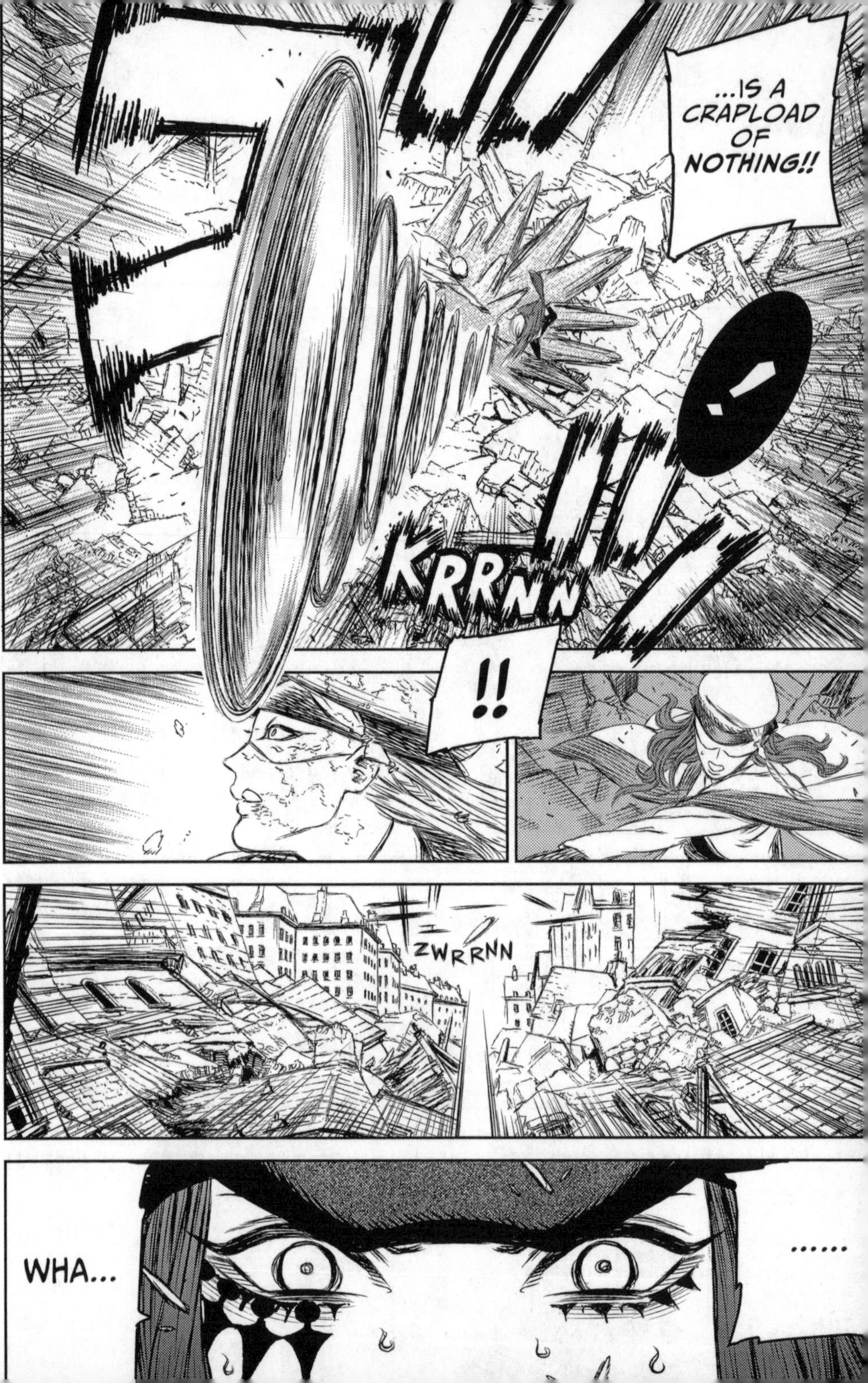
...IS A CRAPLOAD OF NOTHING!!
!
KRRNN
!!
ZWRRNN
......
WHA...

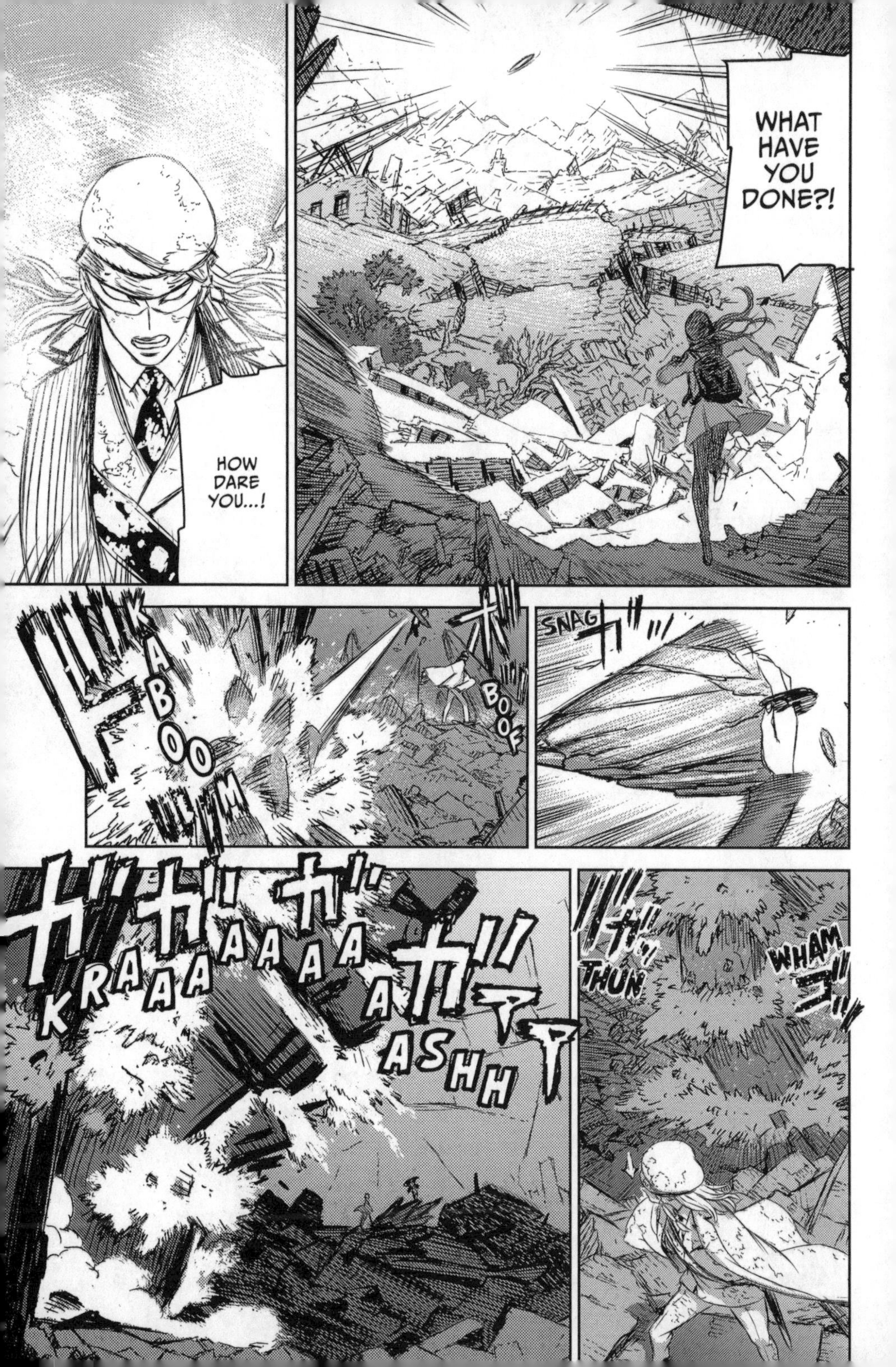
WHAT HAVE YOU DONE?!
HOW DARE YOU...!
SNAG
BOOF
KABOOM
WHAM
THUN
KRAAAAAAAASHH

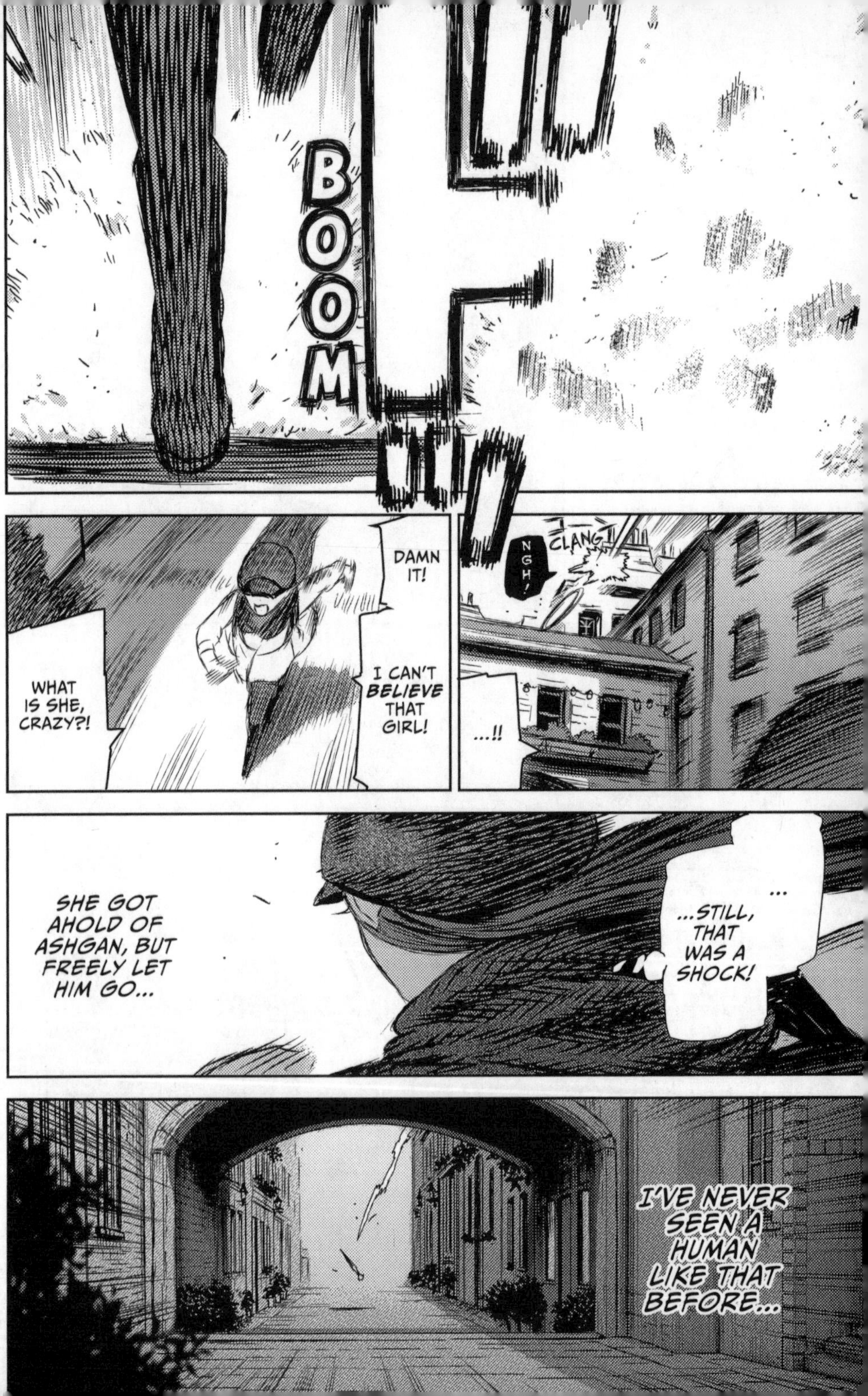
BOOM
NGH!
CLANG!
...!!
DAMN IT!
I CAN'T *BELIEVE* THAT GIRL!
WHAT IS SHE, CRAZY?!
...
...STILL, THAT WAS A SHOCK!
SHE GOT AHOLD OF ASHGAN, BUT FREELY LET HIM GO...
I'VE NEVER SEEN A HUMAN LIKE THAT BEFORE...

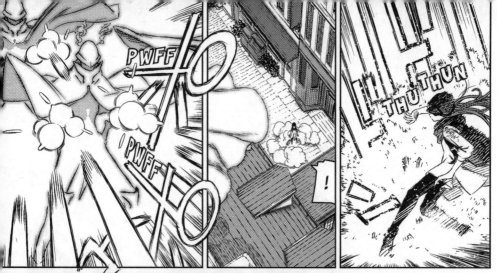

PWFF

PWFF

THUN THUN

!

HOW MANY OF THEM *ARE* THERE?!

THUN THUN THUN

THUN

OH, COME ON!

LEAP

...!!

!

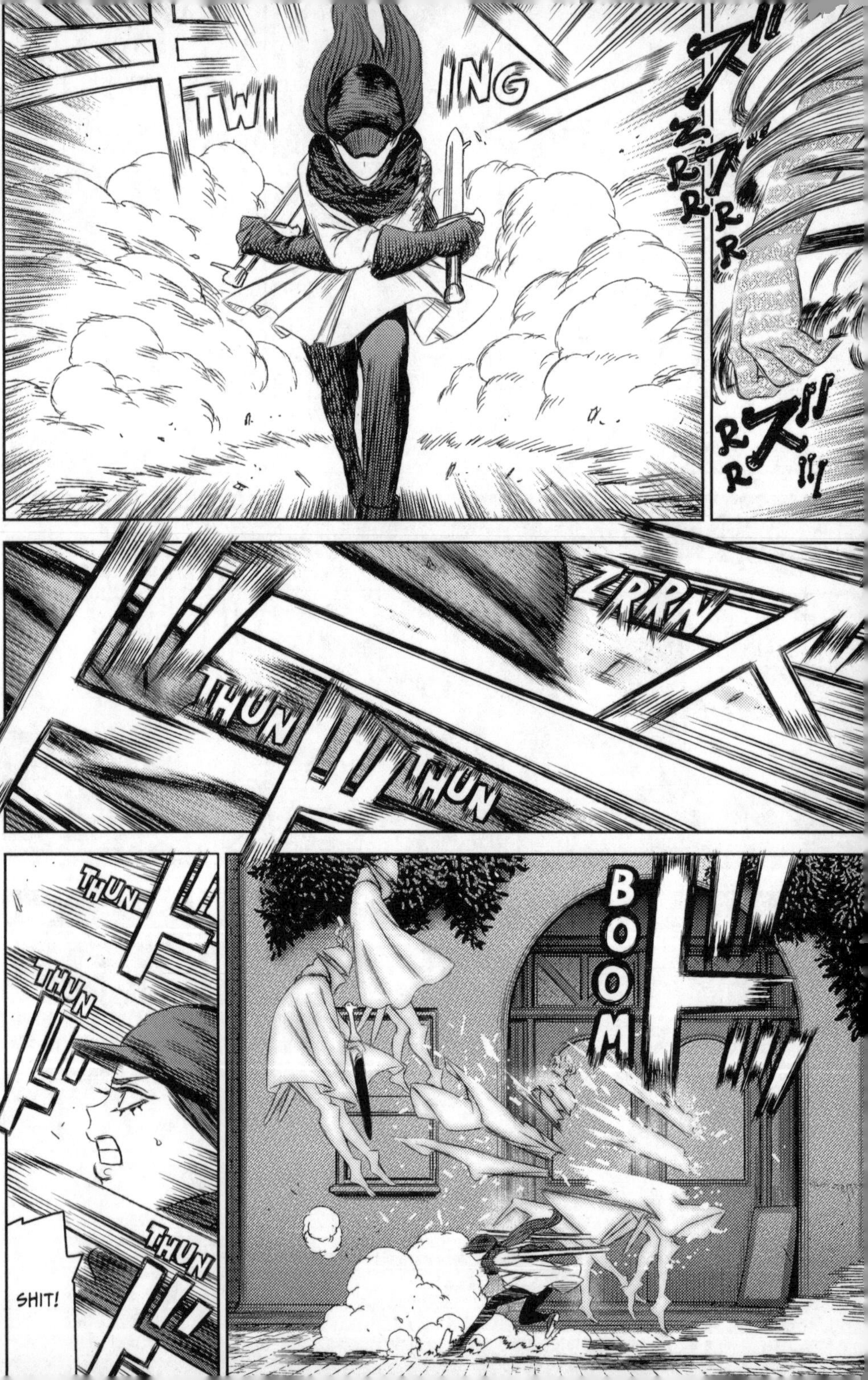

ZRRR
RRR
RRR
TWI ING
ZRRN
THUN
THUN
BOOM
THUN
THUN
THUN
SHIT!

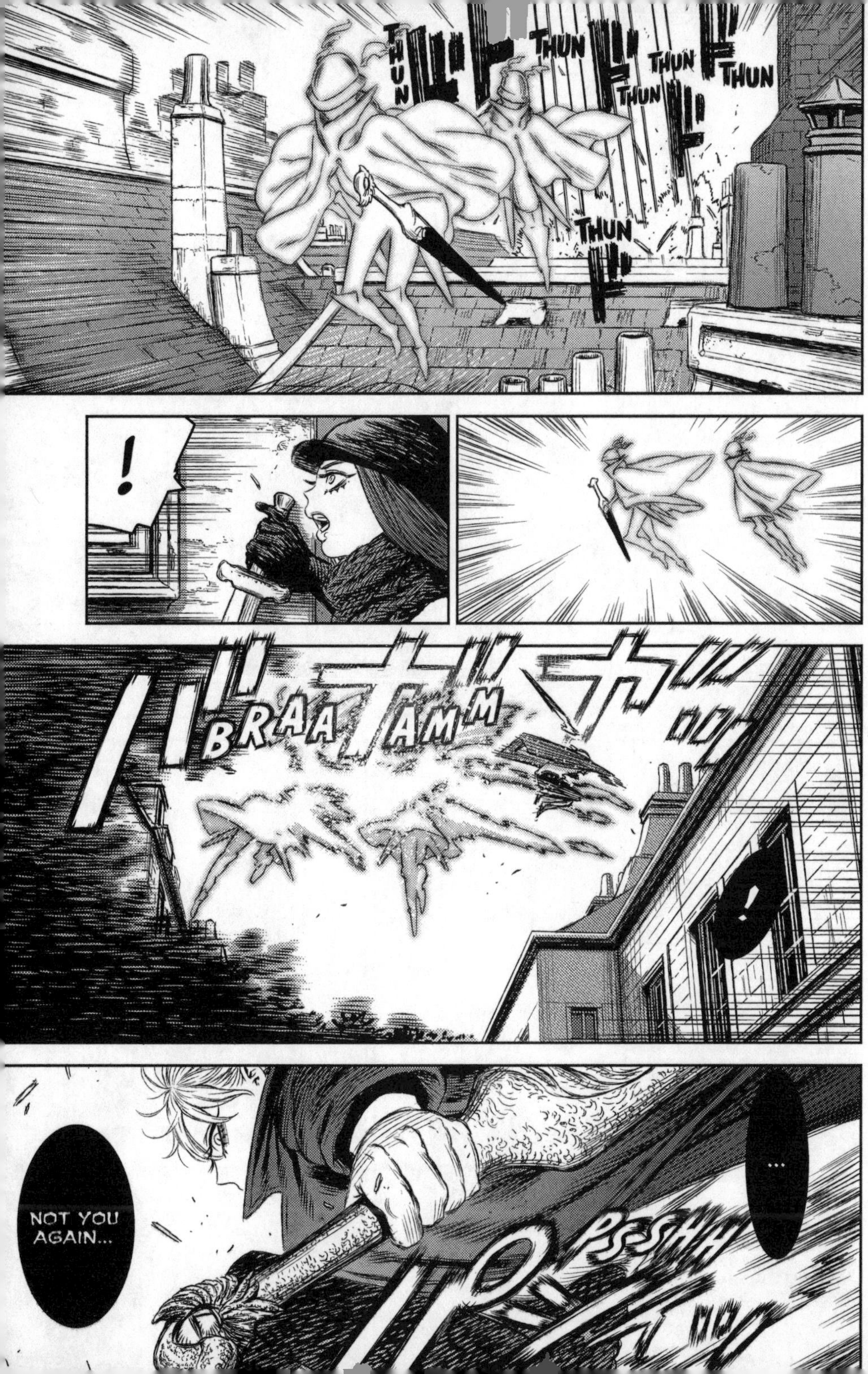
THUN
THUN
THUN
THUN
THUN
THUN
!
BRAAAMM
...
PSSHH
NOT YOU AGAIN...

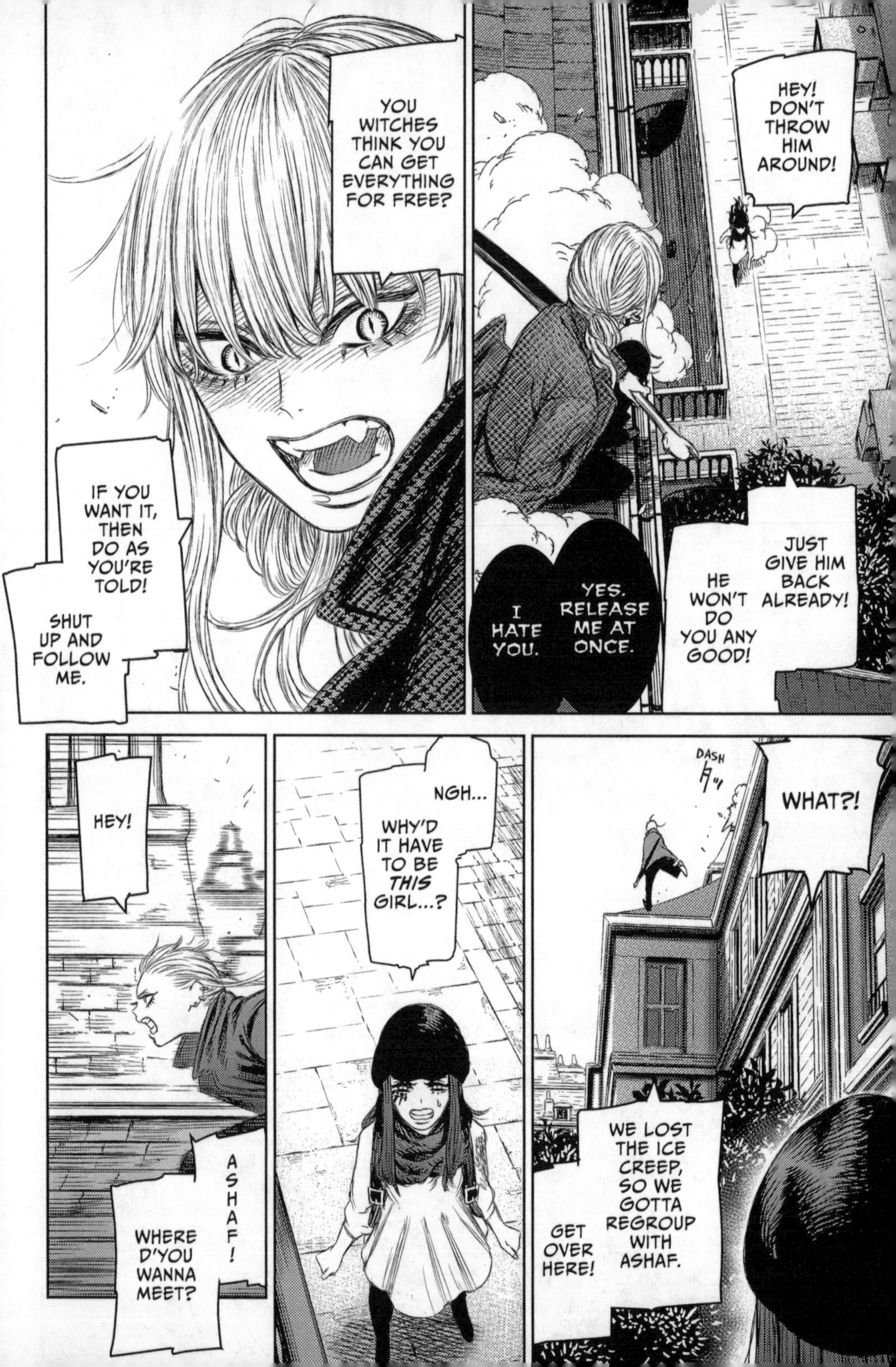
HEY! DON'T THROW HIM AROUND!
JUST GIVE HIM BACK ALREADY!
HE WON'T DO YOU ANY GOOD!
YES. RELEASE ME AT ONCE.
I HATE YOU.
YOU WITCHES THINK YOU CAN GET EVERYTHING FOR FREE?
IF YOU WANT IT, THEN DO AS YOU'RE TOLD!
SHUT UP AND FOLLOW ME.
DASH
WHAT?!
WE LOST THE ICE CREEP, SO WE GOTTA REGROUP WITH ASHAF.
GET OVER HERE!
NGH...
WHY'D IT HAVE TO BE *THIS* GIRL...?
HEY!
ASHAF!
WHERE D'YOU WANNA MEET?

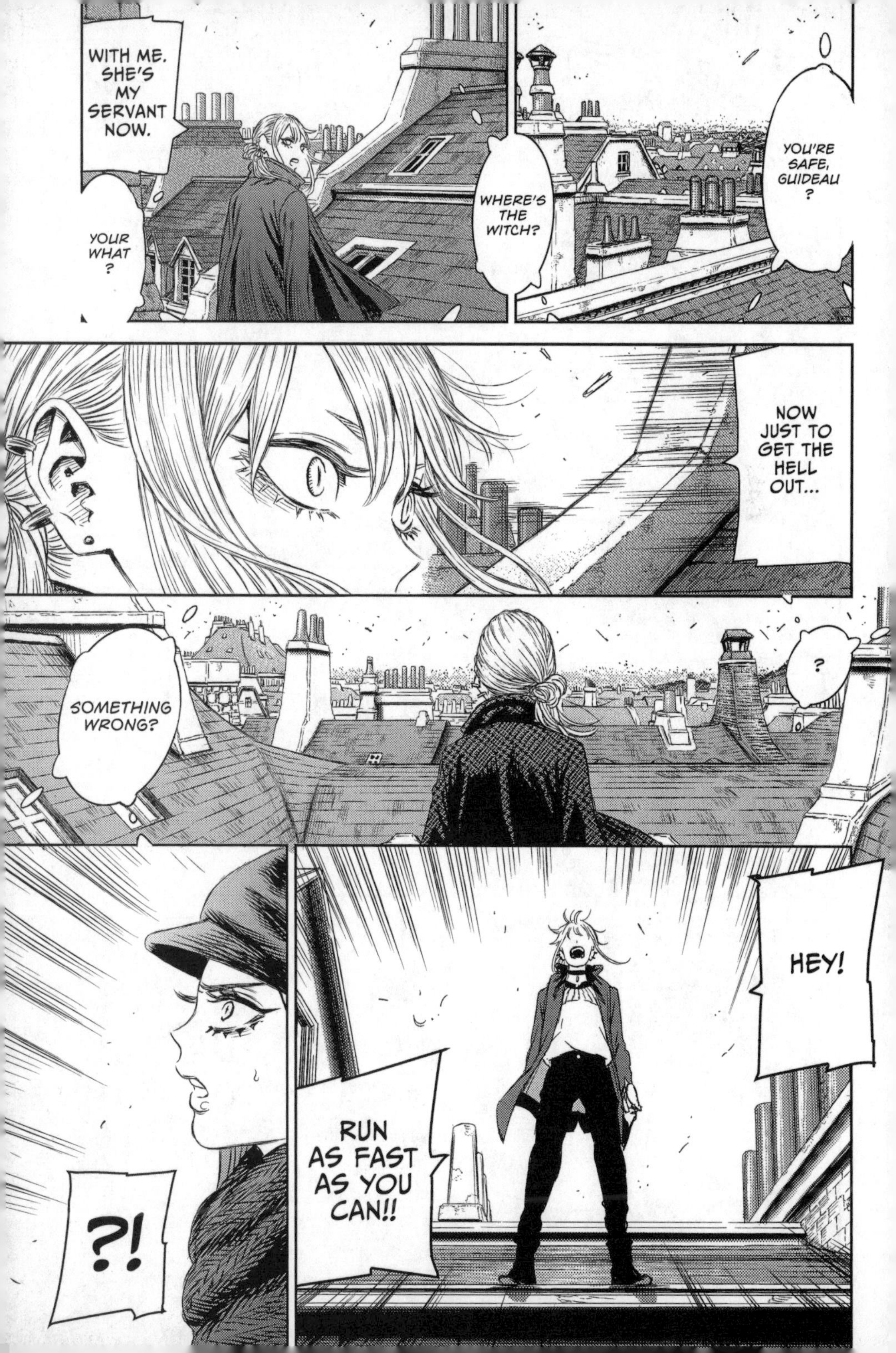

YOU'RE SAFE, GUIDEAU?
WHERE'S THE WITCH?
WITH ME. SHE'S MY SERVANT NOW.
YOUR WHAT?
NOW JUST TO GET THE HELL OUT...
?
SOMETHING WRONG?
HEY!
RUN AS FAST AS YOU CAN!!
?!

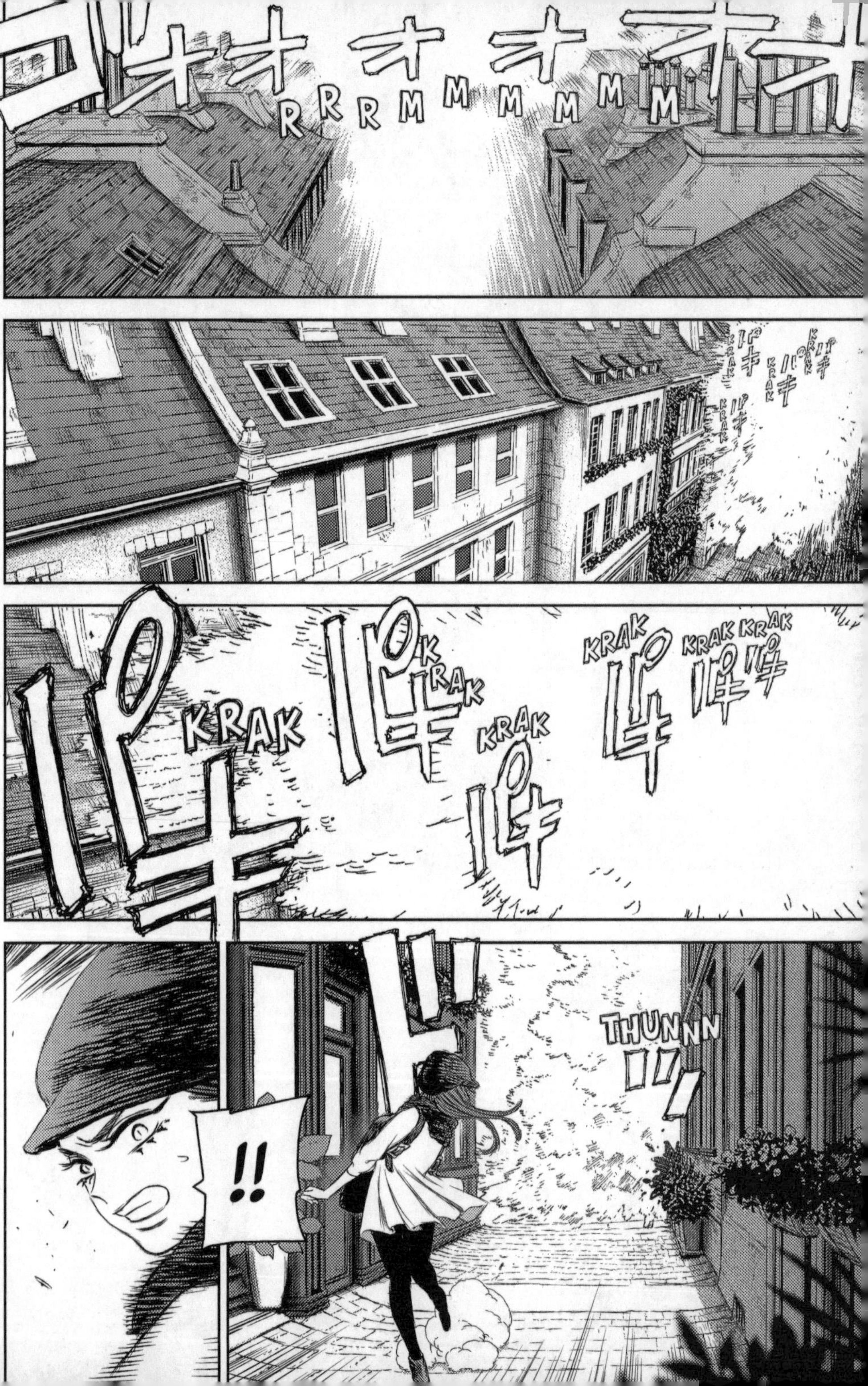
RRRMMMMMM
KRAK KRAK KRAK KRAK KRAK
KRAK
KRAK
KRAK
KRAK
KRAK
KRAK KRAK
THUNNN
!!

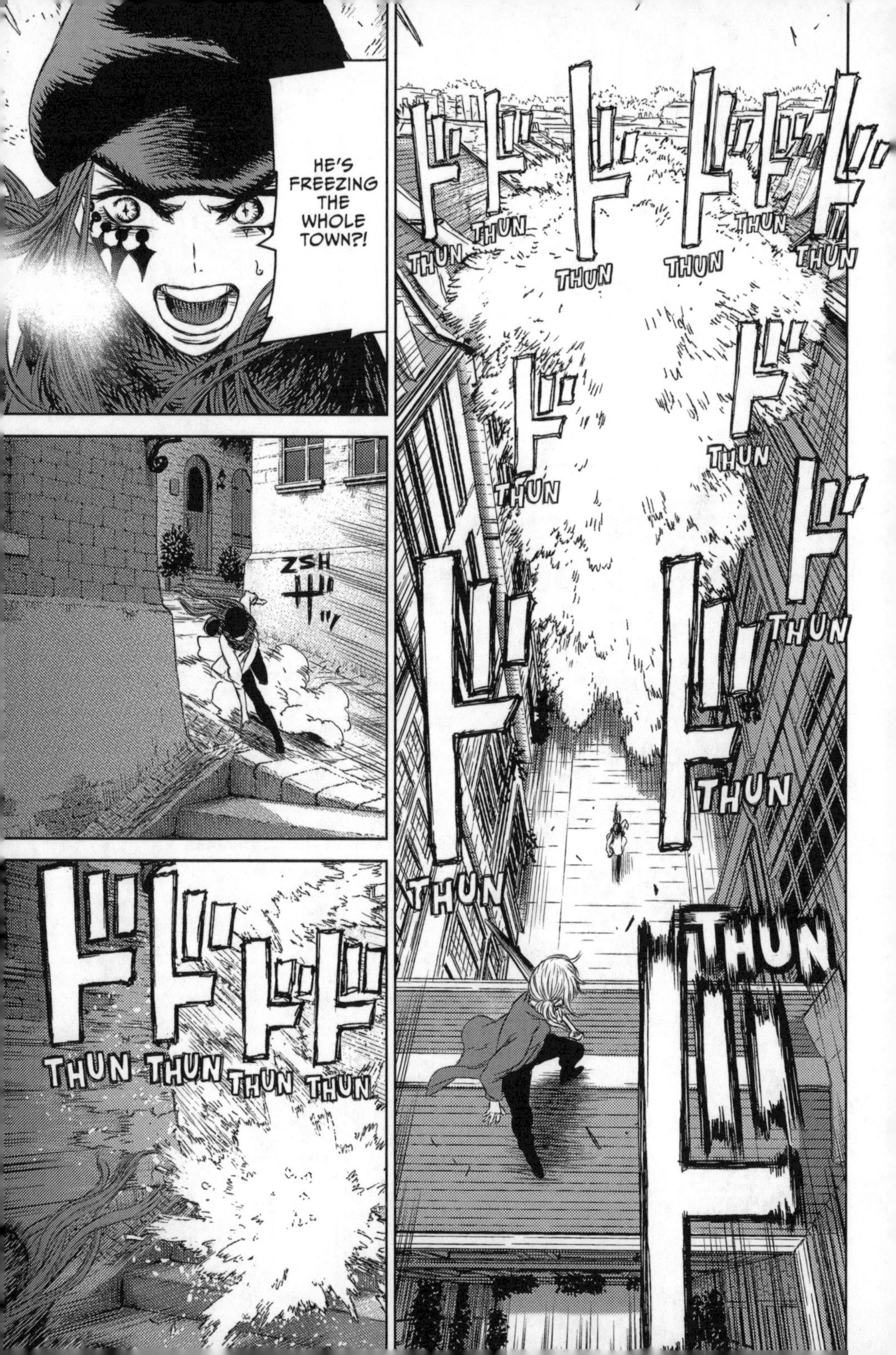
THUN THUN THUN THUN THUN THUN
THUN
THUN
THUN
THUN
THUN
THUN
HE'S FREEZING THE WHOLE TOWN?!
ZSH
THUN THUN THUN THUN

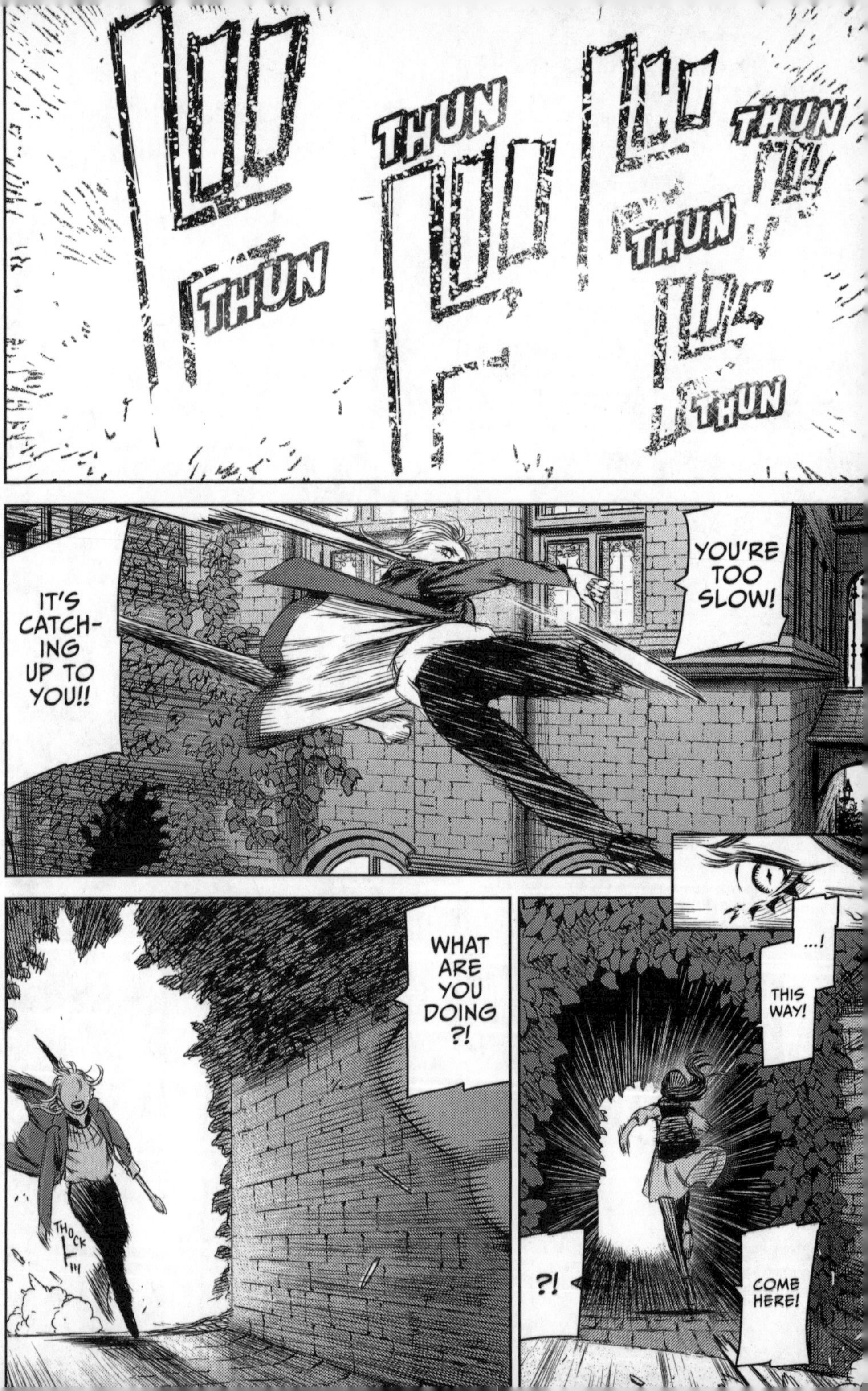
THUN
THUN
THUN
THUN
THUN
YOU'RE TOO SLOW!
IT'S CATCHING UP TO YOU!!
...!
THIS WAY!
?!
COME HERE!
WHAT ARE YOU DOING?!
THOCK

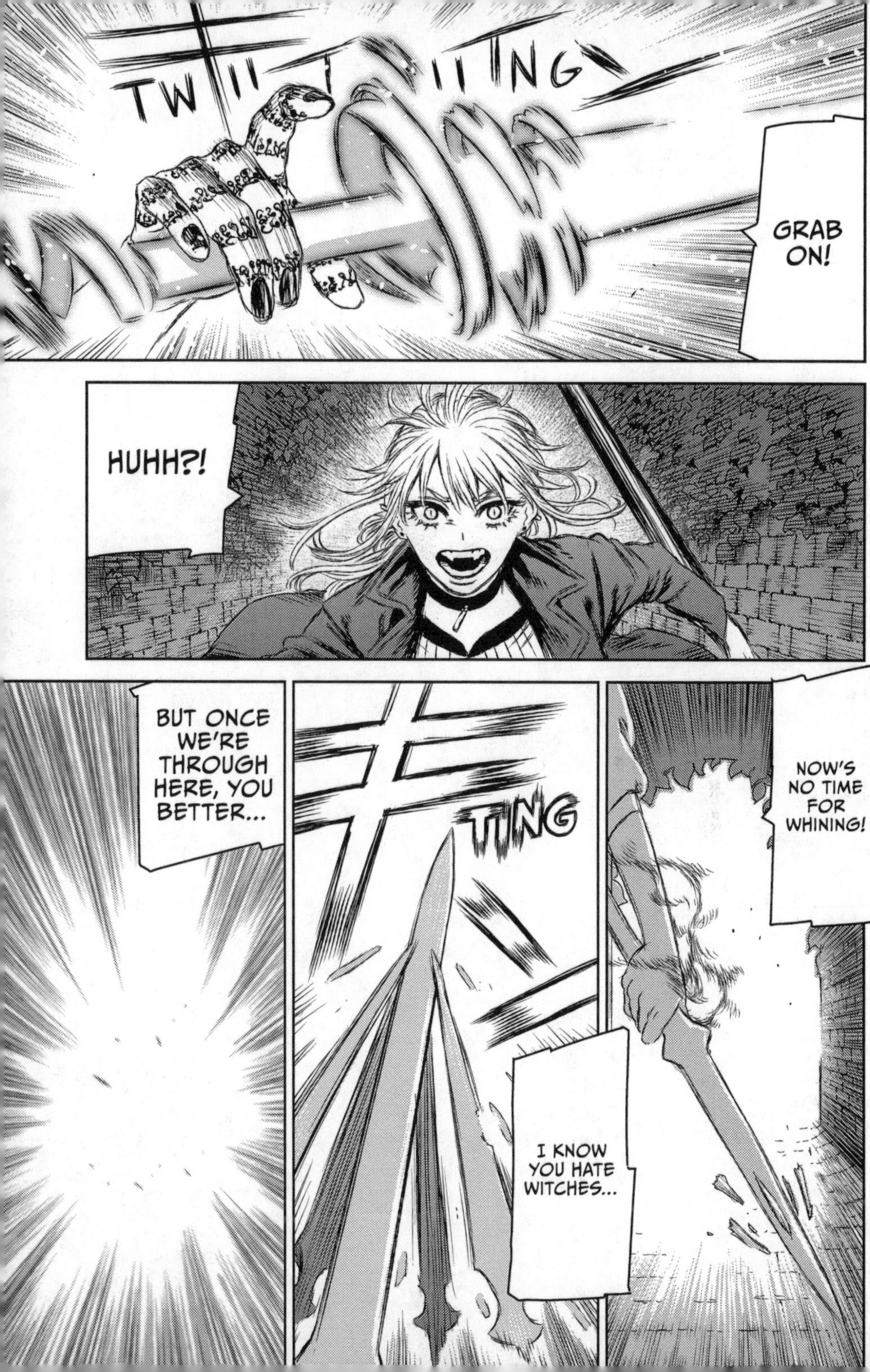
TWIIIIING
GRAB ON!
HUHH?!
NOW'S NO TIME FOR WHINING!
I KNOW YOU HATE WITCHES...
TING
BUT ONCE WE'RE THROUGH HERE, YOU BETTER...

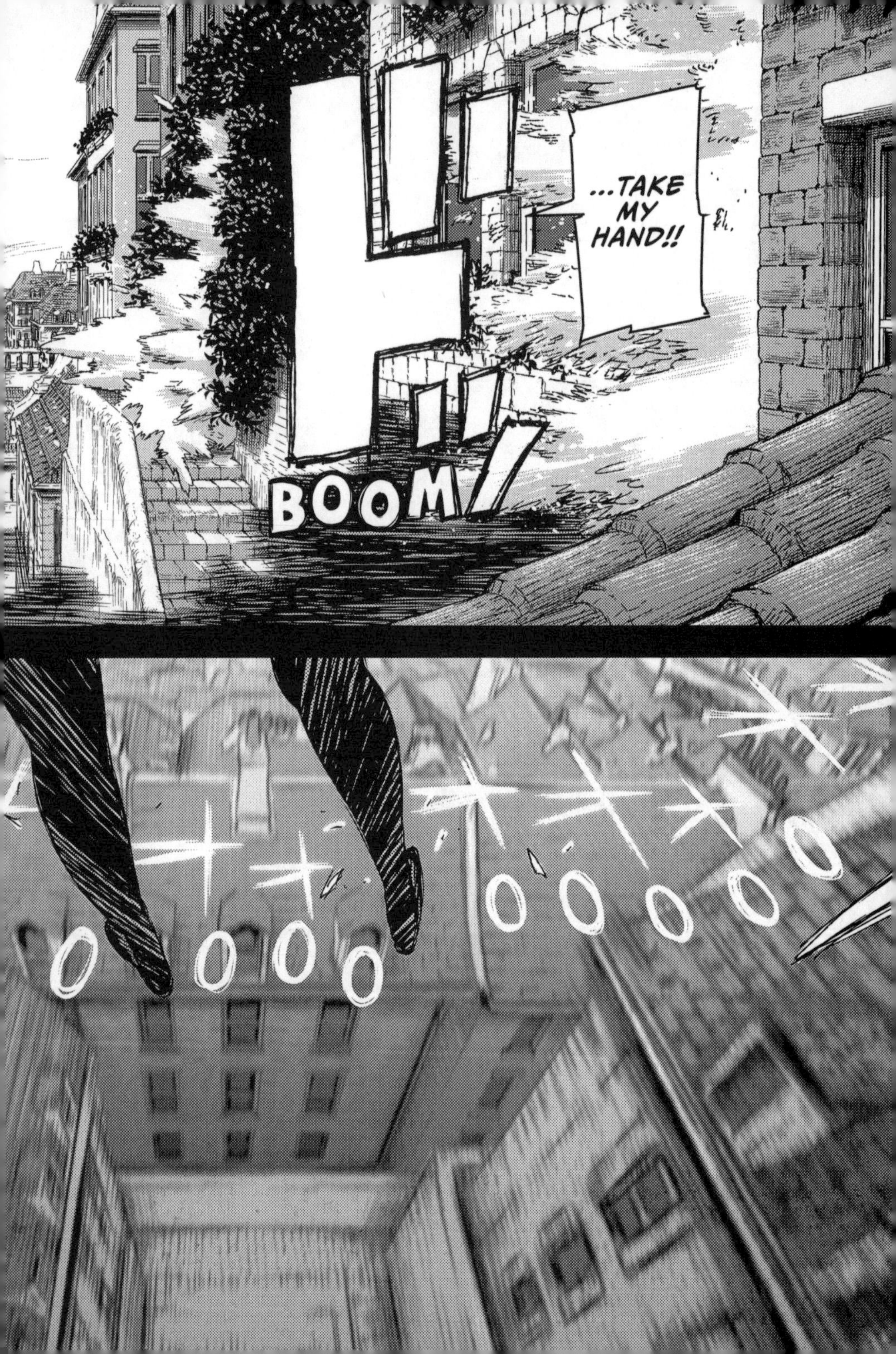
...TAKE MY HAND!!
BOOM

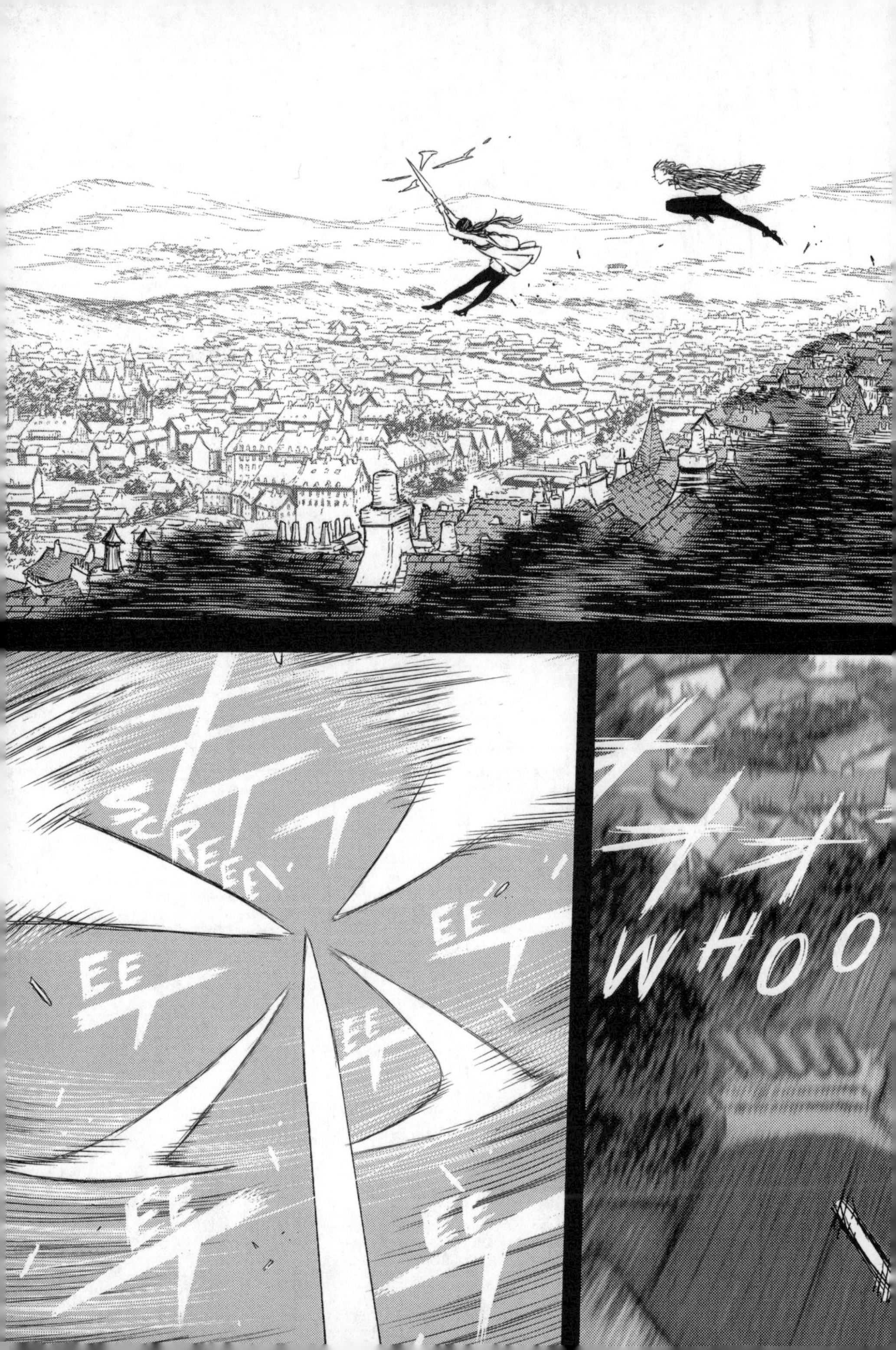
WHOO
SCREEEE
EE
EE
EE
EE
EE

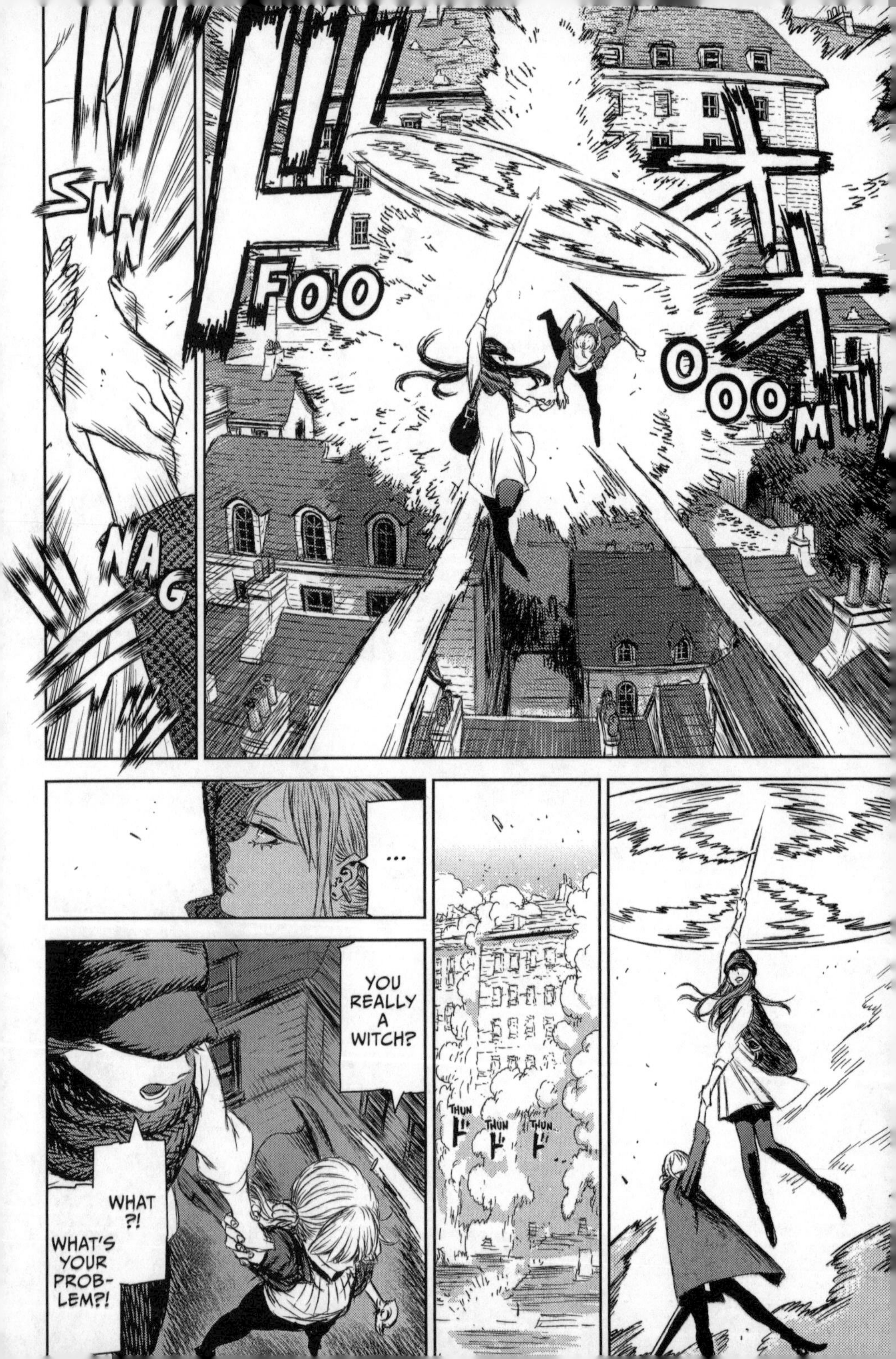
FOO
OOOM
SNN
NAG
THUN
THUN
THUN
...
YOU REALLY A WITCH?
WHAT?! WHAT'S YOUR PROB-LEM?!

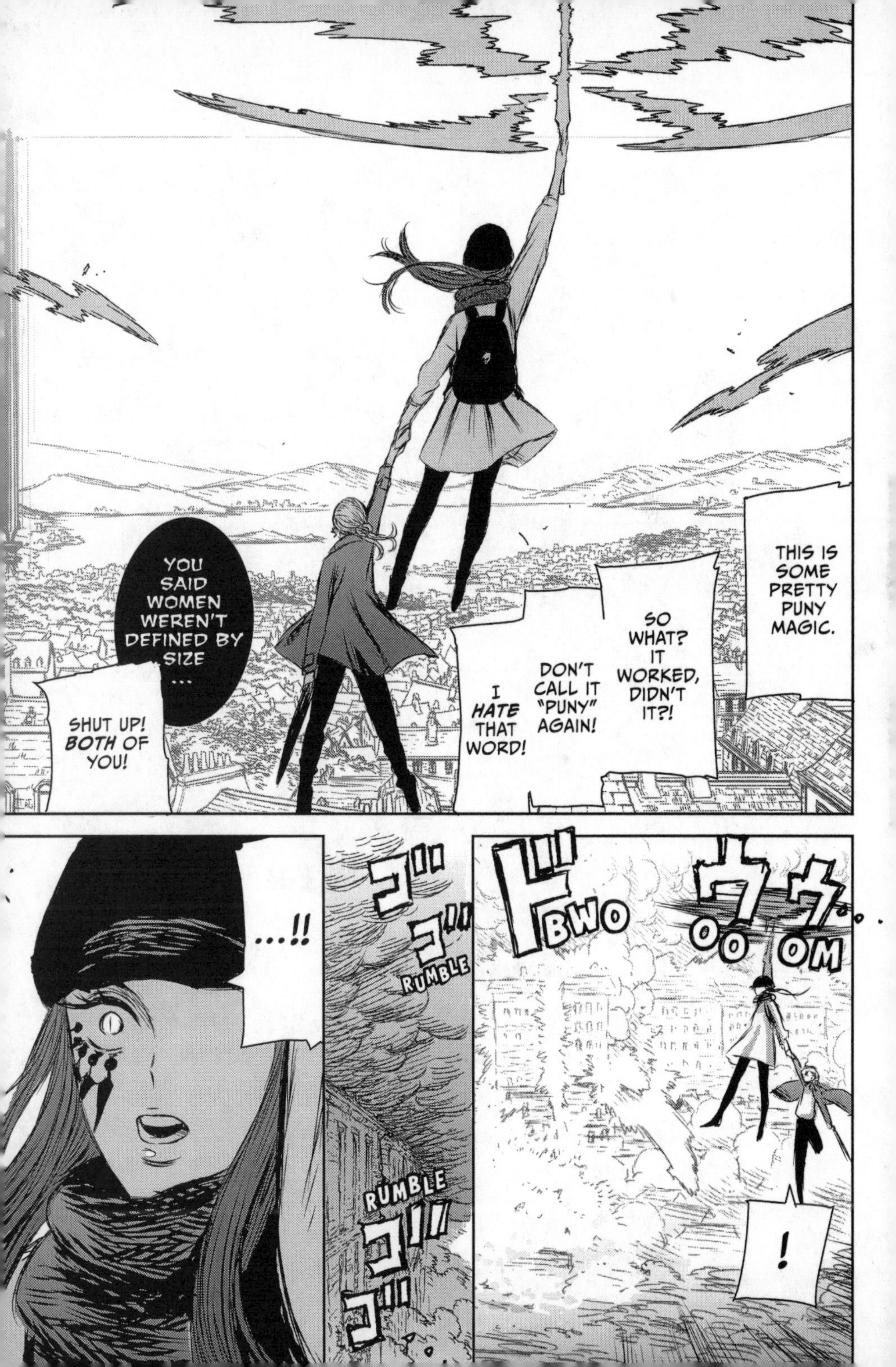
THIS IS SOME PRETTY PUNY MAGIC.
SO WHAT? IT WORKED, DIDN'T IT?!
DON'T CALL IT "PUNY" AGAIN!
I *HATE* THAT WORD!
YOU SAID WOMEN WEREN'T DEFINED BY SIZE ...
SHUT UP! *BOTH* OF YOU!
BWOOOOM
!
...!!
RUMBLE
RUMBLE

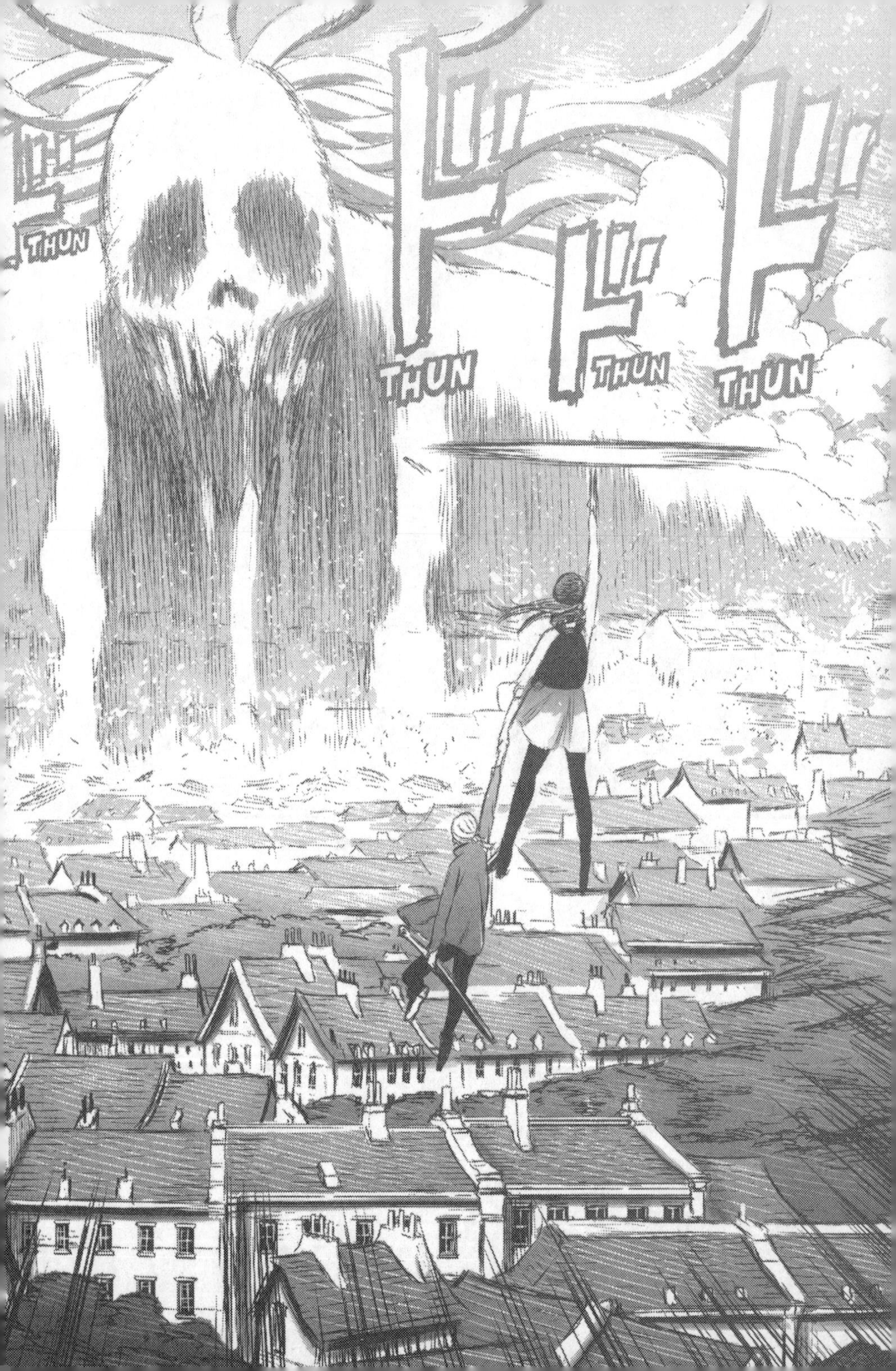
THUN
THUN
THUN
THUN

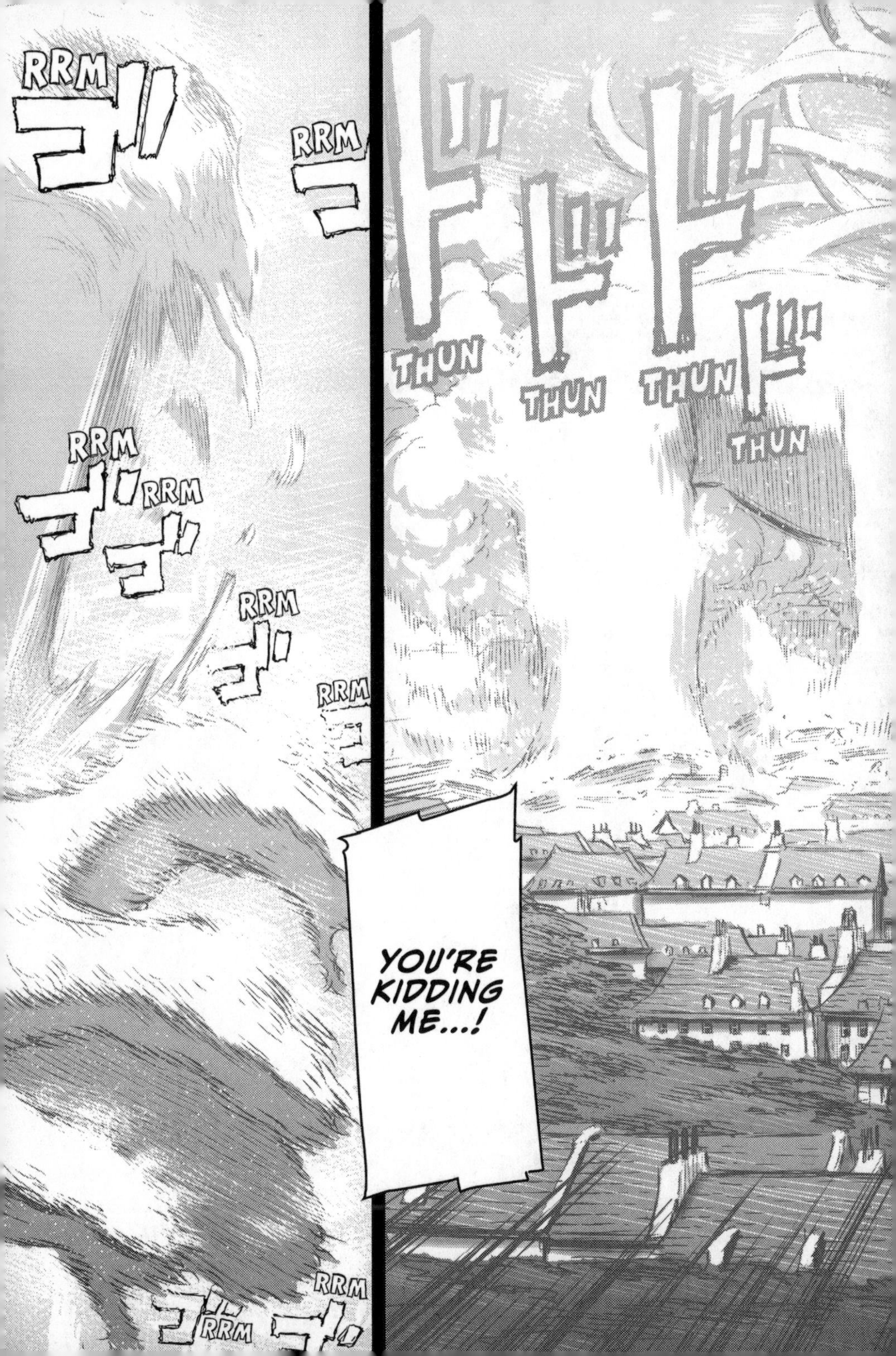
THUN
THUN
THUN
THUN
YOU'RE KIDDING ME...!
RRM
RRM
RRM
RRM
RRM
RRM
RRM
RRM

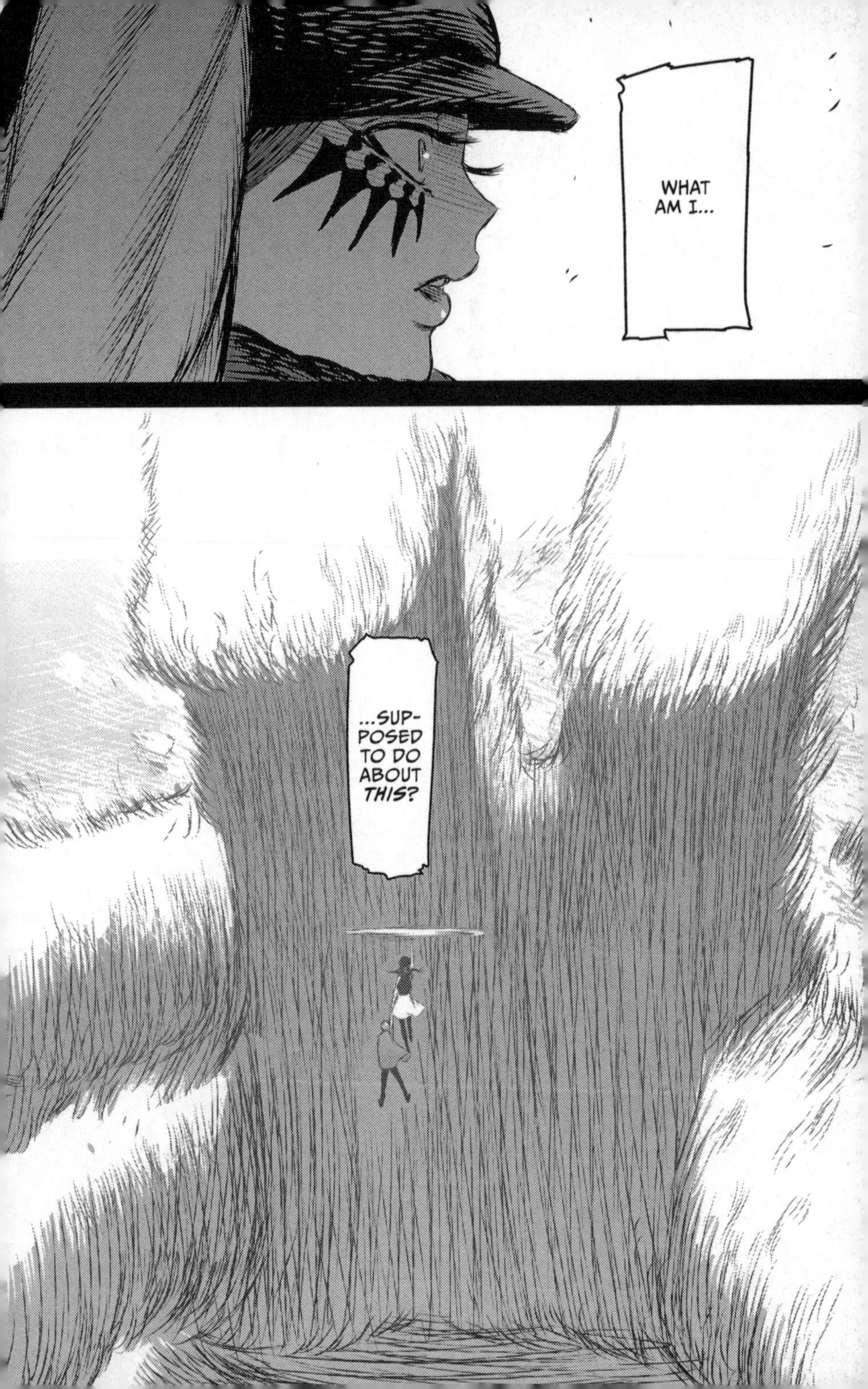
WHAT AM I...
...SUP-POSED TO DO ABOUT *THIS?*

THE WITCH AND THE BEAST

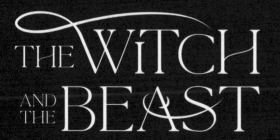

THE WITCH AND THE BEAST

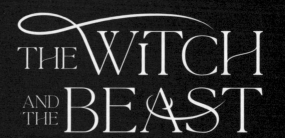

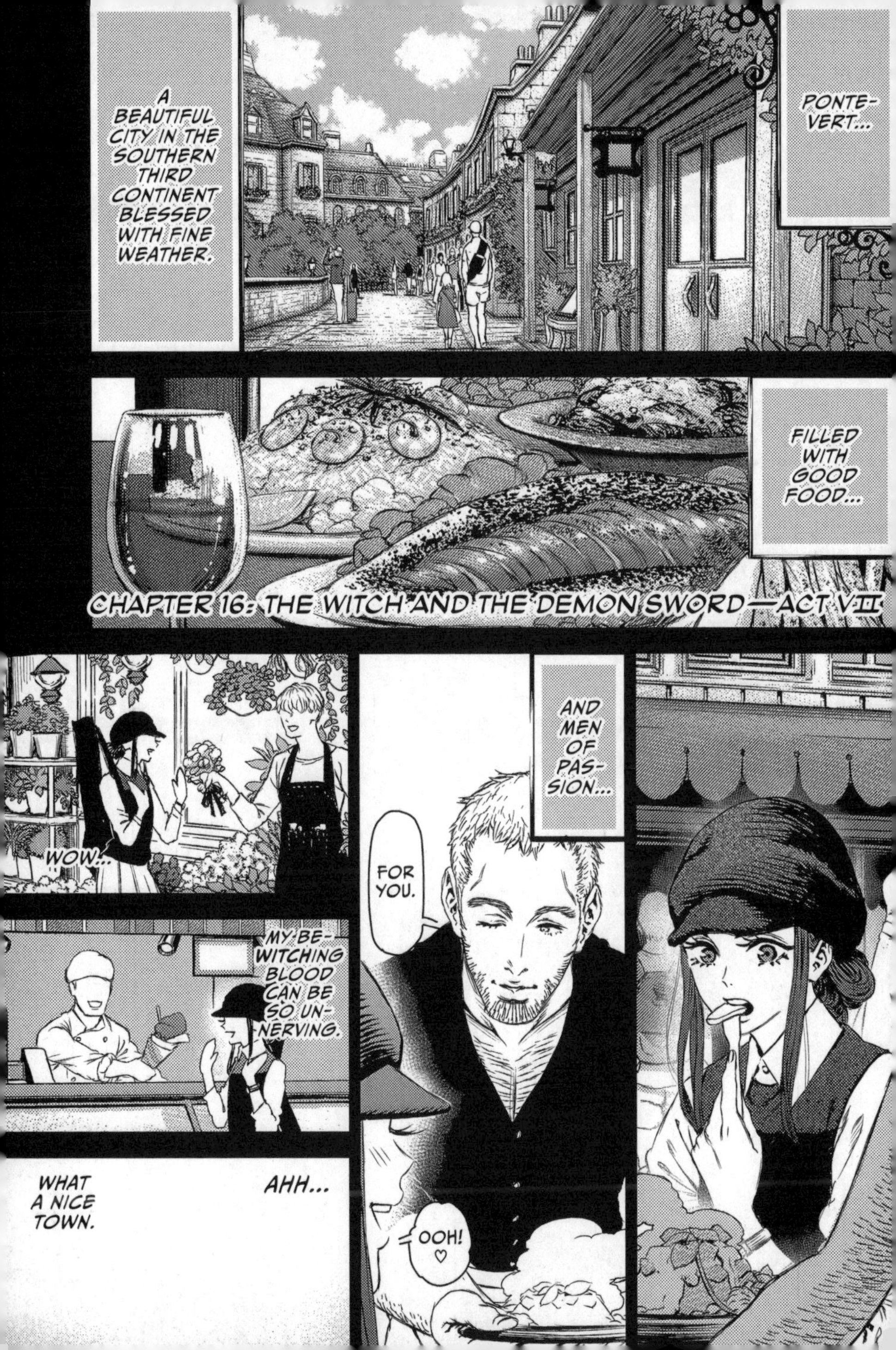

PONTEVERT...
A BEAUTIFUL CITY IN THE SOUTHERN THIRD CONTINENT BLESSED WITH FINE WEATHER.
FILLED WITH GOOD FOOD...
CHAPTER 16: THE WITCH AND THE DEMON SWORD—ACT VII
AND MEN OF PASSION...
FOR YOU.
OOH! ♡
WOW...
MY BEWITCHING BLOOD CAN BE SO UNNERVING.
AHH...
WHAT A NICE TOWN.

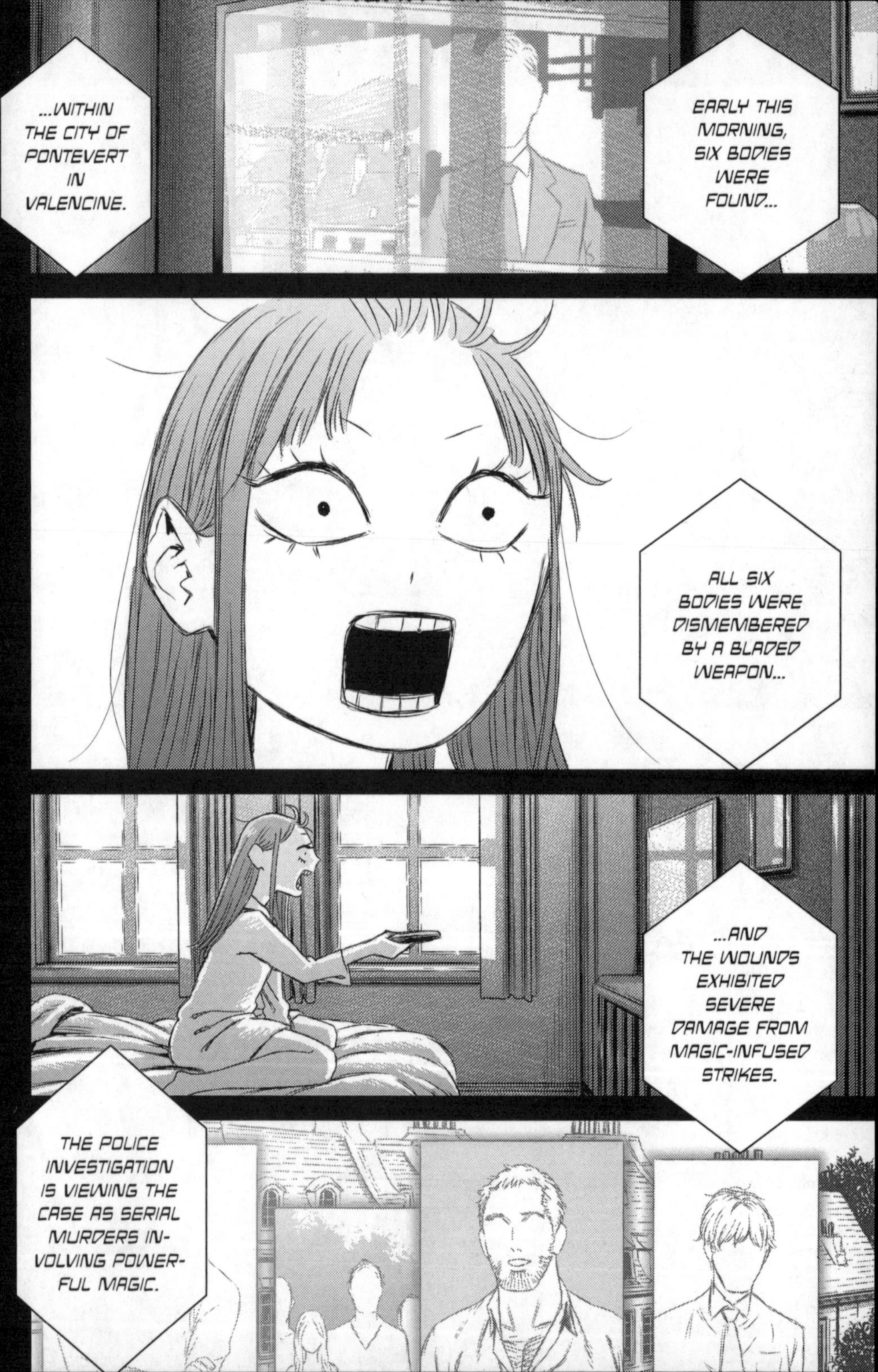
EARLY THIS MORNING, SIX BODIES WERE FOUND...
...WITHIN THE CITY OF PONTEVERT IN VALENCINE.
ALL SIX BODIES WERE DISMEMBERED BY A BLADED WEAPON...
...AND THE WOUNDS EXHIBITED SEVERE DAMAGE FROM MAGIC-INFUSED STRIKES.
THE POLICE INVESTIGATION IS VIEWING THE CASE AS SERIAL MURDERS IN-VOLVING POWER-FUL MAGIC.

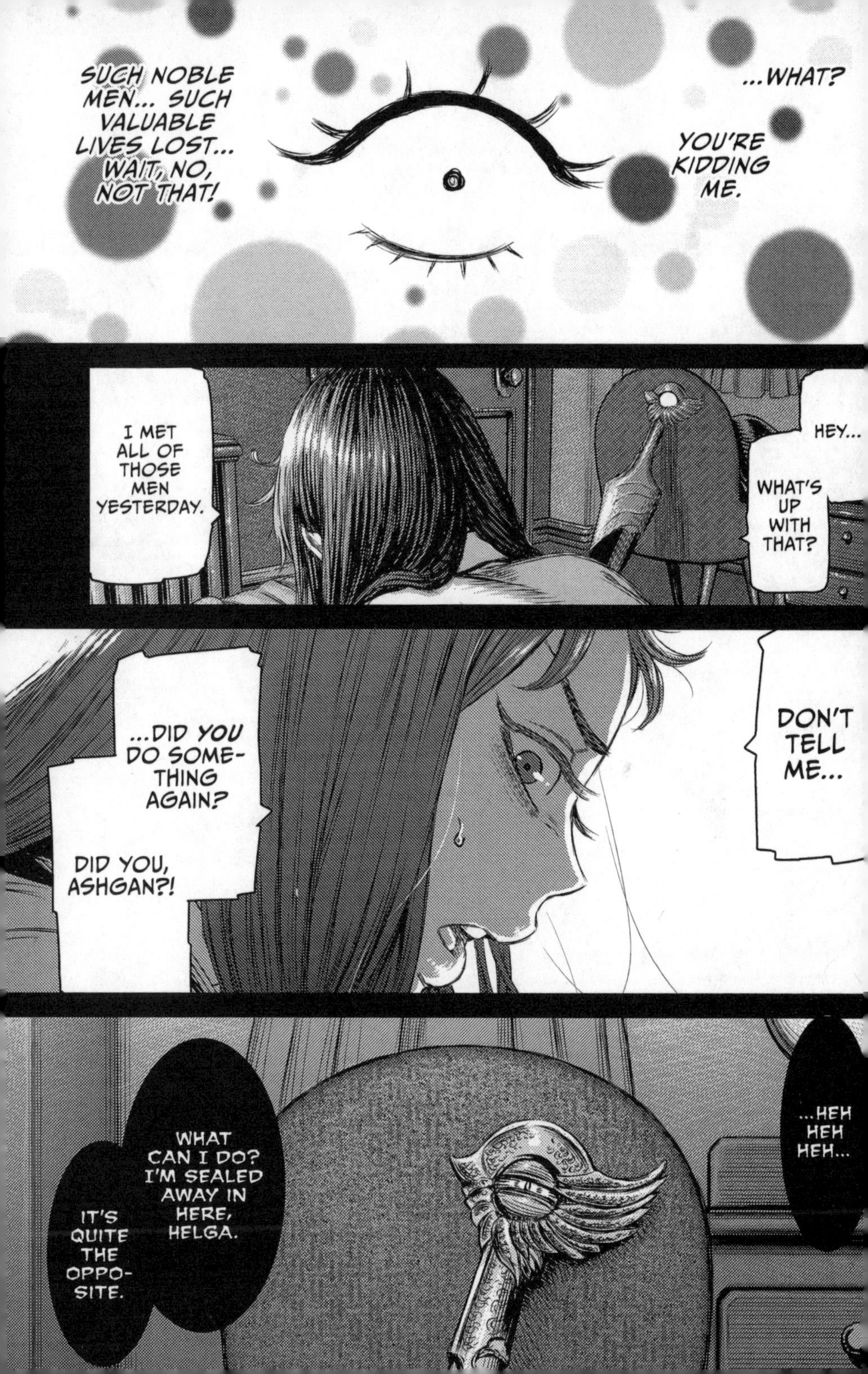
...WHAT?
YOU'RE KIDDING ME.
SUCH NOBLE MEN... SUCH VALUABLE LIVES LOST... WAIT, NO, NOT THAT!
HEY... WHAT'S UP WITH THAT?
I MET ALL OF THOSE MEN YESTERDAY.
DON'T TELL ME...
...DID YOU DO SOMETHING AGAIN?
DID YOU, ASHGAN?!
...HEH HEH HEH...
WHAT CAN I DO? I'M SEALED AWAY IN HERE, HELGA.
IT'S QUITE THE OPPOSITE.

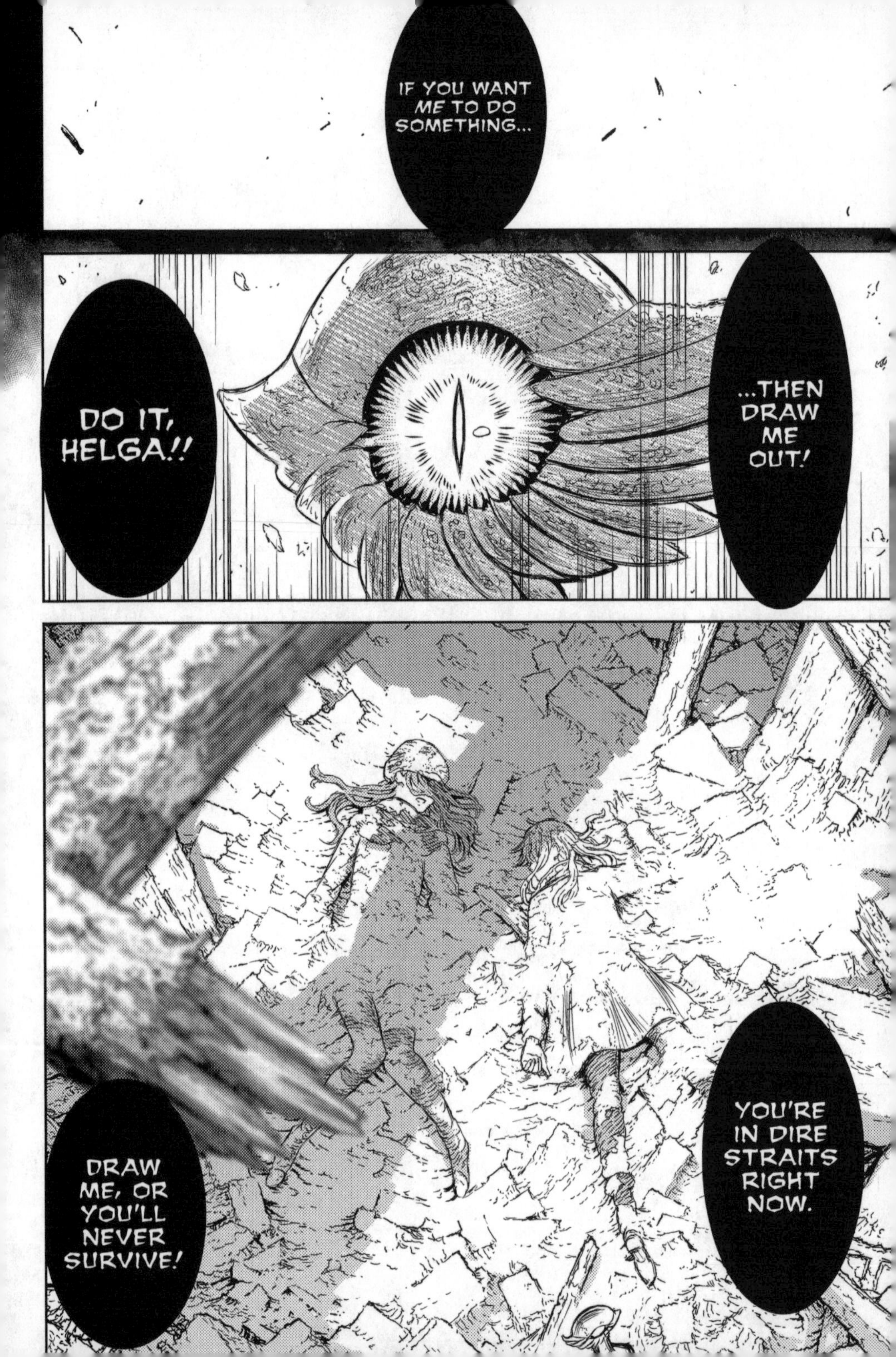
IF YOU WANT ME TO DO SOMETHING...
...THEN DRAW ME OUT!
DO IT, HELGA!!
YOU'RE IN DIRE STRAITS RIGHT NOW.
DRAW ME, OR YOU'LL NEVER SURVIVE!

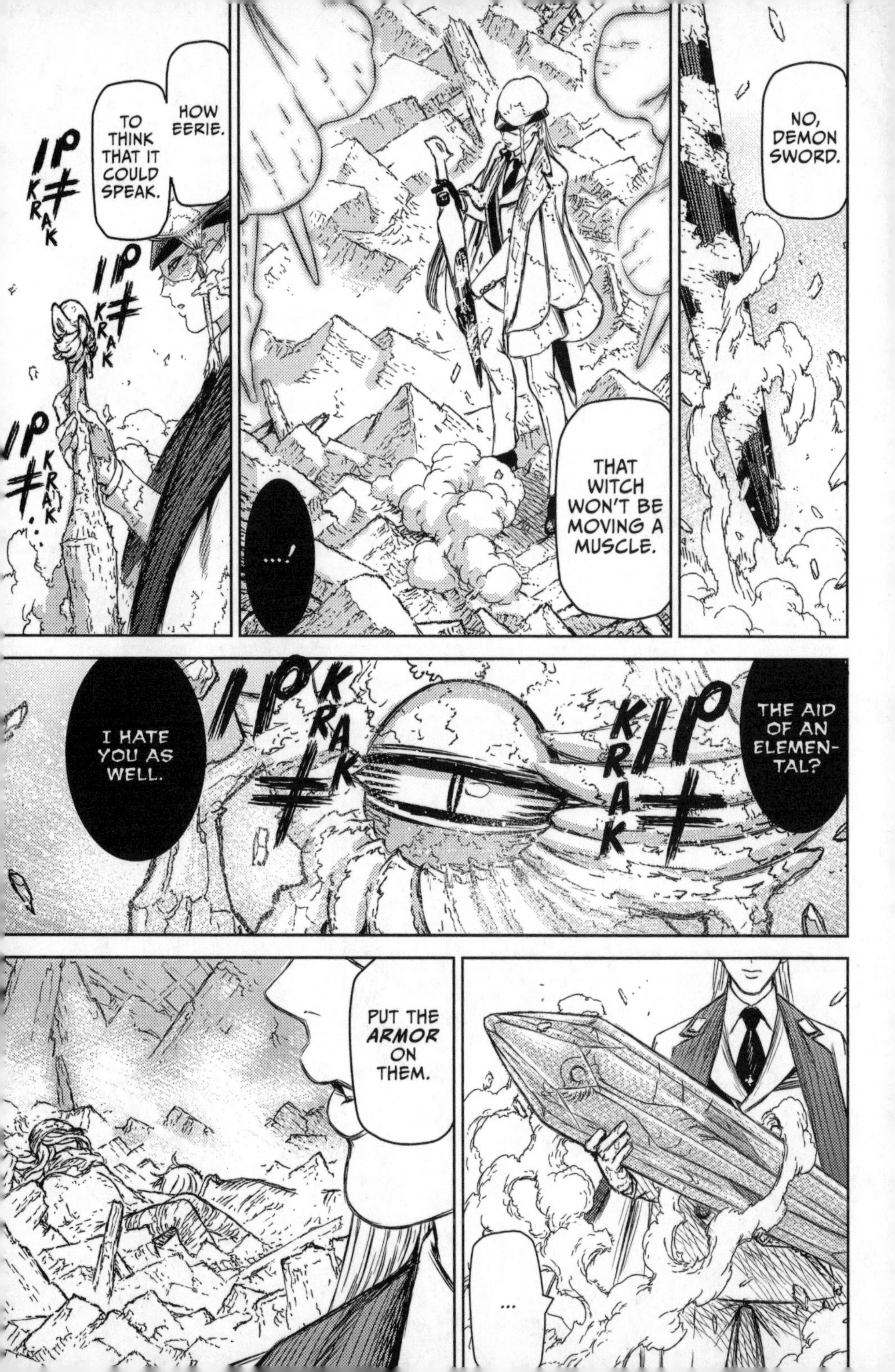
NO, DEMON SWORD.
THAT WITCH WON'T BE MOVING A MUSCLE.
...!
HOW EERIE.
TO THINK THAT IT COULD SPEAK.
KRAK
KRAK
KRAK
THE AID OF AN ELEMEN-TAL?
KRAK
KRAK
I HATE YOU AS WELL.
...
PUT THE ARMOR ON THEM.

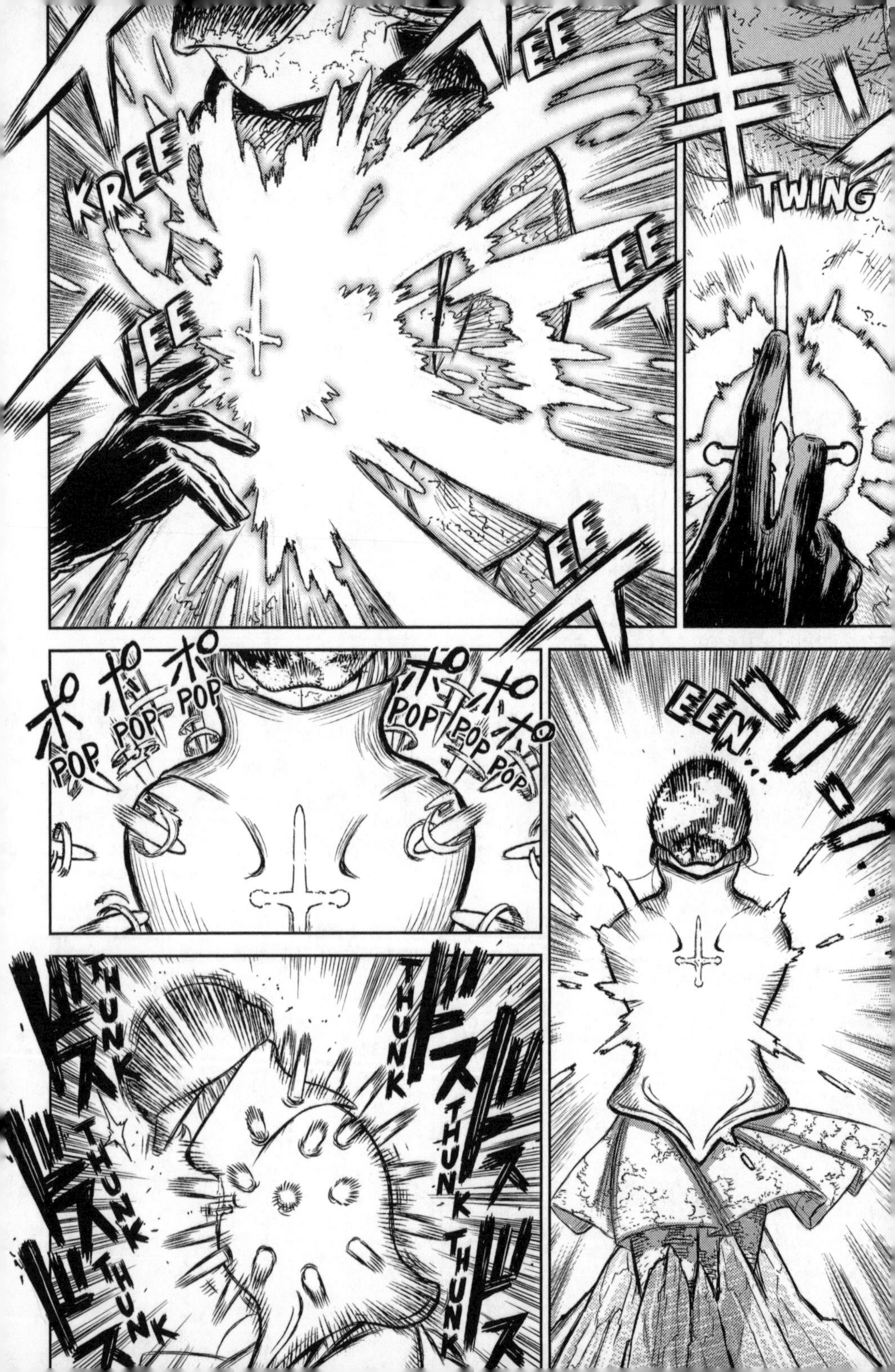

TWING
EE
KREE
EE
EE
EE
EEN...
ポポポ POP POP POP
ポポポ POP POP POP
ドスドス THUNK THUNK THUNK
ドスドス THUNK THUNK THUNK

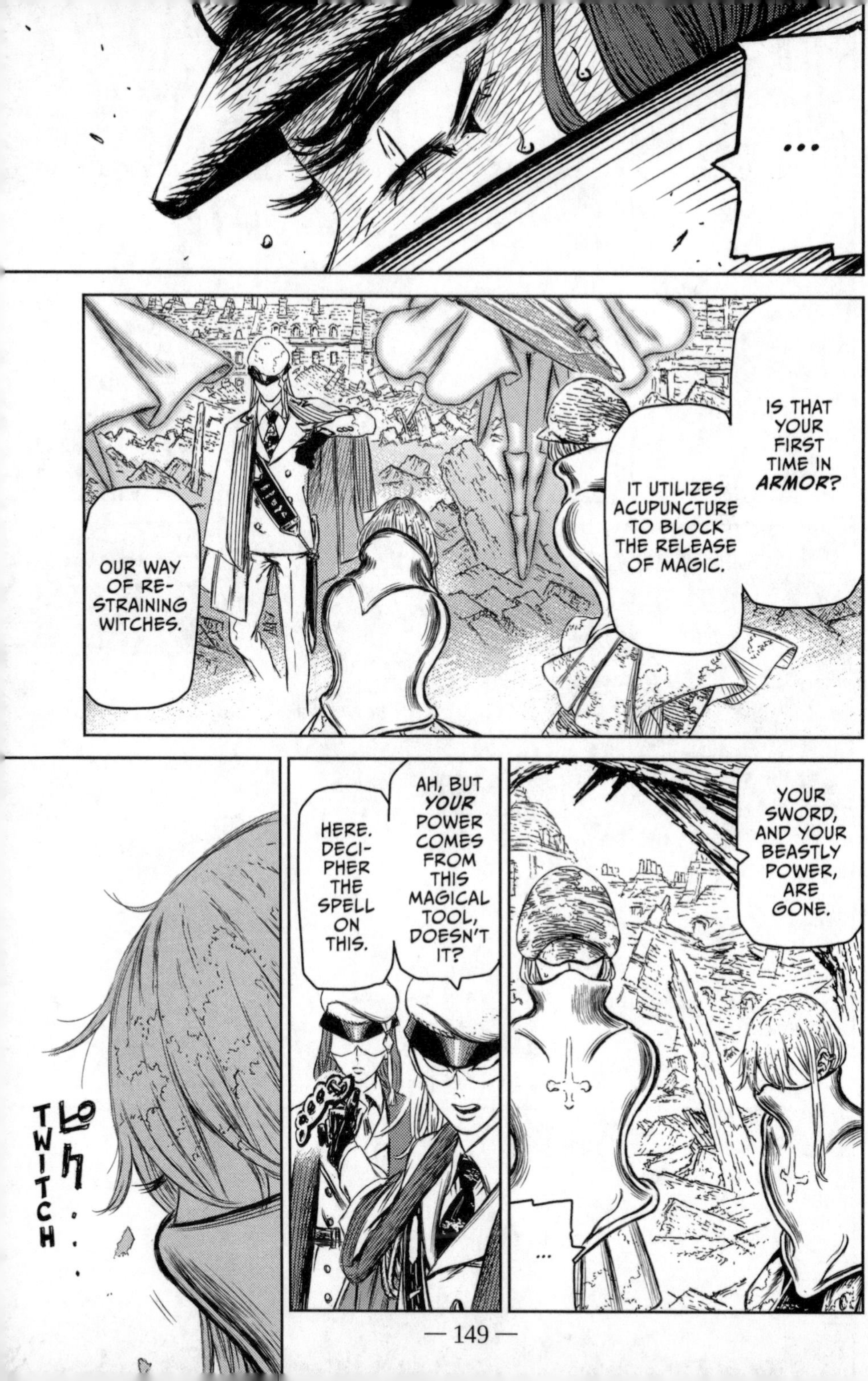
...
IS THAT YOUR FIRST TIME IN *ARMOR*?
IT UTILIZES ACUPUNCTURE TO BLOCK THE RELEASE OF MAGIC.
OUR WAY OF RE-STRAINING WITCHES.
YOUR SWORD, AND YOUR BEASTLY POWER, ARE GONE.
...
AH, BUT *YOUR* POWER COMES FROM THIS MAGICAL TOOL, DOESN'T IT?
HERE. DECIPHER THE SPELL ON THIS.
TWITCH

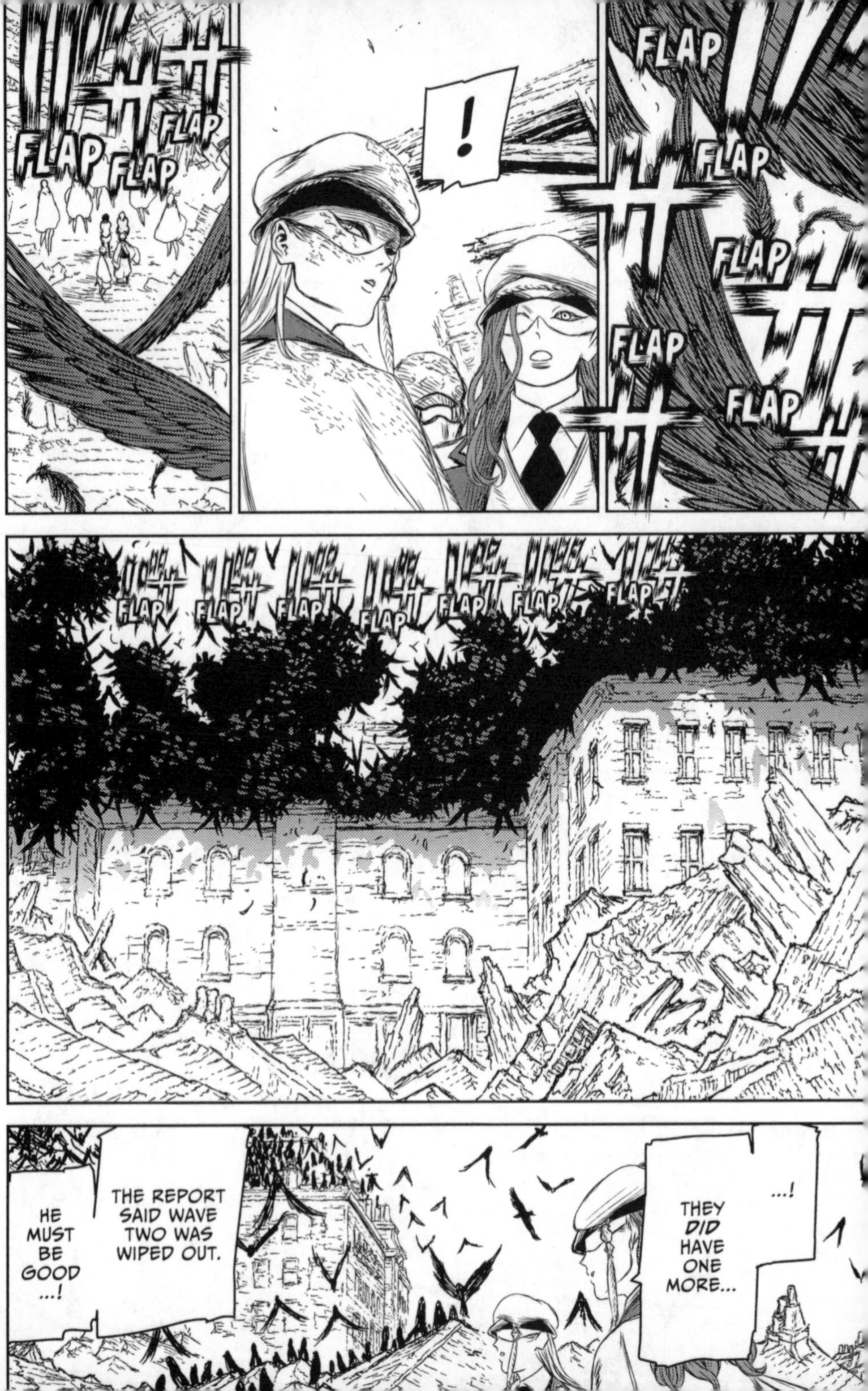
FLAP
FLAP
FLAP
FLAP
FLAP
!
FLAP
FLAP
FLAP
FLAP
FLAP
FLAP
FLAP
FLAP
FLAP
FLAP
...!
THEY DID HAVE ONE MORE...
THE REPORT SAID WAVE TWO WAS WIPED OUT.
HE MUST BE GOOD ...!

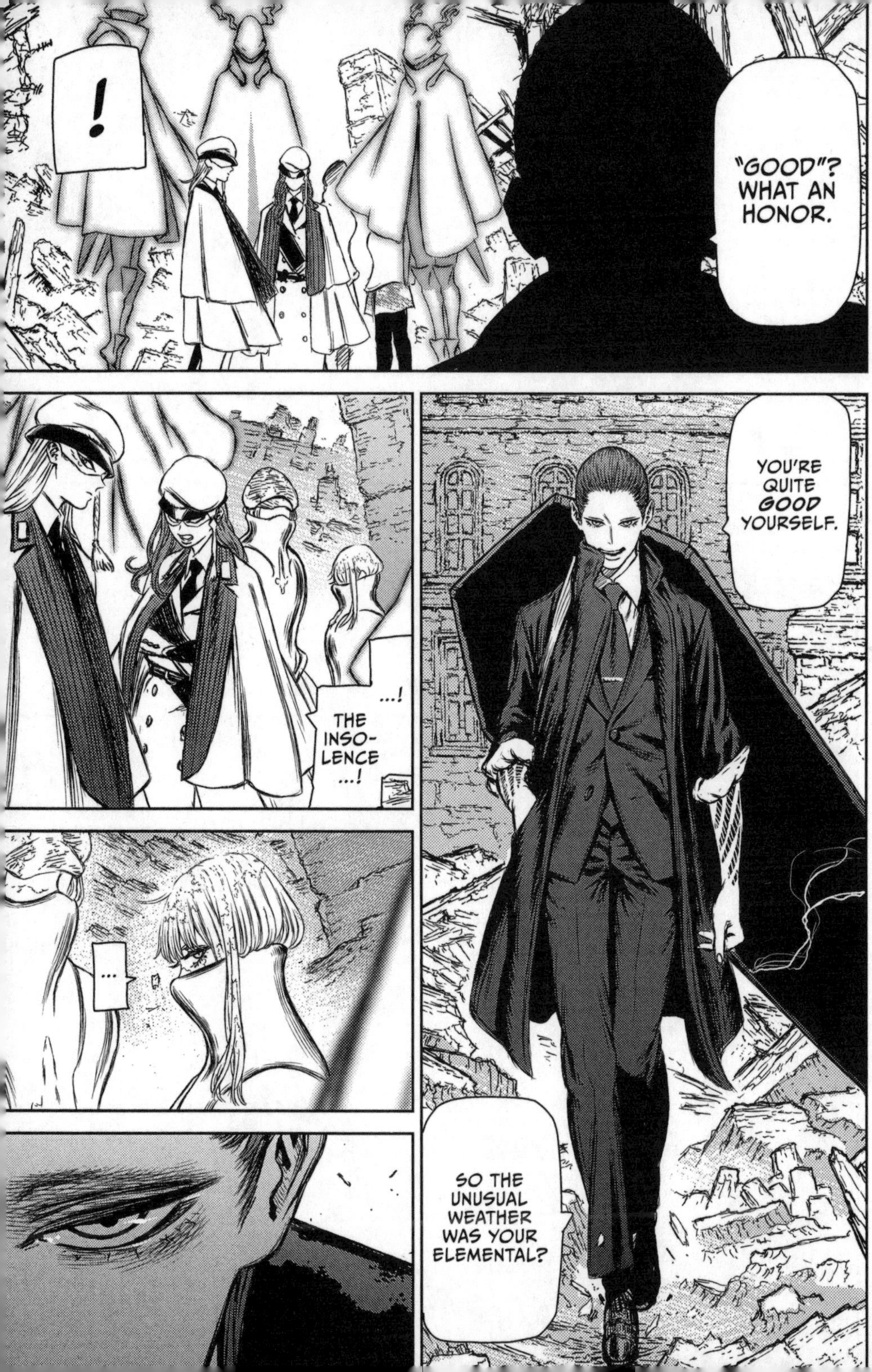
"GOOD"? WHAT AN HONOR.
!
YOU'RE QUITE *GOOD* YOURSELF.
SO THE UNUSUAL WEATHER WAS YOUR ELEMENTAL?
...! THE INSOLENCE ...!
...

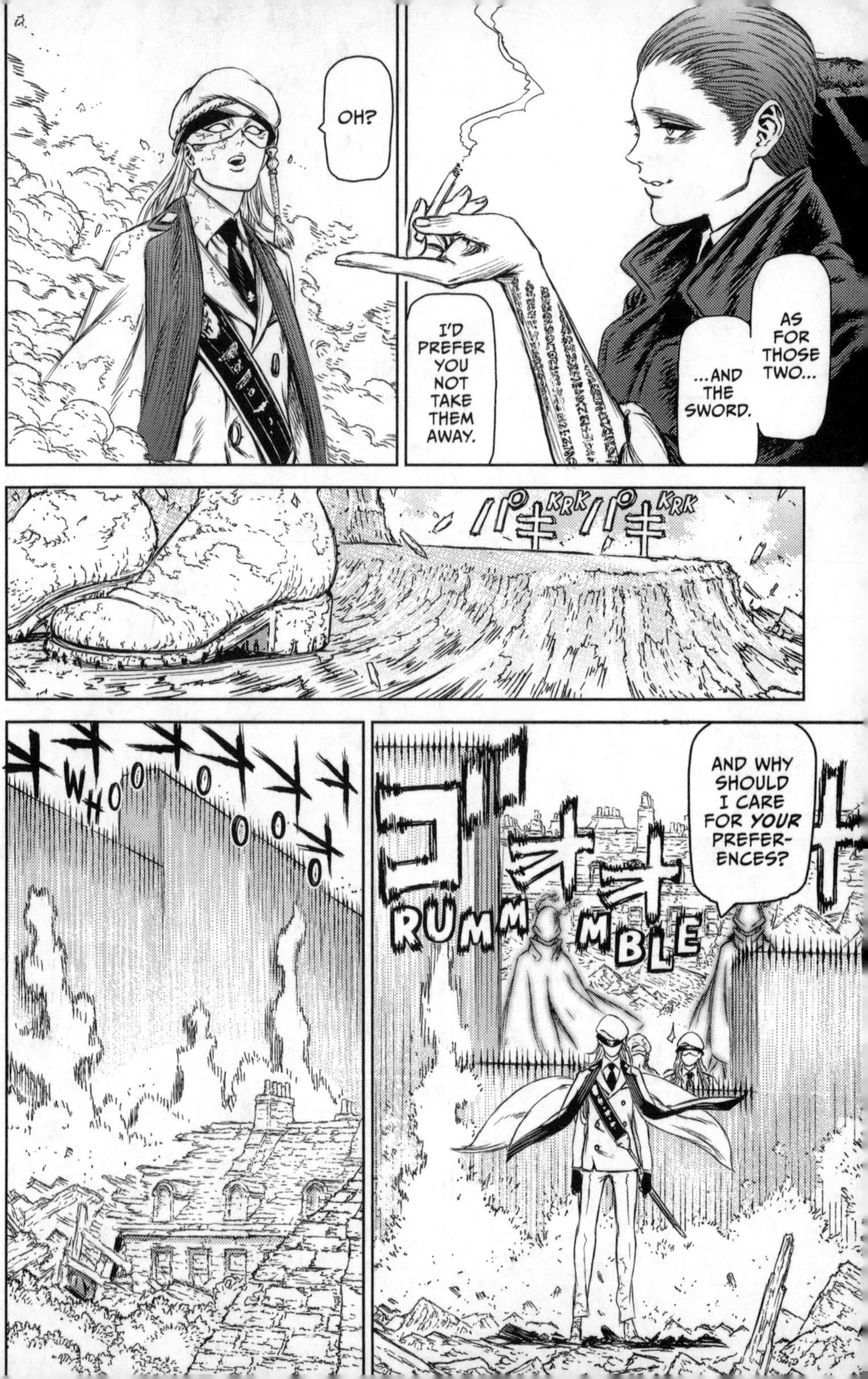
AS FOR THOSE TWO...
...AND THE SWORD.
I'D PREFER YOU NOT TAKE THEM AWAY.
OH?
パキ KRK パキ KRK
AND WHY SHOULD I CARE FOR *YOUR* PREFERENCES?
RUMM MBLE
WHOOOOOO

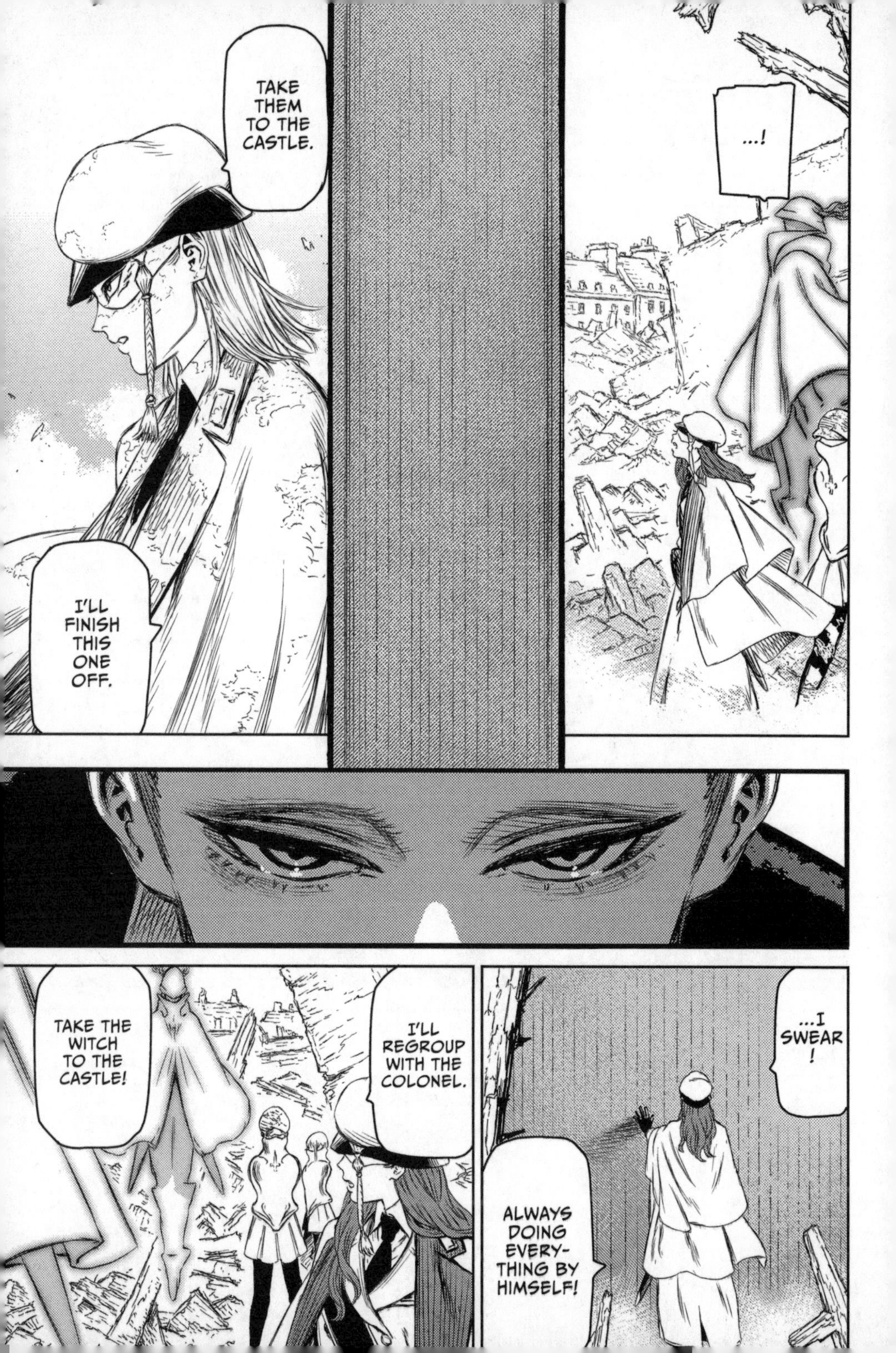
...!
TAKE THEM TO THE CASTLE.
I'LL FINISH THIS ONE OFF.
...I SWEAR!
ALWAYS DOING EVERY-THING BY HIMSELF!
I'LL REGROUP WITH THE COLONEL.
TAKE THE WITCH TO THE CASTLE!

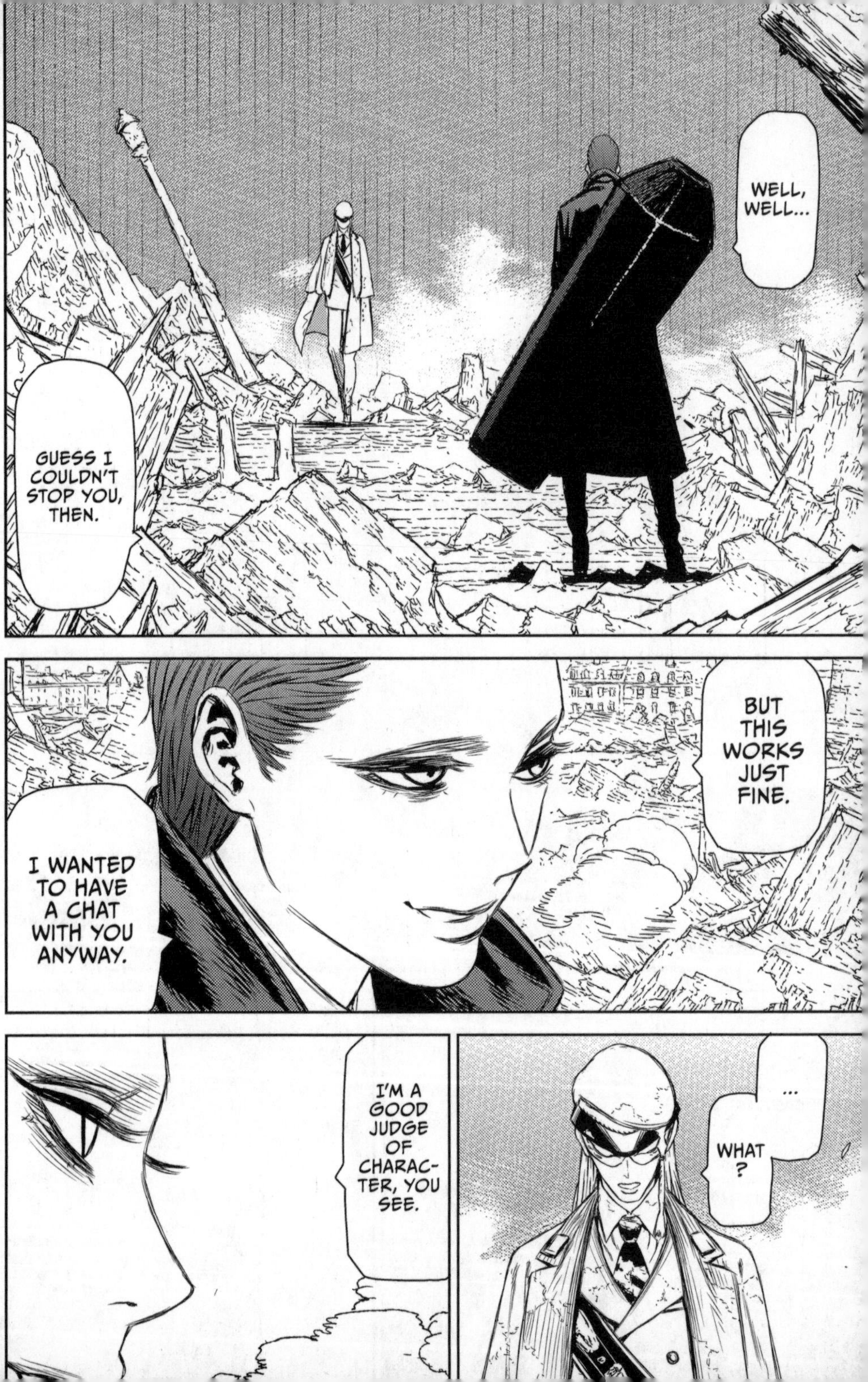
WELL, WELL...
GUESS I COULDN'T STOP YOU, THEN.
BUT THIS WORKS JUST FINE.
I WANTED TO HAVE A CHAT WITH YOU ANYWAY.
... WHAT?
I'M A GOOD JUDGE OF CHARACTER, YOU SEE.

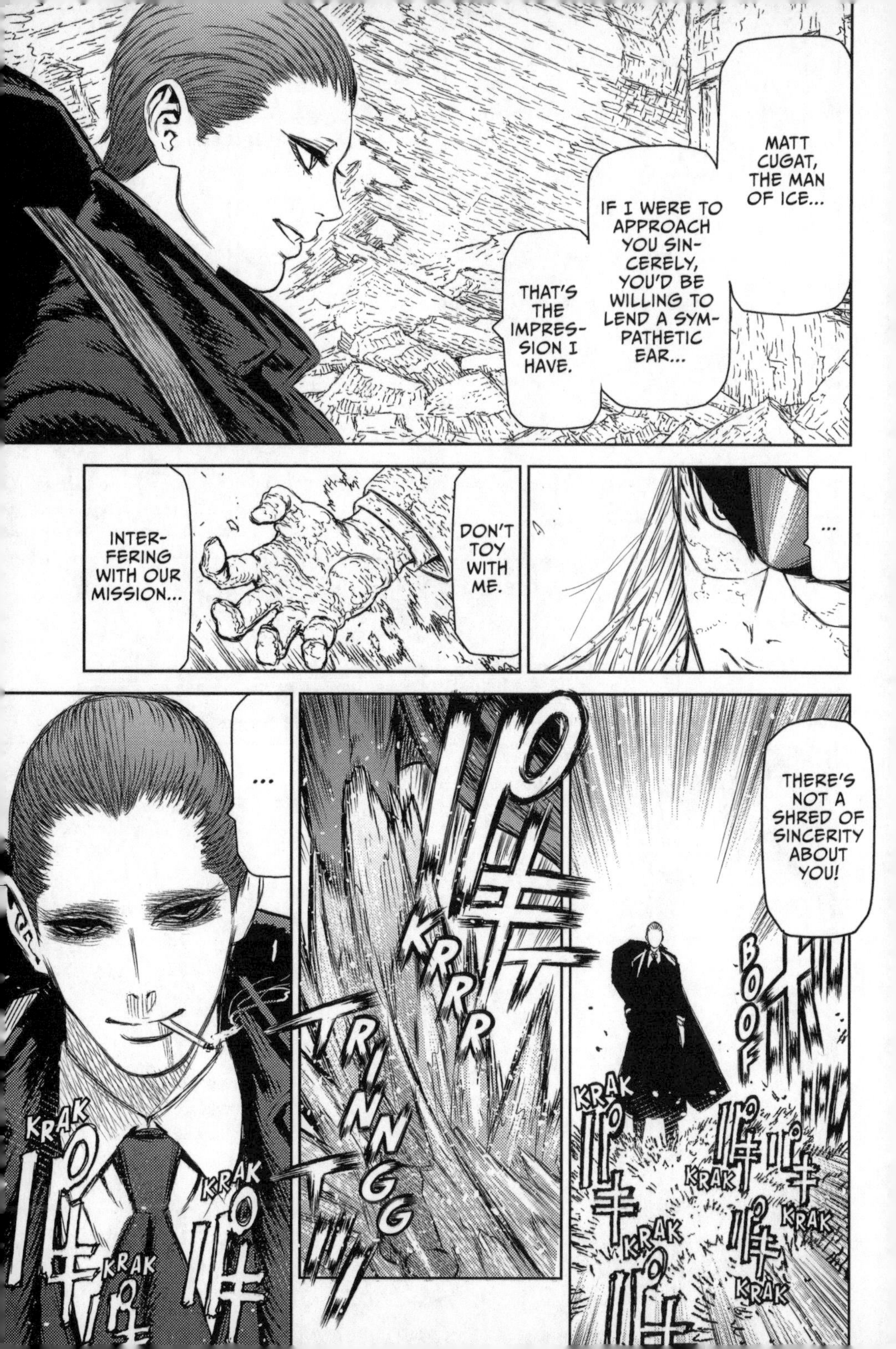
MATT CUGAT, THE MAN OF ICE...
IF I WERE TO APPROACH YOU SINCERELY, YOU'D BE WILLING TO LEND A SYMPATHETIC EAR...
THAT'S THE IMPRESSION I HAVE.
...
DON'T TOY WITH ME.
INTERFERING WITH OUR MISSION...
THERE'S NOT A SHRED OF SINCERITY ABOUT YOU!
BOOOF
KRAK
KRAK
KRAK
KRAK
KRAK
KRRRR
TRINNNGG
...
KRAK
KRAK
KRAK

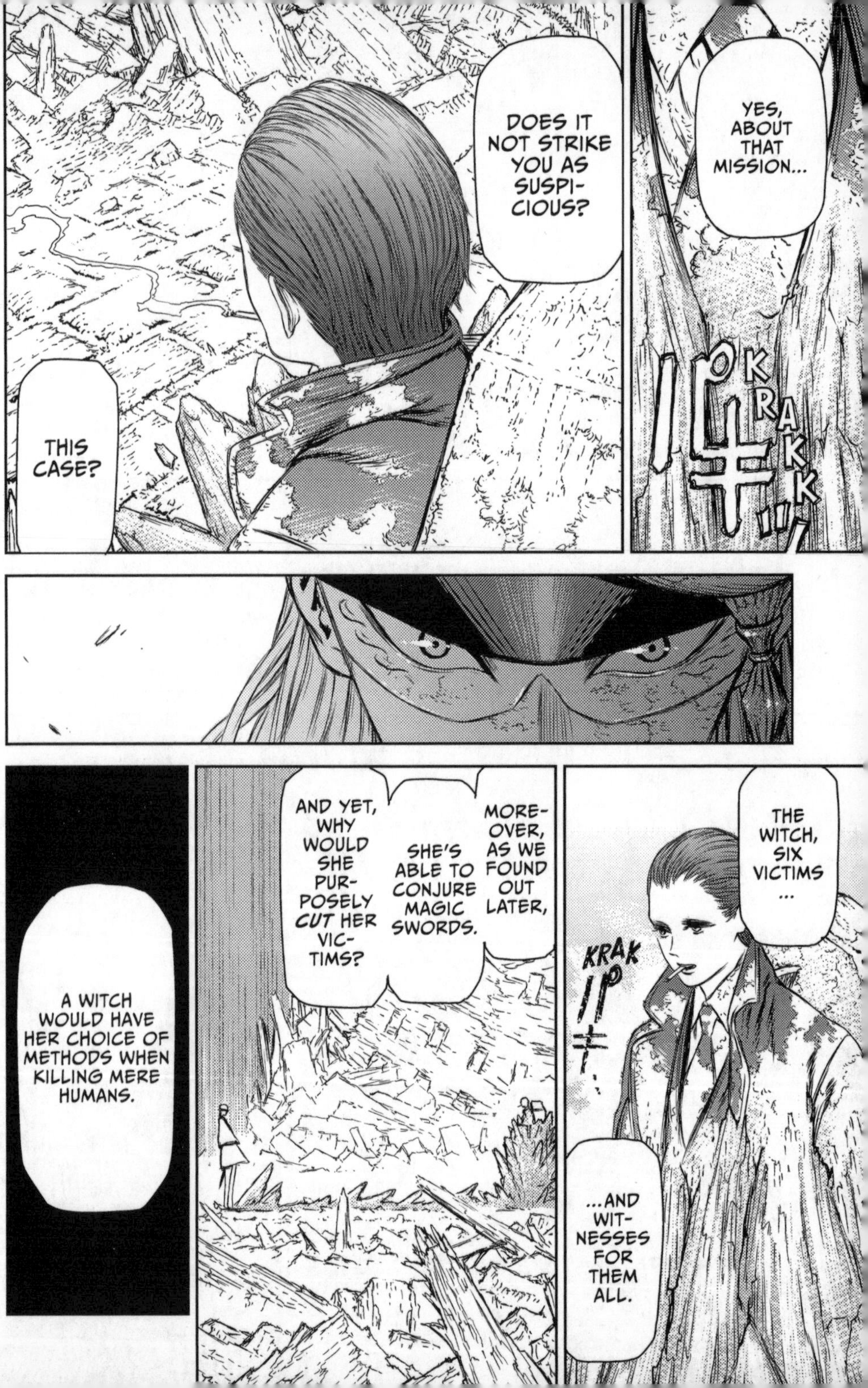
YES, ABOUT THAT MISSION...
KRAKK
DOES IT NOT STRIKE YOU AS SUSPICIOUS?
THIS CASE?
THE WITCH, SIX VICTIMS ...
KRAK
...AND WITNESSES FOR THEM ALL.
MOREOVER, AS WE FOUND OUT LATER,
SHE'S ABLE TO CONJURE MAGIC SWORDS.
AND YET, WHY WOULD SHE PURPOSELY *CUT* HER VICTIMS?
A WITCH WOULD HAVE HER CHOICE OF METHODS WHEN KILLING MERE HUMANS.

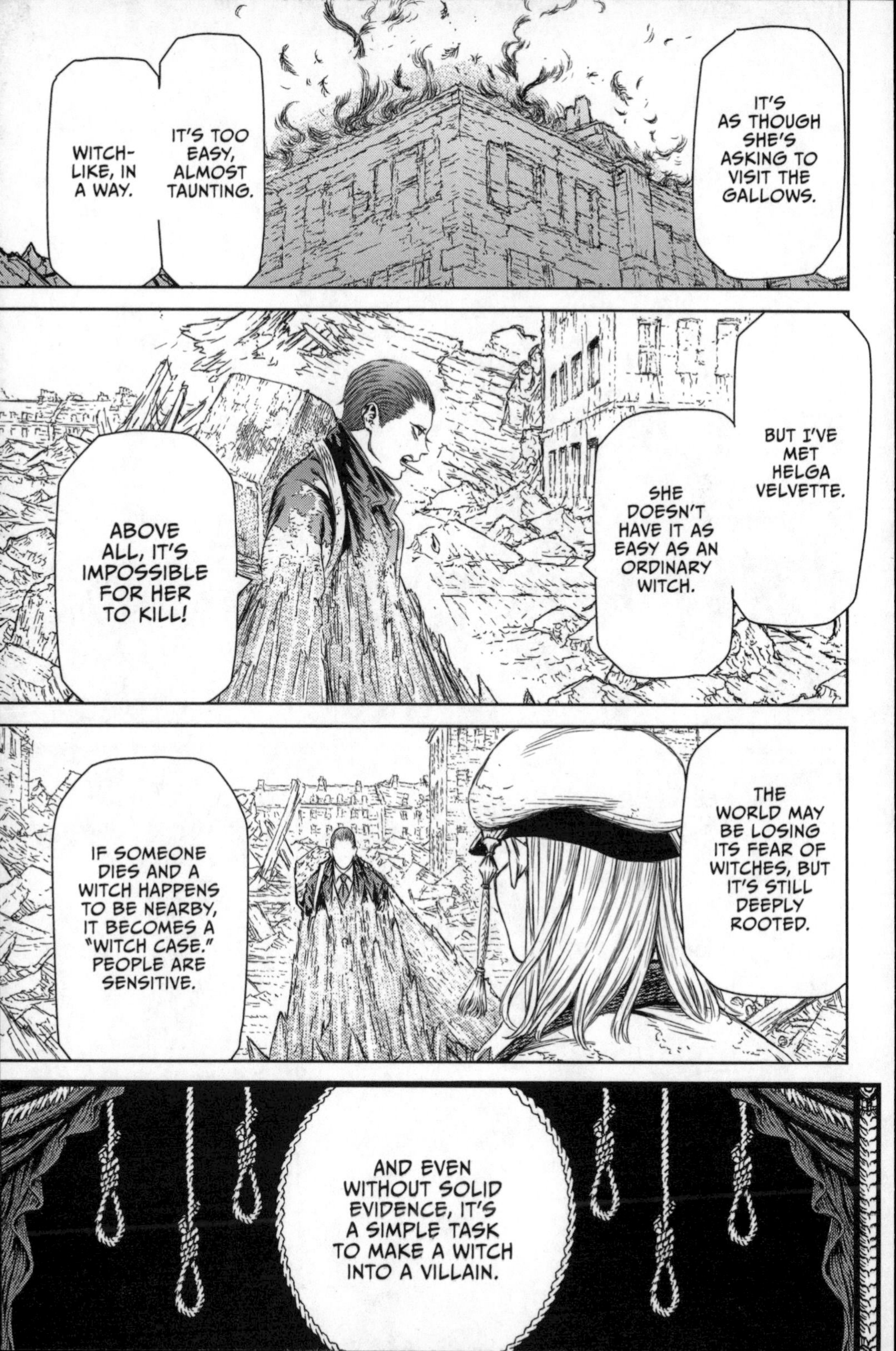
IT'S AS THOUGH SHE'S ASKING TO VISIT THE GALLOWS.
IT'S TOO EASY, ALMOST TAUNTING.
WITCH-LIKE, IN A WAY.
BUT I'VE MET HELGA VELVETTE.
SHE DOESN'T HAVE IT AS EASY AS AN ORDINARY WITCH.
ABOVE ALL, IT'S IMPOSSIBLE FOR HER TO KILL!
THE WORLD MAY BE LOSING ITS FEAR OF WITCHES, BUT IT'S STILL DEEPLY ROOTED.
IF SOMEONE DIES AND A WITCH HAPPENS TO BE NEARBY, IT BECOMES A "WITCH CASE." PEOPLE ARE SENSITIVE.
AND EVEN WITHOUT SOLID EVIDENCE, IT'S A SIMPLE TASK TO MAKE A WITCH INTO A VILLAIN.

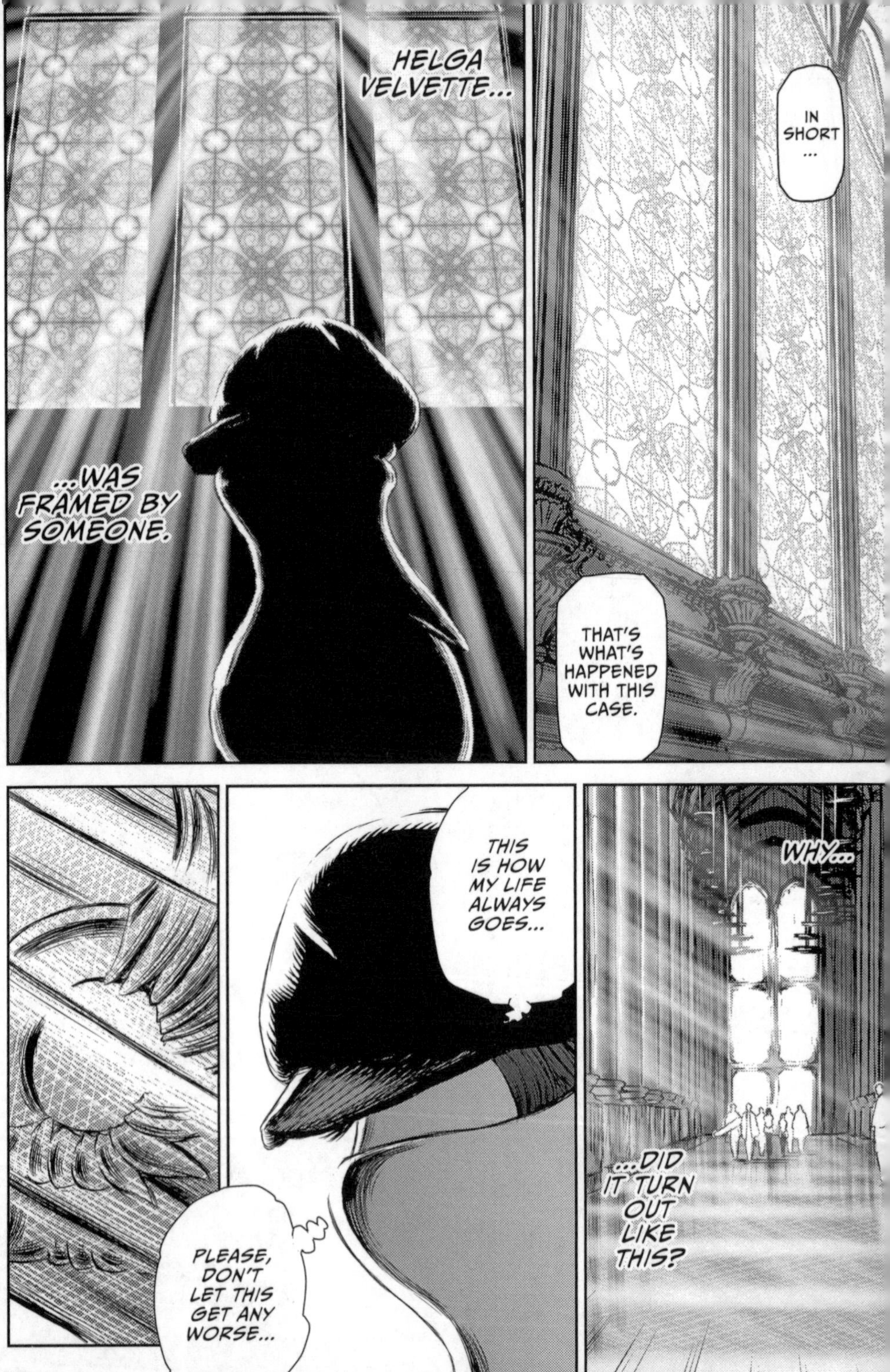
IN SHORT...
THAT'S WHAT'S HAPPENED WITH THIS CASE.
HELGA VELVETTE...
...WAS FRAMED BY SOMEONE.
WHY...
...DID IT TURN OUT LIKE THIS?
THIS IS HOW MY LIFE ALWAYS GOES...
PLEASE, DON'T LET THIS GET ANY WORSE...

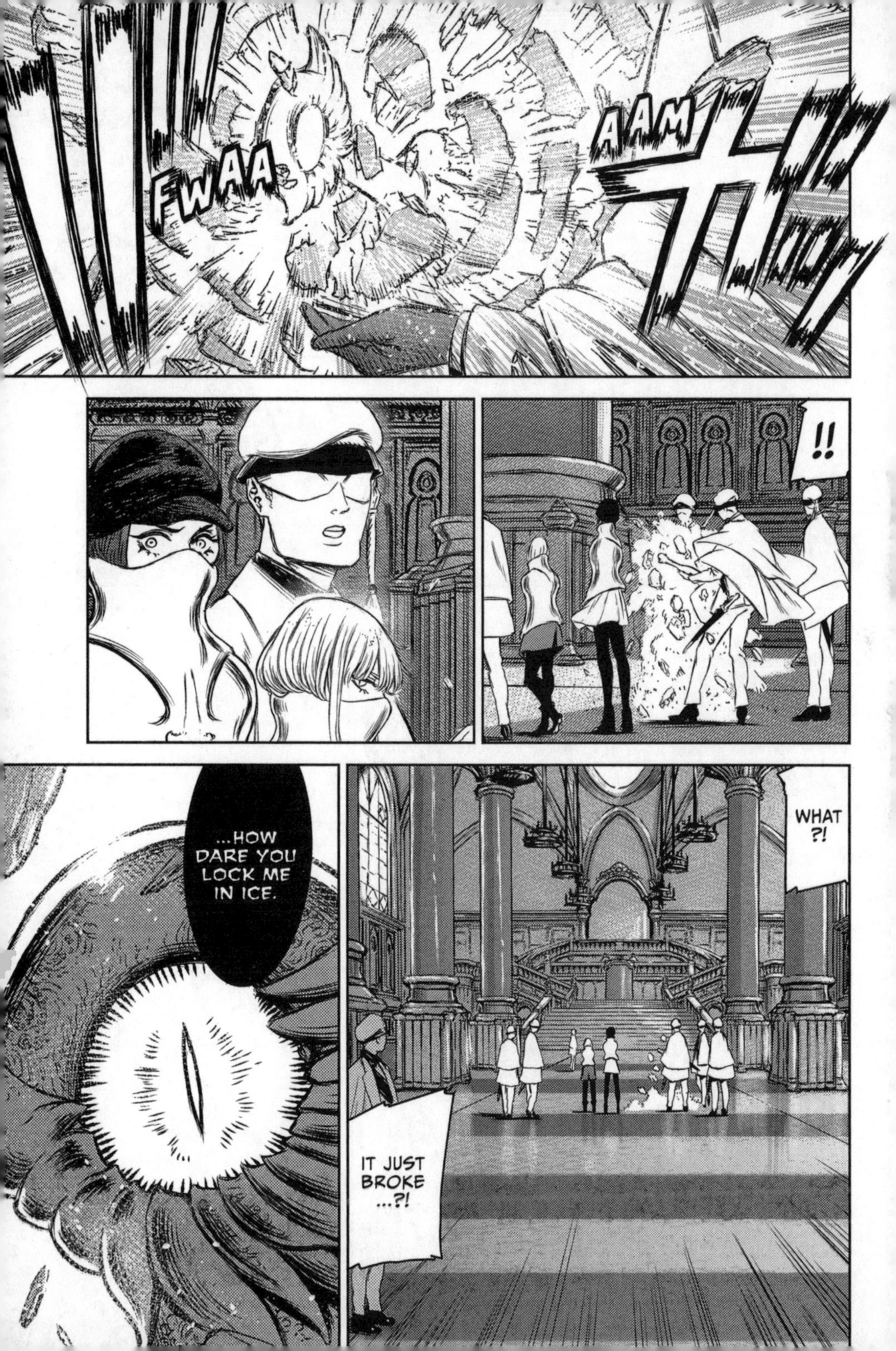
FWAA
AAM
!!
WHAT ?!
IT JUST BROKE ...?!
...HOW DARE YOU LOCK ME IN ICE.

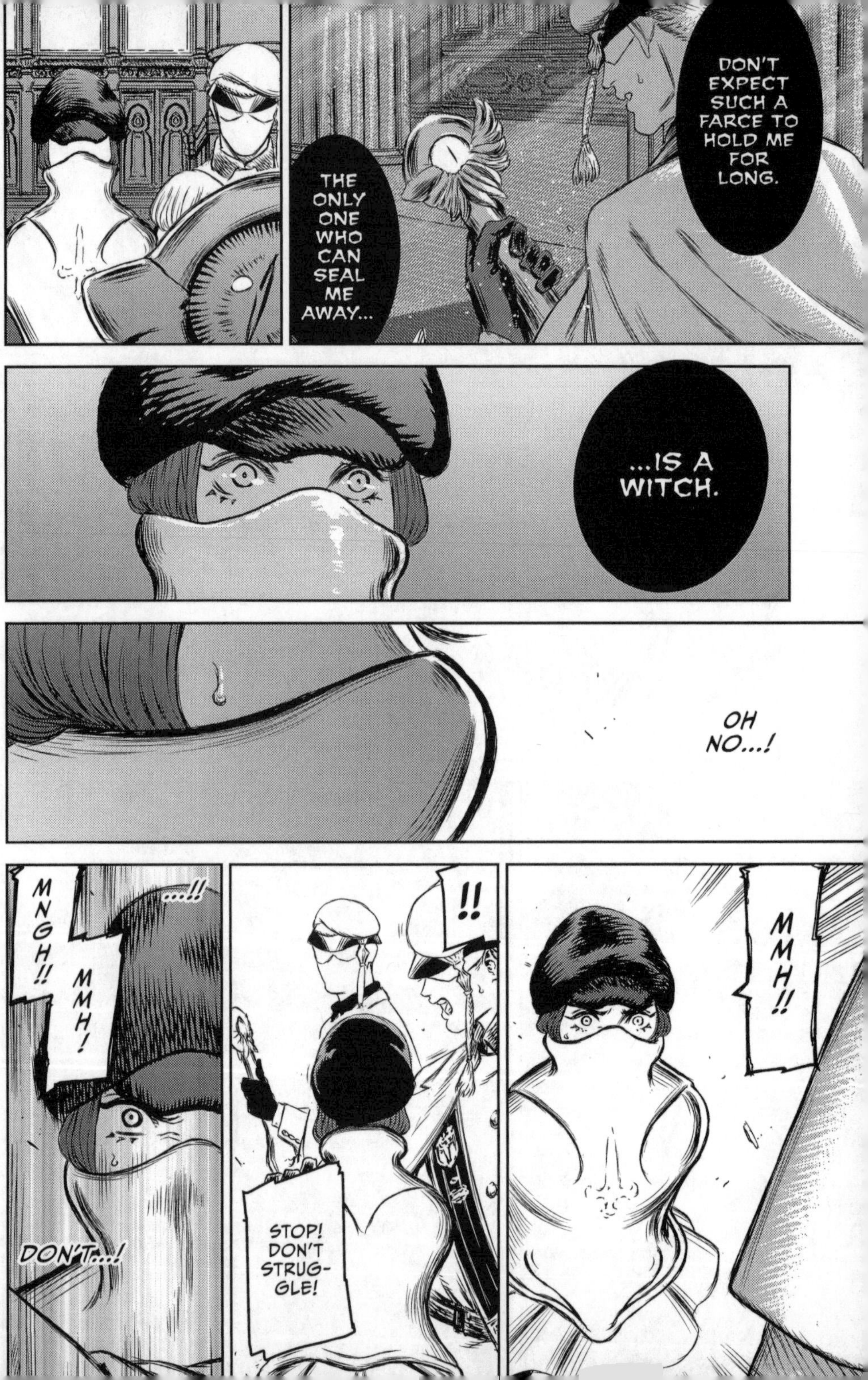
DON'T EXPECT SUCH A FARCE TO HOLD ME FOR LONG.
THE ONLY ONE WHO CAN SEAL ME AWAY...
...IS A WITCH.
OH NO...!
MMH!!
!!
STOP! DON'T STRUG-GLE!
...!!
MNGH!!
MMH!
DON'T...!

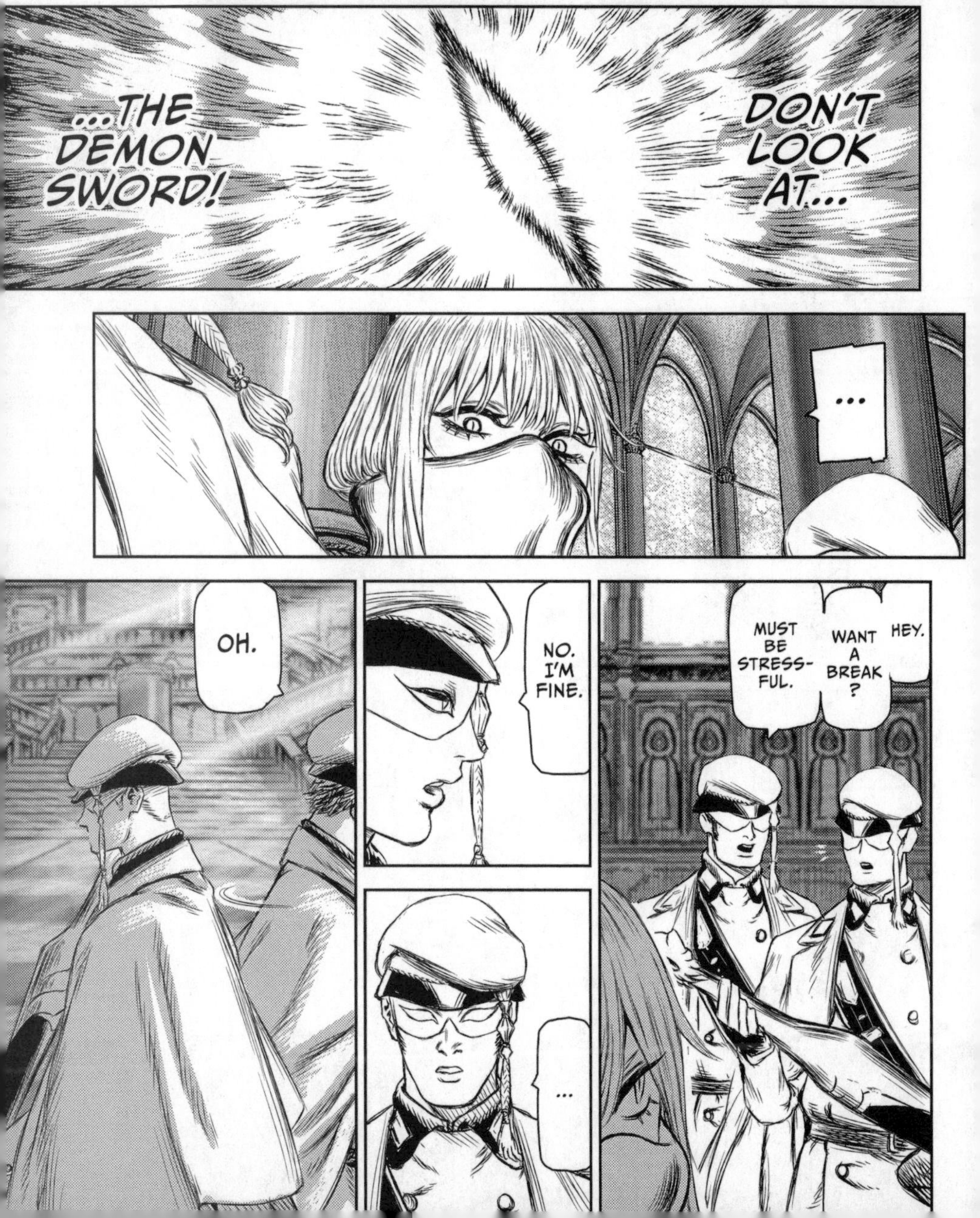
DON'T LOOK AT...
...THE DEMON SWORD!
...
HEY.
WANT A BREAK?
MUST BE STRESSFUL.
NO. I'M FINE.
...
OH.

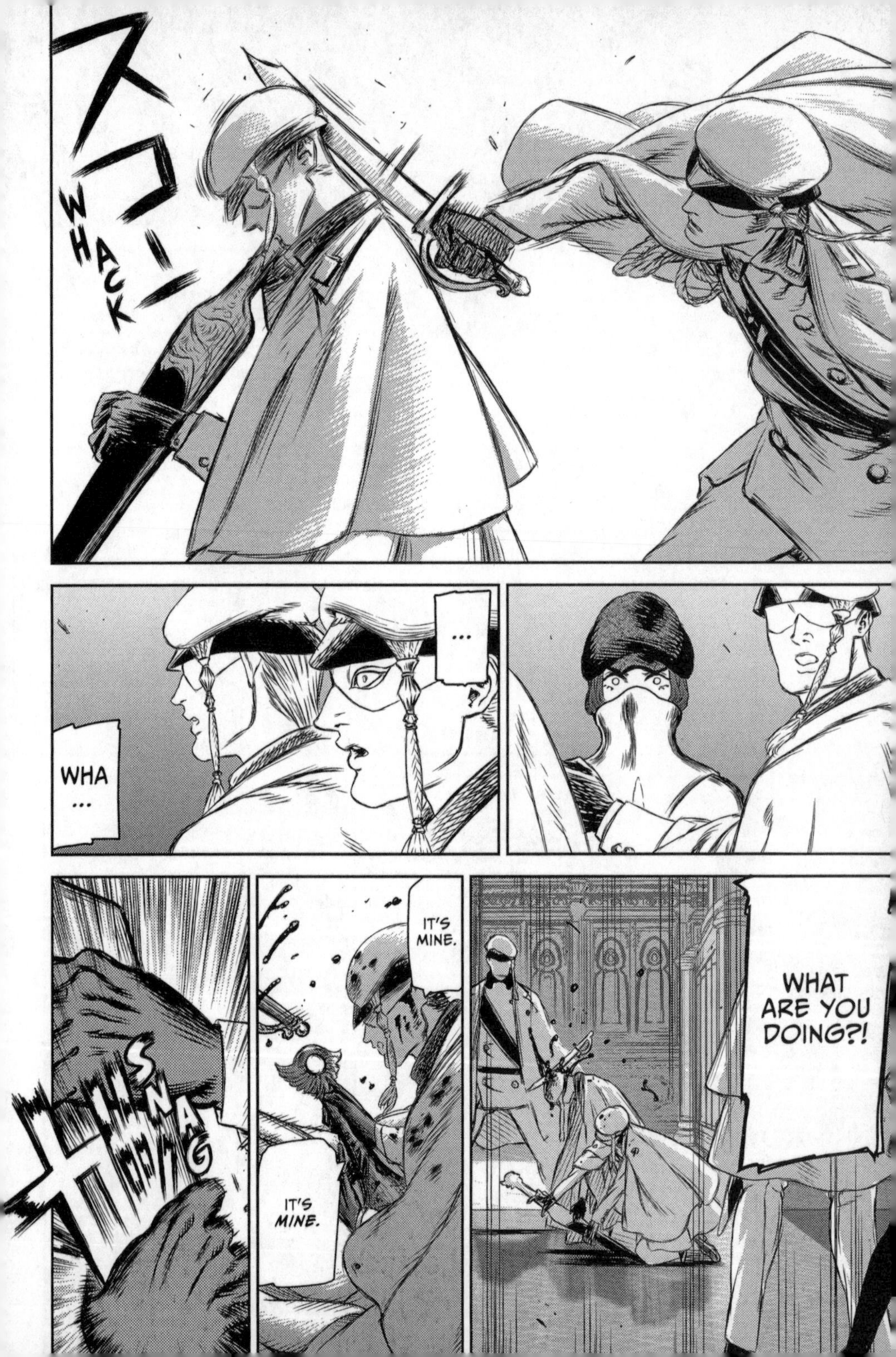
WHACK
...
WHA ...
WHAT ARE YOU DOING?!
IT'S MINE.
IT'S MINE.
SNAG

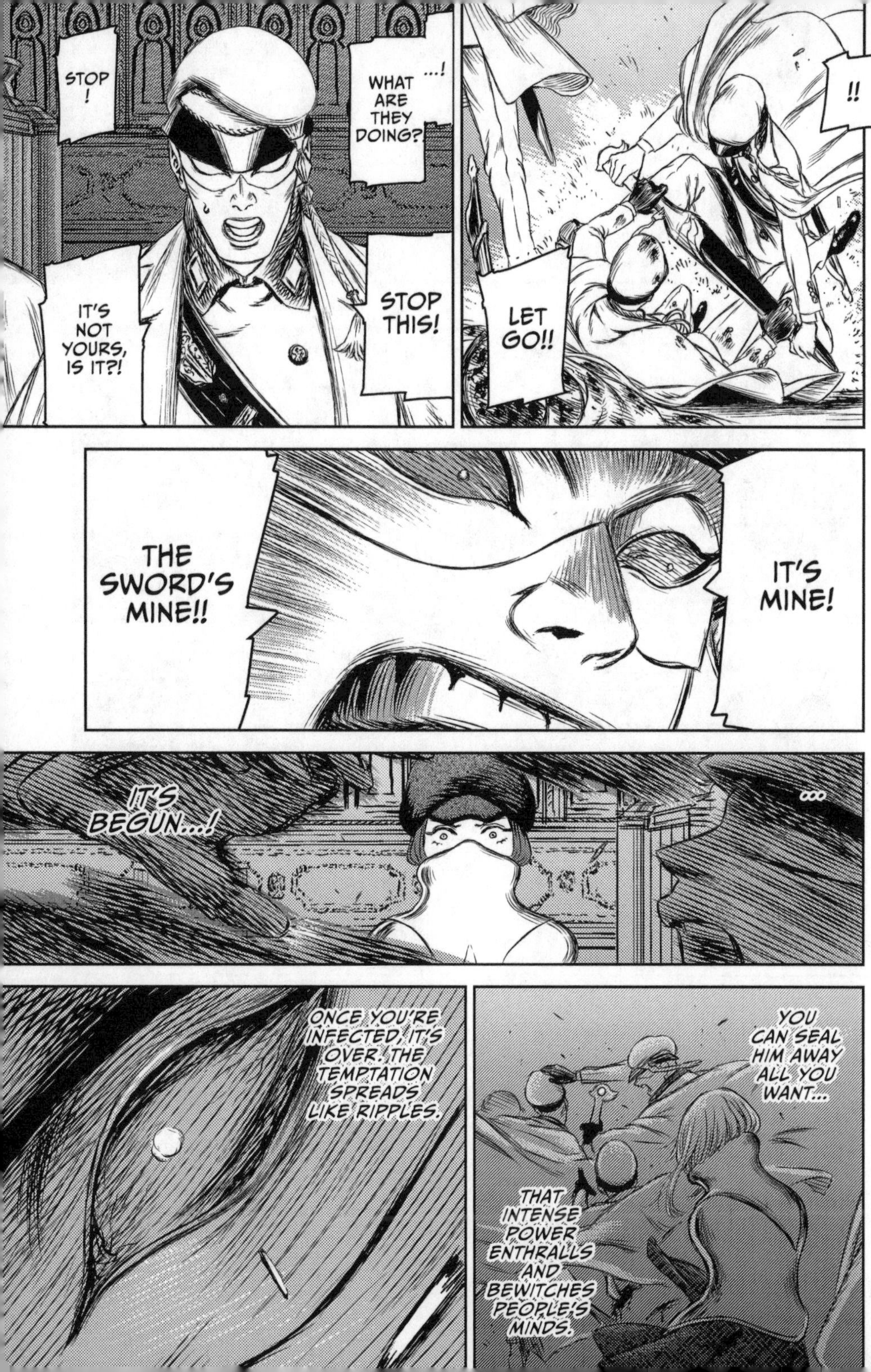
!!
LET GO!!
...!
WHAT ARE THEY DOING?!
STOP!
STOP THIS!
IT'S NOT YOURS, IS IT?!
IT'S MINE!
THE SWORD'S MINE!!
...
IT'S BEGUN...!
YOU CAN SEAL HIM AWAY ALL YOU WANT...
THAT INTENSE POWER ENTHRALLS AND BEWITCHES PEOPLE'S MINDS.
ONCE YOU'RE INFECTED, IT'S OVER. THE TEMPTATION SPREADS LIKE RIPPLES.

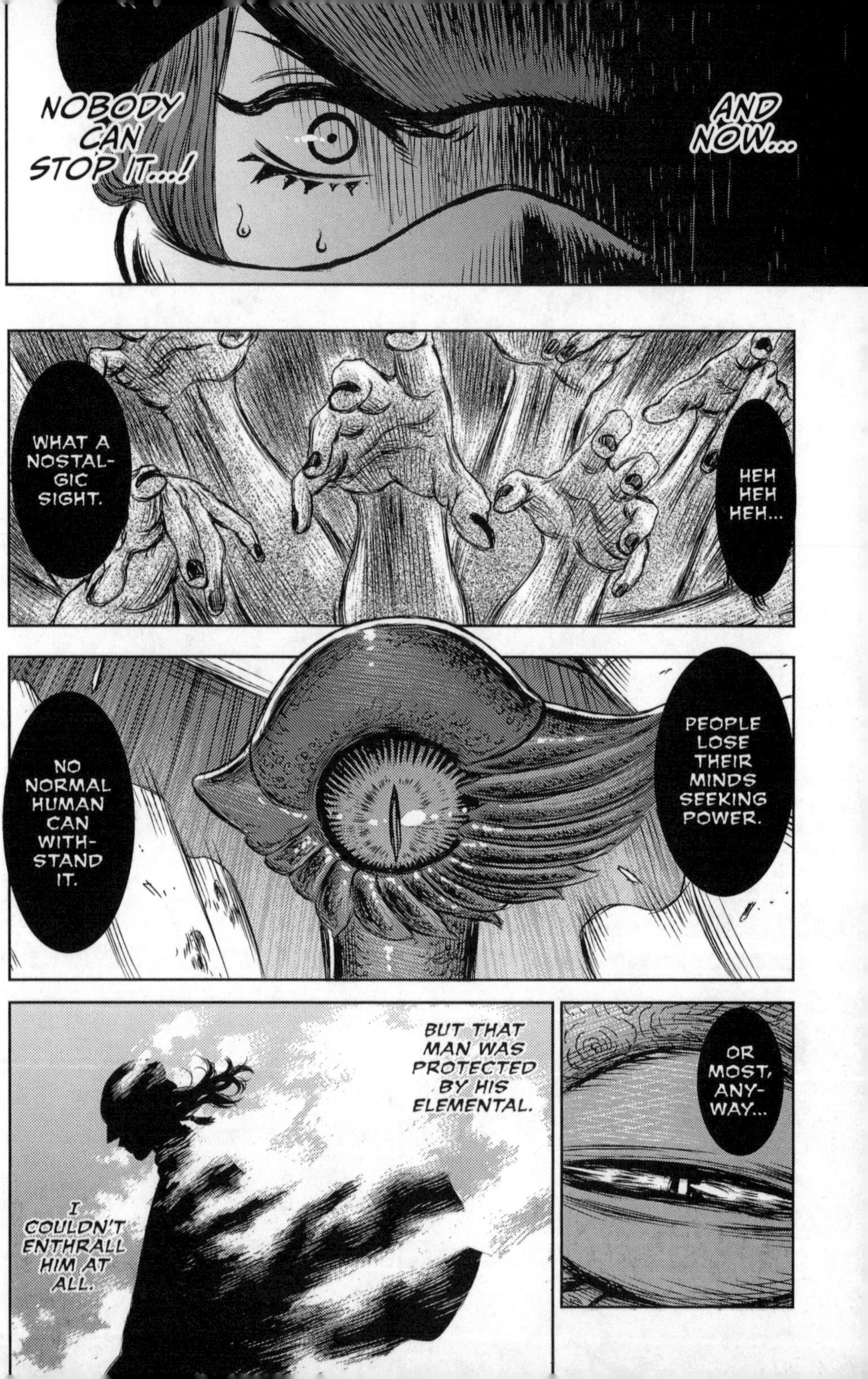
AND NOW...
NOBODY CAN STOP IT...!
HEH HEH HEH...
WHAT A NOSTALGIC SIGHT.
PEOPLE LOSE THEIR MINDS SEEKING POWER.
NO NORMAL HUMAN CAN WITHSTAND IT.
OR MOST, ANYWAY...
BUT THAT MAN WAS PROTECTED BY HIS ELEMENTAL.
I COULDN'T ENTHRALL HIM AT ALL.

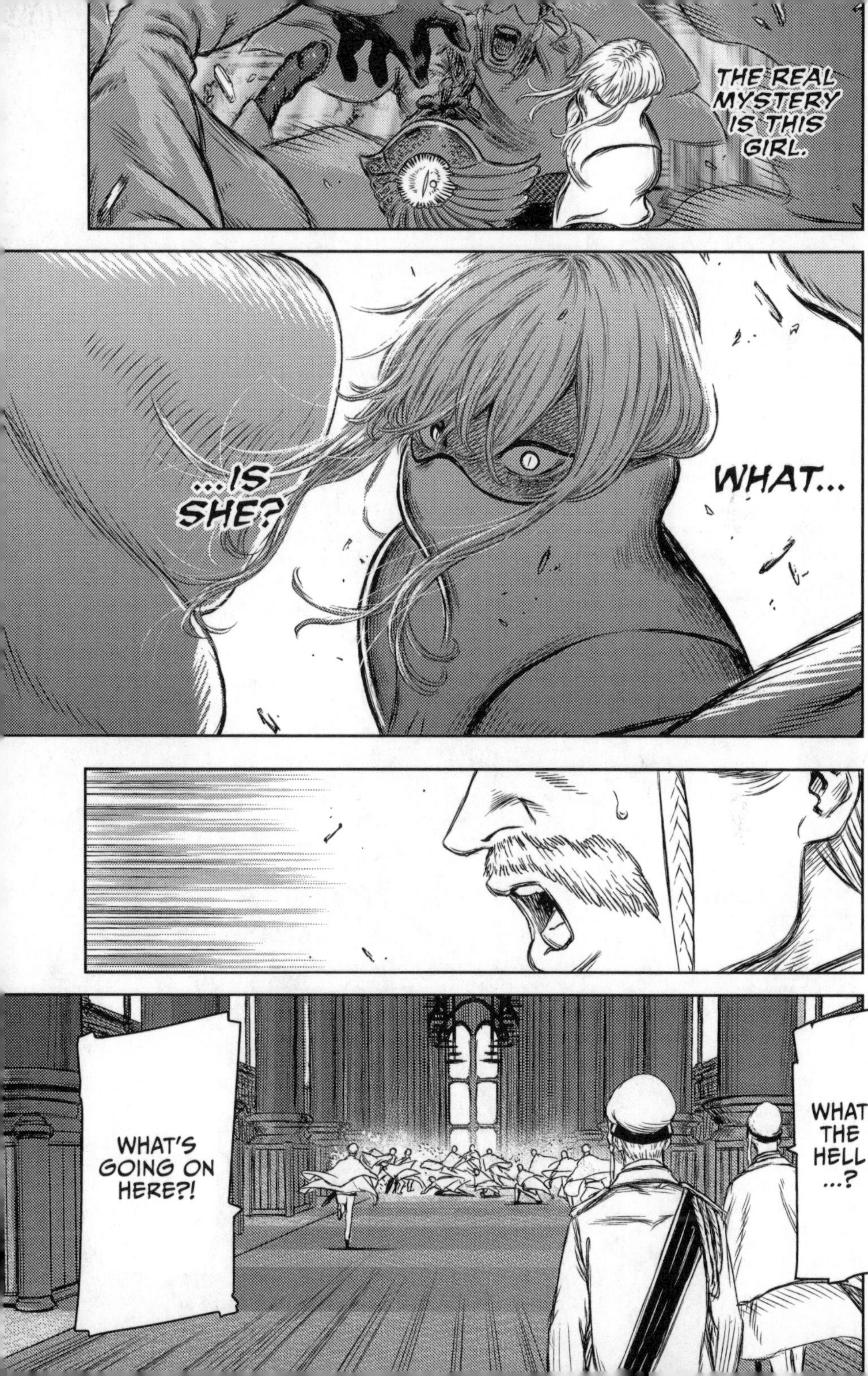
THE REAL MYSTERY IS THIS GIRL.
WHAT...
...IS SHE?
WHAT THE HELL ...?
WHAT'S GOING ON HERE?!

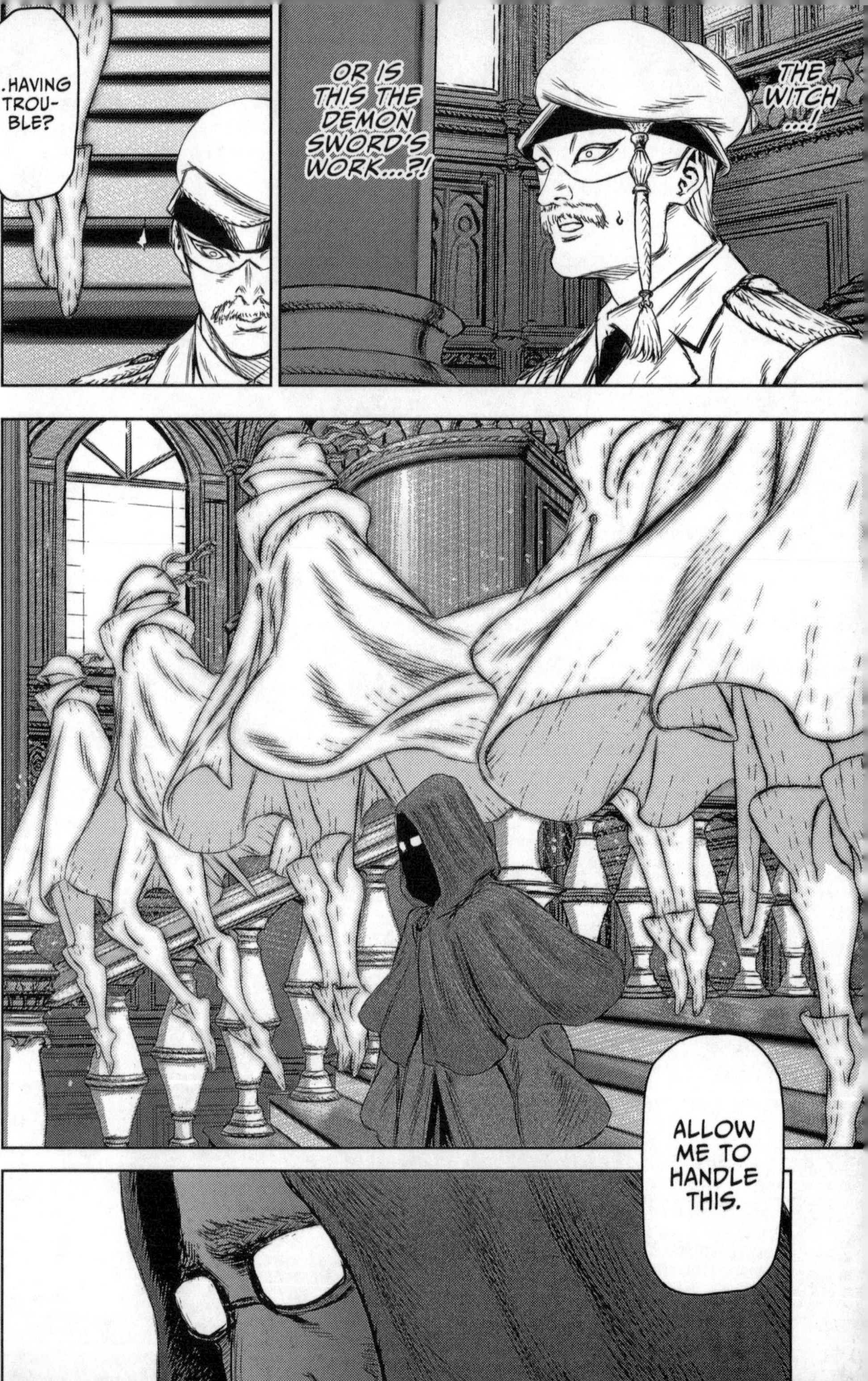
THE WITCH ...!
OR IS THIS THE DEMON SWORD'S WORK...?!
...HAVING TROU-BLE?
ALLOW ME TO HANDLE THIS.

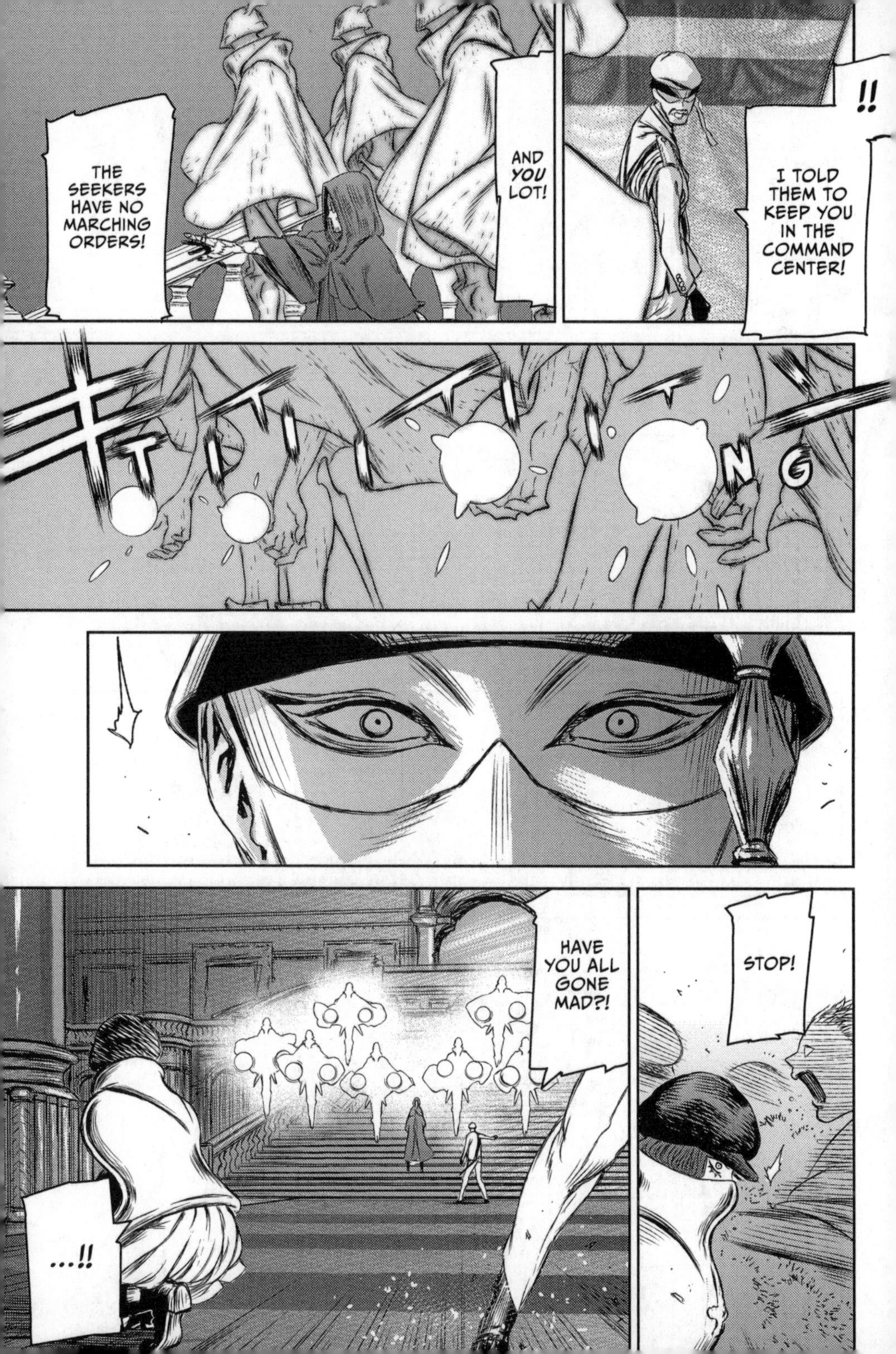
!!
I TOLD THEM TO KEEP YOU IN THE COMMAND CENTER!
AND *YOU* LOT!
THE SEEKERS HAVE NO MARCHING ORDERS!
TIIING
STOP!
HAVE YOU ALL GONE MAD?!
...!!

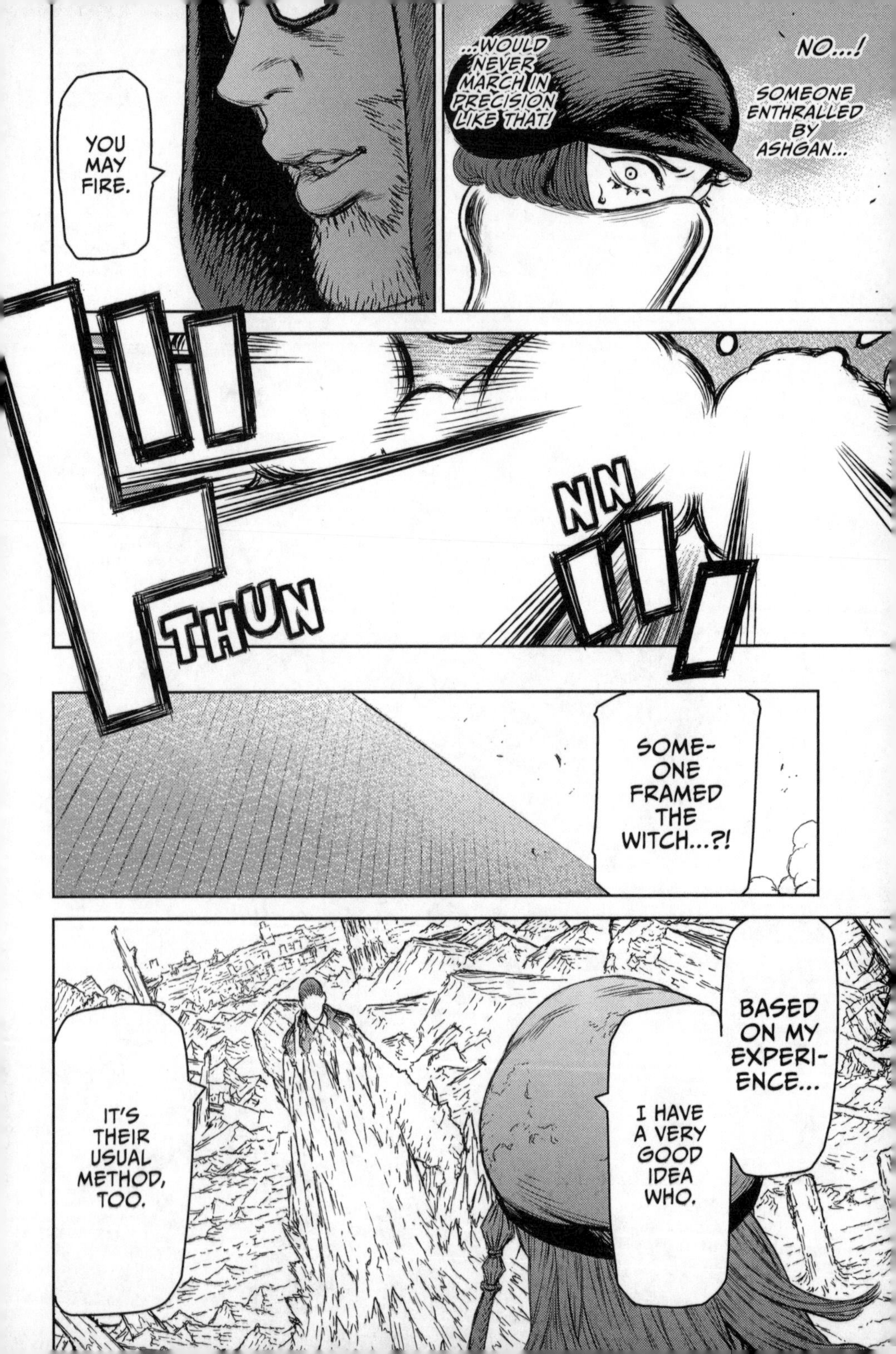
NO...!
SOMEONE ENTHRALLED BY ASHGAN...
...WOULD NEVER MARCH IN PRECISION LIKE THAT!
YOU MAY FIRE.
THUN
NN
SOME-ONE FRAMED THE WITCH...?!
BASED ON MY EXPERI-ENCE...
I HAVE A VERY GOOD IDEA WHO.
IT'S THEIR USUAL METHOD, TOO.

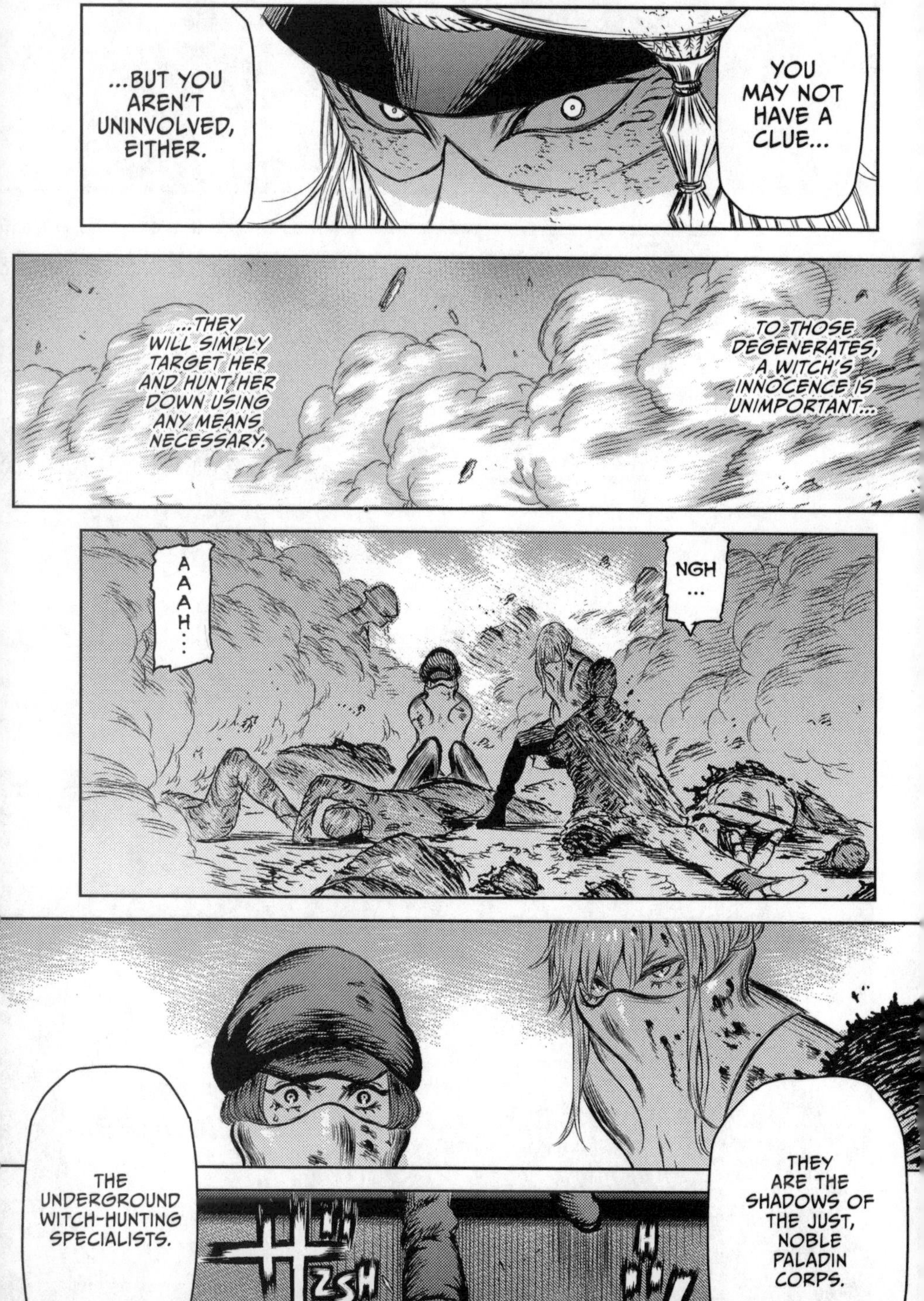
YOU MAY NOT HAVE A CLUE...
...BUT YOU AREN'T UNINVOLVED, EITHER.
TO THOSE DEGENERATES, A WITCH'S INNOCENCE IS UNIMPORTANT...
...THEY WILL SIMPLY TARGET HER AND HUNT HER DOWN USING ANY MEANS NECESSARY.
NGH ...
AAAH...
THEY ARE THE SHADOWS OF THE JUST, NOBLE PALADIN CORPS.
THE UNDERGROUND WITCH-HUNTING SPECIALISTS.
ZSH

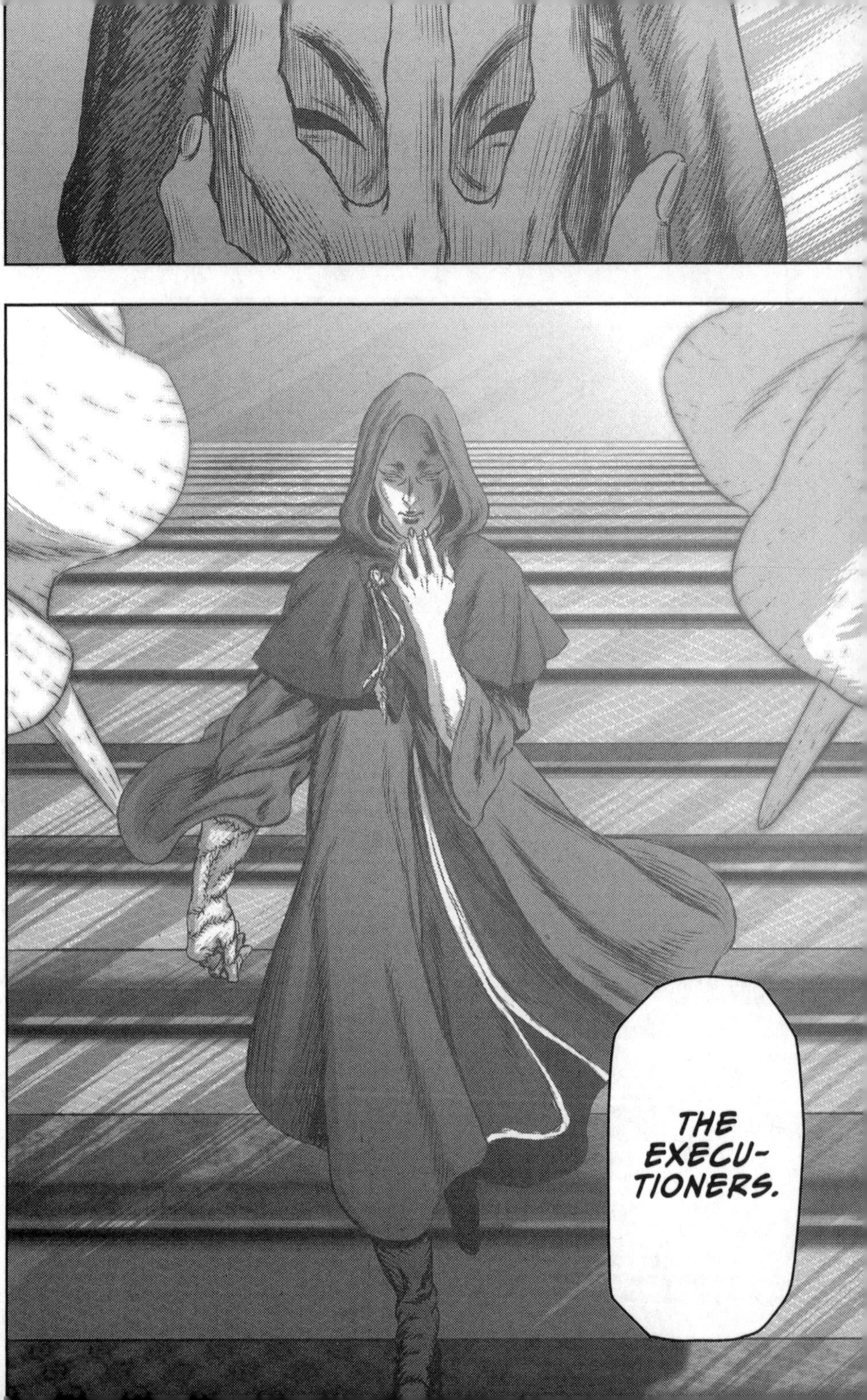
THE EXECU-TIONERS.

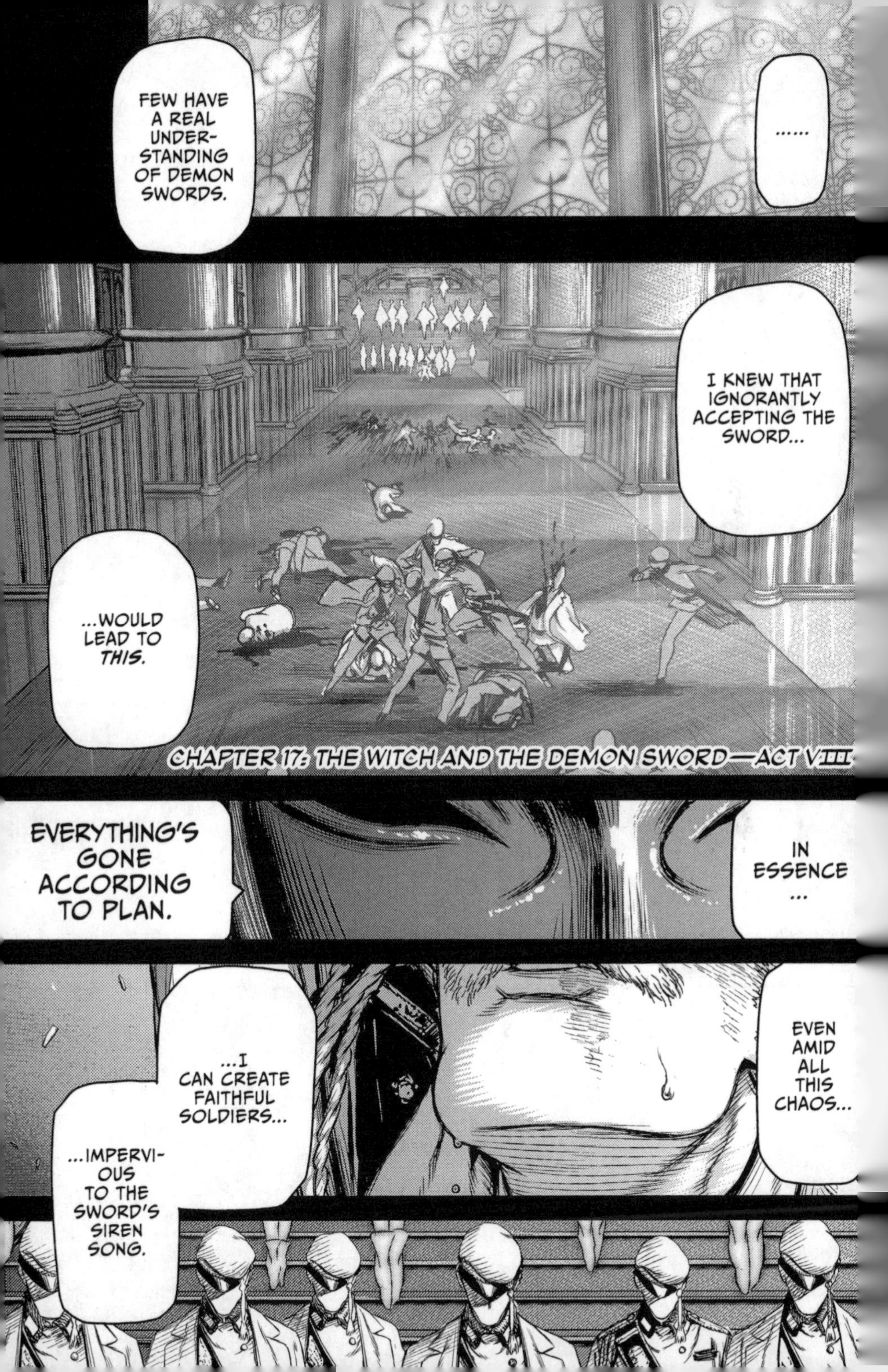
......
FEW HAVE A REAL UNDER-STANDING OF DEMON SWORDS.
I KNEW THAT IGNORANTLY ACCEPTING THE SWORD...
...WOULD LEAD TO *THIS*.
CHAPTER 17: THE WITCH AND THE DEMON SWORD—ACT VIII
IN ESSENCE...
EVERYTHING'S GONE ACCORDING TO PLAN.
EVEN AMID ALL THIS CHAOS...
...I CAN CREATE FAITHFUL SOLDIERS...
...IMPERVI-OUS TO THE SWORD'S SIREN SONG.

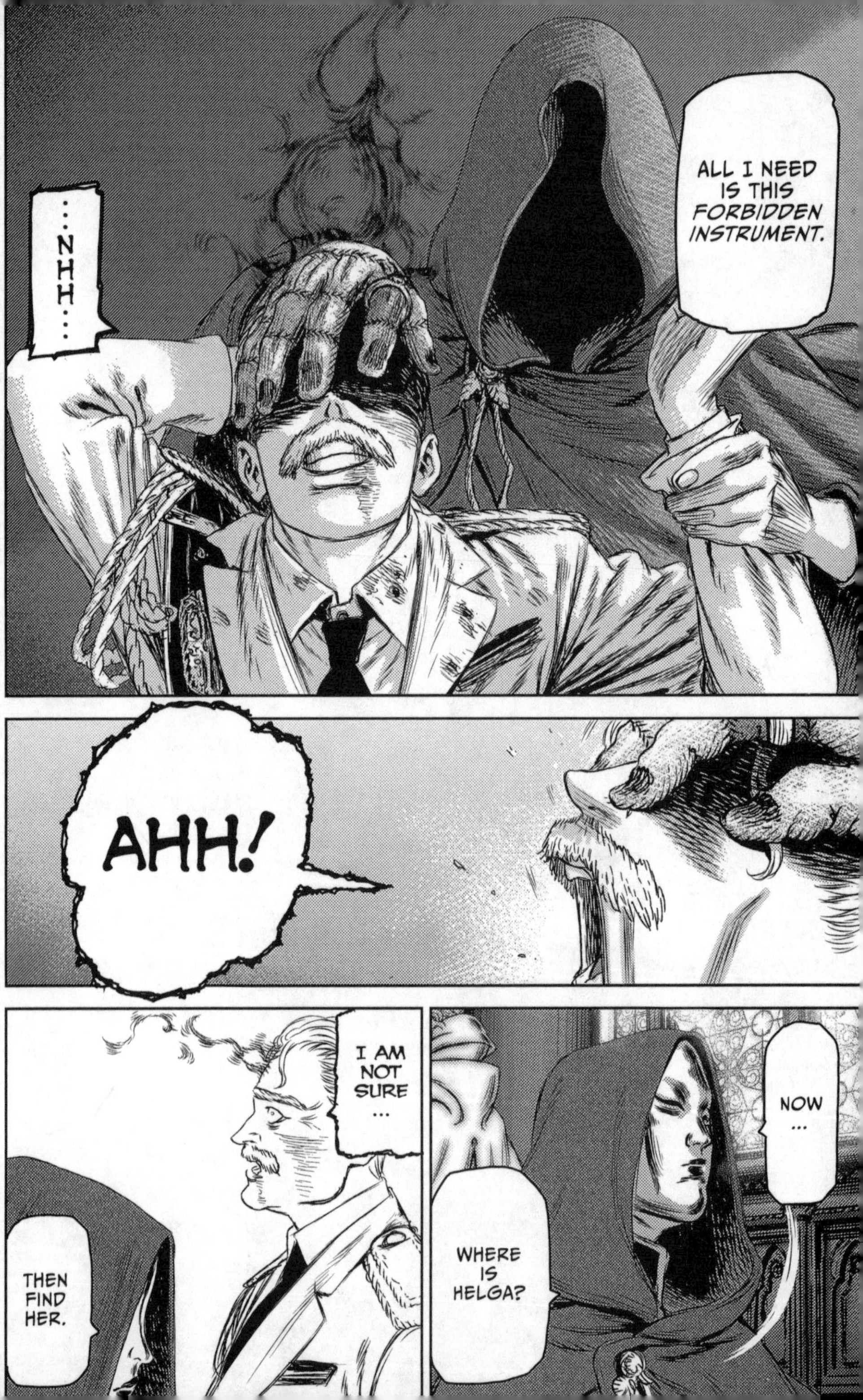
ALL I NEED IS THIS FORBIDDEN INSTRUMENT.
...NHH...
AHH!
NOW ...
WHERE IS HELGA?
I AM NOT SURE ...
THEN FIND HER.

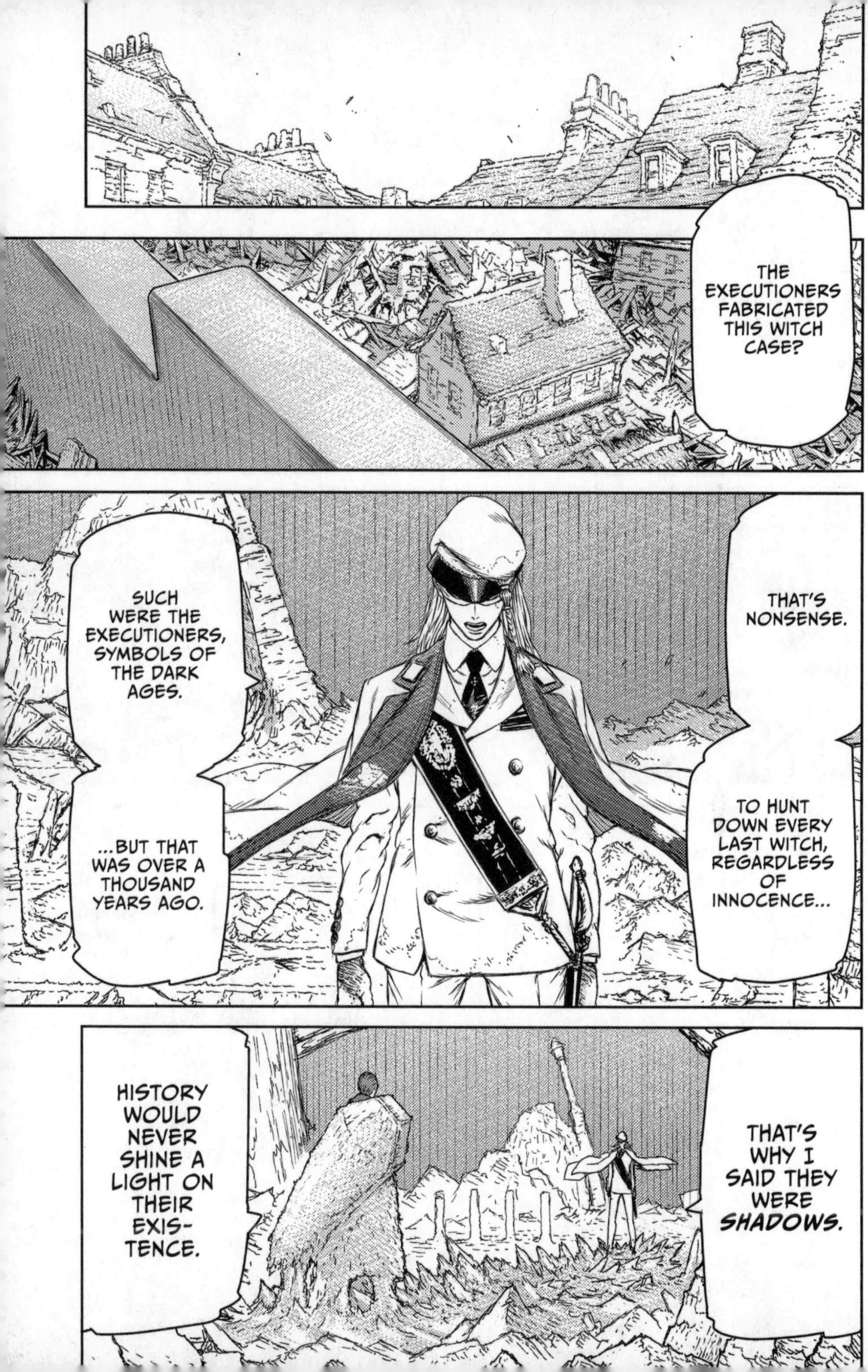
THE EXECUTIONERS FABRICATED THIS WITCH CASE?
THAT'S NONSENSE.
TO HUNT DOWN EVERY LAST WITCH, REGARDLESS OF INNOCENCE...
SUCH WERE THE EXECUTIONERS, SYMBOLS OF THE DARK AGES.
...BUT THAT WAS OVER A THOUSAND YEARS AGO.
THAT'S WHY I SAID THEY WERE *SHADOWS*.
HISTORY WOULD NEVER SHINE A LIGHT ON THEIR EXIS-TENCE.

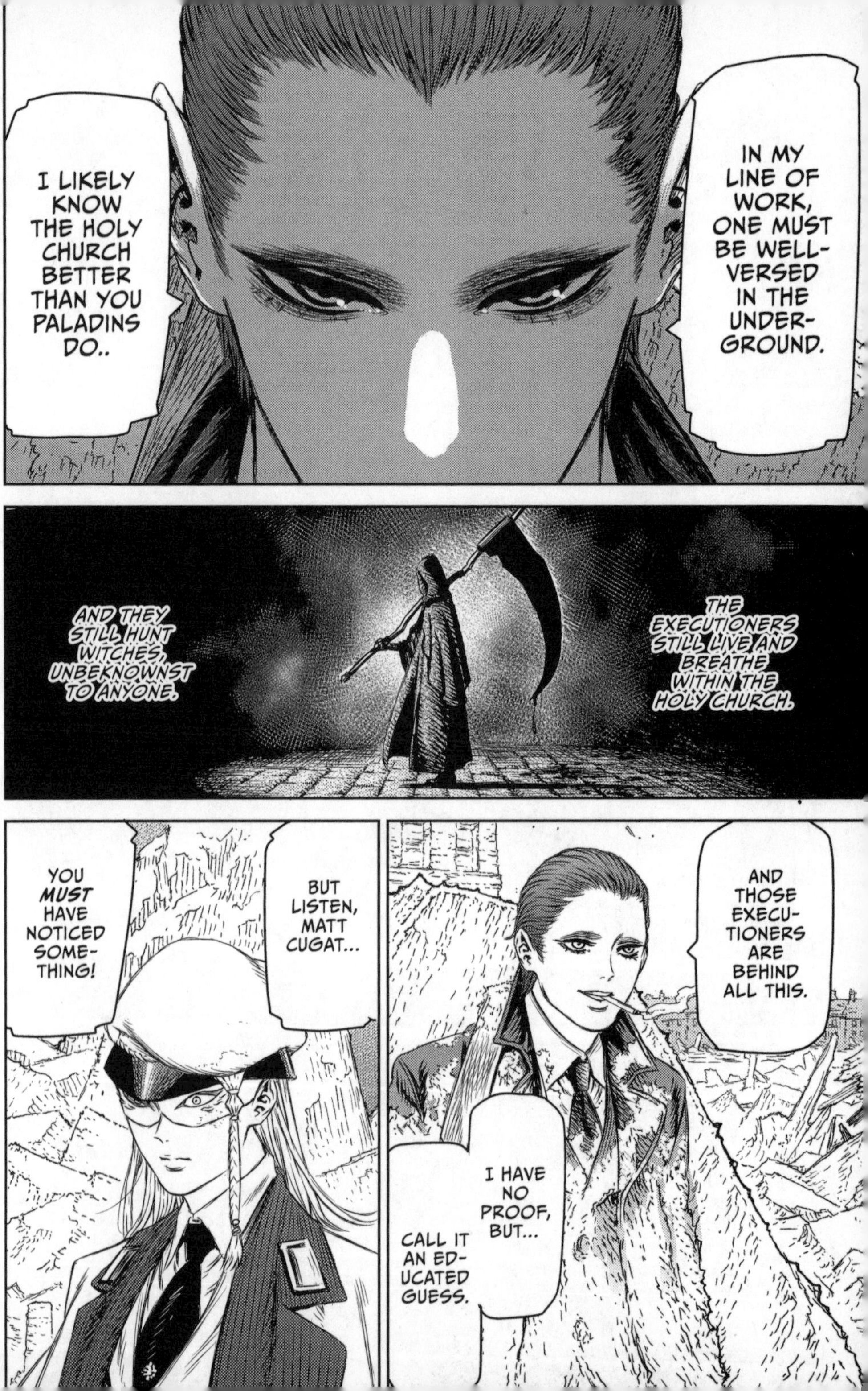
IN MY LINE OF WORK, ONE MUST BE WELL-VERSED IN THE UNDERGROUND.
I LIKELY KNOW THE HOLY CHURCH BETTER THAN YOU PALADINS DO..
THE EXECUTIONERS STILL LIVE AND BREATHE WITHIN THE HOLY CHURCH.
AND THEY STILL HUNT WITCHES, UNBEKNOWNST TO ANYONE.
AND THOSE EXECUTIONERS ARE BEHIND ALL THIS.
I HAVE NO PROOF, BUT...
CALL IT AN EDUCATED GUESS.
BUT LISTEN, MATT CUGAT...
YOU *MUST* HAVE NOTICED SOMETHING!

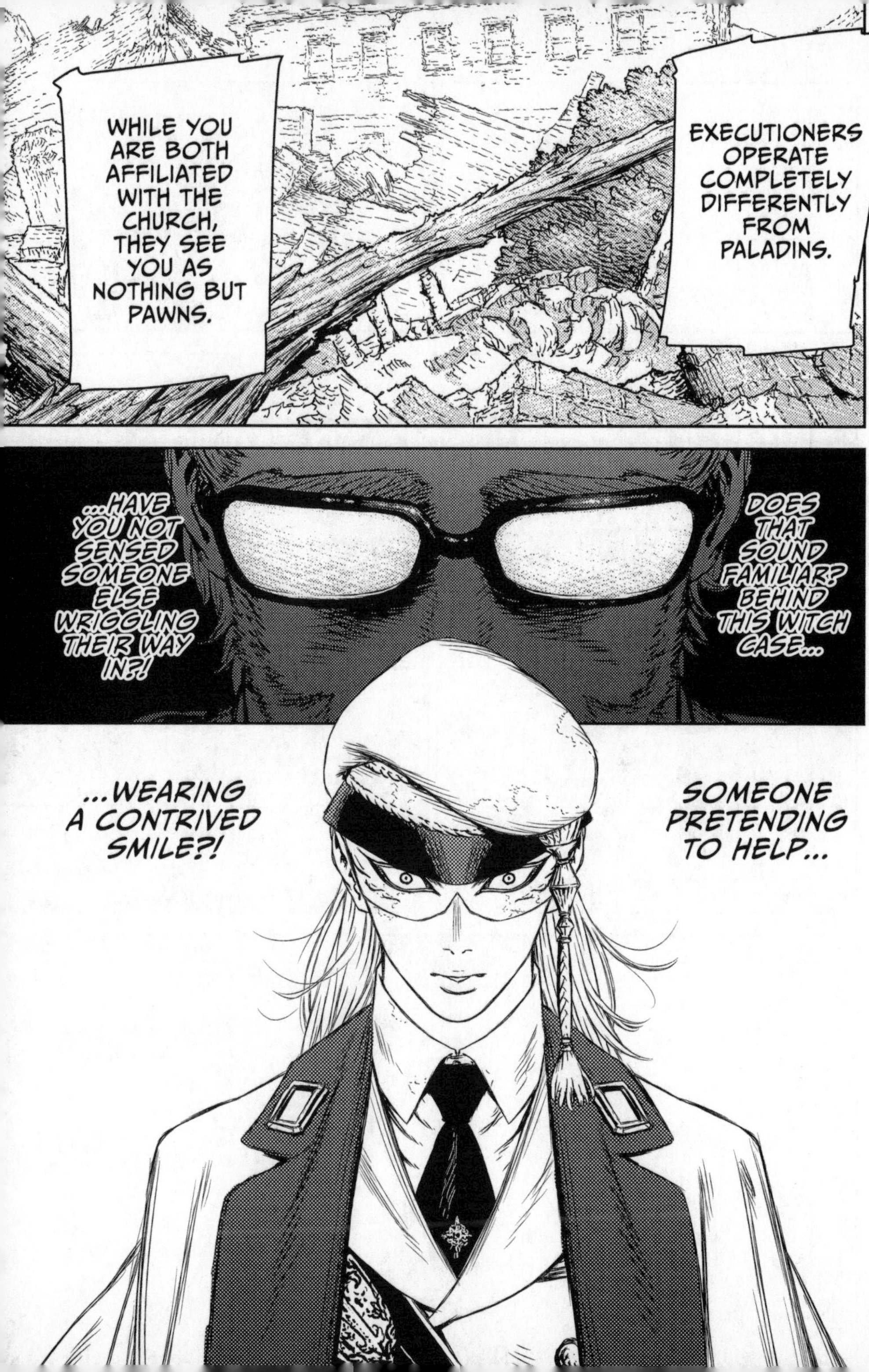
EXECUTIONERS OPERATE COMPLETELY DIFFERENTLY FROM PALADINS.
WHILE YOU ARE BOTH AFFILIATED WITH THE CHURCH, THEY SEE YOU AS NOTHING BUT PAWNS.
DOES THAT SOUND FAMILIAR? BEHIND THIS WITCH CASE...
...HAVE YOU NOT SENSED SOMEONE ELSE WRIGGLING THEIR WAY IN?!
SOMEONE PRETENDING TO HELP...
...WEARING A CONTRIVED SMILE?!

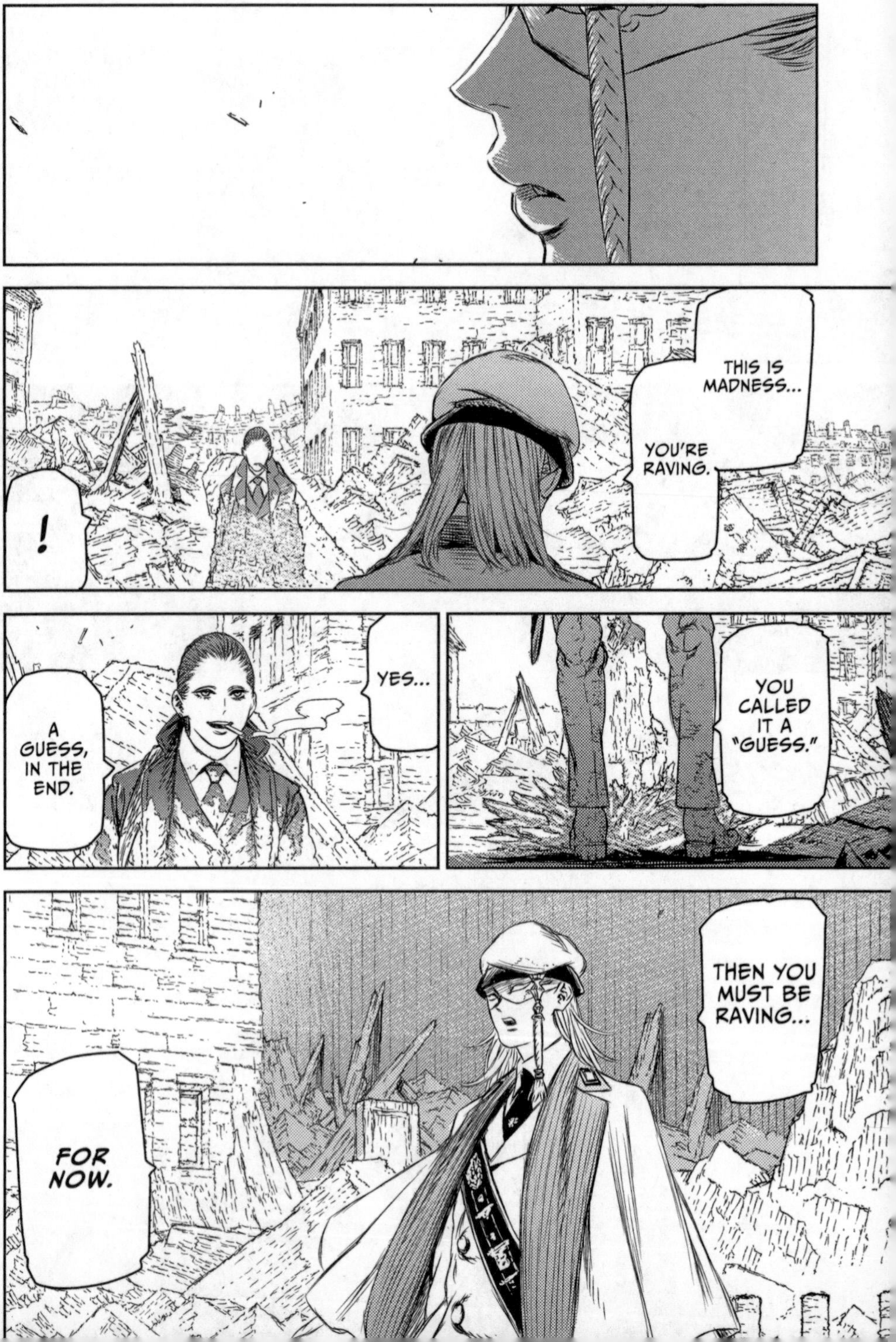
THIS IS MADNESS...
YOU'RE RAVING.
!
YOU CALLED IT A "GUESS."
YES...
A GUESS, IN THE END.
THEN YOU MUST BE RAVING...
FOR NOW.

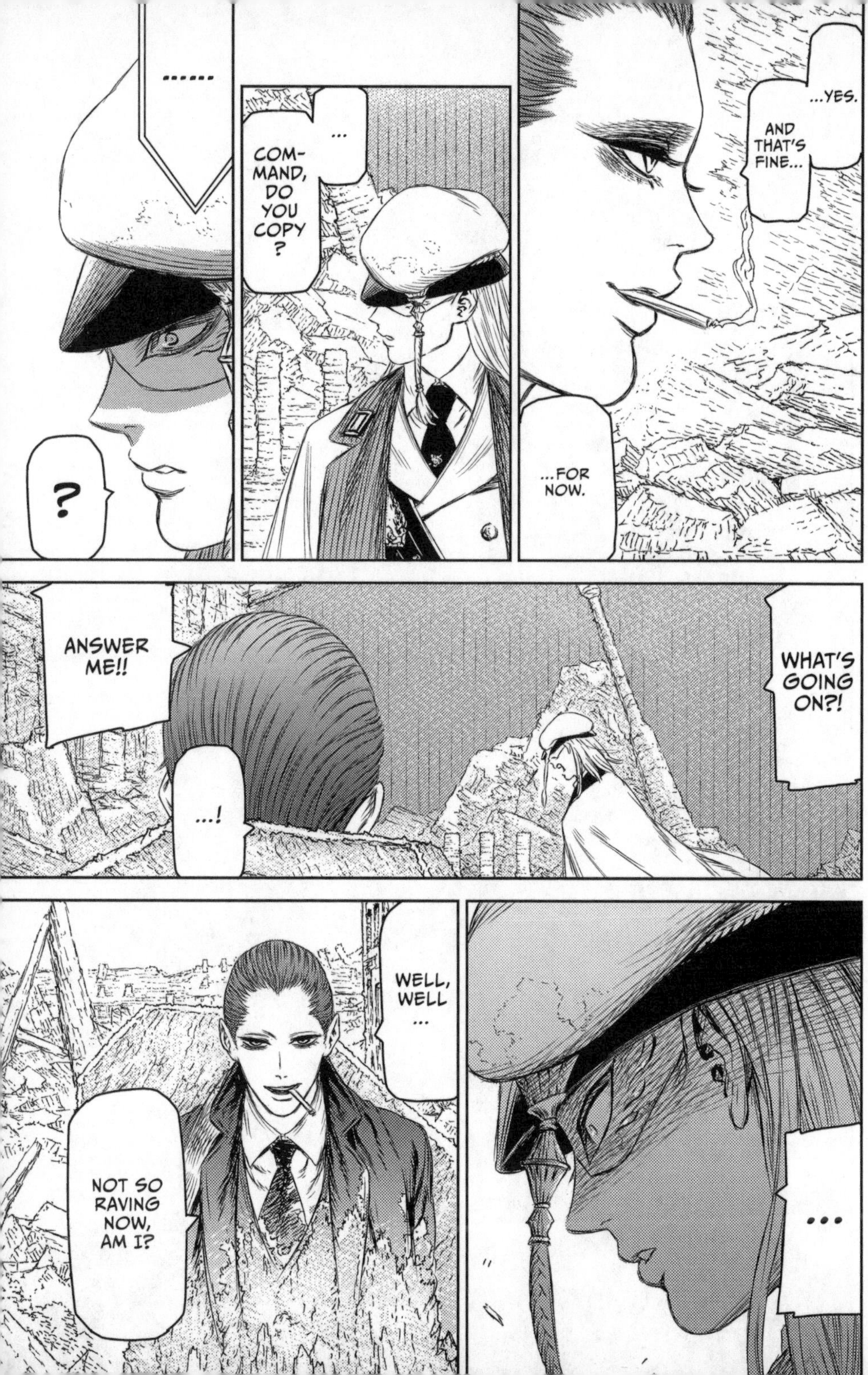
...YES.
AND THAT'S FINE...
...FOR NOW.
...
COM-MAND, DO YOU COPY?
......
?
WHAT'S GOING ON?!
ANSWER ME!!
...!
...
WELL, WELL...
NOT SO RAVING NOW, AM I?

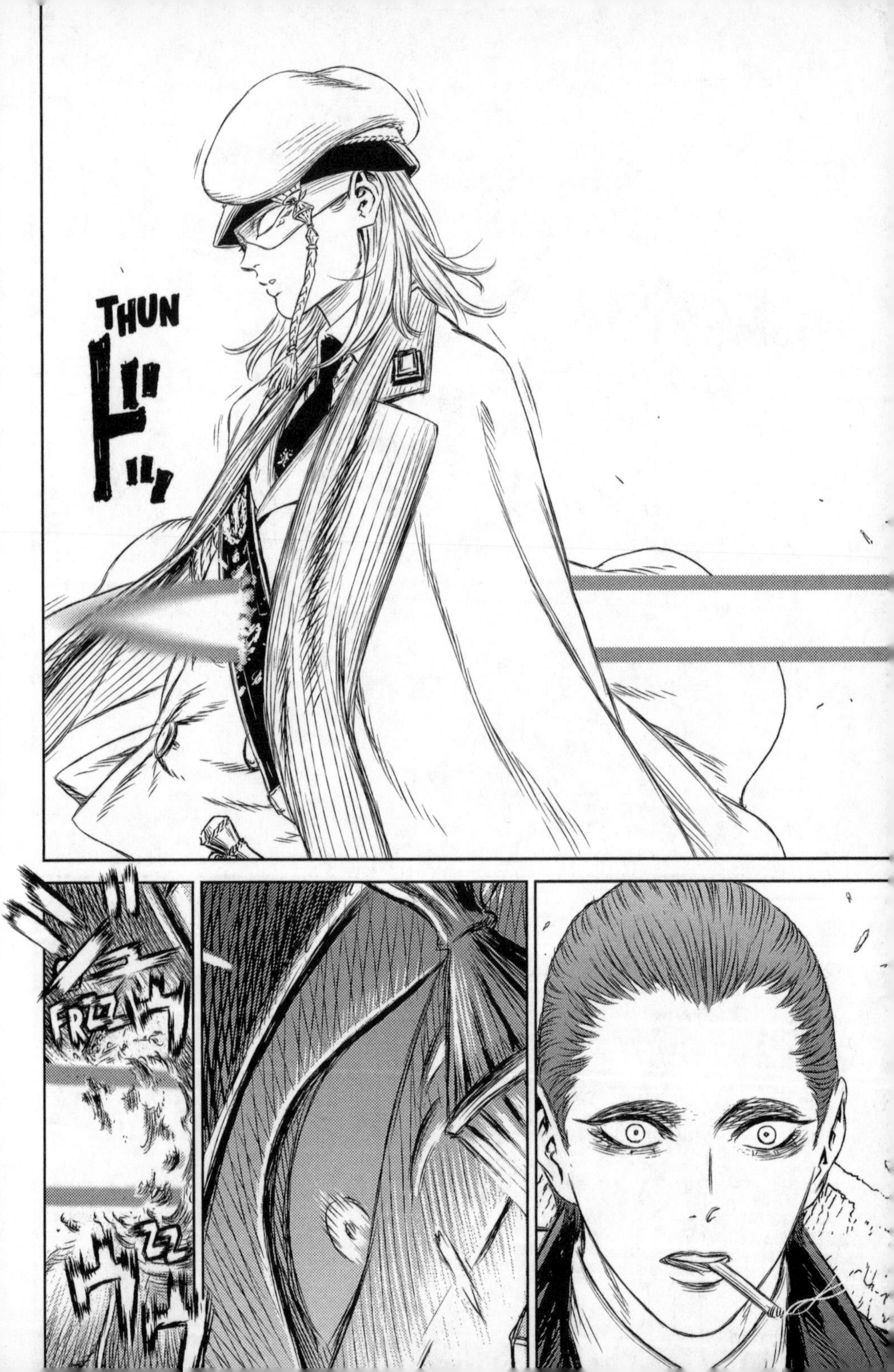
THUN
FRZZ
ZZZ

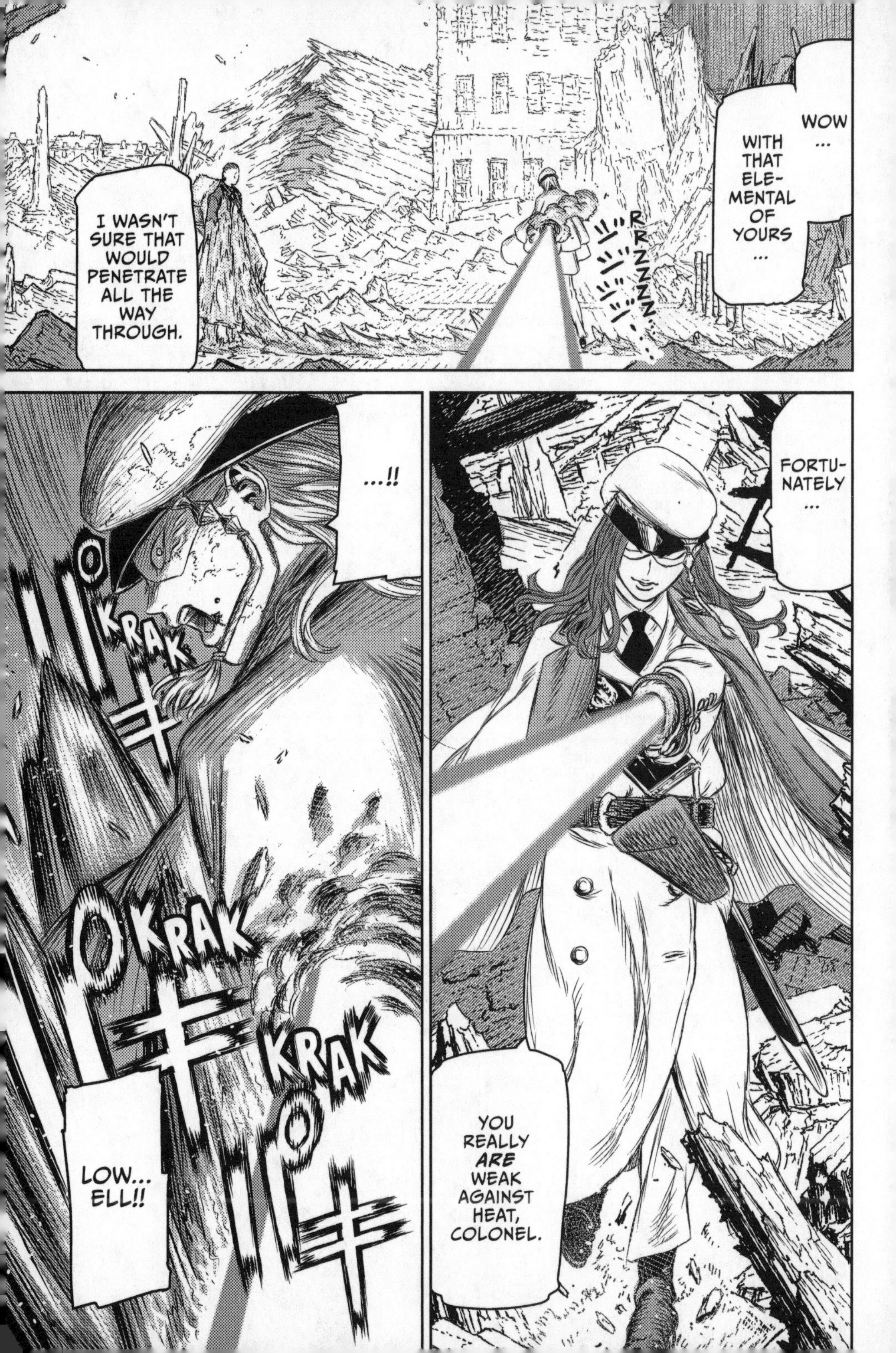
WOW... WITH THAT ELEMENTAL OF YOURS...
RRZZZZ...
I WASN'T SURE THAT WOULD PENETRATE ALL THE WAY THROUGH.
FORTUNATELY...
YOU REALLY *ARE* WEAK AGAINST HEAT, COLONEL.
...!!
KRAK
KRAK
KRAK
LOW... ELL!!

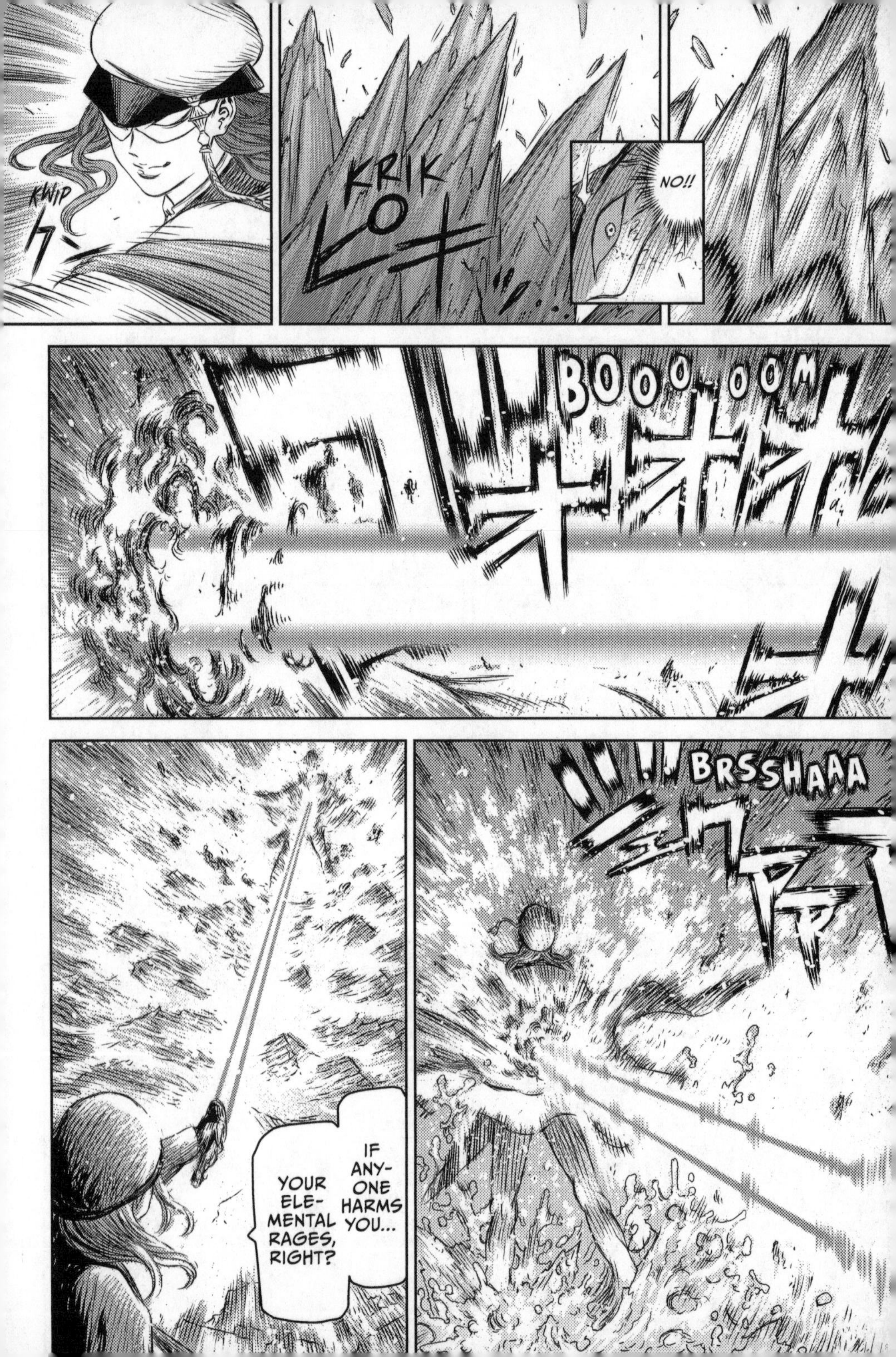
NO!!
KRIK
KWIP
BOOO-OOM
BRSSHAAA
IF ANY-ONE HARMS YOU...
YOUR ELE-MENTAL RAGES, RIGHT?

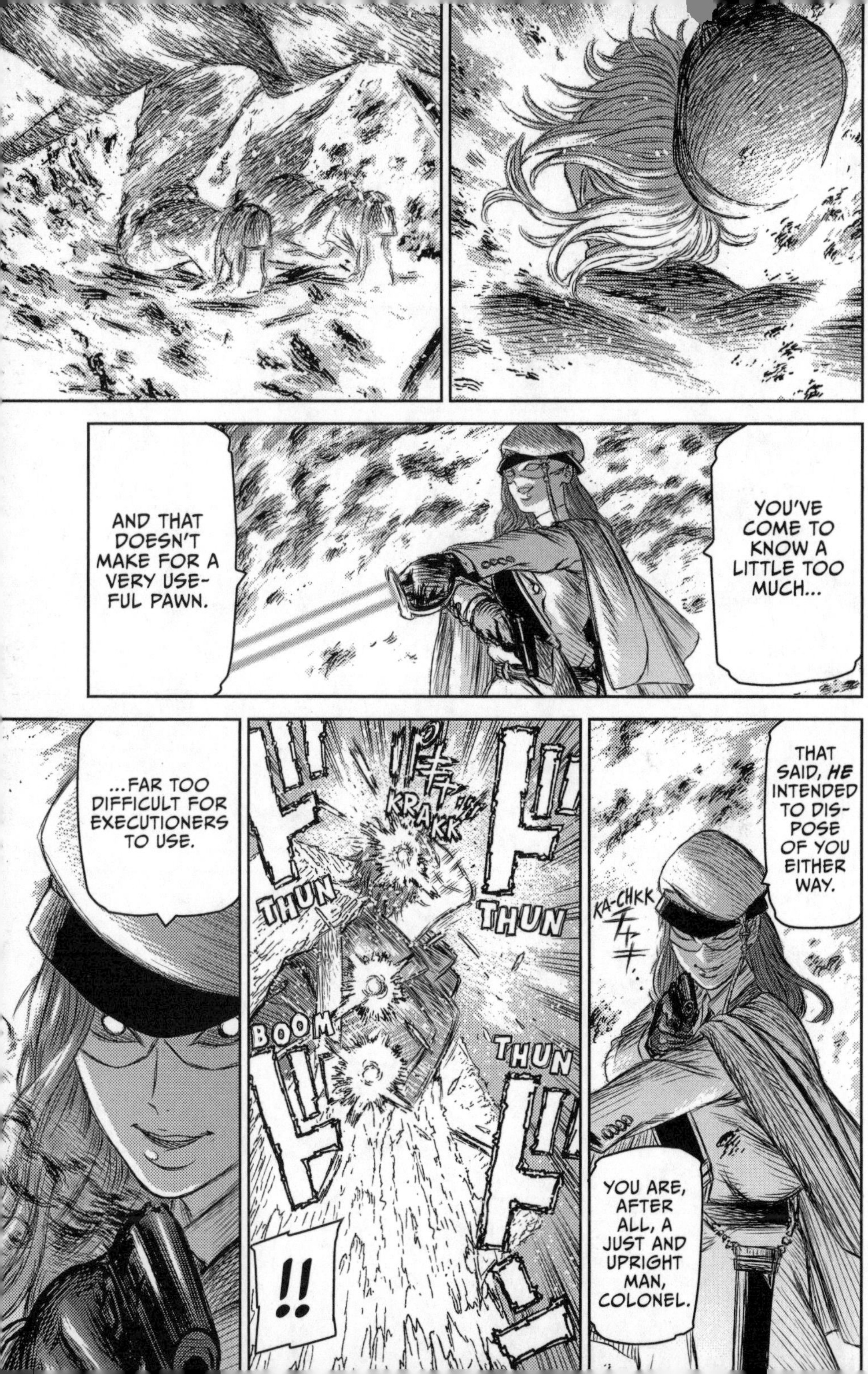
YOU'VE COME TO KNOW A LITTLE TOO MUCH...
AND THAT DOESN'T MAKE FOR A VERY USE-FUL PAWN.
THAT SAID, *HE* INTENDED TO DIS-POSE OF YOU EITHER WAY.
KA-CHKK
YOU ARE, AFTER ALL, A JUST AND UPRIGHT MAN, COLONEL.
KRAKK
THUN
THUN
BOOM
THUN
!!
...FAR TOO DIFFICULT FOR EXECUTIONERS TO USE.

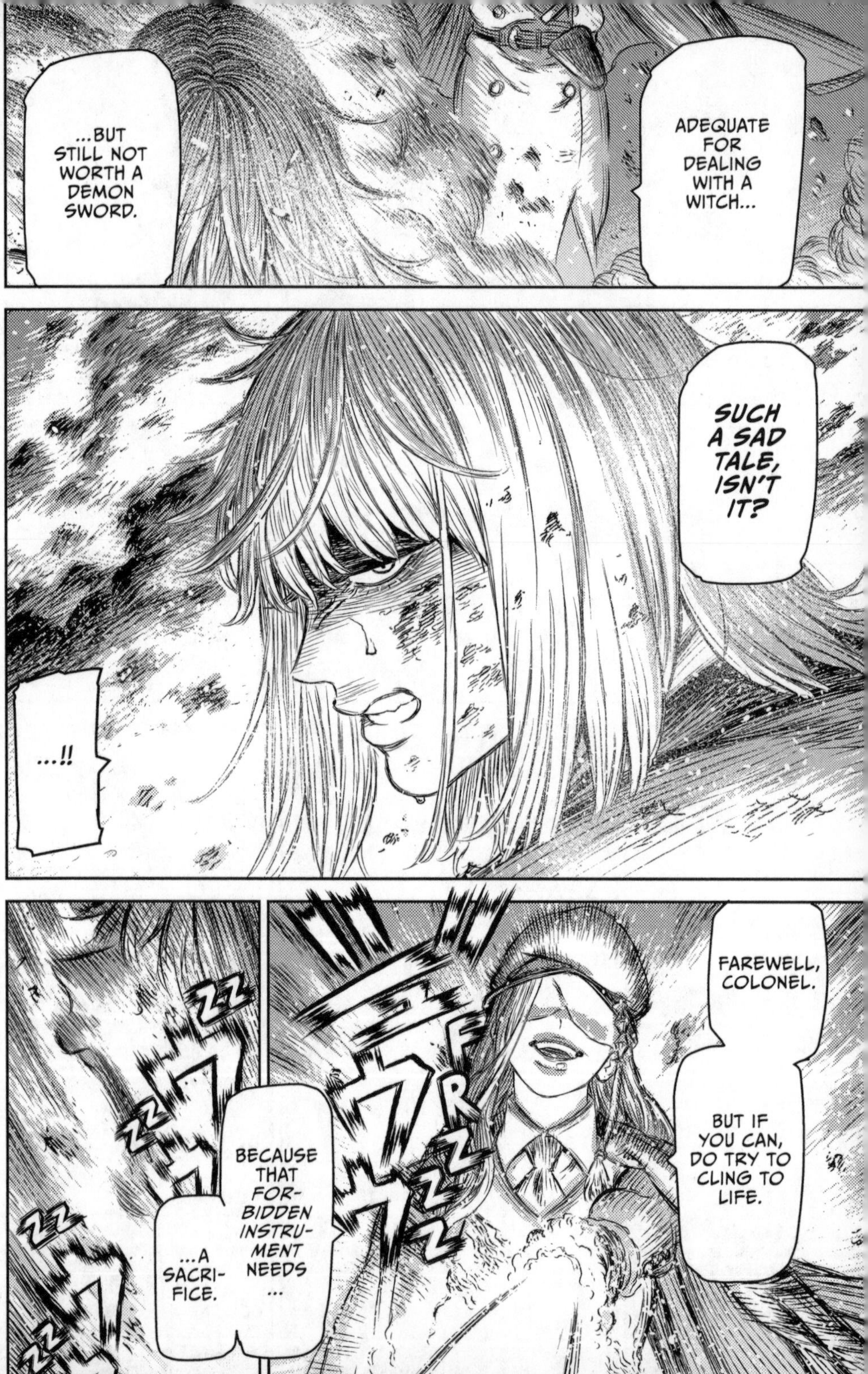
ADEQUATE FOR DEALING WITH A WITCH...
...BUT STILL NOT WORTH A DEMON SWORD.
SUCH A SAD TALE, ISN'T IT?
...!!
FAREWELL, COLONEL.
BUT IF YOU CAN, DO TRY TO CLING TO LIFE.
FRZZZZ
BECAUSE THAT FOR-BIDDEN INSTRU-MENT NEEDS...
...A SACRI-FICE.
ZZ
ZZ
ZZ
ZZ

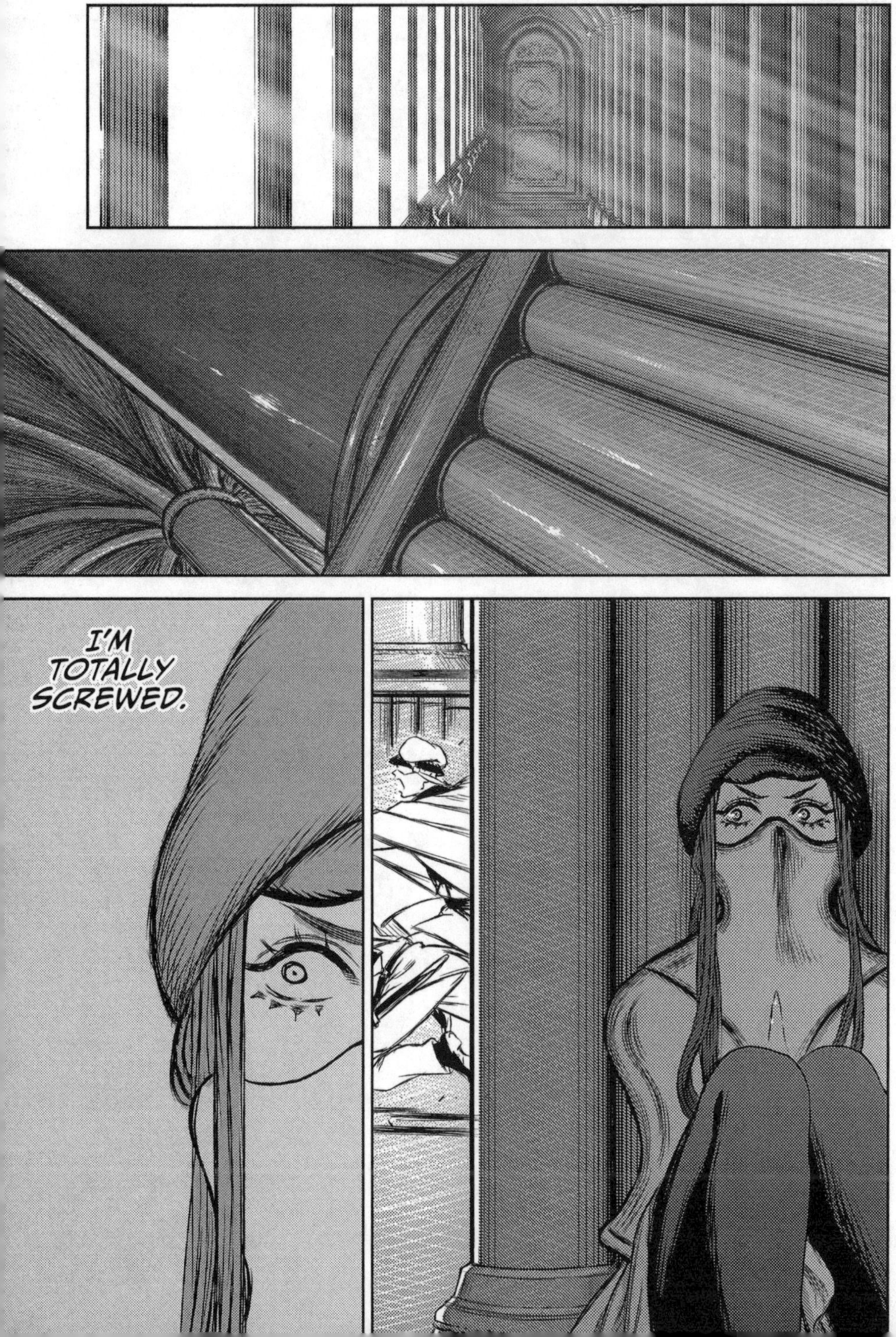
I'M TOTALLY SCREWED.

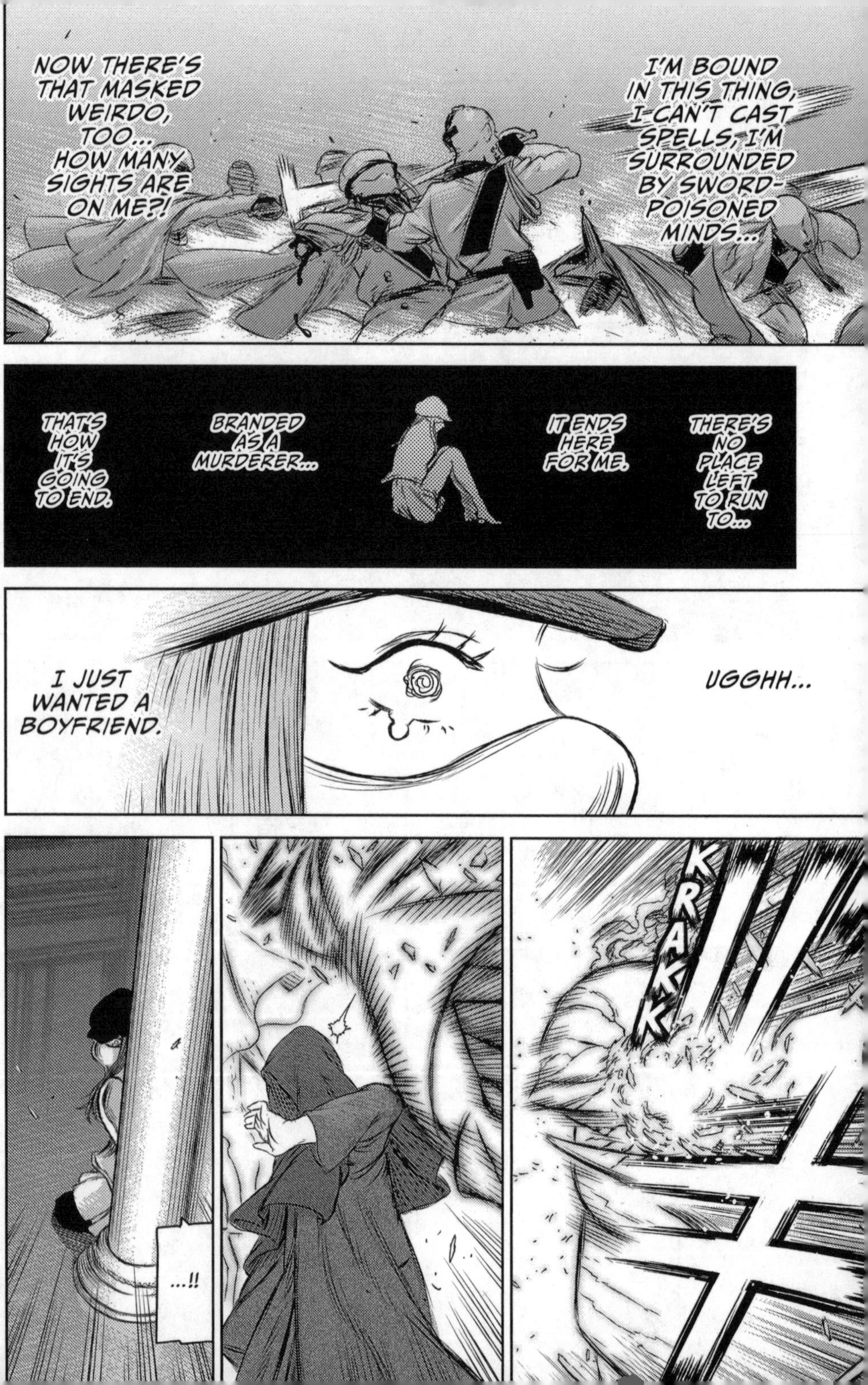
I'M BOUND IN THIS THING, I CAN'T CAST SPELLS, I'M SURROUNDED BY SWORD-POISONED MINDS...
NOW THERE'S THAT MASKED WEIRDO, TOO... HOW MANY SIGHTS ARE ON ME?!
THERE'S NO PLACE LEFT TO RUN TO...
IT ENDS HERE FOR ME.
BRANDED AS A MURDERER...
THAT'S HOW IT'S GOING TO END.
UGGHH...
I JUST WANTED A BOYFRIEND.
KRAKK
...!!

HEH
...

WHILE BOUND, TOO? WELL DONE.

VICE-CAPTAIN...

IT'S YOUR TURN.

......

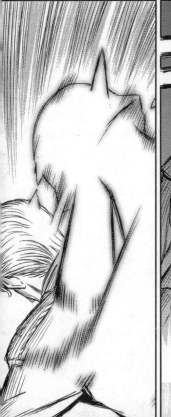

TING

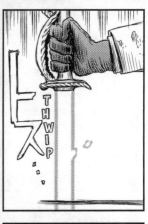

THWIP

TAP

TAP

SCREEEE

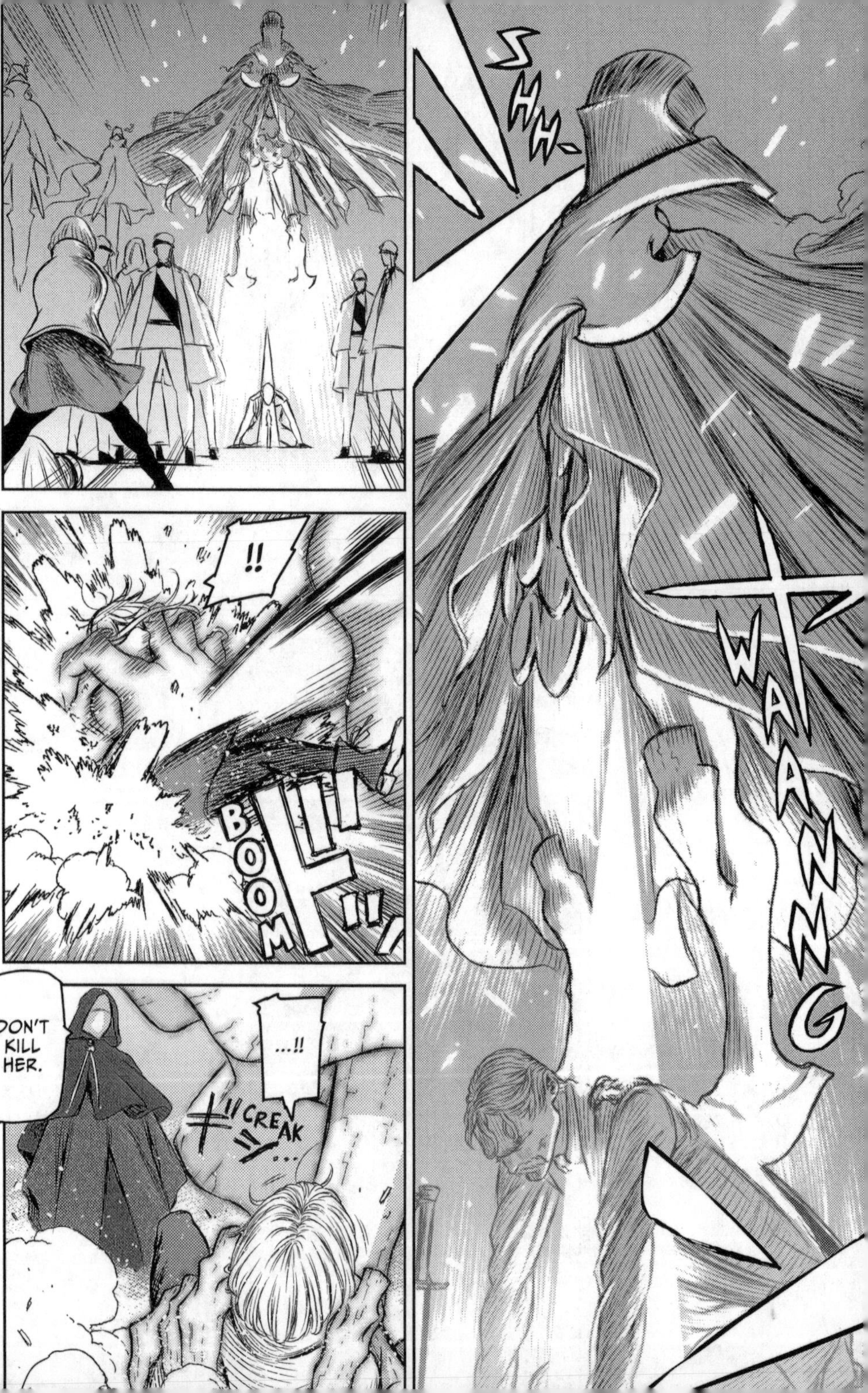
SHH-
WAANNG
!!
BOOM
DON'T KILL HER.
...!!
CREAK

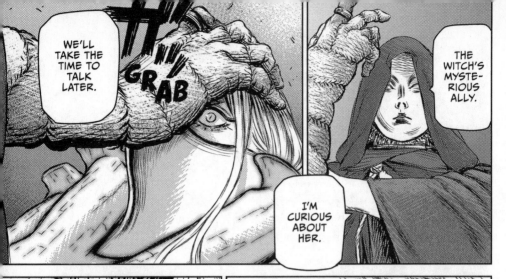

THE WITCH'S MYSTE-RIOUS ALLY.
I'M CURIOUS ABOUT HER.
GRAB
WE'LL TAKE THE TIME TO TALK LATER.
ZRR...
NNAAGGHH!!
HNNNNGH!!
NNNGH!!
...!!

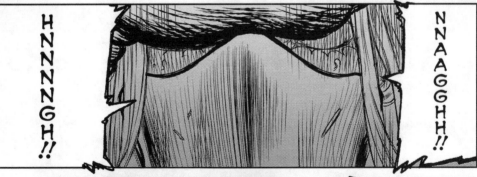

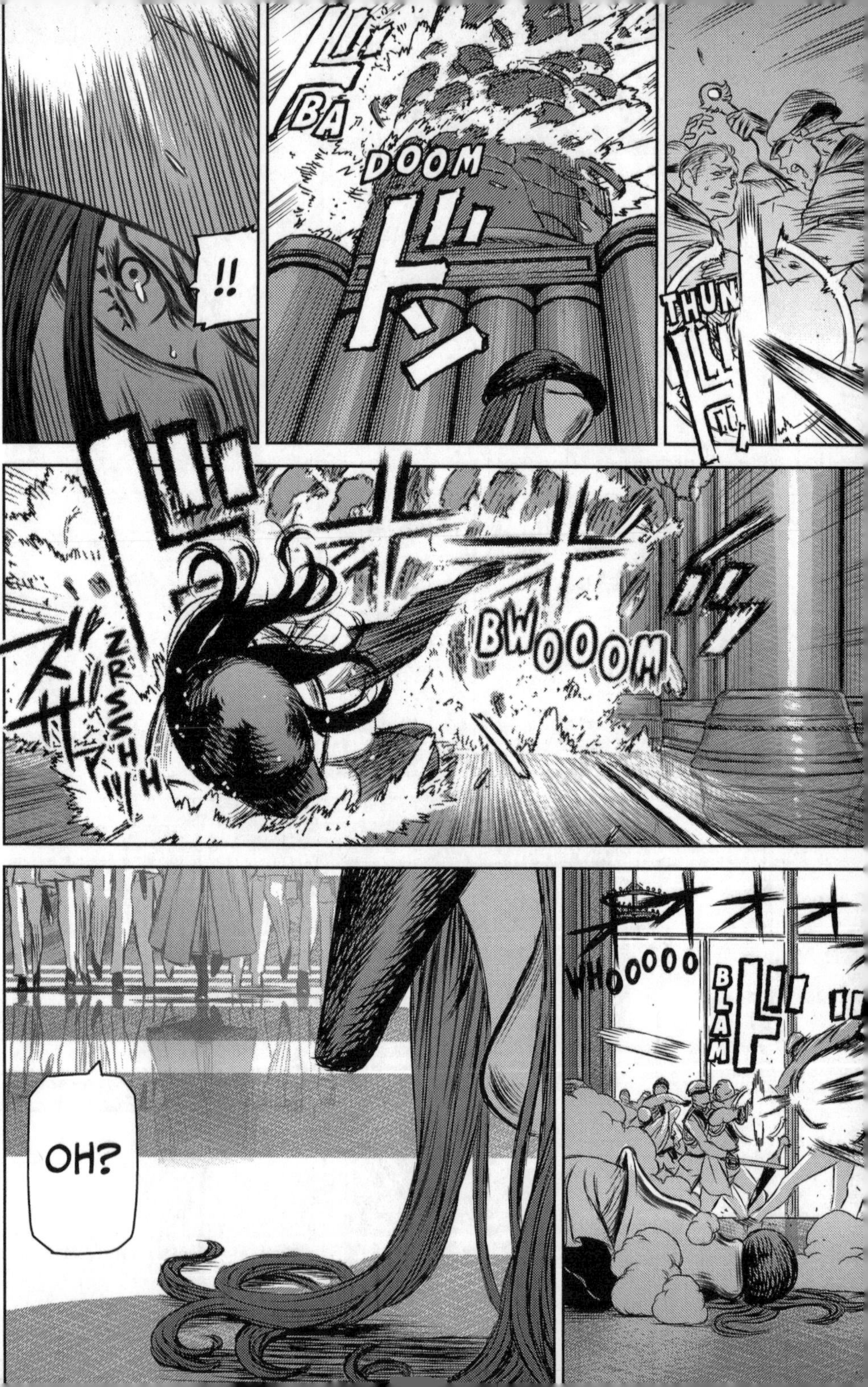

THUN
BA DOOM
!!
BWOOOM
ZRSSHH
WHOOOOO
BLAM
OH?

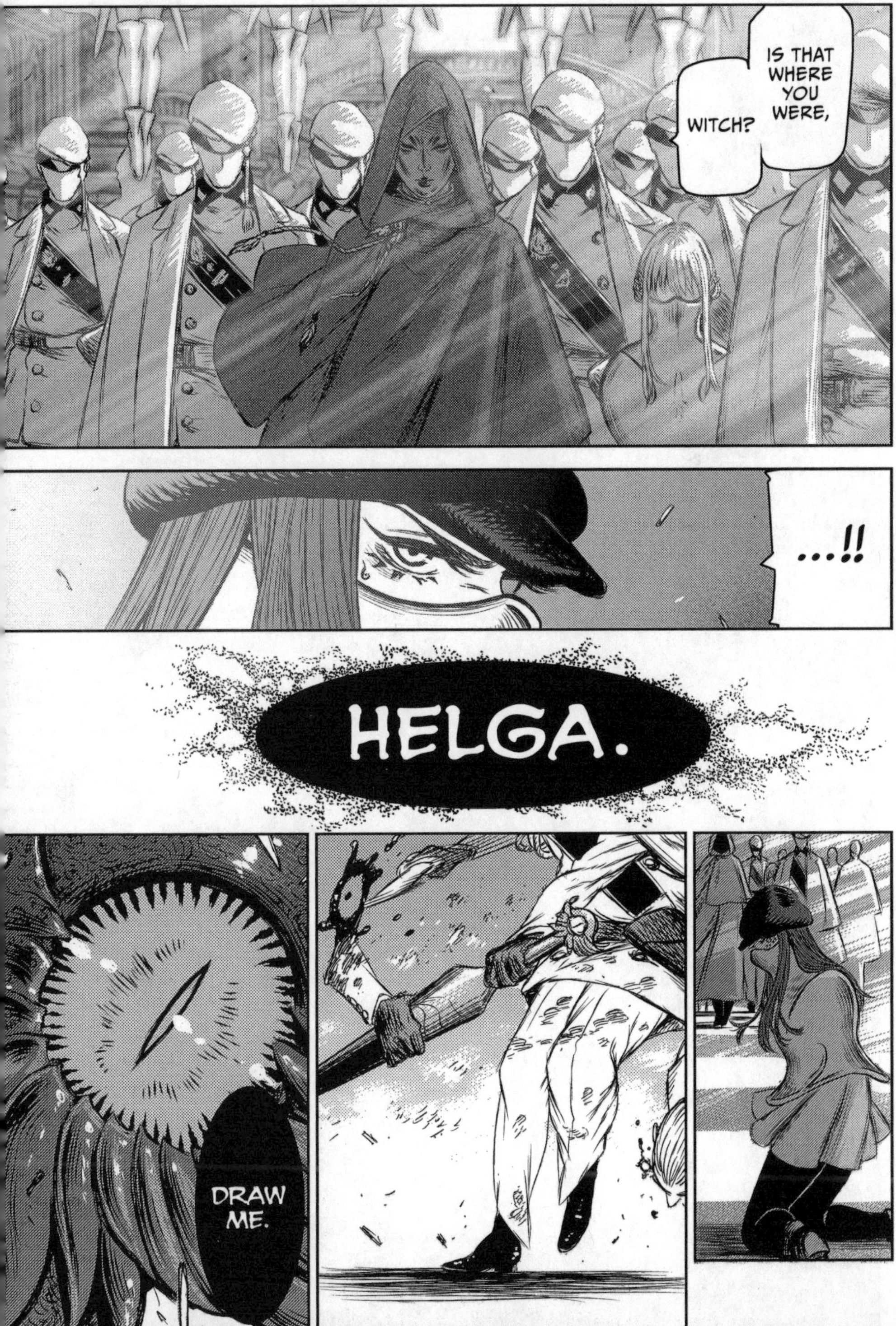
IS THAT WHERE YOU WERE,
WITCH?
...!!
HELGA.
DRAW ME.

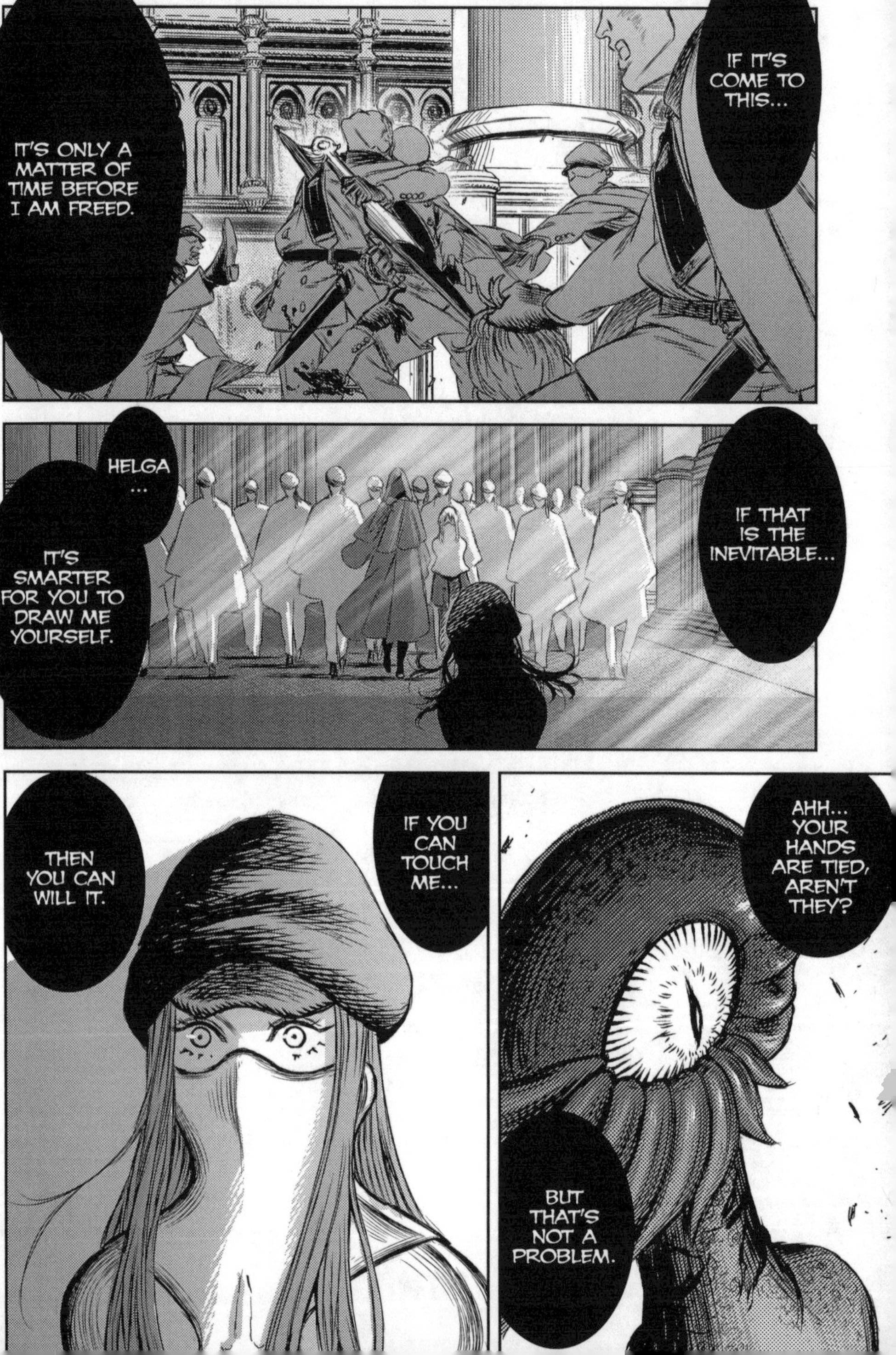
IF IT'S COME TO THIS...
IT'S ONLY A MATTER OF TIME BEFORE I AM FREED.
IF THAT IS THE INEVITABLE...
HELGA...
IT'S SMARTER FOR YOU TO DRAW ME YOURSELF.
AHH... YOUR HANDS ARE TIED, AREN'T THEY?
BUT THAT'S NOT A PROBLEM.
IF YOU CAN TOUCH ME...
THEN YOU CAN WILL IT.

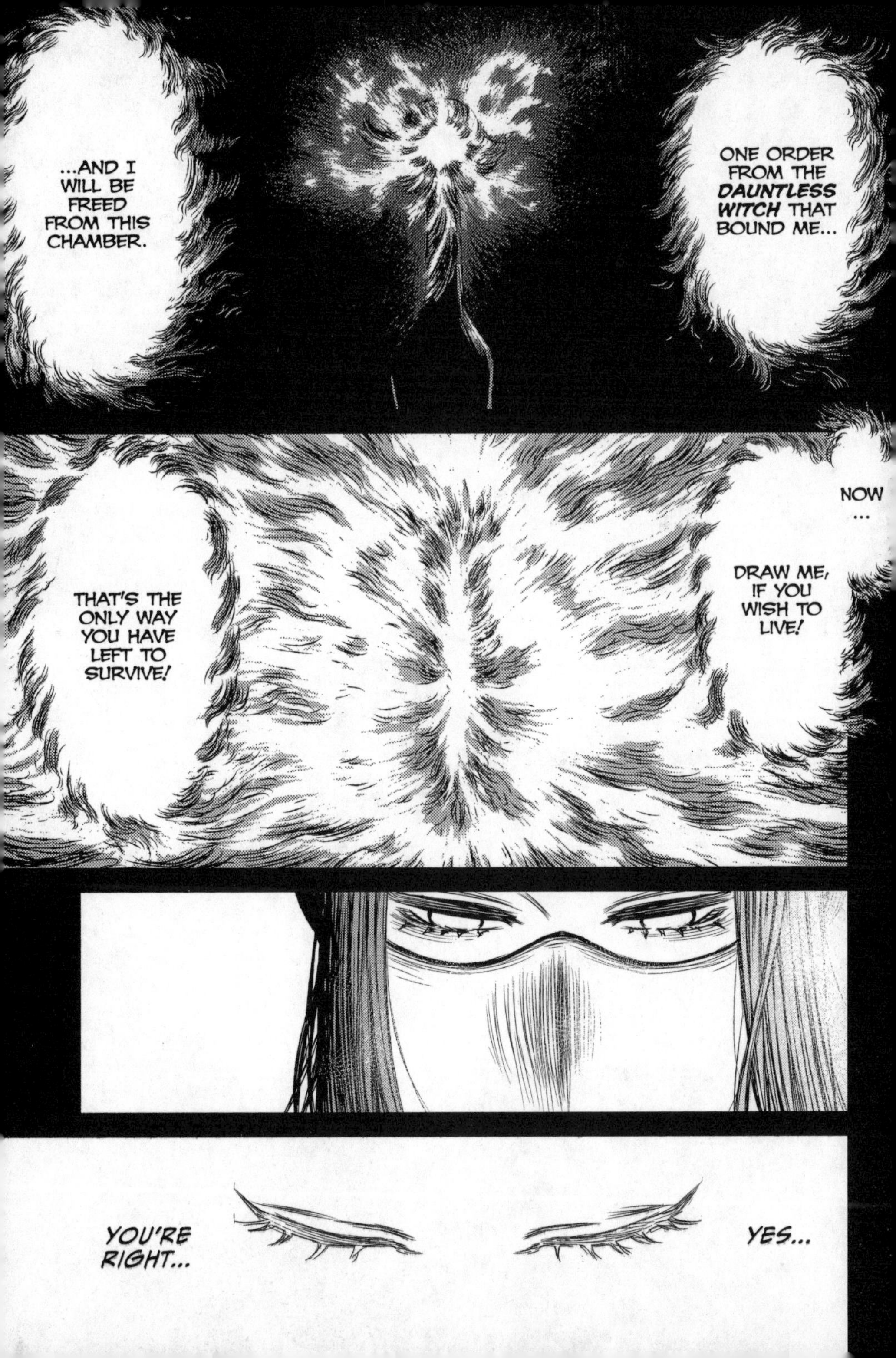
ONE ORDER FROM THE ***DAUNTLESS WITCH*** THAT BOUND ME...
...AND I WILL BE FREED FROM THIS CHAMBER.
NOW...
DRAW ME, IF YOU WISH TO LIVE!
THAT'S THE ONLY WAY YOU HAVE LEFT TO SURVIVE!
YES...
YOU'RE RIGHT...

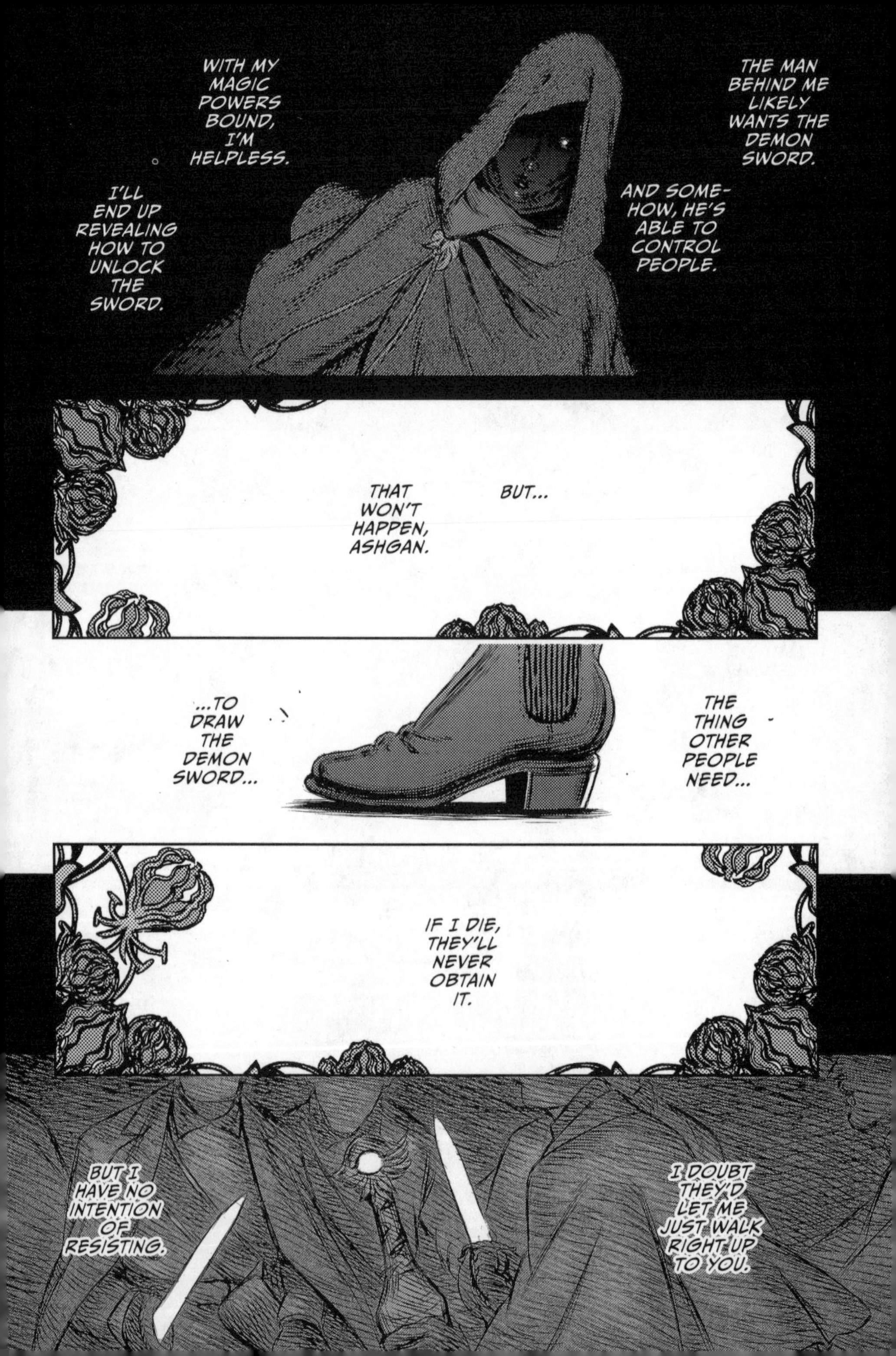
THE MAN BEHIND ME LIKELY WANTS THE DEMON SWORD.
AND SOMEHOW, HE'S ABLE TO CONTROL PEOPLE.
WITH MY MAGIC POWERS BOUND, I'M HELPLESS.
I'LL END UP REVEALING HOW TO UNLOCK THE SWORD.
BUT...
THAT WON'T HAPPEN, ASHGAN.
THE THING OTHER PEOPLE NEED...
...TO DRAW THE DEMON SWORD...
IF I DIE, THEY'LL NEVER OBTAIN IT.
I DOUBT THEY'D LET ME JUST WALK RIGHT UP TO YOU.
BUT I HAVE NO INTENTION OF RESISTING.

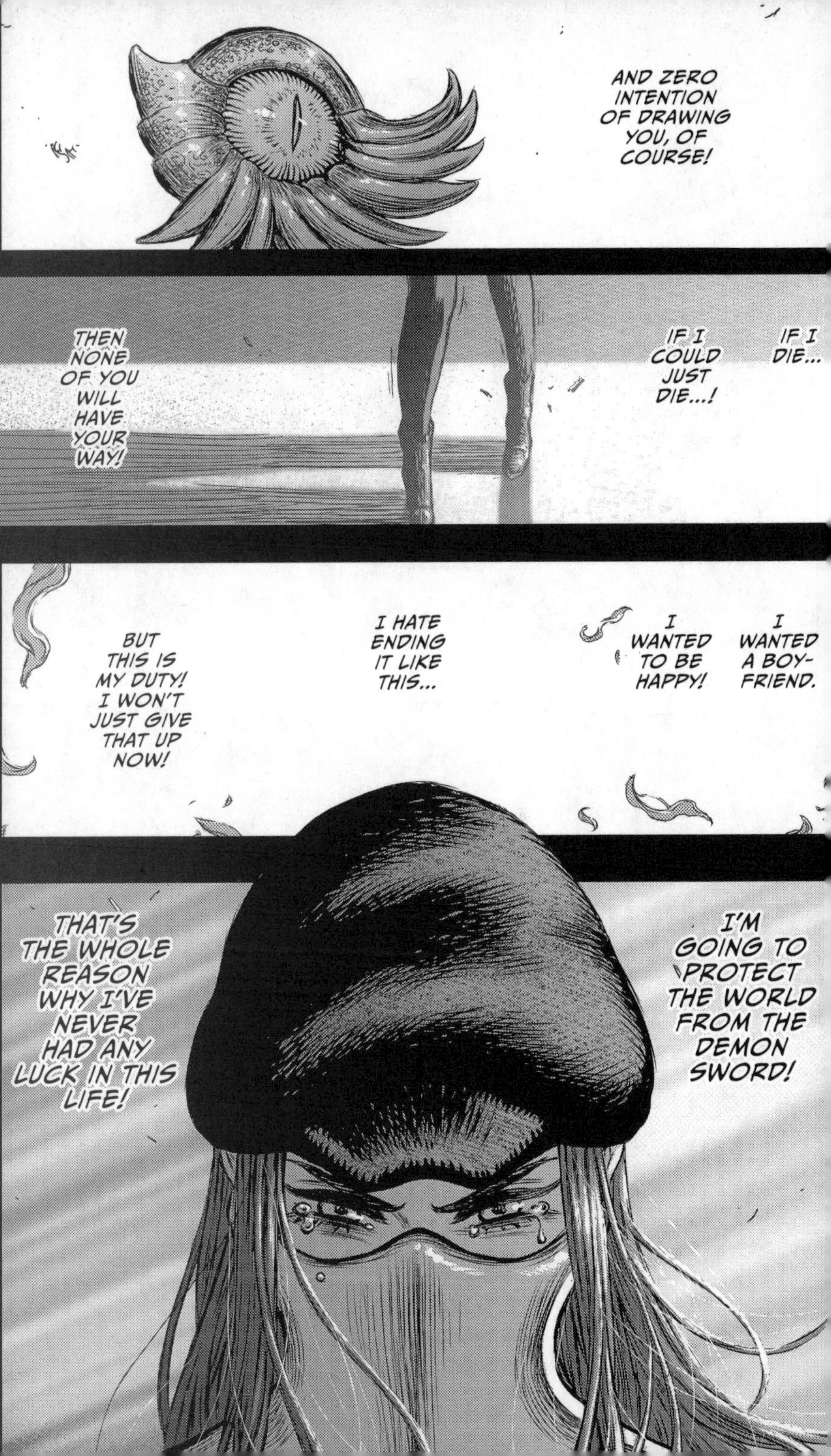
AND ZERO INTENTION OF DRAWING YOU, OF COURSE!
IF I DIE...
IF I COULD JUST DIE...!
THEN NONE OF YOU WILL HAVE YOUR WAY!
I WANTED A BOY-FRIEND.
I WANTED TO BE HAPPY!
I HATE ENDING IT LIKE THIS...
BUT THIS IS MY DUTY! I WON'T JUST GIVE THAT UP NOW!
I'M GOING TO PROTECT THE WORLD FROM THE DEMON SWORD!
THAT'S THE WHOLE REASON WHY I'VE NEVER HAD ANY LUCK IN THIS LIFE!

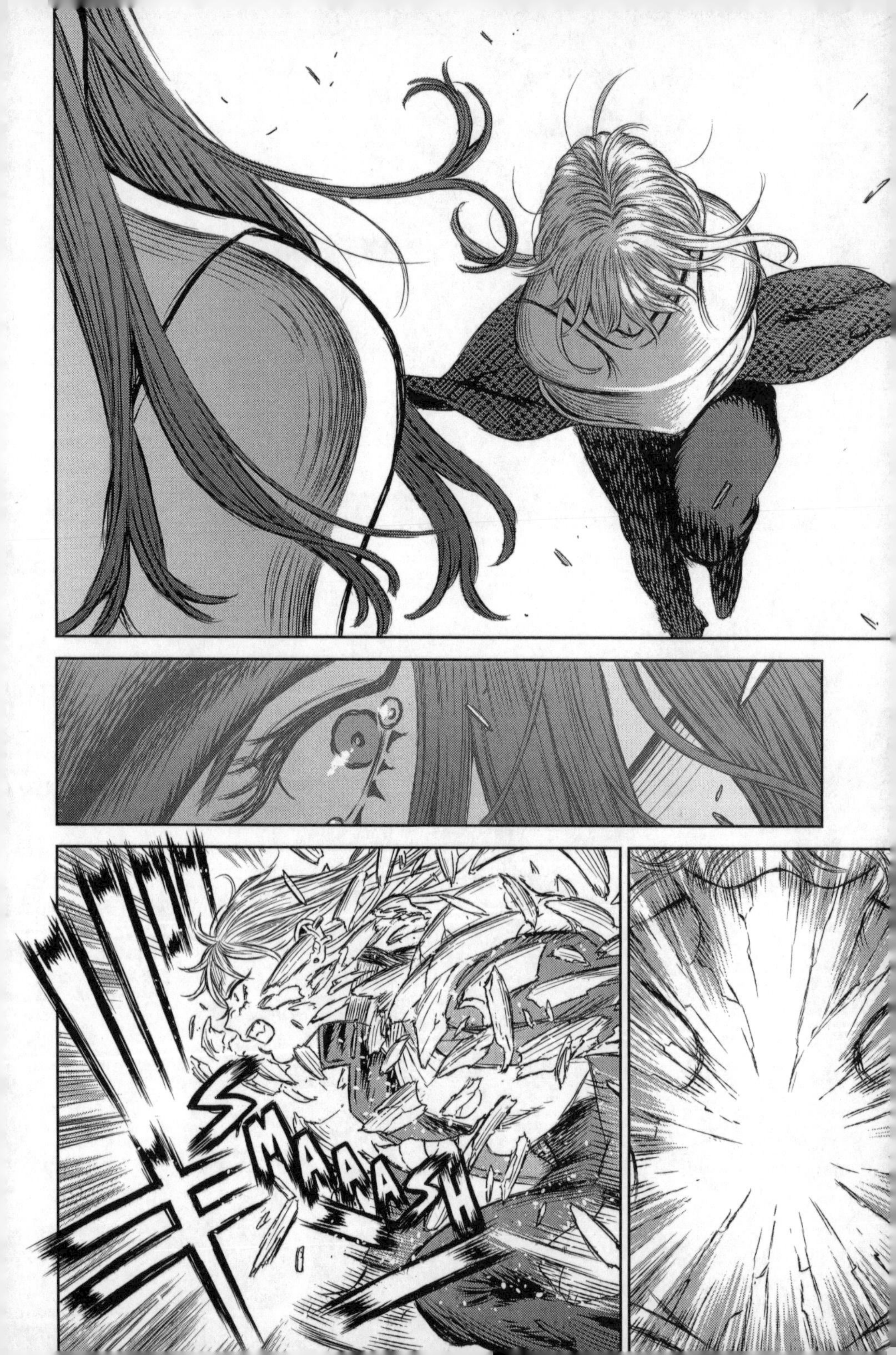
SMAAASH

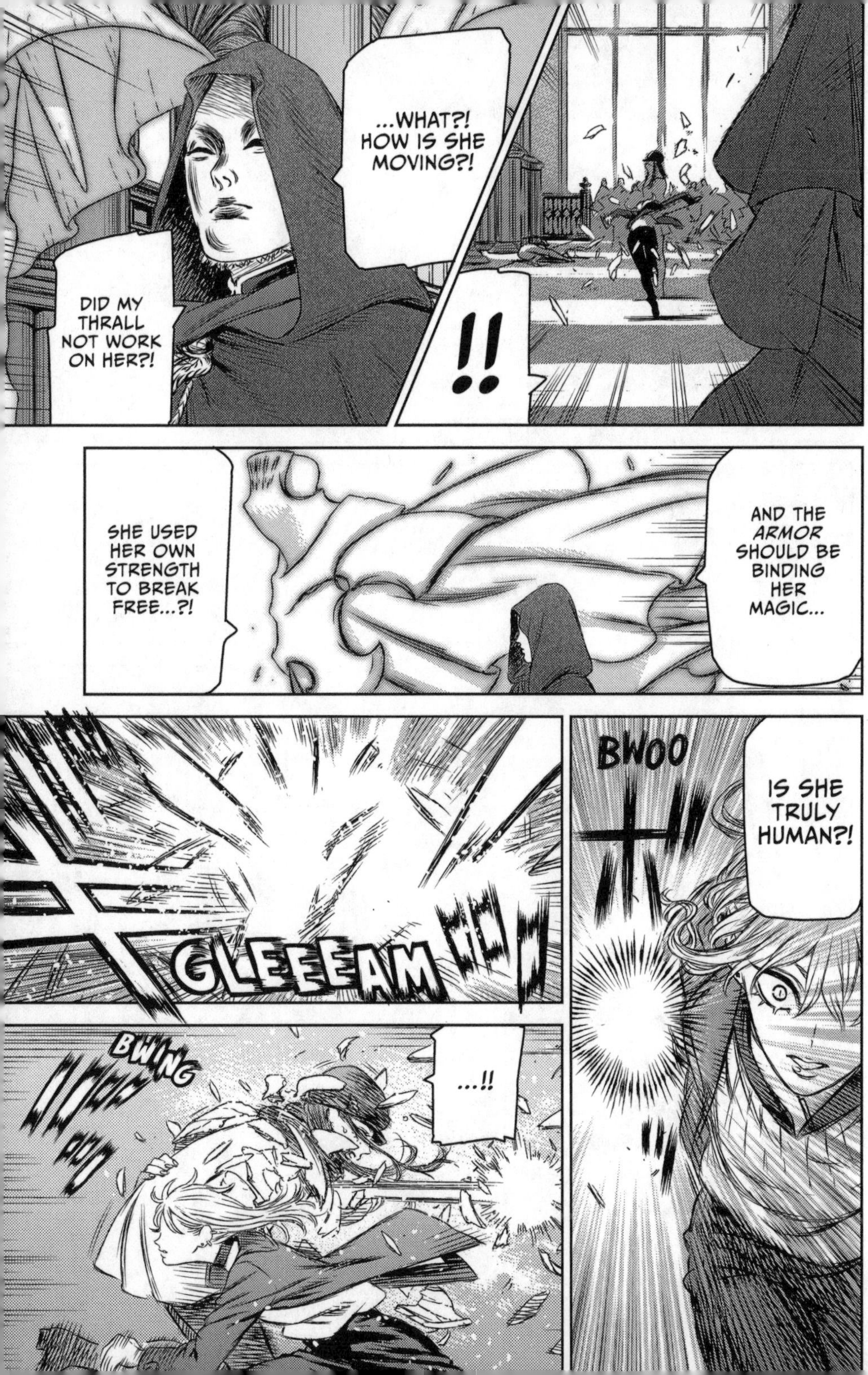
!!
...WHAT?! HOW IS SHE MOVING?!
DID MY THRALL NOT WORK ON HER?!
AND THE *ARMOR* SHOULD BE BINDING HER MAGIC...
SHE USED HER OWN STRENGTH TO BREAK FREE...?!
BWOO
IS SHE TRULY HUMAN?!
GLEEEAM
BWING
...!!

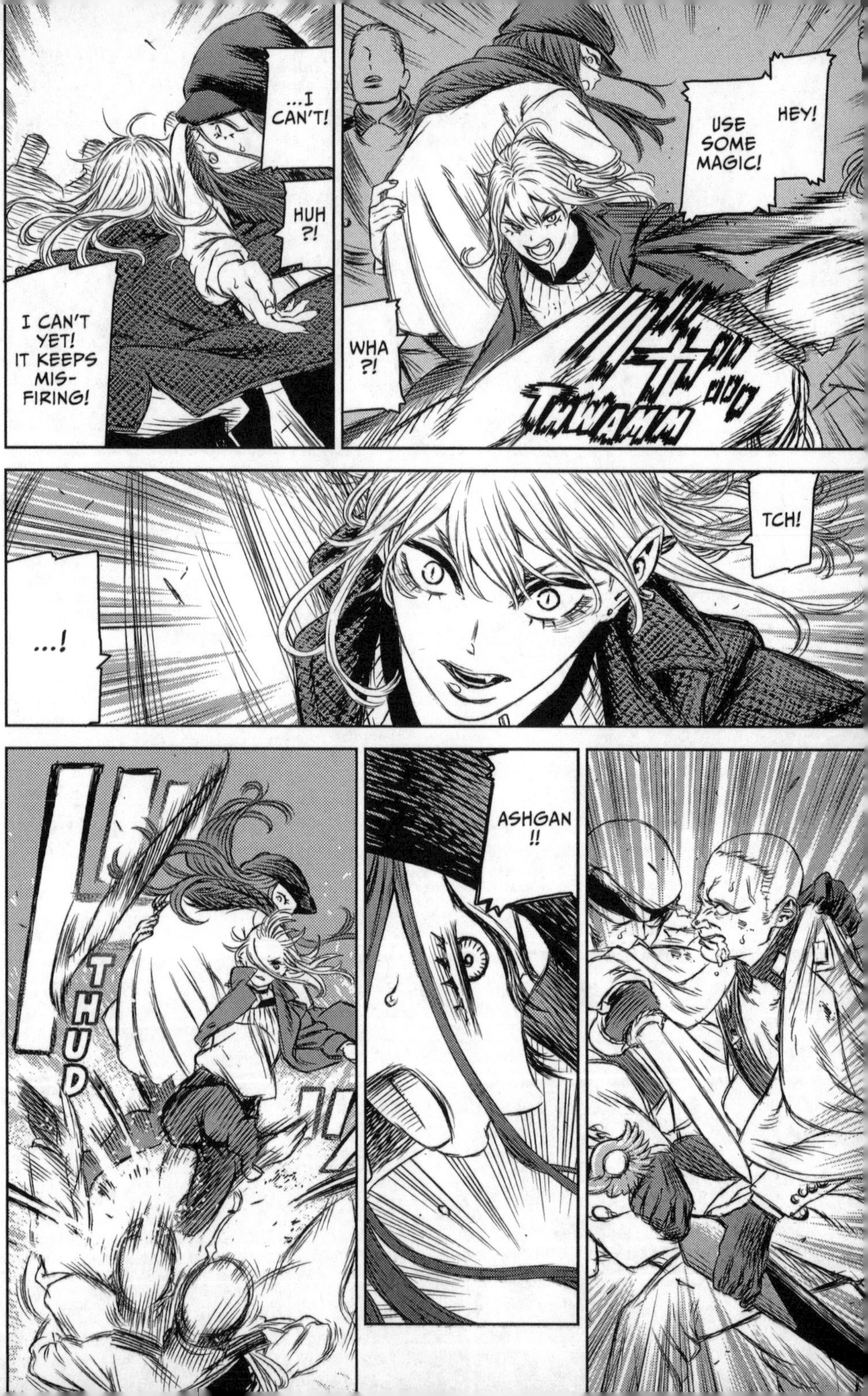
HEY! USE SOME MAGIC!
WHA ?!
THWAMM
...I CAN'T!
HUH ?!
I CAN'T YET! IT KEEPS MIS- FIRING!
TCH!
...!
ASHGAN !!
THUD

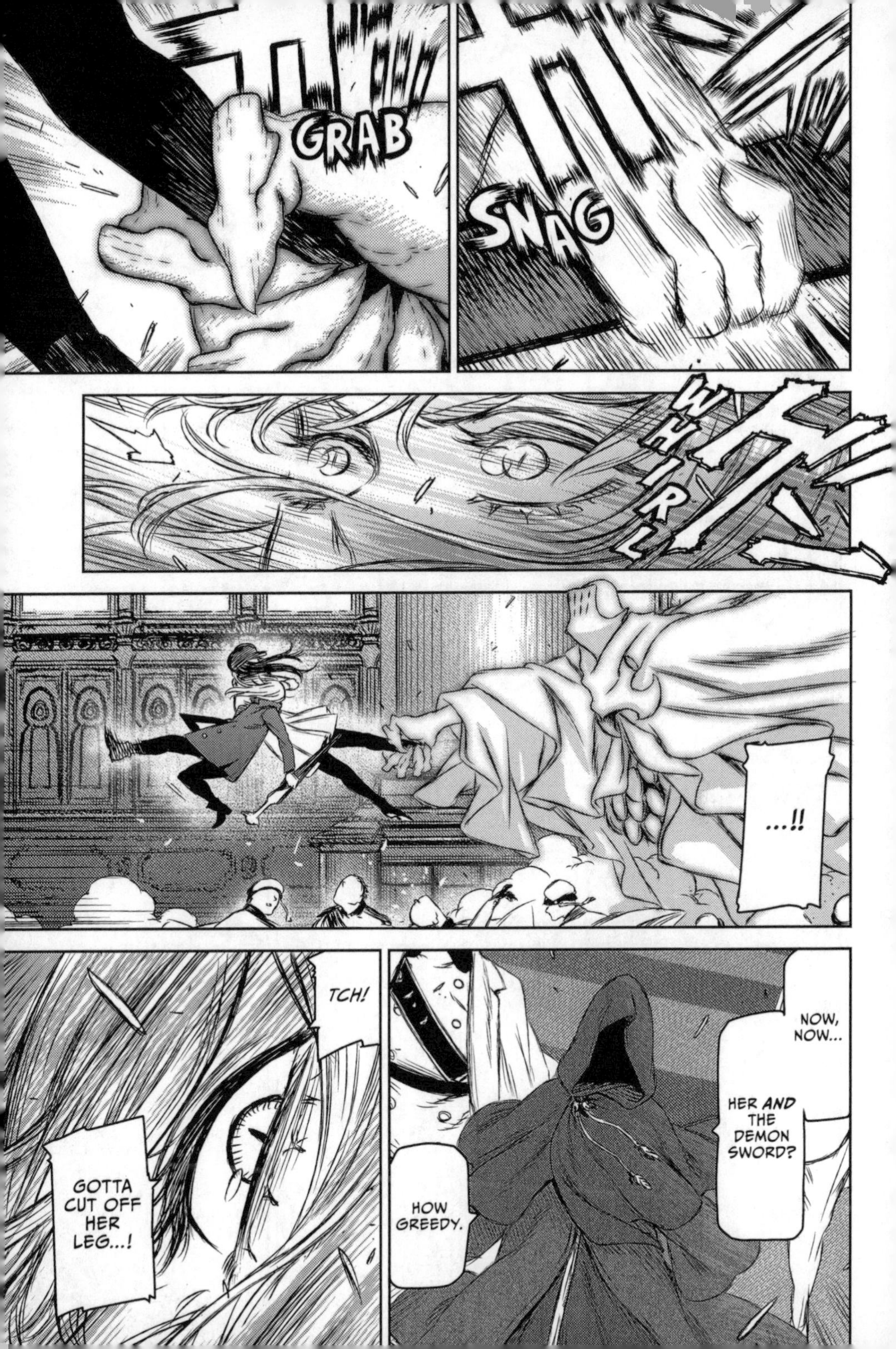
SNAG
GRAB
WHIRL
...!!
NOW, NOW...
HER AND THE DEMON SWORD?
HOW GREEDY.
TCH!
GOTTA CUT OFF HER LEG...!

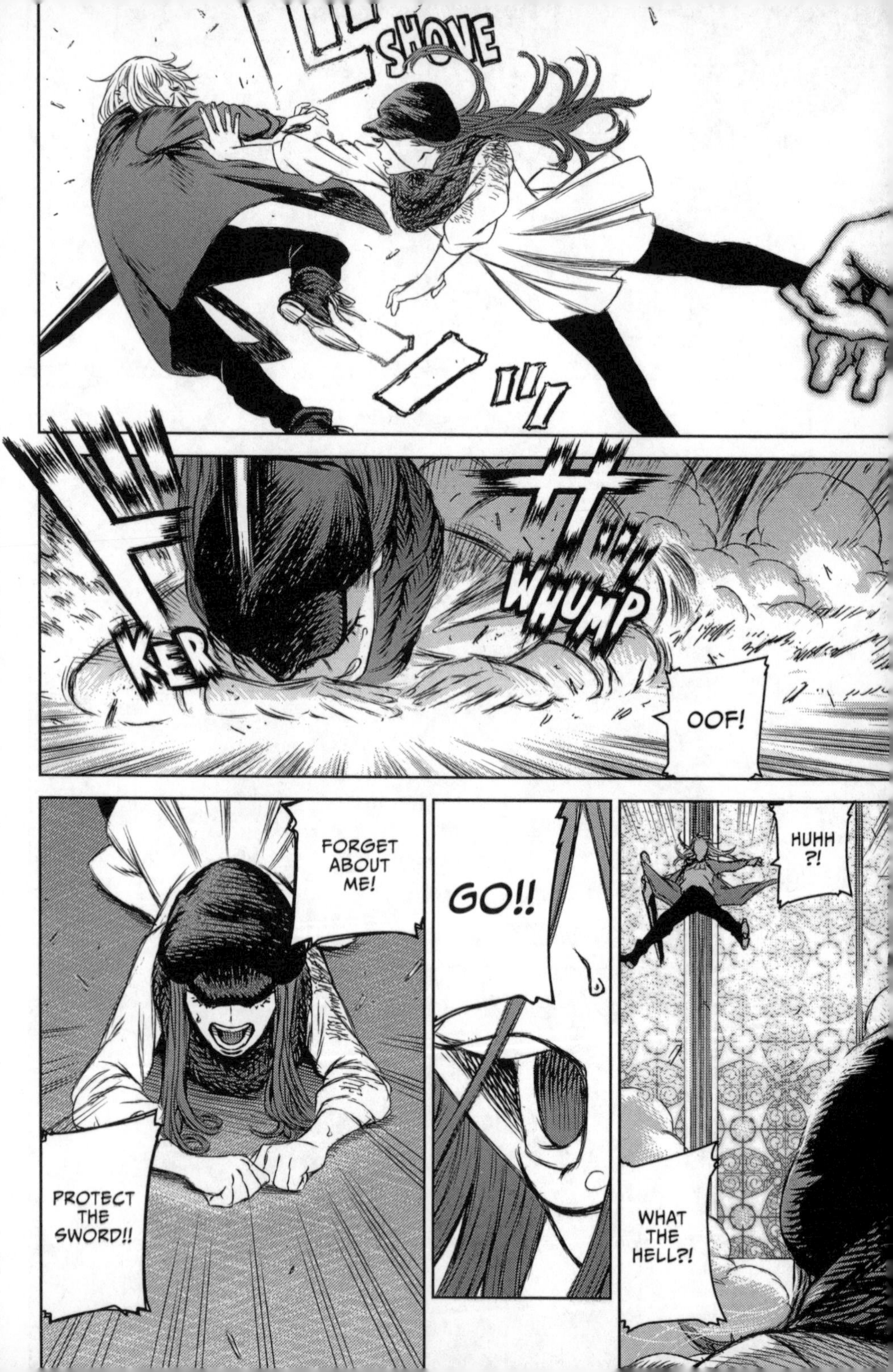
SHOVE
WHUMP
OOF!
KER
HUHH?!
WHAT THE HELL?!
GO!!
FORGET ABOUT ME!
PROTECT THE SWORD!!

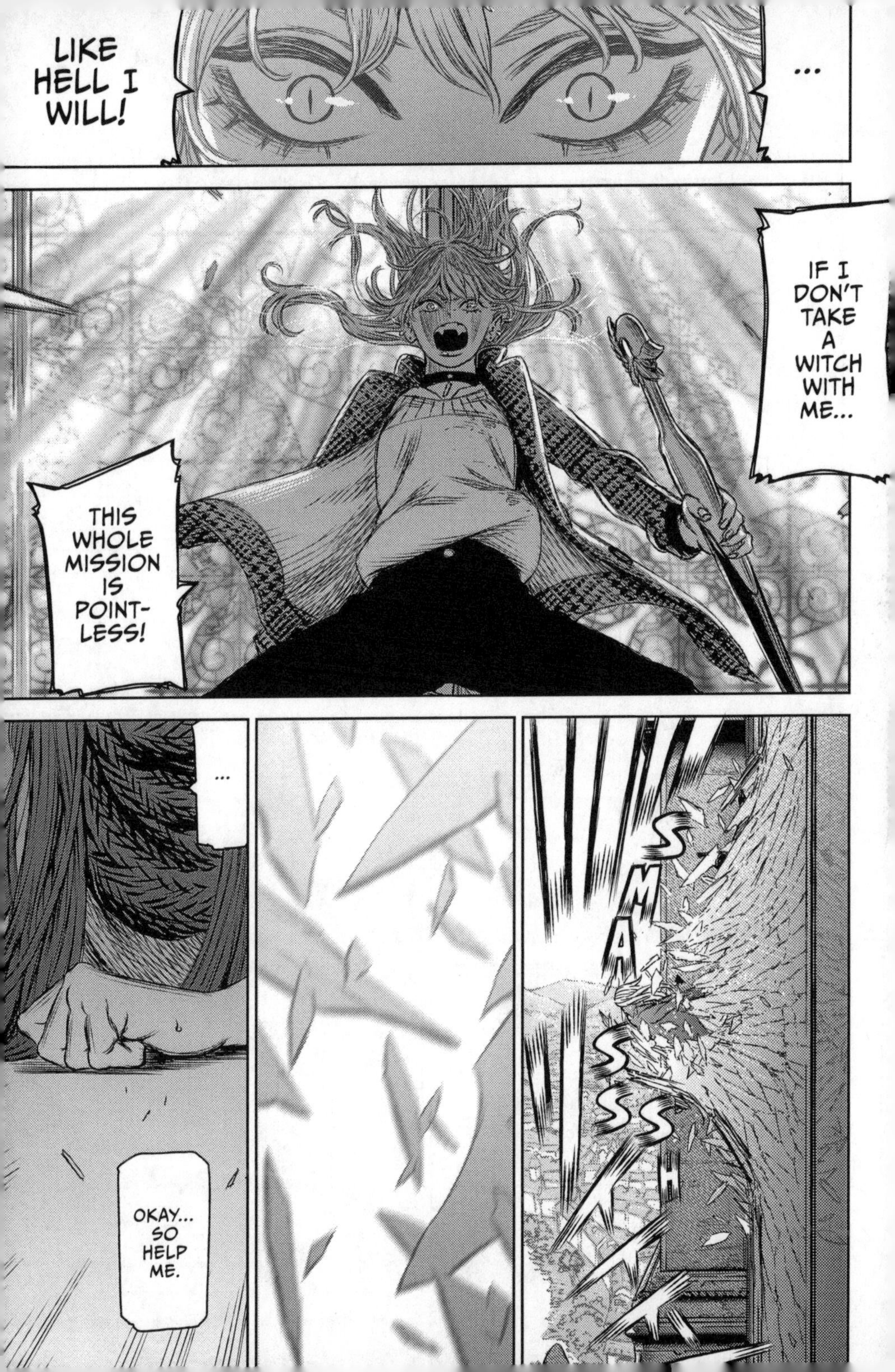
...
LIKE HELL I WILL!
IF I DON'T TAKE A WITCH WITH ME...
THIS WHOLE MISSION IS POINT-LESS!
SMASSSSH
...
OKAY... SO HELP ME.

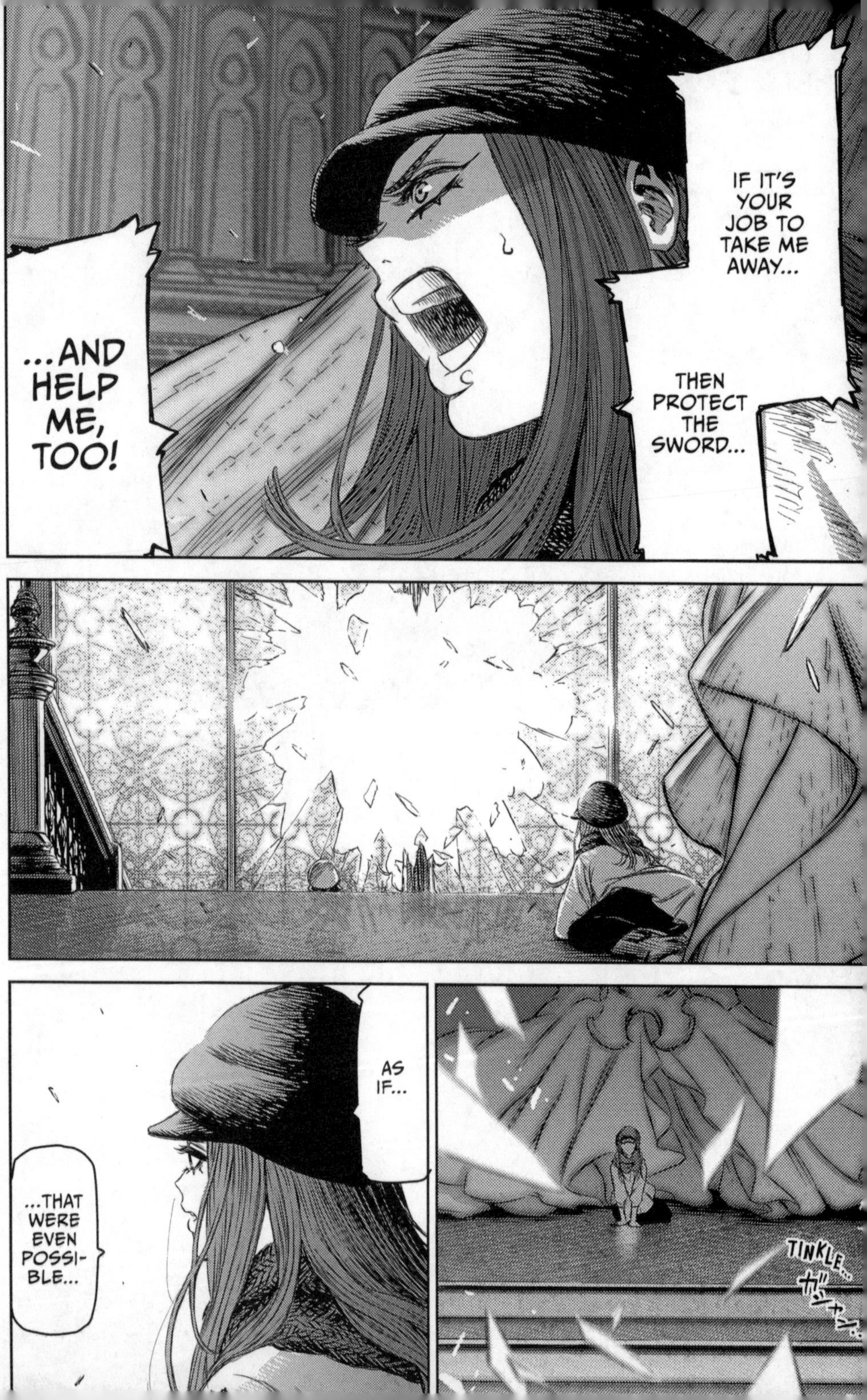
IF IT'S YOUR JOB TO TAKE ME AWAY...
THEN PROTECT THE SWORD...
...AND HELP ME, TOO!
TINKLE...
AS IF...
...THAT WERE EVEN POSSI-BLE...

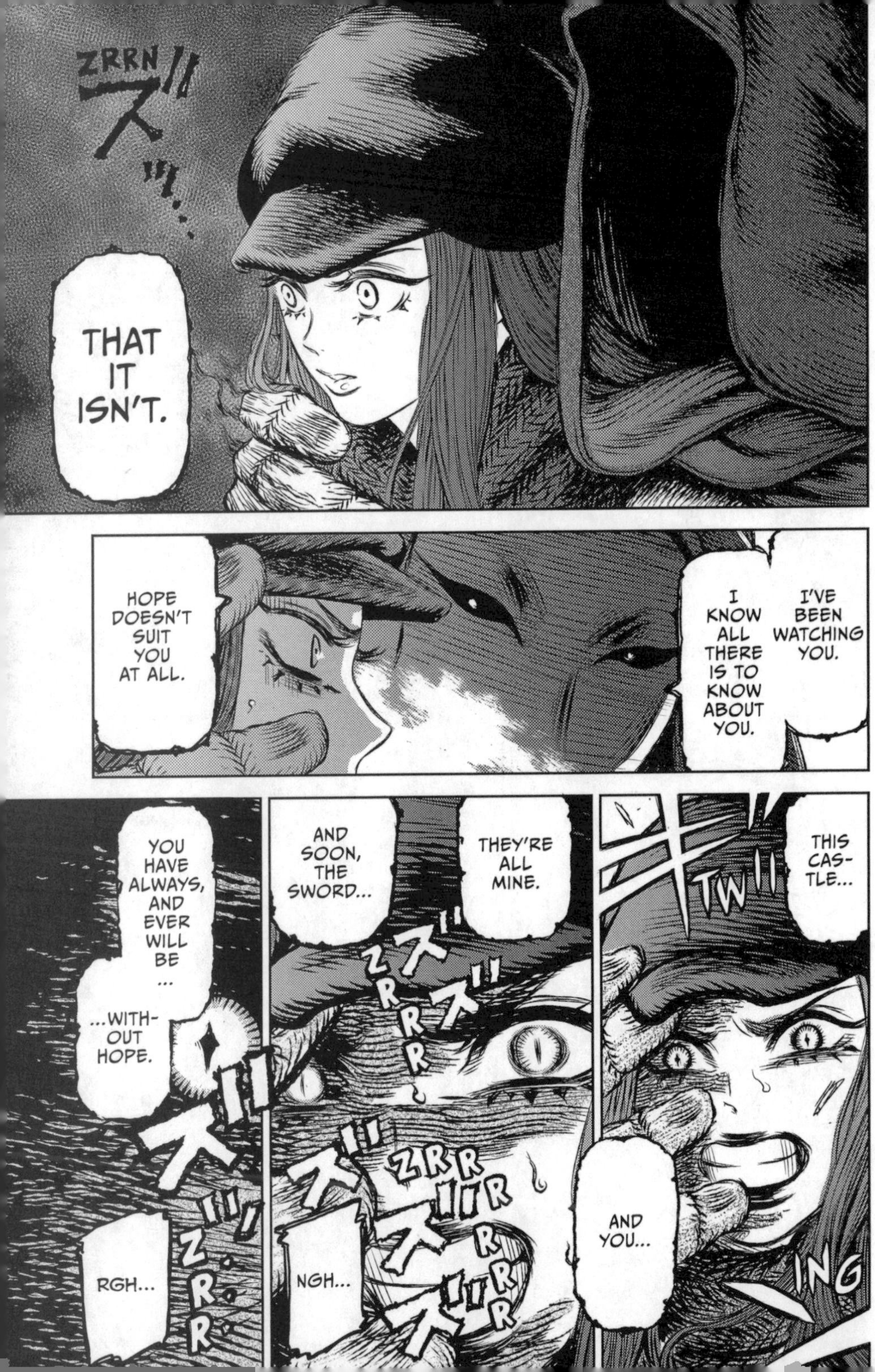
ZRRN
THAT IT ISN'T.
I'VE BEEN WATCHING YOU.
I KNOW ALL THERE IS TO KNOW ABOUT YOU.
HOPE DOESN'T SUIT YOU AT ALL.
THIS CAS-TLE...
TW ING
AND YOU...
THEY'RE ALL MINE.
AND SOON, THE SWORD...
ZRRRR
ZRR
NGH...
YOU HAVE ALWAYS, AND EVER WILL BE ...
...WITH-OUT HOPE.
ZRR
RGH...

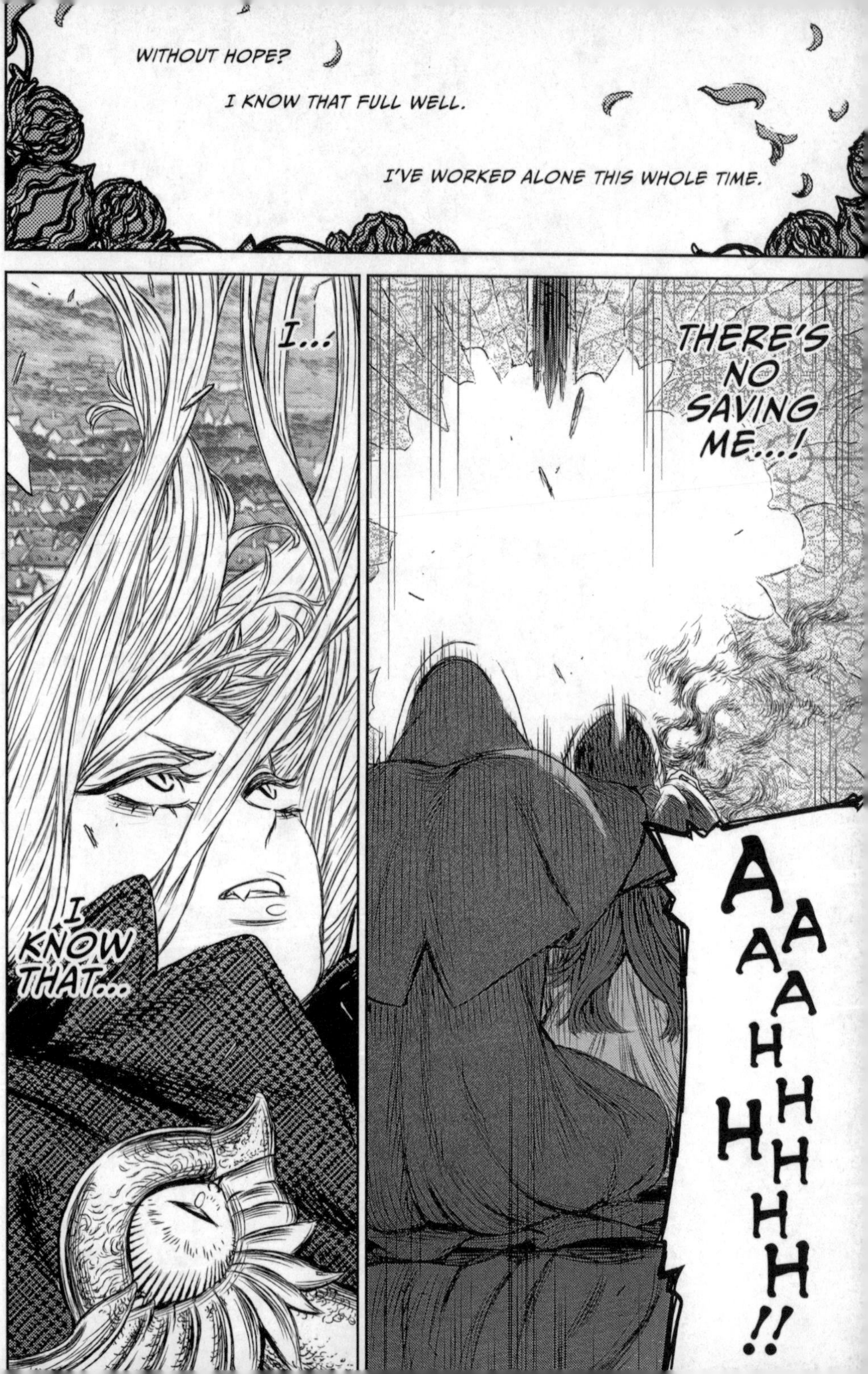
WITHOUT HOPE?
I KNOW THAT FULL WELL.
I'VE WORKED ALONE THIS WHOLE TIME.
THERE'S NO SAVING ME...!
AAAAHHHHHHH!!
I...!
I KNOW THAT...

THE WITCH AND THE BEAST

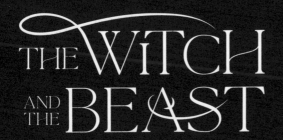

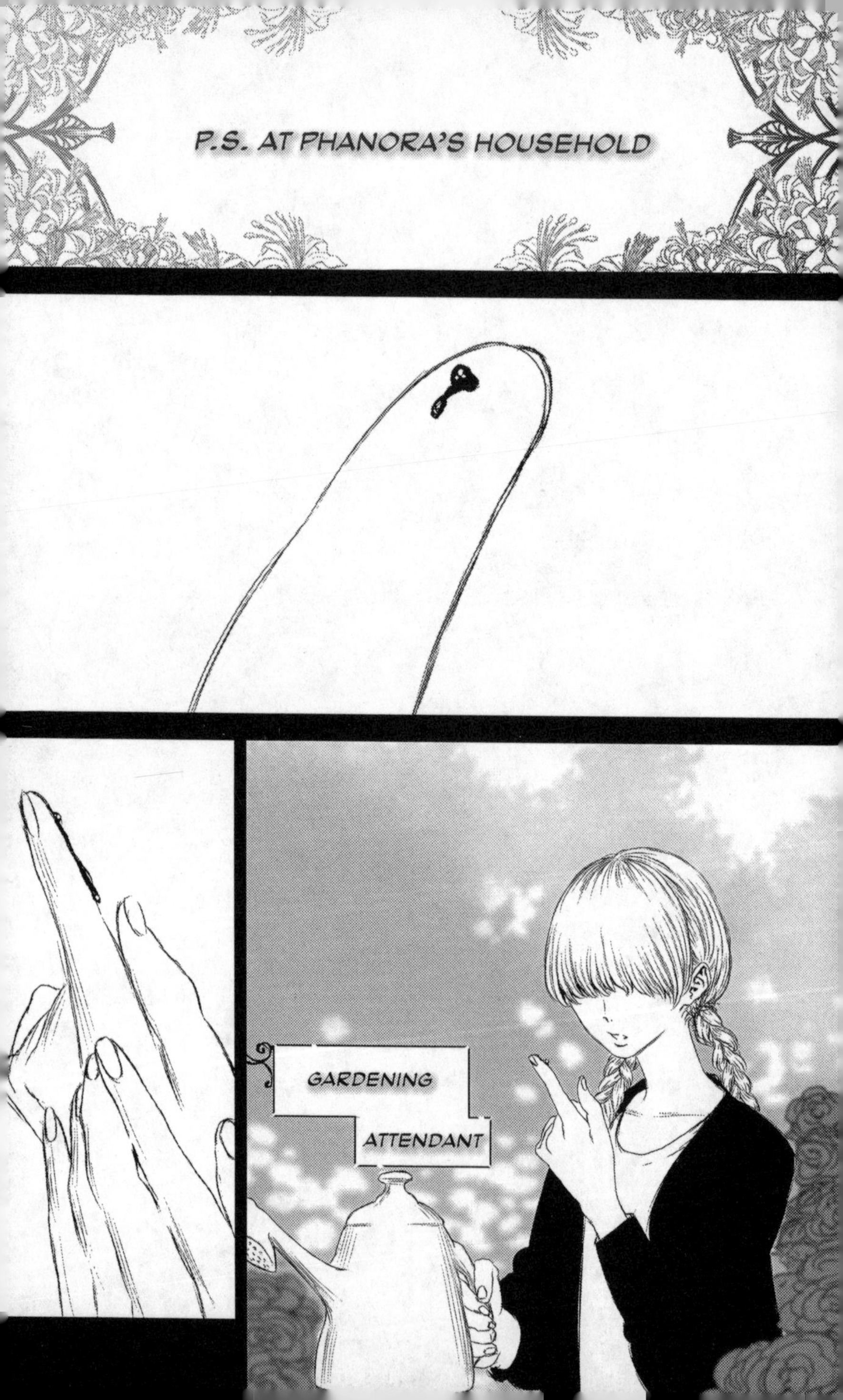
P.S. AT PHANORA'S HOUSEHOLD
GARDENING
ATTENDANT

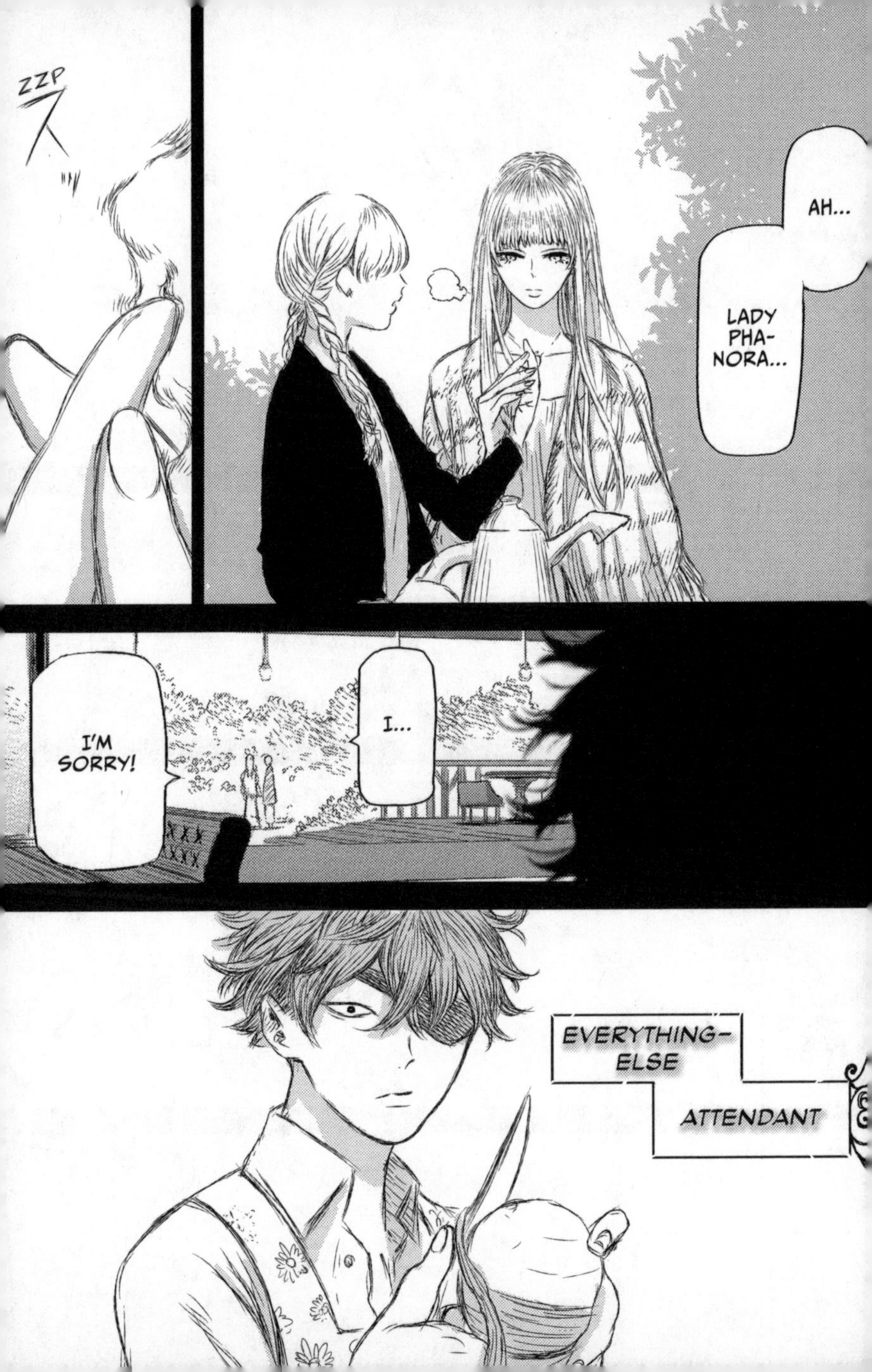
AH...
LADY PHA-NORA...
ZZP
I...
I'M SORRY!
EVERYTHING-ELSE
ATTENDANT

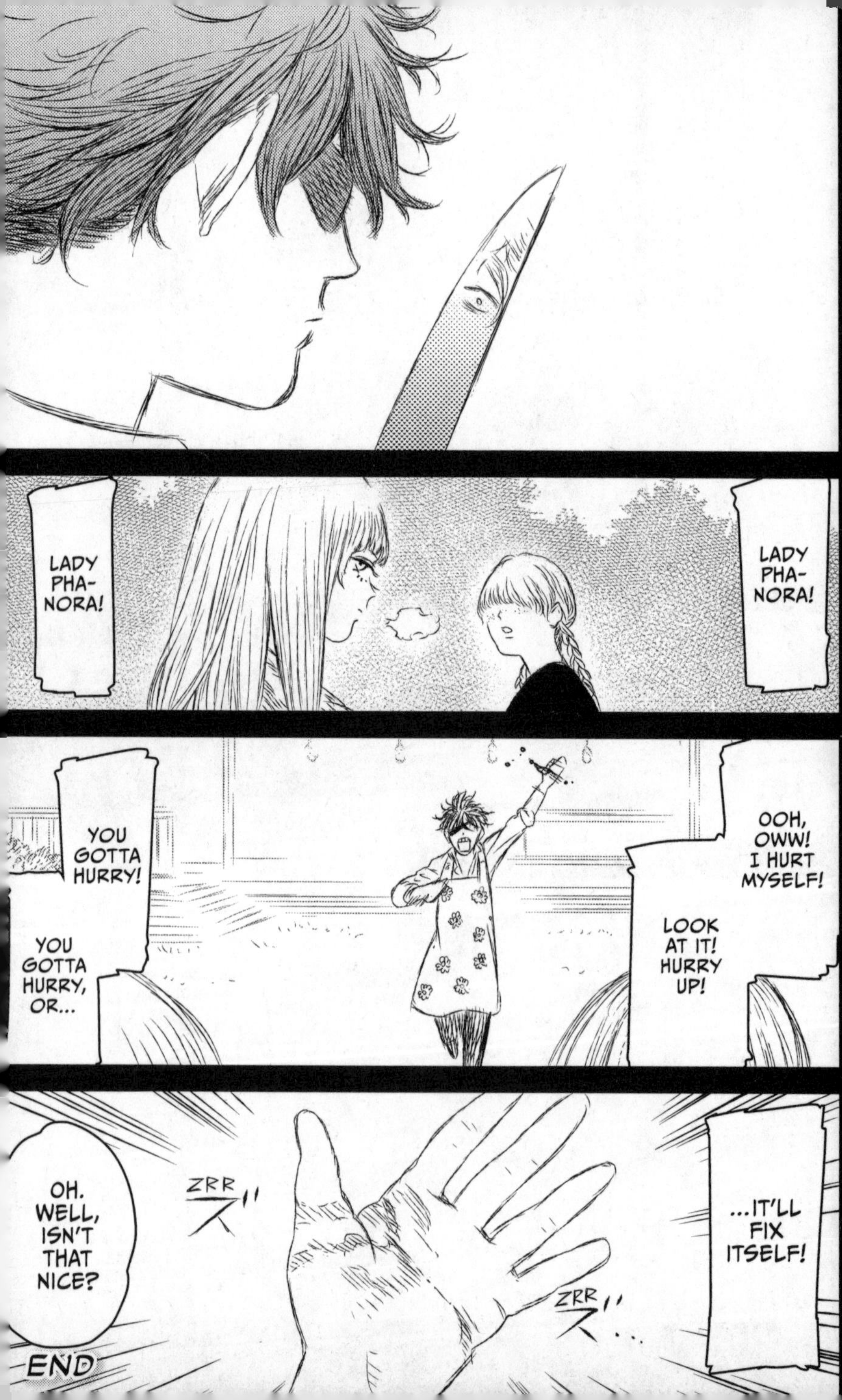

LADY PHA-NORA!
LADY PHA-NORA!
OOH, OWW! I HURT MYSELF!
LOOK AT IT! HURRY UP!
YOU GOTTA HURRY!
YOU GOTTA HURRY, OR...
...IT'LL FIX ITSELF!
ZRR
ZRR
OH. WELL, ISN'T THAT NICE?
END

THE WITCH AND THE BEAST

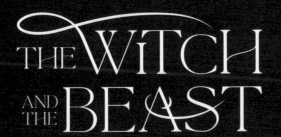

A Kodansha Comics Trade Paperback Original
The Witch and the Beast 3 copyright © 2018 Kousuke Satake
English translation copyright © 2020 Kousuke Satake

Publish   print of

Pub   ugh

Fir   kyo

ISBN 978-1-64651-023-8

Original cover design by Yusuke Kurachi (Astrorb)

Printed in the United States of America.

www.kodanshacomics.com

9 8 7 6 5 4 3 2 1
Translation: Kevin Gifford
Lettering: Phil Christie
Editing: Vanessa Tenazas
Kodansha Comics edition cover design by My Truong

Publisher: Kiichiro Sugawara

Director of publishing services: Ben Applegate
Associate director of operations: Stephen Pakula
Publishing services managing editor: Noelle Webster
Assistant production manager: Emi Lotto, Angela Zurlo
Logo and character art ©Kodansha USA Publishing, LLC